Social-Scientific Approaches
to
New Testament Interpretation

Social-Scientific Approaches
to
New Testament Interpretation

Edited by
DAVID G. HORRELL

T&T CLARK
EDINBURGH

T&T CLARK LTD
59 GEORGE STREET
EDINBURGH EH2 2LQ
SCOTLAND

First published 1999

ISBN 0 567 08658 5

British Library Cataloguing-in-Publication Data
A catalogue record for this book is available from the British Library

Typeset by Waverley Typesetters, Galashiels
Printed and bound in Great Britain by Page Bros, Norwich

Contents

Preface

Selecting essays for inclusion in a collection is inevitably difficult: from a vast array of potential items a small number must be selected, and many important contributions to the subject must of necessity be left out. Any editor's decisions are to a degree personal, and therefore different from those which others would have chosen to make. Nevertheless, I hope that this collection will prove valuable for students, teachers and researchers, and will be regarded as appropriately representing the diversity of work produced in the last twenty-five years in this field of New Testament studies. In selecting items for inclusion three main criteria have been employed. First, that the collection should contain the work of a wide range of authors, including at least some of the most prominent proponents of a broadly social-scientific approach to New Testament interpretation (the list of worthy authors could, of course, have been multiplied many times). I have also sought to incorporate some essays which, due to books going out of print, journals being hard to access, etc., might otherwise be difficult for students and teachers to obtain. Also presented here is a previously untranslated essay by Luise Schottroff, published originally in German. Second, that the essays should focus on a wide range of New Testament texts, so that the book might provide both a valuable teaching resource and a series of leads for further reading and research. Third, that all of the essays included should develop and apply a social-scientific approach to some New Testament text(s) or some aspect of early Christianity. In other words, there are no survey-type articles (except the *Introduction*) nor essays whose main purpose is methodological reflection or critique. Both of these types of essay are of course important, and are frequently referred to in the book, but I wanted the collection primarily to demonstrate the range of interpretations and perspectives which the social sciences have fostered within the field of New Testament studies. As the book is intended as a resource for teaching and to stimulate research I have written brief introductions to each of

1

the essays, indicating some of the issues and questions which arise, and have provided suggestions for further reading at the end of each chapter. I have tried to be balanced in my assessment of the range of approaches, but inevitably my own judgments and commitments have influenced that assessment. I have also shortened some of the footnotes to the essays and conformed all references to a standard (social-scientific) style. Readers should consult the original publications to see the notes in full. All bibliographical references have been collated in the final Bibliography.

In the course of preparing this publication I have incurred many debts, for which I should like to express my thanks. First of all I must thank the publishers and authors who have given their permission for work to appear here. Details of the original publications and copyright holders are given at the beginning of each chapter. I am also indebted to the University of Exeter Research Selectivity Fund for financing research support in connection with this project. Those who have provided assistance are: Helen Fry, who organised some of the initial correspondence before moving to London; Stuart Dewar, who undertook most of the work involved in translating the essay by Luise Schottroff; and Louise Lawrence, my main research assistant, who has undertaken a variety of tasks, including the indexing, with efficiency and good cheer, and has been invaluable throughout. I am most grateful to them all, especially Louise. I am also very grateful to those who have offered comments on the list of essays to be included, on various of my chapter introductions, and on my introductory essay: John Barclay, Andrew Chester, Justin Meggitt, Todd Still, and Nicholas Taylor.

Finally I would like to thank the students and staff of the Department of Theology here at Exeter, who together provide such a congenial atmosphere in which to work. A particular word of appreciation is due to the students who were the 'guinea pigs' for the module on 'Social Aspects of Early Christianity' which I taught in 1996–97 and from which this book developed. I would like to dedicate this book specifically to the person who has done so much to cultivate the research and teaching of the Department and whose pastoral concern and personal warmth are deeply appreciated: Professor David Catchpole.

April 1998

Introduction

Social-Scientific Interpretation of the New Testament: Retrospect and Prospect

DAVID G. HORRELL

The last twenty-five years or so have seen the introduction of a wide variety of new methods in biblical studies. In both Hebrew Bible/Old Testament and New Testament studies, alongside the established methods of historical criticism, new approaches have been developed using theoretical traditions from other disciplines, such as literary criticism and the social sciences.[1] Social-scientific interpretation of the New Testament, then, is a part of this wider trend in biblical studies as a whole, reflecting increased diversity within the discipline and greater interdisciplinarity within the humanities and social sciences. Unlike some forms of literary criticism, the wide variety of social-scientific approaches to the Bible retain a close link with the aims of historical criticism; the intention is that the use of the resources which the social sciences offer, alongside the other methods of textual and historical criticism, may enable a fuller and better appreciation of the biblical texts and communities within their historical, social, and cultural setting (see Elliott 1993, 7–8; p. 341 below). John Elliott's recent definition of contemporary social-scientific criticism offers a clear summary of the approach:

> Social-scientific criticism of the Bible is that phase of the exegetical task which analyzes the social and cultural dimensions of the text and of its environmental context through the utilization of the perspectives, theory, models, and research of the social sciences. As a component of the historical-critical method of exegesis, social-scientific criticism investigates biblical texts as

---

I am very grateful to Harriet Harris, Todd Still, and especially John Barclay for comments on a draft of this introduction. Any errors or indiscretions naturally remain my own responsibility.

[1] On the Hebrew Bible/Old Testament, see e.g. Mayes 1989; Osiek 1989; Chalcraft 1997. On the diversity of methods now practised in New Testament studies see e.g. Anderson and Moore 1992; McKenzie and Haynes 1993; Green 1995; Porter 1997.

> meaningful configurations of language intended to communicate between composers and audiences. (Elliott 1993, 7)

In the essay that follows, I shall set the modern development of social-scientific criticism in its historical context, summarise the different approaches currently represented in New Testament studies, and explore the areas of contemporary debate and the prospects for future development.

1. The revival of interest in the social world of early Christianity

Interest in social aspects of early Christianity is certainly nothing new.[2] Indeed, from the later years of the nineteenth century into the early decades of the twentieth, scholars representing a variety of perspectives devoted considerable attention to social questions about the New Testament. A number of different approaches may be identified. One is the development of form criticism, pioneered by the German Old Testament scholar Hermann Gunkel (1862–1932) and applied to the New Testament especially by Martin Dibelius (1883–1947) and Rudolf Bultmann (1884–1976). Form criticism was concerned to relate different types of textual material to their particular *Sitz im Leben,* or setting in life; it aimed to recover the earliest form of a tradition by relating the development of textual traditions to their use in specific social settings. Hence in 1925 Oscar Cullmann insisted that form criticism would require the development of a 'special branch of sociology devoted to the study of the laws which govern the growth of popular traditions'.[3]

A notable representative of another approach is Adolf Deissmann (1866–1937), an influential German scholar who in the early decades of this century made an important contribution to the social history of early Christianity. Deissmann paid particular attention to the recently discovered papyri and their implications for understanding the social world of the New Testament, especially of Paul (see Deissmann 1911; 1927). German interest in the social dimensions of early Christianity is also evident, from a very different perspective, in the work of early Marxist scholars, including Friedrich Engels (1820–95) himself, and perhaps most notably Karl Kautsky, author of a large work published in 1908

---

[2] This point is often made; see e.g. Scroggs 1980, 164; Theissen 1979, 3–6.
[3] Cullmann 1925, quoted from MacDonald 1988, 19; see also Maier 1991, 5. See also Esler in ch. 4 below, pp. 127–28.

on the origins of Christianity.[4] In America interest in the sociology of early Christianity was pursued especially in the work of the so-called Chicago school, whose most prominent members included Shirley Jackson Case and Shailer Mathews (see further Keck 1974; Funk 1976; Scroggs 1980, 164–65).

However, from the 1920s until the 1970s, interest in the social dimensions of early Christianity declined.[5] There were a number of reasons for this. One was the failure of form criticism, particularly in the hands of its most prominent exponent, Rudolf Bultmann, to explore the social context in which the traditions were preserved and developed. It is often remarked that Cullmann's call for a sociological dimension to form criticism went virtually unheeded. In practice form criticism focused not on the wider social context, as might be implied in the term *Sitz im Leben*, but on the *Sitz im Glauben,* the setting in faith, or the setting in the life of the church (Theissen 1993, 9–10; also n. 3 above). Also significant was the fact that Bultmann's interests developed in the direction of a hermeneutic of demythologisation and a concern to formulate the word of the Gospel in existentialist terms, as a challenge to the 'I' to a radically new self-understanding (see Bultmann 1960; 1985). Thus in Bultmann's work the New Testament kerygma becomes essentially detached from its socio-historical context, just as does its contemporary reformulation (see Kee 1989, 4–5). Another important reason was the influence, indeed an influence on Bultmann, of Karl Barth's (1886–1968) dialectical theology, a break with the then established theological liberalism first announced in his Tambach lecture of 1919 and in the successive editions of his famous commentary on Romans (first edn 1918; second edn 1922; see further Scholder 1987, 40–45). For Barth the revealed Word of God is radically 'other' than all humanly and socially constructed patterns of religiosity. The Gospel stands as a radical challenge to all forms of human society and can never be identified with any particular social organisation. As Gerd Theissen points out, this aversion to a connection between theology and society was profoundly related to the specific social context in which Barth was

[4] See Marx and Engels 1957 for essays by Engels published in the 1880s; Kautsky 1908 (ET: 1925); see also Schottroff in ch. 10 below.
[5] Theissen 1993, 1–29, divides his survey of the interest in the sociological interpretation of the New Testament into three phases: 1870–1920; 1920–1970; 1970s onwards. Theissen's analysis, which focuses on German scholarship, perceptively relates the various approaches adopted by scholars to their social and political contexts.

located, and the struggles of the Confessing Church against National Socialism and the German Christians (Theissen 1993, 8–15; see further Scholder 1987).

The tide began to turn in the 1960s, and a revival of interest in the social aspects of early Christianity began. One landmark was the publication in 1960 of Edwin Judge's short book, *The Social Pattern of the Christian Groups in the First Century*, which, in the following decade or two, played a significant role in encouraging this renewed interest.[6] Other notable works of social history were published, for example, by Martin Hengel (e.g. 1969; 1973; see Scroggs 1980, 168–71). However, in distinction from the work undertaken earlier in the century, what was new in the early 1970s was the creative and varied use of methods, models and theories from the social sciences in New Testament studies.

Why, then, the revival of interest in social aspects of early Christianity, and why the experimentation with new methods? Undoubtedly one major factor was dissatisfaction with the established methods of New Testament study. This dissatisfaction is perhaps best summarised in the oft-quoted words of Robin Scroggs:

> To some it has seemed that too often the discipline of the theology of the New Testament (the history of *ideas*) operates out of a methodological docetism, as if believers had minds and spirits unconnected with their individual and corporate bodies. Interest in the sociology of early Christianity is no attempt to limit reductionistically the reality of Christianity to social dynamic; rather it should be seen as an effort to guard against a reductionism from the other extreme, a limitation of the reality of Christianity to an inner-spiritual, or objective-cognitive system. In short, sociology of early Christianity wants to put body and soul together again. (Scroggs 1980, 165–66)

The new interest in the sociology of early Christianity must also be understood in the light of wider developments in society at the time. The dissatisfaction of which Scroggs speaks, for example, may perhaps be linked with the widespread protests of the 'radical' 1960s (cf. Theissen 1993, 16). At least partly as a product of the communitarian and radical concerns of this period, there was something of a shift in the methods of

---

[6] Judge 1960a. Cf. Theissen 1993, 19 n. 23: 'This little book deserves a place of honor in the history of modern sociological exegesis.' Judge was Professor of Ancient History at Macquarie University in Sydney, Australia, where since the 1960s interest in the social history of early Christianity has been energetically pursued.

doing history, away from a focus on the 'great' figures and towards a concern with communities, with social relations, with popular movements and popular culture: in short, history not 'from above' but 'from below' (cf. Barton 1997, 278). The 1960s also witnessed an expansion in the disciplines of the social sciences and an increase in their influence and prominence in the Universities and in society (see Barton 1992, 401). All that happened in the 1970s, Theissen suggests, was that 'exegesis caught up with what had already developed elsewhere' (Theissen 1993, 18). The interest in the use of social-scientific methods in biblical studies thus stems from a particular social context, which also gave rise to feminist and political/liberationist hermeneutics, for example, and more generally to a period of widespread and creative experimentation with a whole range of 'new methods' in biblical studies.[7] Social-scientific approaches to the Bible retain a much closer connection with the concerns of historical criticism than many of these other new methods, particularly some of the forms of literary criticism (Barton 1995).

2. Innovative studies of the 1970s; assessment and criticisms

Two 'events' of the early 1970s, one in the U.S.A., the other in Germany, deserve particular notice in a review of social-scientific study of the New Testament. One is the formation in 1973 of a SBL[8] group devoted to the study of the social world of early Christianity (see Smith 1975). One of the group's founding members was Wayne Meeks, who had already (in 1972) published a ground-breaking essay on John's gospel, using perspectives from the sociology of knowledge to argue that the Christology of the fourth gospel reflects and legitimates the social situation of a sectarian community which is alienated and isolated from the world.[9] Another founder member was Jonathan Smith, who offered an outline of what he saw as the major tasks and opportunities in the field (Smith 1975). The group devoted a number of years to the study of early Christianity in a particular location, Antioch, seeking to give

---

[7] See further Barton 1992, 399–406, for a more extensive list of the influences on the renewed interest in the 'communal dimension of earliest Christianity'.

[8] SBL denotes the Society of Biblical Literature, the major U.S.-based organisation for Biblical Studies. On the various SBL groups that have since been formed see Osiek 1989, 268–69.

[9] See esp. Meeks 1972, 70; further Scroggs 1980, 176–77; Holmberg 1990, 125–28; Barton 1993, 145–52.

concrete and specific focus to their studies of the social context in which the early Christians lived (see Meeks and Wilken 1978).[10]

The second notable event (not strictly a single 'event') was the publication of a series of articles between 1973 and 1975 by Gerd Theissen, then of the University of Bonn, now at Heidelberg. These articles, which encompass both the Palestinian Jesus movement and the Pauline church at Corinth, remain among the most influential and ground-breaking contributions to the sociology of early Christianity.[11] They combine a detailed and careful use of historical evidence with a creative and eclectic use of sociological theory (see chs 3 and 9 below). Notably, the essays on the synoptic material demonstrate a close connection with the methods and concerns of form criticism, while exploring the sociological questions about *Sitz im Leben* which form criticism evidently failed to do (see ch. 3). The detailed methodological and exegetical reflections in these essays (see Theissen 1979) underpin the more popular presentation in Theissen's much discussed *Soziologie der Jesusbewegung,* translated into English as *Sociology of Early Palestinian Christianity* (U.S.A.) or *The First Followers of Jesus* (U.K.; see Theissen 1978).[12]

Other notable ground-breaking publications in this period include Robin Scroggs' essay of 1975, the first systematic attempt to apply the sociological model of the religious 'sect' to early Christianity (see ch. 2 below), and John Gager's book *Kingdom and Community* (1975). In this book Gager sketched the ways in which a number of different social-scientific theories might be applied to early Christianity. These include the models resulting from studies of millenarian movements and Melanesian cargo cults, undertaken by anthropologists in the 1950s and 1960s; Max Weber's concept of charisma and its routinisation; the process of institutionalisation; and cognitive dissonance theory, developed by Leon Festinger and others in the 1950s through the study of groups that predicted the end of the world but which did not disappear when their prediction failed to come true (see ch. 6 below). Although the brevity of Gager's studies left him open to criticism, notably by Smith

---

[10] Gager's failure (in his 1975 book) to relate his social-scientific analyses to specific locations or communities elicited sharp criticism from Smith 1978.

[11] Note the comments of Scroggs 1980, 174–75; Holmberg 1990, 44–54, 119–25; Elliott 1993, 21–23. Theissen's work was collected in book-form as Theissen 1979 (3rd edn, 1988). The essays on Corinth are available in English in Theissen 1982; the essays on the Jesus movement and other more recent articles in Theissen 1993.

[12] Among the important critiques of this book see Stegemann 1984; Elliott 1986a; Horsley 1989.

(1978),[13] many of his suggested avenues have been explored in more detail in subsequent work. Bengt Holmberg (1978), for example, has applied Weber's notions of charisma and its routinisation to the structures of authority in the primitive church, and Margaret MacDonald (1988; see ch. 8 below), influenced in part by Holmberg, has undertaken a detailed study of institutionalisation in the Pauline churches. Robert Jewett (1986) has applied the 'millenarian model' to the Thessalonian churches. The theory of cognitive dissonance has also proved fruitful in further studies (see ch. 6 below).

In the late 1970s and early 1980s interest in the field continued to grow, and an increasing number of widely varied publications appeared.[14] Book-length introductions to the area were written by Derek Tidball (1983) and Carolyn Osiek (1984), both of which remain useful entrées into the subject.[15] More recently, as well as New Testament scholars developing an interest in the social sciences, some sociologists have turned their attention to early Christianity (e.g. Blasi 1988; Stark 1986; 1996). A number of attempts have been made to classify this varied and ongoing work according to the method employed and the scope of the investigation. John Elliott (1993, 18–20), for example, distinguishes the following five categories: (i) 'investigations of *social realia* . . . generally to illustrate some feature or features of ancient society but with no concern for analyzing, synthesizing, and explaining these social facts in social-scientific fashion'; (ii) studies which seek 'to construct a *social history* of a particular period or movement or group' but with a predominantly historical conceptual framework and 'an eschewing of social theory and models'; (iii) studies of 'the social organisation of early Christianity', and of 'the social forces leading to its emergence and its social institutions', which include '*the deliberate use of social theory and models*'; (iv) studies which focus on '*the social and cultural scripts* influencing and constraining social interaction' in the 'cultural environment of the New Testament'; (v) studies which use 'the research, theory, and models of the social sciences . . . in the *analysis of biblical texts*'.[16]

---

[13] See also Bartlett 1978; Tracy 1978 (all three review essays in the same issue of *Zygon*).

[14] Useful surveys and assessments of this early period are provided by Scroggs 1980; Harrington 1980; Judge 1980; Best 1983b; Edwards 1983; Richter 1984. Richter in particular offers extensive and classified bibliographical information. Elliott 1993, 17–35 also offers a comprehensive survey.

[15] Tidball's book was reissued in 1997; a second edition of Osiek's was published in 1992.

[16] Similar classifications are offered, e.g., by Smith 1975; Richter 1984.

Any categorisation can of course be questioned, since the boundaries between types of work are never neat or clear. There are also relevant theoretical debates, for example, concerning the adequacy of any methodological distinction between history and social science (see Horrell 1996a, 26–31). However, in terms of the assessment of published work, there clearly is a significant distinction to be drawn between works of social history which explicitly eschew the use of social-scientific theories or models (e.g. Clarke 1993; Gooch 1993)[17] and those which employ them as tools in the task of historical investigation (e.g. Meeks 1983). Also significant is the distinction which has emerged between those who may be termed 'social historians' (yet who use social-scientific methods) and the 'social scientists' who have developed a rigorous and model-based approach (see §3 and §4 below; Martin 1993, 107). What may be questioned, though, is the legitimacy of a claim to eschew the discussion of theory. Any approach to history is guided by the methods, presuppositions and convictions of the researcher, and the adoption of a merely empirical interest in the data must be seen as a concealment of (implicit) theory, which theoretically-conscious works aim to render perspicuous and therefore open to critical scrutiny (see Horrell 1996a, 27–28, in criticism of Clarke 1993). Indeed, the desire to be open and explicit about methods and models has been a motivation in much social-scientific exegesis (see Esler ch. 4 below, p. 140; Elliott 1993, 36–59).

Those who promote the use of the social sciences in New Testament studies maintain that the fruit of a variety of social-scientific research offers new ways of framing questions, new perspectives, critical theoretical resources, and alerts the researcher to previously unexplored aspects of social behaviour. The question then, as posed by Philip Esler, is 'not "Do we need the social sciences?" but rather "How can we get along without them?"' (Esler 1994, 18). Nevertheless objections to the enterprise have been raised.[18] Cyril Rodd (1981), for example, has questioned whether the ancient sources yield adequate data of a kind suitable for sociological analysis (compared with the contemporary opportunities for interviews, observation, etc.). He highlights the danger that a theory or model may be used to fill in the gaps and assume things for which evidence is lacking. Edwin Judge (1980) similarly expresses the concern that sociological models or theories may be imposed upon

---

[17] Note also the comments of Garrett 1992, 94, on Malherbe 1977a.
[18] See the summary in Osiek 1989, 275–77.

the ancient evidence, without the painstaking study of that evidence necessary to ascertain the 'social facts of life characteristic of the world to which the New Testament belongs' (Judge 1980, 210). Philip Esler rightly questions Judge's apparently empiricist presuppositions; namely the idea that one can simply search for social facts, for uninterpreted data, innocent of the need for theoretical discussion or reflection on the presuppositions of particular approaches to history (see below ch. 4, pp. 138–41; MacDonald 1988, 25–27). For Esler, social-scientific models should not predetermine the results of an enquiry, but rather serve as heuristic tools, suggesting new perspectives and illuminating comparisons. Nevertheless, there is an important debate – a debate within the social sciences and within New Testament studies – about the appropriate methods for social-scientific research and about the philosophical and epistemological assumptions which underpin different types of approach. While an untheoretical empiricism of the kind Judge seems to advocate is to be rejected, there are still important questions to be asked about the ways in which particular methods and approaches shape the way in which the evidence is interpreted (see §6.1. below).

A second criticism often mentioned is that of reductionism, that is, the idea that social-scientific theories will 'explain' religious phenomena purely in terms of social or economic forces.[19] Certainly some traditions of social theory – some forms of Durkheimian or Marxist sociology, for example – are more crudely reductionist and deterministic than others. Yet even if such traditions are avoided, the reductionist criticism cannot be dismissed quite as easily as some suppose.[20] The social sciences prioritise certain aspects of human experience and interaction – the 'social' – and regard human knowledge and culture as essentially 'socially-constructed' (see Berger 1969). Hence their stance is one of what Peter Berger calls 'methodological atheism' (Berger 1969). Although dialogue between theology and sociology is not, in my view, to be brought to an end, as John Milbank has suggested (1990), nevertheless, there are important theoretical presuppositions underpinning various forms of social theory which should be carefully and critically appraised. While there is more variety within the traditions and contemporary formulations

---

[19] See e.g. Scroggs 1980, 166–67; Malina 1982, 237–38; Meeks 1983, 2–4; Esler (below pp. 137–38); Holmberg 1990, 149–50; Theissen 1979, 58–60; 1993, 187–88; Horrell 1996a, 18–22.

[20] E.g. Malina 1982, 237–38; Esler (below p. 137): 'There is little to be said for the reductionist criticism.'

of social theory than Milbank acknowledges, it is certainly the case, as Milbank argues, that sociology and theology offer 'narratives' about human society with fundamentally different priorities and assumptions at their heart, and that *some* forms of social science offer explanations of early Christianity which stand in tension with 'theological' perspectives (see e.g. ch. 6 below). Whether that tension or opposition is an attraction or a problem for the New Testament scholar will of course depend upon personal commitments and beliefs, but what should certainly be avoided is the naive belief that any form of social science can be used to study the early church without any serious theoretical conflict between that perspective and more theological understandings.[21]

These various criticisms should not therefore be too lightly dismissed. But neither do they require the abandonment of the enterprise. Those who practise social-scientific criticism, in whatever form, themselves often stress the need for ongoing methodological reflection and critical discussion. Important theoretical issues need to be clarified, but in the context of ongoing and creative attempts to use social-scientific resources in New Testament studies. At the very least, the social sciences surely offer tools for exploring the social context within which the 'theology' of the New Testament was forged, and resources for investigating the ways in which early Christian writings formed and shaped patterns of interaction within the congregations.

In the following sections (§3–§5), rather than attempt again to survey and classify the existing body of relevant work, I shall focus on three types of approach which have emerged as significant in the 1980s and 1990s and between which there are important differences. This will prepare the ground for a brief overview of areas of current debate and prospects for future development (§6).

3. Cultural anthropology and the Context Group

In 1981 Bruce Malina published his ground-breaking book *The New Testament World: Insights from Cultural Anthropology,* in which he outlined a series of models derived from the work of various anthropologists for understanding the pivotal values of Mediterranean culture – the social world inhabited by the first Christians. Malina's concern

---

[21] See further Milbank 1990, and the range of critical reactions presented in Gill 1996, 429–70, especially that by sociologist Kieran Flanagan. Gill's articles are extracts from fuller presentations in *New Blackfriars* 73 (June 1992).

was to enable his readers to appreciate the strangeness and difference of that cultural context from that of twentieth-century U.S.A. In order to displace the implicit ethnocentric and anachronistic assumption that people then were pretty much like modern Americans, Malina sought to provide models of a culture that operated in very different ways. The central features and values of that culture, he proposed, were honour and shame, dyadic rather than individual personality,[22] the perception of limited good,[23] distinctive norms of kinship and marriage, and a set of purity rules to distinguish clean and unclean (see Malina 1981).

In 1986 Malina published another book of models, drawn from the work of various anthropologists, notably Mary Douglas, and intended to provide further resources for study of the social and cultural world of the New Testament (Malina 1986a). Also in 1986 the 'Context Group' was formed, with Bruce Malina as a prominent and founding member. This group, formally organised in 1989, comprises an international (though largely American) group of scholars who meet 'annually to plan, mutually discuss, and evaluate their individual and collaborative work in social-scientific exegesis' (Elliott 1993, 29). In the words of the announcement for their 1997 conference, 'the Context Group is dedicated to understanding and interpreting the Biblical text within the context of the social and cultural world of traditional Mediterranean society'. The pivotal values of Mediterranean society as outlined in Malina's 1981 book have remained foundational to the Context Group's work (see e.g. Esler 1994, 19–36; Rohrbaugh 1996) and a basic motivation for their work remains the avoidance of ethnocentric and anachronistic readings of biblical texts (see e.g. Elliott 1993, 11). Drawing on studies of the Mediterranean, both ancient and modern, and using models developed by anthropologists, they have consistently developed and applied a range of reading strategies to illuminate the foreign world of the New Testament. Contrasts between Mediterranean and American society are often explicitly detailed or tabulated (e.g. Malina and Neyrey 1988, 145–51; Malina 1993, 56–58, 82–86; Malina and Neyrey 1996, 227–31).

---

[22] That is, where persons form their notion of self-identity in terms of what others perceive and relate to them: 'A dyadic personality is one who simply needs another continually in order to know who he or she really is' (Malina 1981, 55). For Malina, this stands in contrast with modern (U.S.) individualism.

[23] That is, where all goods are deemed to be finite and thus where 'an individual, alone or with his family, can improve his social position only at the expense of others' (Malina 1981, 75).

Another early and influential member of the group is Jerome Neyrey, whose many publications since the mid-1980s have also pursued this approach to the New Testament, often in collaboration with Malina and other members of the Context Group.[24] Others whose interest in social-scientific methods began independently but who have since become closely involved with the group's work include John Elliott, who in 1981 published a pioneering study of 1 Peter using what he then termed 'sociological exegesis',[25] and Philip Esler.[26] Recent products of the group's collaborative efforts include the collection of essays on Luke–Acts, edited by Neyrey (1991a), Malina and Richard Rohrbaugh's *Social-Scientific Commentary on the Synoptic Gospels* (1992), and an accessible presentation of the Context Group's models edited by Rohrbaugh (1996), which now provides the best place to begin an encounter with their approach. Their individual and collaborative output has been impressive and extensive, and can hardly be summarised here.[27]

The main achievements of their approach encompass both method and results. First, by elucidating a clear and explicit set of models they have set out openly the basis for their studies, thus enabling readers both to appraise the results and to employ the models experimentally for themselves, should they so wish (see Elliott 1993, 48). Second, the results of their studies have served to illuminate the strikingly different social dynamics at work in the biblical texts and thus to guard against any hermeneutic which elides the distinction between ancient and modern contexts.

However, critical comments may also be made. First, there seems to be an over-dependence on the basic set of models outlined in Malina's work of 1981, which in any case lack the reference to extra-biblical ancient sources necessary to demonstrate the models' validity as a representation of ancient Mediterranean culture (see Gager 1983, 195–96).[28] Some of these models, notably that of honour and shame, and the

---

[24] See e.g. Neyrey 1990; ch. 5 below. In collaboration with Malina: Malina and Neyrey 1988 (see ch. 1 below); 1991a; 1991b; 1996, etc.

[25] See Elliott 1981, 7–11; 1986a, 1; see also ch. 13 below. For more recent reflections and approach see Elliott 1986a; 1993; 1995a; 1995b.

[26] Esler 1987 (see ch. 4 below); compare more recently Esler 1994 esp. 19–36; 1995a and 1995b.

[27] See Elliott 1993, 29–30. Many articles have been published in the *Biblical Theology Bulletin*; for a recent collection of some of Malina's articles see Malina 1996a.

[28] Note, however, the detailed use of ancient sources in e.g. Neyrey (ch. 5 below); Elliott 1995b; Malina and Neyrey 1996.

idea that contests for honour are played out in public encounters of challenge-riposte, have been repeatedly cited and applied (e.g. Malina and Rohrbaugh 1992; Malina and Neyrey 1991a; ch. 5 below). Certainly these studies have helped to show the extent to which such social values are visible in the biblical texts, but the illumination is not necessarily increased with frequent repetition. It may also be suggested that the models have sometimes become somewhat inflexible tools, which lead to a rather 'homogenised' view of 'Mediterranean culture' and give too little opportunity for the subtleties and variations of local contexts to emerge (see Garrett 1988; 1992; Chance 1994, 146–49; Meggitt 1998a). This is especially to be noted since recent anthropological studies stress the variety of ways in which honour or shame (and not necessarily both) may be instantiated in particular contexts, and encourage the researcher to be open to the rich diversity of local cultures, rather than adopt or assume a single model.[29] Moreover, a number of the anthropological studies employed by Malina *et al.* are of the modern Mediterranean, and the implicit assumption that modern and ancient Mediterranean cultures are broadly continuous and similar may be sharply questioned (Meggitt 1998a). To a considerable extent the underlying issue and point of debate is a methodological one: Should a social-scientific approach involve the testing of cross-cultural models or a more inductive, interpretive approach (see §6.1 below)?[30]

4. Historical sociology/social history

All proponents of the use of the social sciences in New Testament studies acknowledge that such work stands in close connection with historical-critical study. The social-sciences provide a further (and, many would argue, essential) component of historical study, enabling the social context, dynamics and impact of the texts to be better understood (see

[29] See esp. Herzfeld 1980; Chance 1994; Gilmore 1987; Peristiany and Pitt-Rivers 1992. Peristiany and Pitt-Rivers (1992, 6) for example, referring to the use of the term 'Mediterranean Society' in the subtitle of their earlier work (Peristiany 1965) state that this 'led sometimes to the misunderstanding that we were proposing to establish the Mediterranean as a "culture area". This was not the case . . . In fact we were as much interested in the differences of culture as in the similarities among the peoples surrounding the Mediterranean'. I am also indebted here to Louise Lawrence's research on honour and shame in anthropology and biblical studies.
[30] See also the critical comments of Sanders 1993, 100–14, relating particularly to the use of Mary Douglas's theory by Malina and Neyrey [see ch. 1 below].

e.g. Elliott 1993, 7–16; Esler 1994, 2–3). However, in contrast to the Context Group, who have developed a particular set of social-scientific models and applied them consistently, others have adopted social-scientific methods in a more eclectic and piecemeal way, regarding themselves primarily as social historians, or have used social theory to develop a theoretical or research framework, but have rejected a specifically model-based approach.[31] The work of Gerd Theissen, for example, already mentioned above (§2), may appropriately be described in this way. Certainly Theissen is acutely theoretically conscious (see 1979, 3–76; 1993, 231–87), yet his use of sociological (and psychological – see 1987) theory is eclectic and experimental, and often linked closely with other historical studies. Particular mention should also be made of the magisterial study by Wayne Meeks, *The First Urban Christians* (1983; see ch. 7 below). In this wide-ranging study of the Pauline churches, Meeks explicitly declares his identity as 'social historian', and states that he adopts his social-scientific theory – both sociological and anthropological – 'piecemeal, as needed, where it fits' (1983, 6). Meeks is concerned to appreciate the particularities of the early Christian communities, something he sees as essentially a historian's concern, which he contrasts with the social-scientist's search for law-like generalisations (1982, 266; see 1983, 1–7). However, in my view, the contrasts between a search for what is distinctive or for what is typical, between open-ended theoretical frameworks or cross-cultural models, may be related to two sides of a debate *within* the social sciences about the nature of social science, rather than to a supposed contrast between history and social science (see Garrett 1992; Horrell 1996a, 9–32). Furthermore, it is not surprising that this debate is played out also in New Testament studies (see further §6.1 below): Elliott (1985) and Malina (1985b), for example, have criticised Meeks' book for its lack of consistent theoretical foundation, while Theissen declared himself 'deeply impressed' (1985, 113).

Other studies which use social-scientific theory yet remain closely connected with historical scholarship and concerns include those of Howard Kee (1980), Francis Watson (1986), Philip Esler (1987), and Margaret MacDonald (1988). More recently, among a number who could be mentioned, John Barclay has employed the social sciences to

---

[31] See Osiek 1989, 268–74; Martin 1993, 107–10; both of whom refer to the different groups now constituted under the auspices of SBL and representing the differences of approach between the 'social historians' and the 'social scientists'.

provide fruitful and heuristic lines of questioning and enquiry, new ways of seeing and conceptualising old issues, yet is concerned primarily to be a historian, and so to wrestle with the scanty and often ambiguous evidence from the period, and to appreciate the distinctiveness and variety in patterns of social interaction and practice (see ch. 11 below; Barclay 1992; 1995; 1996). While there clearly is a difference between such an approach and the work of those social historians who reject the use of contemporary social theory, and while there clearly have been differences in approach between historians, sociologists, and anthropologists, I follow those who argue that there is no sustainable methodological distinction between history and social science and therefore maintain that the distinction between historical sociology and social history is, or should become, meaningless.[32] Historical studies which avoid any discussion of theory or any use of social-scientific insights, as I suggested above, merely impoverish their analyses, or conceal the implicit theoretical presuppositions of their approach.

5. Radical social history and emancipatory theologies

Just as Marxist scholars in the late nineteenth and early twentieth centuries were among those who demonstrated an interest in the social dimensions of early Christianity (see §1 above), so in recent years a number of scholars have developed a variety of what may be termed 'radical' socio-political perspectives on early Christianity, often allied to the concerns of some form of emancipatory theology.[33] Not all radical approaches to the New Testament are in any sense social-scientific, but a good number are. Some derive theoretical resources from Marxist traditions of sociology, and thus develop a 'materialist' reading of the New Testament (e.g. Belo 1974). Also indebted at least indirectly to Marxism, as well as to other versions of critical social theory, are approaches which employ a critical conception of 'ideology' and thus attempt to unmask the ways in which language/texts are used to legitimate and sustain relations of power and domination (see further §6.3 below).

[32] E.g. Anthony Giddens, Philip Abrams, Peter Burke, etc.; see Horrell 1996a, 29–30.
[33] A concern with human emancipation, or liberation, is shared by a range of perspectives, including those of feminism and liberation theology. For examples in New Testament studies see Schottroff and Stegemann 1978; Schottroff and Stegemann 1984; Gottwald and Horsley 1993; Myers 1988; Rowland and Corner 1990; Elliott 1994; further ch. 10 below.

One prominent achievement is the development of feminist social-historical perspectives on the New Testament. Feminist studies represent one form of ideology-critique, in that they seek to expose patriarchal structures of domination in both past and present and to call them into question. A landmark publication in this regard is Elisabeth Schüssler Fiorenza's *In Memory of Her: A Feminist Theological Reconstruction of Christian Origins* (1983 / 1995a). Although Fiorenza does not explicitly adopt social-scientific methods,[34] her work does represent a creative attempt to recover the social history of the early Christian movement, and especially of women within that movement, from behind the veil of androcentric texts and the tradition of androcentric interpretation. She argues that an early 'discipleship of equals' was gradually marginalised by a process of patriarchalisation within the first-century church. Among the many and varied contributions that might also be mentioned, the writings of Luise Schottroff represent notable studies in feminist social history (see Schottroff 1993; 1995). As the essay in chapter 10 below reveals, Schottroff's feminist commitment is closely allied to a commitment to the cause of liberation theology, the emancipation of the poor from structures of oppression.

While these varied radical approaches make clear their socio-political commitments, it is perhaps misleading to refer to them as 'committed' readings, at least if that is taken as an implicit contrast with supposedly 'uncommitted' readings. As Schottroff points out in the essay below (p. 285) the claim to objectivity in much New Testament scholarship is a claim which conceals the interests and commitments which actually underpin the perspective which is adopted. One may perhaps feel that some of the radical readings present a 'history' which is an idealised reflection of contemporary commitments more than of historical reality – such as the utopian ideal of the discipleship of equals, or the egalitarian church of the poor in which the rich abandoned their social privileges. Nevertheless, they represent an important challenge to 'bourgeois' interpreters to consider the possibility of other perspectives on the history of early Christianity, perspectives which may perhaps sit less comfortably with the presuppositions of their socio-economic location and commitments. Moreover, they challenge interpreters to

---

[34] For this reason Fiorenza's claim, based on the omission of mention of her book in recent overviews of social-scientific approaches by Kee 1985 and Martin 1993, that: 'According to such "scientific" historical records of the discipline, feminist historical and social-scientific work still does not exist' (1995a, xxxv n. 2) is hardly justified.

confront the unacknowledged commitments which inevitably mean that evidence is seen from a particular perspective – or sometimes overlooked altogether – because of the interpreter's own context.

6. Significant areas of current debate and prospects for future development

In such a rich and diverse field of scholarship there are numerous differences and disagreements that could be highlighted. In what follows I focus on certain important points of contemporary debate and on what seem to me the main areas for future development in social-scientific study of the New Testament.

6.1. Theory, methods and models

Many of those who have written about the use of social-scientific methods in New Testament studies have stressed the importance of ongoing methodological reflection (e.g. Stowers 1985; Elliott 1986a). Susan Garrett, for example, writing on the sociology of early Christianity, insists: 'It is . . . increasingly urgent that scholars of Christian origins engage in sustained reflection on the philosophical implications of the perspectives and models they choose to employ' (Garrett 1992, 93). In Garrett's article a contrast is drawn between 'a rigorous model-testing approach' – characteristic, as we have seen, of the work of the Context Group – and the more 'interpretive' approach adopted by 'ethnographic' anthropologists (i.e. those who seek to immerse themselves in the culture of the people they are studying and then to offer a 'thick description'; see Garrett 1992, 92). Garrett sees Meeks' book (1983) as a fine example of the latter approach, which she favours (Garrett 1992, 95–96).

This, then, is an important point of contemporary debate and disagreement (see Martin 1993, 107–10). On the one hand there are those who insist that a social-scientific approach should involve the employment and testing of models which have been formulated on the basis of cross-cultural research. Malina, a prominent practitioner of this approach, defines a model as 'an abstract, simplified representation of some real world object, event or interaction' (1982, 231). Equipped with an appropriate set of social-scientific models the researcher can approach the evidence and test whether the data fit. Those who advocate a model-based approach insist that their use of models is heuristic and not prescriptive, and that only if the data fit the model will its use be justified

(Esler 1994, 12–13; 1995a, 4). But any particular model *shapes* the way in which evidence is selected and interpreted; theoretical questions about the nature of a model or research framework are therefore as crucial as the pragmatic question as to how well the data fit.

Others have doubts about this 'scientific' approach to the study of human societies, and consider that a model-based approach can result in the evidence being fitted into a particular mould which insufficiently allows for variations across space and change over time. They argue instead for an approach which, while theoretically informed, uses theory as a 'sensitising' tool and seeks to explore the particularities of each specific socio-cultural context (see Garrett 1992; Horrell 1996a, 9–18; Barclay below pp. 296–97).

A comparable division among classicists influenced by anthropology is noted by Paul Cartledge (1994):

> On the one hand, there are those who believe it is possible and fruitful to generalize across all modern Greece (and sometimes, more broadly still, to 'the Mediterranean world,' for example) and to use such generalized comparative data to supplement as well as interpret the lacunose primary data of antiquity . . . On the other hand, there are those who . . . believe . . . that such comparison should be used chiefly to highlight fundamental cultural difference rather than homogenize heterogenous cultures, or fill gaps in the extant primary sources. (Cartledge 1994, 5)

This debate reflects a similar one within the social sciences themselves, where some (e.g. Turner 1987, 156–94) advocate an approach which seeks to generalise and explain human behaviour in laws and precise models, while others argue for a more interpretive, or hermeneutically-informed version of social science, which emphasises rather the uniqueness of particular contexts and seeks explanations in those particularities rather than in generalisations (e.g. Giddens 1984, xiii-xxxvii, 1–40; see further Horrell 1996a, 9–32). In the current 'post-modern' climate there has certainly been a move away from grand theory and model-building. Some contemporary anthropologists, for example, have specifically criticised 'generalisations' about supposed cultural zones, such as 'the Mediterranean', calling instead for 'ethno-graphic particularism' (Herzfeld 1980, 349; see Peristiany and Pitt-Rivers 1992, 5–6; n. 29 above).

Such philosophical and theoretical issues are an important area of current debate, with implications for the way in which a historical approach informed by the social sciences should be developed. It is hardly to be expected, nor necessarily to be desired, that the current diversity of method and practice will disappear. But it is important to explore and debate the theoretical issues which underpin the variety of approaches, in order to clarify what is basically in dispute and to refine and reformulate new directions for research.[35]

6.2. Anthropology and the understanding of the ancient Mediterranean context

As outlined in §3 above, members of the Context Group have developed and applied a consistent set of models based on the work of various anthropologists, which, they propose, enables the interpreter to avoid the perils of anachronism and ethnocentricism and to appreciate the cultural dynamics of the ancient Mediterranean. Certainly the group's work has done much to draw attention to the social and cultural dynamics of the New Testament world and to highlight the differences between that world and the twentieth-century West. However, critical questions concerning both the model-based method and the actual depiction of Mediterranean culture (and its diversity across time and space), already raised above, lead some to doubt whether it is as successful as its practitioners claim. On the other hand, members of the group are robust in their defence of the approach (Esler 1995a, 4–8; 1998a), and (sometimes) overly dismissive of work which adopts a different perspective.[36] Balancing the questions posed concerning the Context Group's work, a counter-question should certainly be considered: Have other socio-historical studies failed to find and employ the social-scientific resources which would enable them to grasp the distinctive culture reflected in the New Testament texts and hence perpetuated anachronistic and

---

[35] See Osiek 1989, 269–74, 277; Martin 1993, 107–10. For the two sides of the ongoing debate see Garrett 1992 with response in Esler 1995a, 4–8; Horrell 1996a, 9–32, with critique and response in Esler 1998. For a model-based approach see e.g. Malina 1981; 1986a; Elliott 1986a; Neyrey 1991a; Rohrbaugh 1996.

[36] Malina 1996b, for example, asterisks certain works in his bibliography on 'Understanding New Testament Persons' as 'inadequate for a valid understanding . . . cited as examples of outdated or dead-end approaches to the subject'. The list includes Meeks 1983 and Theissen 1987, both of which, disagreements and criticisms notwithstanding, are generally regarded as important and valuable works. Malina also dismisses the work of Judith Perkins on insubstantial grounds (see Meggitt 1998a, 219). See also his sharply critical review of Stark 1996 (Malina 1997).

ethnocentric readings? [37] Again we may doubt that the debate will somehow be 'resolved', but it is an important one which needs to be pursued so that different approaches may learn from and enrich one another (cf. Osiek 1989, 277).

Furthermore, there is surely much to be gained from continued critical engagement with recent anthropological work on societies which bear closer comparison with the New Testament communities than do the industrialised market economies of the contemporary developed world. Indeed, Dale Martin suggests that 'most scholars engaged in social approaches to the New Testament claim to find sociology less and less helpful and anthropology and ethnography more and more interesting' (Martin 1993, 115). Martin's recent book (1995) represents an interesting and important study, not using a model-based approach, but employing cross-cultural studies and drawing briefly on theories of ideology, which illustrates how ancient sources may be used to reconstruct the diverse and contrasting ancient views of the social and individual body, and of disease in the body, thereby also stressing the gap between that social world and our own. [38]

6.3. Radical or conservative? The New Testament, its interpreters, and the critique of ideology

The work of feminists, liberation theologians, and other radical scholars (see §5 above), has helped to focus attention on particular socio-political questions about the history of early Christianity and the character of the New Testament texts: To what extent and in what sense was the early church egalitarian? To what extent, if at all, did the early Christian communities reject or subvert the dominant social and patriarchal hierarchy of their society? Does the teaching of Jesus, or Paul, or other New Testament witnesses, challenge that patriarchal hierarchy and promote equality and liberation, or does it reinforce established patterns of domination and subordination? Although the presuppositions and commitments of each interpreter undoubtedly affect the ways in which

---

[37] See, e.g. the comments of Malina 1997; the criticism of Malherbe in Malina 1996a, 217–41 and of the use of the Weberian concept of 'charisma' in New Testament studies in Malina 1996a, 123–42; the critique of Horrell 1996a in Esler 1998a; and Elliott's (1993, 97) rejection of certain social-scientific approaches used in New Testament study, because 'they derive from modern social experience with no ancient counterpart'.

[38] See further the review in Horrell 1996b. For another recent book using cultural anthropology see Gordon 1997.

these questions are posed and the style of the answer, a particular perspective by no means necessarily follows from a specific interpretative commitment. Feminist scholars, for example, disagree as to whether the New Testament offers some evidence of, and resources to support, the liberation and equality of women (e.g. Fiorenza 1983; Schottroff 1993) or whether the whole Judaeo-Christian tradition is so irredeemably patriarchal that it must be abandoned altogether (e.g. Daly 1986; Hampson 1996). Radical and Marxist scholars of the New Testament and of ancient history disagree as to whether early Christianity's message challenged the social order of the day, or whether it merely helped to sustain it.[39] What is important is that these critical sociological questions have been placed prominently onto the agenda of New Testament studies, and it is to be hoped that further debate will seek to clarify not only the range of possible answers to such questions, but also the ways in which theoretical resources from the traditions of Marxism and critical social theory might be used to develop historically plausible radical perspectives on the early church (see further ch. 10 below).

Among the wide variety of recent and postmodern approaches to biblical criticism are developments in ideological criticism, where interpreters inquire into the interests which underpin particular textual formulations, and how those texts function in a discourse of power, to sustain hierarchies, to marginalise and exclude, and to conceal or naturalise relations of domination.[40] These critical questions clearly connect with the concerns of feminist and liberation theologies, which seek to unmask the strategies by which men legitimate or conceal their domination of women, or by which the rich maintain and conceal their oppression of the poor. But these questions about (concealed) interests are now being addressed not only to the ancient texts but also to their contemporary interpreters, whose interests and commitments are equally bound up with the perspectives they adopt and promote. Thus a whole series of critical (and sometimes disturbing) questions are beginning to

---

[39] See e.g. the positive view of a 'liberating' Paul in Elliott 1994 (review in Horrell 1997b); the 'love–hate' relationship with the New Testament – essentially positive about Jesus, negative about Paul – expressed by Mayer 1983; and the negative comments on the impact of early Christianity in de Ste Croix 1975; 1981, 103–11, 416–41.

[40] For a brief introduction to ideological criticism see Pippin 1997; also, linked with the wider concerns of postmodern biblical criticism, Adam 1995; Bible and Culture Collective 1995. I have sought to apply a critical conception of ideology in the context of a social-scientific approach in a number of publications: Horrell 1993; 1995; 1996a; ch. 12 below.

be raised and there is the potential for further development of an interesting coalescence of concerns: from ideology-critique, critical social theory, emancipatory theologies, and radical or materialist approaches to history.

6.4. Links with literary and rhetorical approaches

Another major new direction in biblical studies of the last quarter-century or so is the development of a wide variety of literary approaches, ranging from narrative and rhetorical studies to reader-response, post-structuralism and deconstruction (see n. 1 above for surveys). Some of these methods have virtually nothing in common with social-scientific approaches, as they consciously eschew any interest in the social world in which the text was originally produced. However, since the study of the New Testament, whatever else it may be, is certainly the study of literature, tools for literary analysis and criticism can hardly but be important to socio-historical investigations. Any responsible historical or social-scientific study must take account of the literary character of the texts which comprise the primary evidence, and must consider carefully how historical evidence can be drawn from texts that are written to exhort and persuade, often with a polemical and argumentative thrust. In recent years some scholars have sought to develop methods which incorporate both literary and social-scientific approaches to interpretation. Norman Petersen's (1985) study of Paul's letter to Philemon is a good example. Vernon Robbins has given considerable attention to the task of developing an integrated approach to New Testament interpretation which encompasses both literary-rhetorical and social-scientific methods, and has coined the term 'socio-rhetorical criticism' (see Robbins 1996a; 1996b). In two recent 'socio-rhetorical' commentaries, one on the Corinthian letters (1995), the other on Acts (1998), Ben Witherington has independently[41] also sought to combine the insights of social-scientific and rhetorical approaches in a historical analysis of these texts. Such attempts to integrate social-scientific and literary methods are important and timely, and point the way to an important direction for continuing research.

---

[41] Witherington (1995, xii n. 8) does acknowledge: 'It appears that the term "socio-rhetorical" was first used by Vernon K. Robbins.'

6.5. The continued revitalisation of the study of New Testament history, ethics and theology

Since the 1970s 'sociological' perspectives have become increasingly widely infused into New Testament studies. It is now, for example, commonplace to hear about the sectarian character of the Johannine community, or the social function of the Jewish law. Such perspectives have undoubtedly helped to root the discussion of New Testament texts much more concretely in the social situations of human communities and in an appreciation of the social dynamics of human interaction and conflict. In terms of Scroggs' critique of much New Testament study up to the 1970s (cited above, p. 6) it seems that the introduction of social-scientific perspectives has indeed helped 'to put body and soul together again' and has led to the 'revitalising of historical criticism' (Barton 1997, 286; 1995). The continued creative and careful use of a variety of social-scientific approaches – some no doubt yet to be discovered by biblical scholars – should enable this revitalisation to progress further.

At the close of a recent essay introducing social-scientific criticism Stephen Barton suggests that the introduction of social-scientific perspectives may perhaps also bear fruit in revitalising the study of New Testament theology and ethics (Barton 1997, 286: 'it remains to be seen . . .'). Barton mentions the work of William Countryman (1989) and Wayne Meeks (1993) as 'promising beginnings'. Certainly there is an obvious overlap of concern between the study of ethics – if ethics is conceived of as reflection on the ways in which human beings should behave in relation to one another and their environment – and the social-scientific study of patterns of social interaction in communities and of the ways in which texts both arise from and shape their social context. If the social sciences do influence the study of New Testament ethics then they will surely direct the focus away from the individual and her/his decisions of right and wrong on specific moral questions, and towards the ways in which the New Testament texts shape social relationships in particular community contexts (see Barton 1992). Hence Meeks prefers to speak of the New Testament texts as instruments of 'moral formation' (1996, 317). The questions raised by social scientists also have a direct bearing on the critical study of New Testament ethics: Who is urging what particular course or pattern of behaviour, and whose interests does that exhortation reflect? How is power used to manipulate or coerce? There would seem then to be the scope for the fruitful enrichment of the study of New Testament ethics with perspectives and questions from the social sciences.

If theology is seen not as the elucidation of abstract and unchanging truths but as 'a contingent historical construct emerging from, and reacting back upon, particular social practices conjoined with particular semiotic and figural codings' (Milbank 1990, 2), then, *pace* Milbank, the study of theology is surely closely linked with the concerns of social science. In terms of the study of New Testament theology (or theologies) the social sciences offer tools to enrich the historical study of the social context within which such theology was formed, and provide theoretical tools to analyse the ways in which the theology (expressed in texts) acted back upon – i.e. shaped – social interaction in the early Christian communities. In this field of study too, then, the social sciences have an important role to play.

7. Conclusion

The use of the social sciences in New Testament studies is now widespread and firmly established. Whether in the study of the social context behind a text, or of the ideology and impact of a text itself, or indeed of the social location and interests of contemporary interpreters, the social sciences have shown that they offer rich resources to complement both the already established and the newly developing methods of biblical criticism. The sheer diversity of approach, and the increasingly widespread impact of social-scientific study, make the field ever more difficult to survey and assess. With links established to both historical criticism and literary methods, the social sciences have made their presence and their value felt almost right across the board. All the signs indicate that in a wide variety of directions the social sciences will continue to enrich and inform the study of the New Testament.

FURTHER READING

Book-length introductions to the social sciences and New Testament interpretation are Tidball 1983; Osiek 1984 (2nd edn 1992); Holmberg 1990; Elliott 1993. Holmberg and Elliott are especially useful. Shorter introductions and assessments of the field may be found in the dictionary articles by Kee 1985; Garrett 1992; and the articles by Osiek 1989; Barton 1992; 1995; 1997; and Martin 1993. The most accessible and recent introduction to the Context Group's approach is Rohrbaugh 1996. On the wider issues of the relationship between theology and sociology the best place to begin is with the new edition of the reader edited by Gill 1996.

For bibliographical information see Harrington 1988; Theissen 1988, 331–70; May 1991; Barton 1992; and Elliott 1993. May and Elliott offer the most comprehensive and up-to-date coverage.

1

Jesus the Witch:
Witchcraft Accusations in Matthew 12

BRUCE J. MALINA and JEROME H. NEYREY

INTRODUCTION

Bruce Malina and Jerome Neyrey, more than any other New Testament scholars, have worked to explore the ways in which models from the field of cultural anthropology might shed new light upon the texts of the New Testament and the world from which they emerged (see *Introduction* §3). In this essay, the first chapter from their book *Calling Jesus Names: The Social Value of Labels in Matthew* (1988), they draw on the work of the prominent British anthropologist Mary Douglas in order to establish a model which will help to illuminate the 'social script' – the set of social and cultural values, assumptions, etc. – reflected in a certain layer of Matthean tradition. This layer of tradition is one in which 'witchcraft accusations', 'a technical anthropological term' (p. 33) describing the labelling of enemies as 'demonic', are exchanged between members of the Jesus-movement and 'outsiders', notably the Pharisees.

First, using Douglas' grid-group model, Malina and Neyrey sketch the characteristics of a 'high-group/low-grid' culture, which is, they argue, the type clearly represented in the Matthean tradition and descriptive of the early Jesus-movement group within its Mediterranean context. Then, in the second major part of the essay, they outline the specific characteristics of 'witchcraft societies' and consider the nature and intentions of the accusations of witchcraft which are made in such societies, and specifically as they appear in Matthew's gospel. In the rest of the book they study the 'labelling' of Jesus, both positive and negative, from the perspective of deviance/labelling theory (cf. ch. 11 below).

The result is a very different perspective on the Matthean text from that found in much conventional exegesis. The cultural values and social dynamics operative in the early Christian communities are seen to be quite unlike those which dominate modern Western societies, though, at the same time, previously unconsidered similarities with other cultures and contexts may become apparent. Indeed one of Malina and Neyrey's main concerns, as of the 'Context Group' to which they belong, is to interpret the New Testament in the light of its (Mediterranean) cultural context, and thus to avoid 'ethnocentric' and 'anachronistic' readings which implicitly view the text through the lens of North American cultural and social assumptions (see *Introduction* §3).

One of the problems in using Mary Douglas' grid-group model is that the way in which the terms are defined by Douglas has evolved through the course of her publications (see Carter 1997, 45–46). New Testament scholars adopting her work need therefore to make clear the sense in which they are using the terms (see Atkins 1991, 70; for other presentations of Douglas' model, see Carter 1997, 70; Atkins 1991, 54–75). Here (see p. 37) Malina and Neyrey follow the presentation of her model in Malina (1986a, 1–97), and their picture of Mediterranean culture follows, like much of the Context Group's work, the 'pivotal values' set out in Malina's ground-breaking book *The New Testament World* (1981; see also ch. 5 below). Although such models often help to emphasise the 'strangeness' of the New Testament world (see Nineham 1976, 1–39; 1982), one may perhaps question whether they allow the interpreter sufficiently to appreciate the distinctiveness of the particular context being investigated. Cross-cultural comparisons and models may of course be illuminating, but may also lead to an approach which is most concerned with what is generalisable and typical (see Horrell 1996a, 9–26). It has been suggested that Malina's work has produced a rather 'homogenised' view of 'Mediterranean culture' which pays insufficient attention to the variations across time and space (see Meggitt 1998a; further *Introduction* §3). Jack Sanders has also questioned Malina's and Neyrey's applications of Douglas' model, and argued that it is unable to offer adequate explanations or to incorporate change, and thus that it is not useful for the study of early Christianity (Sanders 1993, 100–14).

Douglas' grid-group model has also been applied to the study of Paul and the Pauline churches (see e.g. Neyrey 1986a; 1990; Atkins 1991; Carter 1997; Gordon 1997; cf. also Barton 1986). Robert Atkins, for example, concludes that the Pauline churches are (like the early Matthean group, according to Malina and Neyrey) high-group/low-grid communities characterised by strong group boundaries but 'little concern for internal division or hierarchy' (Atkins 1991, 186): they may be described as 'egalitarian communities'. Timothy Carter, in dialogue specifically with Neyrey (1986a) and focusing on the church at Corinth, argues that 'Paul should in fact be located in the sectarian 'high-group/low-grid' quadrant, while the Corinthians themselves should be located in the 'high-grid/low-group' quadrant of competitive individualism' (Carter 1997, 47–48).

Does Mary Douglas' model provide an adequate scheme for categorising types of community and culture and for theorising change? Do the New Testament texts provide enough of the kind of information that can be used to classify reliably the group culture which they reflect? Are the negative labels exchanged between hostile parties recorded in Matthew's gospel rightly seen as 'witchcraft accusations' arising within a 'witchcraft society'? These are just some of the questions which readers may consider as they study this essay. In my view, however, what is beyond doubt is that Malina and Neyrey have helped to illuminate a social dynamic, reflected in the Matthean tradition, which operates on the basis of cultural values and assumptions quite different from those which underpin modern Western societies, and in which conflict and hostility are dealt with in very different ways. In that particular social context, the conflict between the Jesus-movement and the Pharisees was expressed in the attempt to exclude and demonise the other, at least partly through the use of 'witchcraft accusations'.

1.1. The evidence: accusations

Matthew's gospel is remarkable in that it contains numerous accusations of demonic possession and / or collaboration. To begin with, the Pharisees' accusations against Jesus are quite familiar. Twice they interpret Jesus' healing actions negatively: 'He casts out demons by the prince of demons' (9:34) and 'It is by Beelzebul, the prince of demons, that this man casts out demons' (12:24). They even call him 'Beelzebul,' a terrible accusation that extends also to Jesus' disciples: 'If they have called the master of the house Beelzebul, how much more will they malign those of his household' (10:25). Further, John the Baptizer is dismissed as an imposter with this slur: 'He came neither eating nor drinking, and they say he has a demon' (11:18). In turn, members of Matthew's community accuse the Pharisees and other enemies of being possessed by demons. The inimical Pharisees, who were once exorcised of a demon, are accused of being repossessed by that demon and 'seven others more evil than itself' (12:43–45). They are identified as the tares among the wheat, 'the sons of the evil one' (13:38), because 'the enemy who sowed them is the devil' (13:39). They are more fearsome than those who cause physical pain and misfortune because they also kill and so 'destroy both life and person (= soul and body) in Gehenna' (10:28). And when they find a proselyte, they make of him 'twice as much a child of Gehenna' as themselves (23:15). Finally, Jesus himself is alleged to have called Peter 'Satan,' perhaps metaphorically, but perhaps not (16:23). The point is that accusations of demon possession and/or collaboration pervade the gospel, reflecting not just the Pharisees' label for Jesus and his followers, but also the reaction of members of Jesus' group to the Pharisees and other non-members.

Comparable accusations are made in John's gospel as well. We are all familiar with the verbal affront to Jesus: 'Are we not right that you are a Samaritan and have a demon?' (8:48) and 'Now we know that you have a demon' (8:52). In another place, a charge is made against Jesus: 'He has a demon, and he is mad' (10:19). But Jesus himself is credited with accusing his opponents of the same thing: 'You are of your father the devil, and your will is to do your father's desires' (8:44). The accusations, then, are mutual, and they continue among adherents of the Johannine tradition (see 1 John 3:8–10). Thus, the gospels do not have a monopoly on this sort of labelling.

Paul, too, was accustomed to attacking opponents such as the 'super apostles' in 2 Corinthians 11 with a similar charge (Neyrey 1986c). Regarding rival preachers in Corinth, Paul remarked:

> For such men are false apostles, deceitful workmen, disguising themselves as apostles of Christ. And no wonder, even Satan disguised himself as an angel of light. So it is not strange if his servants also disguise themselves as servants of righteousness. (2 Cor 11:13–15)

Whatever the circumstances of Paul's accusations, he considered his rivals as demonic figures who were seducing the pure bride of Christ, just as the serpent deceived Eve by his cunning (11:3).

Although this study will concentrate on the accusations in Matthew's story of Jesus, it is evident that followers of Jesus charged others – even other members of various Jesus groups – with the same charge of demonic possession and / or collaboration with which they were charged. Such accusations were a recurring phenomenon in the time and place occupied by the persons described in the New Testament.

How can readers of the New Testament understand and interpret the experience of those persons? It is the purpose of this discussion to suggest a set of models developed in the field of cultural anthropology that can offer an adequate scenario for a reader to interpret this evidence. The charges mentioned above may be labeled 'witchcraft accusations,' a technical anthropological term that concretely points to a specific situation in a village or small group where a charge is made that (1) one's enemies or rivals are actually the forces of evil or are demonically controlled by them, (2) they are thoroughly evil and so (3) should be expelled from the village or group. The 'witchcraft accusation,' then, while it focuses on the charge of demonic possession, implies much more. For example, it implies a social script based on enemies in constant conflict, on the perception of enemies as fully evil and friends as totally good, on exile and expulsion as the main forms of extreme punishment. Furthermore, the way the witch works, his sources of power and the nature of his attack all relate to an image of the community, the way it works, the sources of power that control it and the kind of attack to which community values are subject. Thus, the evidence of witchcraft accusations implies that the charge arises from a specific type of social script and that it serves to maintain meaningful behavior for persons living according to that sort of script.

What is needed for appreciating the import of these witchcraft accusations is a set of models that might provide insight into the cultural directives of the group in which the accusations occur. The models would thus serve to explain the meaning of such accusations within that context. We turn first to the works of the British anthropologist Mary Douglas for a model that will deal with the general social context within which witchcraft might be understood in a comparative way. This model has two parts. First, Douglas argues that witchcraft accusations occur within a certain type of cultural system (1982, viii–ix, 107–24). Accurate description of that system, then, is an integral part of the model. Second, within that cultural system, it is possible to describe who or what is a 'witch,' how this figure is perceived, and how a 'witchcraft accusation' functions in that system. Elsewhere, we consider another model that deals with the process by means of which persons are labelled as 'witch' or 'demon-possessed.' Such titles, once successfully attached, serve to identify the whole personhood of the one thus labelled. Since such negative labelling is part of a degradation process by means of which a person is judged to be deviant, the model within which these elements fit is called a deviance model (see Malina and Neyrey 1988, 35ff).

The reason for mentioning these models here is that accusations of deviance along with the labelling process and accompanying rituals are part and parcel of what goes on when one accuses or acclaims. Hence, they have always been part and parcel of traditional Christology. We begin here with those typically Mediterranean accusations of witchcraft (Murdock 1980, 21).

1.2. Text and data

Before we begin our anthropological study of the gospel, there is a technical, historical problem to be dealt with. It concerns the text of Matthew itself and the proper data for this study. It is common knowledge that a document such as Matthew presents what an anonymous author says that people before him said that Jesus said and did. The Lukan prologue (Luke 1:1–4) spells this out in detail. The time lag between Jesus' actual career and the writing of the document called Matthew might be some fifty to sixty years. During that period, information about Jesus was 'traditioned,' i.e. selectively remembered and forgotten, successfully applied to new situations and perhaps even misrepresented. While all this is nothing new in historical gospel scholarship, we are suggesting that the witchcraft accusations are found primarily in a stage of Matthew's history considerably earlier than its final form produced by the anonymous evangelist we call 'Matthew.' New Testament criticism can identify many of the sources of this gospel: a Q tradition, Mark's gospel, and special M materials, some of which come from the final author/editor but by no means all, for some of the special M materials may be very early. It is necessary to discriminate among these sources, as failure to do so might produce a homogenized view of the gospel as either overly faction-conscious or overly inclusive of Jews and non-Jews alike. This seems to have been the case with an earlier attempt to use Douglas' witchcraft material *vis-à-vis* Matthew (Pamment 1981).

In the sources of Matthew, we can clearly discern radically different attitudes to key topics such as law (5:18–19 versus 12:7), sin and forgiveness (18:15–17 versus 18:21–32), mission (10:5–6 versus 28:19), and the like (Neyrey 1985, 67–94). The differences in attitudes can be credited to different sources or layers of tradition in the gospel that in turn reflect different experiences and interpretations of those experiences. The final edition of the gospel clearly presents a more inclusive, less perfectionistic view of the ideology of the Jesus group than the earlier materials represented in the Q stratum of the gospel traditions. In the final edition Jesus breaks down restrictive traditions by touching the unclean, eating with sinners, preferring mercy to sacrifice, urging love and forgiveness, and accepting all people, good and bad, as his followers.

Yet as we have noted, this is not the only profile of Jesus in the gospel. There are other text-segments in the same gospel that portray Jesus as strengthening Torah, urging separation from sin and sinners, pronouncing judgment, and restricting the mission only to Jews. It is in text-segments belonging to this level that we find witchcraft accusations. These restrictive, factional actions attributed to Jesus are found primarily in the Q traditions. The differences between the two layers of tradition may be summarized in the following chart.

Early Matthean Tradition	Later Matthean Tradition
1. Mission and Membership	
(*a*) Jews only	(*a*) Jews and non-Jews
(*b*) the few, worthy ones	(*b*) good and bad, clean and unclean, saints and sinners
2. Interpretation of Scripture	
(*a*) OT as legal document	(*a*) OT as prophetic document
(*b*) hedged about by tradition and customs	(*b*) rejection of custom and tradition
(*c*) all OT laws in force	(*c*) essential Law of Love in force
3. Eschatological Perspective	
(*a*) imminent and sure judgment	(*a*) future, distant judgment
(*b*) prophetic judgment of the church and by the church	(*b*) all judgment put in Jesus' hands, not the church's

4. *Ethical Directives*

(*a*) virtue: perfection and total separation from sin	(*a*) virtue: mercy and forgiveness
(*b*) vice: hypocrisy and scandal	(*b*) vice: lack of charity

5. *Group Self-Understanding*

(*a*) the reformed, authentic covenant group	(*a*) a new, different covenant group
(*b*) based on the Mosaic model of covenant	(*b*) based on the promises made to Abraham and David

These distinctions have a direct bearing on this project, because the premier passage in which witchcraft accusations are made about Jesus and by Jesus himself comes from the earlier, more faction-focused stratum of the traditions contained in Matthew's gospel. Although the episode is found in Mark 3:21–30, the account of it in Matthew (and Luke) reflects a different and fuller telling of the story, a version that can be identified as stemming from the Q source, as the following argument indicates.

The version of the mutual accusations of witchcraft in Matthew and Luke share notable, additional points that are not found in the Markan version of the episode:

1. Matt 12:22//Luke 11:14 locate the charge of demon-possession after the cure of a 'dumb demoniac,' which is not the case in Mark.

2. Matt 12:25//Luke 11:17 preface the apology of Jesus to the accusation of demon possession with the important remark that 'Jesus knew their thoughts . . .'

3. Matt 12:27//Luke 11:18–19 record a counteraccusation from Jesus: 'If I cast out demons by Beelzebul, by whom do your sons cast them out?'

4. Matt 12:28//Luke 11:20 record a reinterpretation of Jesus' exorcism: 'But if it is by the Spirit (or finger) of God that I cast out demons, then the kingdom of God has come upon you.'

5. Matt 12:30//Luke 11:23 conclude the defensive strategy of Jesus with the dualistic statement that divides the world into irreconcilable camps, believer versus unbeliever, good versus bad: 'Who is not with me is against me, and who does not gather with me scatters.'

The Matthean version of the episode must be identified with the Q source and not with Mark's text.

The material subsequent to the episode of mutual accusations of demon possession is also supportive of this perspective. It too comes from the Q source and appears to have been originally linked to 12:22–32, as its identical content and location in Luke's gospel illustrate:

6. Matt 12:38–42//Luke 11:29–32 record a strong judgment leveled against unbelievers, especially those who 'seek a sign.' Jesus' exorcism ought to be the sign indicating his agency from God (see Matt 12:28//Luke 11:20), but it is rejected by 'an evil and adulterous generation.' Such unbelievers will be judged by the men of Nineveh and the Queen of the South, true 'outsiders' who became 'insiders' because they acknowledged God's prophets and wise men.

7. Matt 12:43–45//Luke 11:24–26 tell a parable about a person once rid of a demon but later repossessed by it and seven others more evil than the first. In the context this contains a charge that those who accuse Jesus of demon possession are themselves possessed.

The importance of these observations on the stratum of the text-segment and the proper data for this study lie in the advantage they yield, for they enable us to come to this material with some clear ideas about the kinds of issues considered important at this stage and the positions the people involved then took. The episode in which the witchcraft accusations are found belongs to a tradition in which factional self-consciousness was high, where judgmental language was common and strident, where hypocrisy and conspiracy were feared, where perfection was prized and where boundaries were clearly and sharply drawn.

1.3. The model: part one
Cultural cosmology of witchcraft societies

Douglas has been concerned throughout her research with describing the degree of control or non-control that is exercised over a social body. In describing social systems, she has set off two variables, which in her jargon are called 'group' and 'grid' (over the years she has readjusted the meanings of the group and grid variables; we follow the model in Malina 1986a, 1–97). Social systems in general exert varying pressure on their members to conform to societal norms. This degree of pressure to conform is what Douglas means by 'group'; it may be *strong* or *weak*. Strong 'group' indicates a high degree of pressure to conform to societal norms, as well as a strong degree of pressure for order and control.

Where there is strong group pressure, the body is imaged as a bounded, controlled system; entrances and exits are guarded; order and discipline are valued; individuals always think of themselves as group members first; hence, group values take precedence over individual desires. Weak 'group' indicates a low degree of pressure to conform to societal norms. Where this pressure is weak, the body is not perceived as a controlled system but as a means to ends chosen by individuals, who are ever in charge of themselves; entrances and exits are left to individual discretion; norms and discipline are not valued; and personality tends to be individualistic.

Douglas' model of social description contains a second variable, 'grid,' which refers to the degree of assent given to the norms, definitions and classifications of a cultural system. 'Grid' may be *high* or *low*. High 'grid' indicates a high degree of fit and compliance between an individual's experience and societal patterns of perception and expectations. Individuals will perceive the world as coherent, consistent and intelligible in its broadest reaches. Low 'grid' indicates a poor degree of fit and match between individual experiences and stated societal patterns of perception and experience. When 'grid' is low, the world seems incomprehensible or fraught with conflict and contradictions.

According to the variables, a possible typology of social systems emerges:

(*a*) strong group/high grid
(*b*) strong group/low grid
(*c*) weak group/high grid
(*d*) weak group/low grid

The cosmology or world view of each of these types can be rather carefully delineated according to a set of categories that anthropologists and others concerned with social meanings consider significant: (1) purity, (2) ritual, (3) personal identity, (4) body, (5) deviance, (6) cosmology and (7) suffering and misfortune. If we follow the grid and group variables, there will be four distinct social scripts or cosmologically rooted social systems. The type that interests us is that of strong group/low grid, which may be briefly described as follows.

Purity is about systematic classification. The existence of dirt, for example, points to purity. Dirt is matter 'out of place.' For there to be dirt, there must be a system of places sufficiently marked off so that matter can be assessed to be 'out of place.' Dirt entails a system of related places so that everything can be seen to belong some place. Cleaning a place is a purification process in which things are returned to where they belong. Thus, dirt is 'removed.' If 'dirt' points to and implies disorder, then 'purity' points to and implies order/system. The existence of purity concerns is revealed in the existence of societal classifications and the 'law and order' deriving from them.

In strong group/low grid, there is a strong concern for an ordered society, with clear classification of persons and things, sexual and role differentiation (Malina 1981, 37–41; Neyrey 1986b, 92–105). Yet this concern is more a desideratum than anything realizable, for the ordered, 'pure' social body is perceived to be under attack. Pollution, the actual or possible state of disorder, of mixed and blurred classifications, is present, and purification rituals are ineffective for expelling the threat. The social body as well as the individual body are perceived to be under siege.

Ritual is behavior concerning the lines that make up the purity or societal system. Line crossings are called *rites*, while the celebration of lines and of those within is called a *ceremony* (Malina 1986a, 139–43).[1] In strong group/low grid, the group's ritual activity is focused on the making and maintenance of boundaries for the rather unsure purity system. This involves the development of tests for outwardly determining who is 'in' and who is 'out' of the group and for internally ordering and ranking people according to desirably clear roles. The threat to boundaries in this script indicates that social energy will be focused there. This means that effort will be expended (1) to identify pollutants that are invading the ordered group and (2) to seek their expulsion from the threatened system. Identifying the invader, however, constitutes one of this group's major problems because the group's internal lines of classification – especially the lines defining the authority structure of the group, the roles and the social ranking of its members – are chronically ambiguous. Who can act as spokesperson for the ordered system so as to know who is true and who is false or what is or is not in place?

Personal identity refers to the way individual humans perceive themselves relative to others in primary group settings. In strong group/ low grid, the individual is enculturated to perceive himself or herself as always embedded in a group. Thus, personal identity is dyadic, assessed in terms of others, located primarily in group membership, with individual

---

[1] [Elsewhere, Malina and Neyrey use *rite* as the overall label, and distinguish between *rituals* of status-transformation/line-crossing and *ceremonies* of status-confirmation; see introduction to ch. 8 below – Ed.]

roles being ill-defined, even confused. As awareness of the threat to the system grows, there is a corresponding awakening to the divergence between the external appearance of things and people and their internal states. Things are not as they seem; deceit is at work everywhere. And because evil is disguised as good, it is very difficult to detect.

Body, that is, the individual physical body, is perceived as a micro-cosm of the social body. As the social body is carefully ordered and structured, so the physical body is tightly controlled. And as the social body is under attack, so the physical body is experiencing assault: invaders and pollutants have broken through the bodily boundaries, especially the oral or sexual orifices. The body, which ideally ought be considered a symbol of life, is now a battleground where disguised and corrupting pollutants are threatening attack.

Deviance refers to the behavior of persons out of place in a negative way. In traditional theological language, deviance is sin. The perception of deviance in this script might surface in two ways. A group with a strong sense of 'purity' tends to be concerned with order and system, that is, with formal rules, the violation of which constitutes deviant behavior, a sin or a crime. But as people with this script perceive themselves under threat of attack from a corrupting force, sin will also be understood as pollution, evil or disease within persons and society. In other words, perceptions of some abiding 'original sin,' 'original corruption,' 'evil impulses in the heart' and the like are typical. Since one cannot trust external appearances, concern will tend to be focused on a person's interior, to see if the heart or intention is still pure and in line.

Cosmology refers to world view, to common beliefs about how the world works. This group's world view is profoundly dualistic, as it perceives the cosmos peopled with warring forces of good and evil. This world, moreover, is anthropomorphic. This means that human or humanlike forces are perceived to stand behind success, as well as illness and failure. The operative question is 'Who did this to me?' Yet, this world is under attack by disguised, evil personal forces, so that ultimate victory may not be apparent.

Suffering and misfortune are meted out quite unjustly. Punishment does not automatically follow transgression, but may well be the result of malevolent forces attacking and harming the ordered world. Suffering, moreover, becomes especially the lot of the good, since they are the natural enemies of the attacking evil forces. Suffering is simply part and parcel of life; it cannot be eliminated but perhaps can be alleviated for a while.

There seems little doubt that the strong group/low grid social script served as the cultural milieu in which the early Matthean group lived, for this much is evidenced by the information presented in the basic strata of Matthew. These strata are undoubtedly representative of early traditions that made up the original gospel story as remembered and interpreted by some of the first members of the Jesus-movement group. To realize this point, simply consider that information provided by these strata in terms of the previous classification.

1.3a. Purity

In a social group the concern for order and system indicates what is permitted or proscribed (Malina 1981, 122–52). A strong emphasis on purity and its opposite, pollution, suggests a highly ordered social group with clear boundaries, a clear classification system, and clear standards of orthodoxy and orthopraxis. The text of Matthew makes this evident. A strong sense of purity is linked, in the first place, with a 'perfect' keeping of the Law. Total purity demands a radical keeping of all the commandments: Jesus will not relax one iota, one dot of the Law: 'Whoever relaxes one of the least of these commandments . . . will be called least in the kingdom' (5:18–20; see Luke 16:17). The demand for obedience extends beyond mere external observance of the commandments to both interior attitudes and derivative behavior. The genuine keeping of 'Thou shalt not kill,' for instance, is abstention not just from homicide, but from anger and abusive language (5:21–22); to refrain from sexual challenges to another's honor entails abstention from lust for his wife in one's heart, as well as in actual behavior (5:27–28). Group members are not only informed about the meaning of genuine obedience to Torah (5:21–47), but are also given an exalted ideal: 'Be perfect as your heavenly Father is perfect' (5:48; see Luke 6:36), a command analogous to Lev 11:44–45, 'Be holy as I am holy.' In short, the ordering of life according to the principle of Torah is complete and systematic, as hedges are constructed around the Law and every ambiguity or detail fully accounted for.

The demand for order and purity is total; even partial evil, or 'darkness,' makes the whole body into darkness. Hence, a pure and perfect 'eye' is demanded; if it is sound, 'your whole body will be full of light,' but if there is pollution in the eye, then 'your whole body will be full of darkness' (6:22–23 // Luke 11:34–36). In this regard, the group is explicitly contrasted with hypocritical Pharisees, who cleanse only the outside of the cup and plate, but neglect the inside (23:25–26 // Luke 11:39–41). Members of the Jesus group must be clean within and without. It is evident, then, that this early stage of Matthew's community strongly emphasized purity, and that this purity was identified with the radical and reformed keeping of Torah as this was interpreted by Jesus and his followers and not by the Pharisees. Called to be perfect, they must be so in every area of life.

But in accordance with the witchcraft perceptions indigenous to the Mediterranean area (Murdock 1980, 58), the social and physical bodies are under attack in the Jesus faction as well. These attacks come from the outside and the inside: (1) *From without* – the Jesus-movement group is challenged by another Jewish reform group, the Pharisees, whose members disparage allegiance to Jesus and his teaching. (2) *From within* – some members are perceived as not living up to Torah perfection, and behavior rooted in undisciplined enthusiasm threatens to displace Torah observance as the group's ideal. Against these it must be affirmed that it is not those who say 'Lord, Lord,' nor those who 'prophesy in my name and do mighty works' who will enter the kingdom, but only those 'who do the will of my father who is in heaven' (7:21–23 // Luke 6:46 and 13:25–27). The system, then, is under siege from within and without.

1.3b. Ritual

The typical or characteristic activity of this society is boundary making and boundary maintenance (Douglas 1966, 114, 123–24; 1982, viii–ix, 113). Consequently, it seems normal to find great concern with boundaries in the sources of Matthew and in the final text itself, where the world is completely divided between friends and enemies, typical of strong group / low grid:

Q Matt 5:43–48:	*On the positive side*: neighbor, those you love, those you pray for, the good, the just, those you greet, brothers
	And on the negative side: enemy, those you hate, those who persecute you, the wicked, the unjust, tax collectors, non-Jews
M Matt 7:6:	Dogs, swine (fit on the negative side)
M Matt 7:15:	False prophets, inwardly ravenous wolves

Q Matt 7:16–17:	*On the positive side*: grapes, figs, good fruit
	On the negative side: thorns, thistles, bad fruit
M Matt 7:18–20:	*On the positive side*: sound tree, good fruit
	On the negative side: bad tree, evil fruit
	Note: thrown into the fire for not bearing good fruit (compare preaching of John the Baptist in Q 3:10: identical)
M Matt 10:17–25:	*On the one side*: 'you,' members of Jesus' household, through whom the Spirit of your Father speaks, hated, persecuted, disciples below their teacher, servants below their master, the maligned for Jesus' name sake
	On the other side: 'they,' fellow Jews with their councils and synagogues, with their kings and governors, along with non-Jews, persecutors and executors, those who label Jesus Beelzebul
Q Matt 12:34:	*On the positive side*: good treasure (of the heart), good things
	On the negative side: evil treasure (of the heart), evil things

The initial action that creates boundaries for those Jews who made up the Jesus-movement group is the alternative group awareness deriving from the group's preaching. Believers are the insiders who accept the preaching and the preacher, and by 'change of heart' restore those limit markers setting off sin from behavior befitting God's coming kingdom. Fellow Israelite unbelievers, who reject the preacher and the preaching, are the outsiders who do not enter the kingdom but go down to destruction. By preaching, then, boundary distinctions are constantly being made. For example, John the Baptizer preaches about Jesus, describing him as a boundary maker with a winnowing fork in his hand to clean his threshing floor. The wheat (believers/insiders) will be gathered into the granary, while the chaff (unbelievers/outsiders) will be cast out and burned in the furnace (3:12//Luke 3:17).

Jesus likewise preaches in such a way as to continue this boundary-making distinction in passages such as 12:38–42 (//Luke 11:29–32): this wicked and illegitimate generation will be confronted by Nineveh and the Queen of the South. Those former outsiders have been transformed into insiders because 'they repented at the preaching of Jonah' and 'they heard the wisdom of Solomon.' They will judge Jesus' un-believing audiences who refuse to listen to the preaching of one who is 'greater than Jonah and greater than Solomon.' As a whole, the people of Chorazin, Bethsaida and Capernaum, too, rejected Jesus' preaching and so find themselves on the wrong side of the boundary of judgment. Instead of being 'exalted to heaven,' they will be 'cast down to Hades' (11:23//Luke 10:15). Jerusalem, which was invited to come 'inside' as a chick under a hen's wing, refused and remained outside, even desolate (23:37–38//Luke 13:34–35).

Becoming a member of the new Jesus faction itself produces boundaries. In the instructions that Jesus is said to have delivered to those who would promote his name, he states that he came to force people to cross boundaries and to shift allegiances. He does not bring 'peace on earth . . . but a sword,' to set 'a man against his father, a daughter against her mother, a daughter-in-law against her mother-in-law' (10:34–35//Luke 12:53). Conversion to the new group, then, will split families and set members on different sides of the boundary. Converts cross family boundary lines – perhaps even expelled by their families (10:21) and so become outsiders. But they become insiders in that they enter the new, fictive family of the Jesus-movement group (12:46–50), and so boundaries are maintained all around.

The ideology of the Jesus movement, as articulated in the teaching of group leaders, also makes boundaries. When it is contrasted with scribal teaching on Torah in the 'Antitheses' of the Sermon on the Mount (5:21–47), the teaching of the Jesus faction establishes clear boundaries distinguishing the two groups. One will never 'enter the kingdom of God' unless one's righteousness in Torah observance exceeds that of the scribes and Pharisees (5:20). The attack on the 'leaven' of the Pharisees (16:6, 11–12) and the long list of woes against their teaching (chapter 23) also serve to draw sharp boundaries between them and the followers of Jesus.

The metaphors used to describe how members of the Jesus movement understood themselves indicate the extent of their appropriation of the boundaries that have been made. Jesus' followers are the 'few who are chosen' out of the many Israelites who were called (22:14); they enter through the narrow gate where the way is hard, while the many go through the wide gate that leads to destruction (7:13–14//Luke 13:23–24). They are the sheep among wolves (10:16//Luke 10:3); they are the wheat growing in a field with tares (13:24–30); they are the obedient sons who go to work in the father's vineyard in contrast to sons who said that they would go, but did not (21:28–31). They are the houses built on rock that survive floods and winds, unlike the houses built on sand (7:24–28//Luke 6:47–49). All of these metaphors point to the clear distinction between those Jews who belonged to the Jesus movement group and all other Jews. They underscore how these followers of Jesus have been singled out from the others who do not share their convictions and their purity.

Yet, boundary lines are likewise drawn to assess pollution within as well as to keep outsiders from entering. Should pollution be found within the group, then the rite appropriate to this condition is the expulsion of the contaminating member. The procedure here was a process of (1) prophetic identification of sin, especially if it were disguised, (2) judgment of it and (3) expulsion of the offender from the group. For example, should some evil occur in the group because of one of its members, it was apparent that the purity boundary had been breached. The group immediately sought to contain and expel the pollutant (18:15–18//Luke 17:3), first by individual action that unmasked the evil, then by the help of two or three other holy members who interpreted and judged the sinner, and finally by submission of the problem to the entire group. If no correction took place (that is, if the polluting person were not purified), then the errant member himself was declared an outsider, 'a non-Jew and a tax collector,' and removed across the group's borders.

This group, in fact, had 'the keys of the kingdom,' exercising power both to enable some to cross into the group and to compel others to cross out of it (18:18, see 23:18). The principle of such action is clear: 'If the salt loses its saltiness it is good for nothing but to be thrown out' (5:13//Luke 14:34–35). Evil had to be identified as such and expelled. For example, enthusiasts who might even make the correct confession ('Lord, Lord'), but who did not subscribe to Torah perfection were especially singled out. They were judged 'unknown' and ended up outside the house where the feast went on (7:23//Luke 13:27), just as the person without a wedding garment at the king's banquet was dishonored in turn by being 'cast out into the outer darkness' (22:13).

The horror of pollution extended even to temptations (18:6–9//Luke 17:12). Violent remedies were proposed to offset the results of disloyalty that such tests entailed. Those who caused fellow group members to deviate from the group's ideology were better removed from the group and cast into the depths of the sea. Contaminating temptations might enter by border areas of the body such as the eye, ear, hand or foot, which are in unavoidable contact with the corrupt 'outside.' Such temptations must be dealt with at once by amputation of the contaminated organ, which is the radical redrawing of the boundaries to exclude the pollutant.

Such judgment was exercised from within the group according to strict standards. The group's would-be judges were told, 'First take the log out of your own eye, and then you will see clearly to take the speck out of your brother's eye' (7:5 // Luke 6:42). Be sure, in effect, that you yourself are within the boundaries of the group's ideology before you accuse anyone else of being outside.

The enemy without is dealt with in an analogous way. Since membership in the Jesus-movement group at this stage was quite small, group members would be in no position to expel their enemies from the boundaries of village and synagogue, which they held in common. Yet their judgment language against such majority outsiders made it clear that God, at least, would expel them from his kingdom. Israel's unbelief would cause 'the sons of the kingdom' to be 'thrown out into the outer darkness' (8:11–12 // Luke 13:28). In this vein, we note how the judgment parables consistently use boundary language: a separation will take place, and what is good will be gathered inside, while the bad will be thrown out, as in the example of the wheat and the chaff already cited. The wheat will be gathered into God's barn, but the tares thrown out and burned (13:30). The wise will enter into the bridegroom's house for the feast, while the foolish remain outside (25:1–13). The profitable servants remain in the master's house and are given greater riches, while the unprofitable are 'cast out into the outer darkness' (25:30). The sheep will be welcomed 'into eternal life,' while the goats are told to 'depart' and to 'go into eternal punishment' (25:46).

The obvious outcome of such boundary-marking activity is space set off as exclusive to the group. But because boundaries are rather porous, such 'sacred space' (also a ritual concern) becomes highly privatized and fluid. Purity and holiness cannot be tied to any regularly acknowledged ritual practice or place, such as a synagogue or temple, but are found in the holy interior of the group itself. Thus, piety was best practiced not in public or in the synagogue, as the Pharisees did (23:6), but 'in secret' (6:1–18). Temple sacrifice was less important than the maintenance of single-mindedness in the 'heart' of believer and group (5:23–24). The group's preachers, as they carried out their mission, were not to go to the official sacred space of the village, the synagogue, but to seek private houses containing the few 'worthy' people (10:11–13), for sacred space is where group members gather for group functions, as in: 'Where two or three are gathered (to decide a case), there am I' (18:18; see Derrett 1979).

1.3c. Personal identity

Individuals in this Mediterranean society are dyadic personalities (Malina 1981, 51–60). They are anti-introspective, not psychologically minded at all. Consequently, persons are known according to stereotyping in terms of locale, trade or class, but especially according to the family, clan or faction in which they are embedded. For example, as regards place, the Simon who carried Jesus' cross was sufficiently identified as 'Simon from Cyrene' (Matt 27:32); Peter was identified as a Galilean because of his accent (Matt 26:73); and Saul was always that fellow from Tarsus (Acts 22:3). 'Cretans,' moreover, were identified as 'liars, evil beasts, lazy gluttons' (Tit 1:12). As regards trade or class, Joseph was always 'the carpenter' (Matt 13:55); Peter and Andrew were 'fishermen' (Matt 4:18). As regards family, it was sufficient to identify Jesus as 'son of Joseph' (Matt 13:55) or 'son of God,' whereas Simon was 'son of Jonah' (Matt 16:17) and James and John were 'sons of Zebedee' (Matt 4:21; 10:2; 20:20; 26:37 and 27:56).

As regards Jesus himself, the fact that studies of the titles of Jesus in the gospels evidence little agreement among scholars, aside from the fact that there are titles, simply points to the conditions typical of strong group/low grid. Since individual roles are ill-defined and even confused, in this social arrangement the linguistic encoding of those roles in titles will reveal ill-defined, even confused, job characteristics.

In the gospel of Matthew, if Jesus embodied any social role, it surely was that of faction founder. The personal identity of individuals in this faction consisted in their group membership as followers of Jesus, the recruiter of the faction. As his followers, they were the salt of the earth and the light of the world (5:13–14//Luke 14:34–35). Since their allegiance placed them in conflict with their natural families, they were described as members of Jesus' new family of 'brothers' (5:22–24; 7:3–5; 18:15; 23:8; 25:40) whose father is God. Thus, they formed a fictive kin group, male-centered with females embedded in males, with fictive kin rights and obligations and with an abiding relationship between father and son. In other words, this fictive kin group undoubtedly mirrored the arrangements of the 'natural' kin group typical of the first-century Mediterranean.

These 'brothers' were the unique recipients of heavenly revelation: blessed are their eyes and ears, which see and hear (13:16–17//Luke 10:23–24). For God hid from the wise and understanding what he revealed to the 'babes' of this group (11:25–26//Luke 10:21–22). The few, the wheat, the sheep, the wise, the obedient – these were the designations that gave group members their identity. The internalization of specific roles within the group could not give personal identity, if only because there do not seem to have been any specific roles.

It would seem that all of the 'brothers' had equal competence in hearing cases of members against each other, for all received the authority to bind and to loose (18:18). Yet, there were conflicting claims to authority. Focal figures who articulated the reformed teaching on Torah were in considerable tension with enthusiastic figures who presumed self-authenticating authority (7:21–23//Luke 6:46). Some of these later were classified within the group as 'false prophets' who seduced the group from Torah perfection (7:15). Even recognized prominent figures were distinguished from their rivals, the Pharisees, by the titles with which they were addressed. Although the teachers of the Jesus movement group and Pharisaic teachers both explained the Law for their respective groups, the former were not to be called 'teacher' or 'master' like the Pharisees, but rather 'servant' (23:8–9). That title, of course, masked the difficult tasks that the central figures in Jesus factions had to perform, such as to define purity and pollution and to erect and maintain boundaries. It is difficult to say, on the basis of explicit statements in the gospel tradition, how such persons gained prominence within Jesus factions, how they derived their authority and how they were replaced. It is difficult, then, to sort out authoritative social roles at this stage of Matthew's community. Although the need for such central figures is obvious, it would seem that the inside/outside conflict absorbed the energy required to establish internal group structures.

Once boundaries are duly established, their continued utility depends on the group's ability to judge an individual's actual state of 'holiness,' i.e. whether a given individual is within or outside, a state based on any perceivable degree of commitment to or solidarity with the group. Ordinarily, one would look to external actions as indicators of heart and intention, but not here. On the contrary, it is critically important to be able to distinguish external appearances, which may be deceptive, from internal realities. The existence of witchcraft accusations indicates that this capacity to distinguish would have been well developed. Consequently, the group could readily identify the primary fault of its enemies as 'hypocrisy,' that is, deviant posturing and play acting, and hence the sin of only appearing to be holy. Such hypocrisy was a great dishonor to God, since it relied upon truly non-existing relationships with God to gain social prominence. These enemies loved external show and the appearance of righteousness; they prayed in public so as to be seen, seeking acclaim for their almsgiving and exaggerating their fasting (23:5–7; 6:1, 2, 5). They aimed to deceive others, not to please God. They were zealous to make converts, but they taught only surface (and so deficient) piety. And so their converts became 'twice as much a child of Gehenna' as they themselves were (23:13–15) because they thought that externals substituted for true interior piety. They cleansed only the outside of the cup (23:25–26 // Luke 11:39–41) as they cleansed only their own outsides (e.g. washed their hands); hence, they were like whitewashed tombs, 'outwardly they appear righteous, but within they are full of hypocrisy and wickedness' (23:28).

If hypocrisy was the worst sin, the highest virtue was integral righteousness. Such righteousness was revealed in right actions accompanied by a pure heart, a correct internal attitude. This combination is best exemplified by the 'Antitheses' (5:21–47), which demanded internal control of eye, tongue and heart, as well as avoidance of the 'external' dishonoring of others in behavior such as murder, adultery and false swearing. To make discernment of these inner states possible, group members were counseled to judge the tree by its fruits and not merely by its foliage (7:16–20; 12:33 // Luke 6:43–45). They were put on their guard against 'false prophets who come in sheep's clothing but inwardly are ravenous wolves' (7:15). Extracting the beam from one's own eye before proceeding to judge a sinner (7:2–5 // Luke 6:41–42) was another safeguard against hypocrisy and another example of wholeness between inside and outside.

1.3d. Body

Douglas' model presupposes a correlation of the physical body and the social body (Douglas 1982, 65–81; Neyrey 1986a). Care of the body, concern about its entrances and exits, attention to socially permitted and forbidden behavior attendant with bodily functions – these are windows into the workings of the social body as well. In witchcraft societies (1) the social and physical body are tightly controlled; and yet, (2) invaders have broken through bodily boundaries. The concern for boundaries that we noted above is replicated in the concern for the boundaries of the individual physical body. Entrances and exits are carefully guarded – the tongue, for example, from anger and abusive language, which endangers the inner heart (5:22). Likewise, one must guard the eye, the entrance to the heart (6:22–23//Luke 11:34). And one must beware of dishonoring one's brother through adultery, by which the genital orifices of the body (5:28) symbolize, in traditional Mediterranean fashion, male honor and female modesty (see Malina 1981, 42–43).

If pollutants do invade the entrances of the body, the advice is simple: get them out! If the eye, hand or foot is an abiding source of dishonorable, unclean behavior, radical amputation is called for (5:29–30; 18:7–9). Much of the boundary language we have seen applied to such situations of endangered purity is, of course, 'body' language as well.

1.3e. Deviance

Consistent with these preoccupations, deviance in this group is not rooted in ignorance, human failure or the violation of formal rules, but rather in some abiding source of corruption. When deviance occurs, it pollutes and contaminates the whole organism; there is no such thing as a slight sin or a minor imperfection. If the eye of the lightsome body is darkened, 'how great is the darkness' (6:23//Luke 11:34–35). If it is admitted, the 'leaven' of the Pharisees will corrupt the whole batch of flour (16:11–12). A bad tree cannot bear good fruit (7:18); evil people out of their evil treasure bring forth evil (12:35//Luke 6:45). Nothing good can come from what is utterly polluted: 'Either make the tree good and its fruit good or make the tree bad and its fruit bad' (12:33//Luke 6:43). There is no grey area, no middle ground.

Again, deviance is determined by inner reality, not outward adherence to rules. In this connection, we have already noted the group's concern for interior purity, both of individuals and of the group, as well as its horror at the hypocritical disguising of an impure interior by exterior piety. Correct piety, then, led to concern about the motivation behind interpersonal behavior between the individual and God, as well as its value when done in public (6:1–18). In contrast, the corrupt Pharisees were concerned rather with such rules as tithing and so neglect 'the weightier matters . . . justice, mercy, and faith' (23:23//Luke 11:42).

The preference for internal states over formal rules is shown most clearly in Matthew's treatment of the exceptions to the Law allowed by the Pharisees. They evidently allowed for divorce (5:31–32; 19:3–9) and swearing and oathtaking (5:33–39; 23:16–22), all of which were rejected by Matthew's group as deviant behavior. Once admitted, such behavior would contaminate the whole and weaken the perfect keeping of Torah. Matthew's own exception to the divorce law (5:33; 19:9), however, demonstrated how this perfection was to be interpreted. Divorce was a matter of exterior social organization. Since interior states take precedence over rules for behavior, divorce must be allowed in cases in which a person is dishonored because someone had sexual union with his wife. For a husband to stay married after such dishonor would point to lack of concern for his honor, that is, to conduct typical of a procurer, hence to an inwardly polluting sin. Thus, it is clear again that at this level of the tradition, the principle of maintaining the group's internal purity supersedes adherence to external rules, even Torah in its most stringent form.

1.3f. Cosmology

The constant distinction between insiders and outsiders points to how members of this group would look at the world from a dualistic perspective. People are either good or bad fish, wheat or chaff, wise or foolish maidens, profitable or profitless traders, sheep or goats, good or bad trees. 'Who is not for us is against us; who does not gather with us scatters!' (12:30//Luke 11:23).

In keeping with the establishment of new and clear boundaries, the group emphatically distinguishes itself from the Pharisees. For the Pharisees were not just rivals of these Jewish followers of Jesus with respect to the reform of Torah. They are the enemy, 'a wicked and adulterous generation' (12:39; 16:4//Luke 11:29) and 'a brood of vipers' (12:34; see 3:7//Luke 3:7). It is here that the accusations of witchcraft possession against the Pharisees come into their own to identify these opponents as an altogether evil group, possessed by Satan. They were the 'sons of the evil one,' whom the devil, the enemy, sowed among the good wheat (13:28, 38–39).

Yet the new and clear boundaries often prove to be the stuff of un-realizable ideals, for the boundaries surprisingly and sporadically develop holes; they fade, become porous or leave room for doubt. The wicked prosper, the good suffer, injustice is rife. Because of this, the believer knew that the universe was unjust and would not reward the good nor requite the evil as they deserved in this world. God's prophets and messengers have always been rejected, from Abel to Zechariah (23:34–35//Luke 11:49–51); the messengers with invitations to the wedding feast were maltreated (22:5–6//Luke 14:17–21). The members of this group, moreover, expected and experienced the same rejection and hostility (5:11–12//Luke 6:22). But this world is, nevertheless, governed by a principle of personal causality, not fate or some impersonal and unpredictable rule. Conformity to the group's classification system was important and will be rewarded eventually 'in heaven,' that is, by God (6:4, 6, 18). Enduring the hostility of unbelievers (5:12), making proper professions of allegiance (10:32; 12:36), receiving a prophet (10:41) – all bring their eventual reward. The reward would not necessarily be experienced now in an unjust age when Satan and his minions prowled about, but rather in the future when God's judgment finally prevails.

1.3g. Suffering and misfortune

The members of this group primarily endured hostility, rejection, failure in their mission (10:14–16//Luke 9:5), and conflict within their synagogue from Pharisees. But these things came to them not as retribution for their wickedness but because of their faithfulness, for doing right (see 'on my account,' 5:11 and 'for my name's sake,' 10:18, 22).

Because it was unlikely that the confrontation with the Pharisees would cease, since the group's claims to righteousness would not allow it to compromise and since the Pharisees could not be quickly expected to look kindly on this Jewish faction focused in Jesus, the result was a series of incidents causing suffering for members of the Jesus-movement group. Such ostensibly unjust suffering might be alleviated by several strategies, such as through a special interpretation of the phenomenon of suffering, notably through an appeal to the classical Israelite social critics of the past – the prophets. Sent by God with a reforming message and with judgment, the prophets were all rejected and persecuted (23:32–35, 37–38//Luke 11:49–51; 13:34–35). So John the Baptizer! So Jesus! Conflict that arose from the reforming and radical posture of the group was to be expected, for Scripture and tradition tell us that prophets suffered. In fact, rejection served as a sort of touchstone of authenticity for the group: this was how they knew that they were right (5:11–12//

Luke 6:22). Since the agents of the suffering were unbelievers, sons of the evil one, oppression from them was another proof of the righteousness of the group's position.

In summary, the Jesus-movement group, which accused the Pharisees of being possessed, looked as follows: It was a small group of Jews who were recruited directly or indirectly by Jesus and who considered themselves as participants in the true reform movement within a Judaism marked by a number of such movements (we thus agree with the intuition of Theissen 1978, 80–87). Considering purity and perfection their chief hallmarks, they established boundaries that distinguished outsiders from insiders. There can be no ambiguity: 'Who is not with us is against us' (12:30 // Luke 11:23). But within these clear lines of demarcation, group members were, of course, still living side by side with other Jews in a Jewish village, still sharing the general symbolic world of Judaism, especially centered in the keeping of Torah. Their reform stance and positive acclamation of Jesus brought them into conflict with a rival reform movement, the Pharisees, whom they considered as hypocrites for failure to espouse total purity of action and heart. Most of their energy was spent maintaining the boundaries between themselves and their rivals. Since they perceived the world through dualistic glasses, all that was not totally pure (that is, in proper time and place in keeping with their interpretation of Torah) was evil and corrupt, and this included the Pharisees, their reform ideology notwithstanding. They cast judgment not only upon the rival Pharisees but also upon imperfect members of their own group whose imperfection threatened to pollute the whole group. And so, the group remained tightly controlled and vigilant against the pollution that constantly threatened its boundaries.

1.4. The model: part two

Witches and witchcraft accusations

Apart from the movement group revealed in the Fourth Gospel (Malina 1985a; 1986a, 37–44), perhaps all of the other communities represented by the various New Testament traditions can rightly be said to share many aspects of the cosmology just outlined. Since those communities were all Mediterranean groups, they would have the distinctive features typical of a Mediterranean 'witchcraft society' to a lesser or greater extent (Murdock 1980, 42). Inasmuch as we are focussing on Christology 'from the side,' i.e. how members of his society labelled Jesus or successfully accused him, it seems useful to consider how a strong-group type of individual might typically assess others. Two preliminary points need to be made: the first pertains to how stereotyping is characteristic of Jesus' world and the second looks to how Jesus' mobility would be labelled as deviance. After clarifying these two points, we will be better able to proceed to a direct examination of the anthropological meaning of accusations of witchcraft.

The strong-group persons described in the pages of the gospels, all typical first-century Mediterraneans, thought about themselves and other persons in a way best described as 'sociological' (see *Personal identity*, 1.3c above). The gospel discussion of witchcraft and demon possession is quite difficult for Americans to follow because whenever anyone starts talking about some individual or other, the inevitable frame of reference in that scenario is psychological. First-century Mediterraneans did not understand the individual as such. They were not concerned with psychological personality, with the person as a unique, individualistic and incommunicable being. Hence, they would find psychological explanations extremely irrelevant and strange. Rather their basic unit of social analysis was the group-oriented person, the dyad, the person considered as embedded in some other person or some other group of persons.

To think of and describe individual persons in terms of the groups to which they belong strikes us as stereotyping, and indeed it is, for every person is judged according to features typical of the group to which she/he belongs. But the kind of stereotyping involved here is far more refined and complex, since it covers constantly verified self-stereotypes along with stereotypes of other individuals in terms of their family, place of origin, place of habitation, sex, age and distinctive features, all correlated and fixed onto some concrete person. And this concrete person, as a rule, agrees with the stereotypical assessment, assuming it as valid self-stereotype.

Contrast, for example, someone living in today's United States and anyone in the first-century Jesus-movement group. The U.S. person will dwell upon inferences about another person's psychological dispositions and could well summarize by saying something such as 'He isn't all there,' or 'She is very neurotic.' Even a word such as 'together,' which in formal speech refers to social relations par excellence, can take on psychological significance, as in 'He's very together.' The first-century Palestinian follower of Jesus would say 'He is a sinner,' 'He submits to the Prince of this world,' or 'She has a demon.' That would not mean that the person in question disregarded some law or commandment of Torah, which behavior she or he personally had the ability to refrain from (although that might be true). And it would equally not mean that that person participated in demon worship (although that might be true also). Rather that the first-century person, with his or her accusation of demon possession and sin, would mean that the accused 'is in an abnormal position because the matrix of relationships in which he is embedded is abnormal' (Selby 1974, 15). In other words, the person is accused of being a deviant.

Consequently, a type of 'sociological' awareness pervades people following the strong group/low grid cultural script. The most significant way in which they differ from typical U.S. people hinges upon 'their predisposition to regard offenses against the social order or conditions that bring about social disorder as being pre-eminently deviant' (Selby 1974, 16). Naturally, the social order in question is that of Roman-controlled Israel, of the aristocratic, Sadducee-controlled temple, of Palestinian towns and villages and of various associations within these units.

Within this cultural scenario, it is not surprising that all the Jesus-movement groups who tell the story of their origins witness to the fact that their central characters clearly behaved as deviants. For if we consider Jesus or the Twelve or Paul from the perspective that boundary making produces interpretations that result in social meaning, we can see that all *acted outside of their inherited social roles and ranks*. A first indication of such social activity is to be found in physical mobility; that is, in the fact that Jesus, his followers and Paul travelled around in socially unexpected and unusual ways. Such physical mobility replicates the social behavior that rejects ascribed status and intimates willingness to be deviant.

Travel on pilgrimage or business, as well as visits to relatives and the like, would be expected, usual and non-deviant. Such travel presupposes a return home, a return to a solid and stable base from and around which boundaries of geographical stability are drawn. However, general geographical mobility, random wandering and moving from place to place all symbolize a break with previous social location and rank. The meaning symbolled by this sort of wandering life, this sort of geographical mobility, would be negatively perceived by first-century Mediterraneans precisely because for them, stability, roots, sedentary living and a stable center were the ideal. These people shared great aversion to geographical mobility that would make one a stranger and foreigner to others (Elliott 1981; Malina 1996a, 217–41). Continued geographical mobility except in the case of forced movement, such as enslavement and exile, or necessity, such as emigration due to famine, war or some other calamity, was a deviant type of behavior, Perhaps the severest sort of punishment at the time, even worse than death, was exile. Consequently, geographical mobility or a wandering way of life would be a social problem requiring comment.

The wandering life undertaken by Jesus within the confines of Palestine, by Paul and others in the Mediterranean basin, or by Cynic and Stoic philosophers in the same area, all symbolize a break with inherited social role and rank. Hence, a wandering lifestyle would call for some sort of social verdict on the part of the publics confronted by wandering persons. In the gospels, it was the sedentary public that assessed Jesus and his first group of wandering followers with such traditional designations as 'prophet,' 'teacher' and 'disciple.' Others, including Jesus' own family from Nazareth, assessed them variously: as imbalanced, possessed by demons, in the service of Beelzebul, seditionists and the like. Witchcraft accusations belong within this sort of scenario. What plausibly triggered them was the deviance involved in attempting change by means of roving agents of change, Jesus included.

With an understanding of stereotypical thinking as typical and mobility as deviant for first-century Mediterraneans, we are ready to probe formally into the meaning of witchcraft accusations. In line with our initial intention, we focus on the early Matthean community. To understand that group from the perspective of witchcraft, we turn again to Douglas' works to complete the model. She provides us with three important elements: (*a*) a list of specific characteristics of witchcraft societies, (*b*) a definition of a 'witch' and (*c*) a description of the function of witchcraft accusations.

1.4a. *Specific characteristics of witchcraft societies*

Douglas identifies six specific characteristics of witchcraft societies. These features are simply more developed aspects of the cosmology discussed in section 1.3 above. They include clearly drawn external boundaries, confused internal relations, close and continual interaction, poorly developed tension-relieving techniques, weak authority and disorderly but intense conflict. We consider each in turn:

(1) External boundaries clearly marked: In a genuine witchcraft society, external boundaries are clearly marked (Douglas 1982, 113). As we noted previously, in Matthew's group there is no ambiguity over who is 'in' or who is 'out,' for the primary ritual concern of this group is the building and maintenance of clear boundary lines to remove that ambiguity. Group members undoubtedly had a rite to mark the passing from outside to inside. Perhaps, given their high assessment of John the Baptist, they borrowed John's repentance washing and adapted it for their own form of line crossing and boundary maintenance. Be that as it may, group members were found in small Jewish villages where movement in and out was restricted. Jewish distinctiveness kept non-Jews at arm's length, and Jews stayed close for purposes of identity.

Matthew's group, moreover, clearly distinguished itself from other Jewish groups in the village by its radical teaching on Torah observance and its polemic against rival groups. Followers of Jesus, at least, can be told from Pharisees and other people in the synagogue. This group found ways to distinguish itself, often accentuating minor differences between itself and other rival reform groups such as the Pharisees (Theissen 1978, 77–87).

(2) Confused internal relations: Internal relations both in the village and in the group are confused (Douglas 1982, 111–14, 119). *Within the synagogue*: Since Judaism in the first century was a religion embedded in kinship, members of the Jesus faction would necessarily continue to believe themselves to be Jews. The Jesus movement that they espoused was a particularistic reform of post-exilic Judaism, meant for Jews alone. Hence, those committed to Jesus' reform knew themselves to be authentic members of the covenant, devoted to the valid reform of contemporary Judaism. In fact, they were, as Jesus said, the salt of the earth and the light of the world. But their claims to be the authentic reform movement were not so appreciated by their equally zealous Jewish neighbors, some of whom (the Pharisees) claimed the same distinction. And there was no socially approved mechanism to test these conflicting claims in some public way. Roles within synagogue and village were undifferentiated: the leadership of the synagogue was vague, for no priest of Levitical pedigree, no student of Hillel or Shammai presided there.

Within the Jesus-movement group: Even within the Jesus-movement group there was role confusion. Leading figures were prohibited from being labelled 'teacher,' 'rabbi' or 'master' (23:8–10); but when they functioned within the group, they exercised just such roles. They claimed to know and to teach the correct way of interpreting the Scriptures and the authentic way of living the Torah. They were told to be 'humble' and 'servants' of the group (23:11–12); they were told that beatitude lies in being meek and humble (5:5; 11:29). Yet they stood in judgment of deviants and those who misled others both within the group and without. They were, after all, leaders of reform and critics of the unreformed. They have, then, ambiguous roles that are impossible to fulfil.

Even within the group, teachers of Torah clashed with prophetic figures who cry 'Lord, Lord' but do not do God's will as the reform teachers would define it (7:21–23). This clash of reformed and prophetic leaders points to further role confusion within the group because the process of aspiring to a lead role, as well as the criteria for that role, were obscure. Given the low level of organization in this society, no machinery existed within the synagogue or the Jesus faction, or beyond both groups, to settle the question of authority or of conflicting claims to competence.

(3) Close, unavoidable interaction: Yet this was a *small* world, where social interaction is unavoidably close (Douglas 1982, 109–14; Mair 1969, 207–13). The Jewish members of the Jesus faction were not numerous; they were the few worthy figures who lived in fractured households. Prospective group members likewise tended to remain in their households in ever-growing tension with their families as a result of their new ideology (10:34–35//Luke 12:51–53). Indicative of this is the passage that warns 'A man's enemies are those of his own household' (10:36; see 10:21).

(4) Tension-releasing techniques underdeveloped: Techniques for distancing, regulating and reconciling these conflicts were little developed here. Because of the crisis in leadership in both synagogue and Jesus faction, the Pharisees could not expel those members who followed Jesus nor could the latter resolve the issue by expelling the Pharisees. Neither group was apparently able to validate its claims to the satisfaction of the other or the rest of the people in the village. There was no procedure for regulating the intense confrontation, adjudicating the rival claims or even separating the parties from one another in village, synagogue or household. And reconciliation would be possible only with the complete capitulation of one side, which was most unlikely, given the loss of honor involved.

(5) Weak authority: The ability to control the behavior of others effectively was obviously not available to village groups (Douglas 1970, xviii; 1982, iii). While the Pharisees seemed to dominate the local synagogue and were admitted to be zealous for the traditional faith, they were not clearly accepted by all as spokespersons for Judaism itself, let alone by a rival reform group that looked to Jesus as Messiah. Leadership in the Jesus group likewise had no authority to settle doctrinal issues with the Pharisees or to establish its reform praxis as village norm. Even within the Jesus groups there was a crisis of authority: we hear of one wing that insists on strict Torah observance, criticizing those who boast of prophetic activity. The procedure for being invested with leadership positions within the Jesus group is not even hinted at in our traditions, another indication of weak authority.

(6) Intense, disorderly competition: Witchcraft accusations are likely in groups best characterized as experiencing intense and disorderly confrontations (Douglas 1982, 109–12; Mair 1969, 208). Jesus' followers versus Pharisees! True Israel versus false Israel! Torah-observing Christians versus Torah-bypassing Christians!

The social environment in which Matthew's group functioned seems fully to meet the criteria of a genuine 'witchcraft society.' It consisted of groups concerned with purity and boundaries, small in size, harboring intense and disorderly confrontations, in unavoidably close interaction with rival reform movements. It had no techniques for regulating disputes, settling claims or confirming authority.

1.4b. Definition of a witch

In general, we might define witchcraft itself as the ascription of some personal misfortune 'to the suspected voluntary or involuntary aggressive action of a member of a special class of human beings believed to be endowed with a special power and propensity for evil' (Murdock 1980, 21). A 'witch,' moreover, is best defined in terms of the misfortune such a person is said to cause and the context in which such misfortune appears. In the gospels, accusations of witchcraft appear in a context of sick care, hence of healing and sickening, of demon possession and demon expulsion. It is rather curious to note in this regard that witchcraft accusations in a health-care context seem typical of the Mediterranean region (Murdock 1980, 42, 57–63).

More specifically, according to Douglas' model, 'witches' appear in groups dominated by a dualistic point of view (Douglas 1982, 114): 'Who is not with me is against me; who does not gather with me scatters' (12:30//Luke 11:23). Only insiders are good, with good fruit, while all outsiders are evil, with only evil fruit (12:33//Luke 6:43). The insiders perceive that they are under attack, especially from hostile outsiders who would condemn it, poison it or seduce it. Lastly, the human wickedness that the group experiences takes on a cosmic dimension: what is bad is all bad and it comes from the Evil One. The 'witch' is a figure who sums up all of the above sense of dualism, cosmic evil and hostility to the group.

According to Douglas' analysis, the 'witch' will be described as having the following characteristics (Douglas 1970, xxvi-xxvii, 1982, 113):

1. The witch is one whose inside is corrupt;
2. the witch has a perverted nature, a reversal of the ways things ought to be; it is a deceiver whose external appearance does not betray its inner nature;
3. if the witch is seen as living within the group, it attacks the pure and innocent by life-sucking or by poison.

Examining the Christian accusations against the Pharisees, these characteristics are plainly evident. (1) The Pharisees' insides were said to be corrupt; they were like whitewashed tombs, which 'outwardly appear beautiful but within they are full of dead men's bones and all uncleanness' (23:27//Luke 11:44). They cleansed the outside of cup and plate, but 'inside they are full of extortion and rapacity' (23:25// Luke 11:39). Even though they appeared righteous, within they were 'full of hypocrisy and iniquity' (23:28).

(2) Their hypocrisy, moreover, in concealing this inner corruption was considered their chief sin. They claimed to teach and practice a reformed Torah; they claimed to build a fence around it; even their name meant 'the Separated Ones.' But they only 'preach and do not practice' (23:3). They were, therefore, deceivers whose external appearance 'whitewashed' the death within, whose external show of piety covered up their actual faithlessness (23:23//Luke 11:42).

(3) Their attacks were those of witches living within the group. When they made converts, they effectively destroyed the interior of their proselytes, making them twice as much children of hell as themselves

(23:15). This happened because they taught the proselytes to worry about externals and not about the core of the Torah, motivation or integrity. The interior was effectively sucked dry. They also spread about a poisonous 'leaven' (16:6, 11, 12), their false teaching, which corrupted and polluted the whole pure batch with which it came in contact. The overall description of the Pharisees, then, is fully consistent with the typology of a witch in a witchcraft society.

It is the nature of the Gospels that we have basically Christian evaluations of Jesus, not those of his opponents. This means a scarcity of data about others' opinions of Jesus, which is never more evident than in assessing the accusation that Jesus is himself a 'witch.' The gospel tersely records in 12:24 the accusation by the Pharisees that Jesus is a 'witch,' an accusation repeated in 9:34 and 10:25. This is the only datum we have from these opponents with which we might understand the full scenario that makes these accusations plausible.

The gospel of John, however, does give us particulars concerning a Jewish accusation that Jesus is demon-possessed. He is regularly called a sinner (John 9:24), a corrupt person. His opponents regularly accuse him of 'deceiving' the crowds (7:12, 47). They regularly expose his duplicity to the crowds. His teaching, then, cannot be from God, for he does not keep God's commandments, in particular the observance of the Sabbath; that teaching must be a poison.

The example of the gospel of John might help us to piece together disparate comments about Jesus in the gospel of Matthew that allow us to see the anthropological understanding of a 'witch' operative there. In addition to several public accusations such as 12:24, 9:34 and 10:25, Matthew records charges that Jesus was a 'deceiver' who worked 'deception' on the people (27:63–64). The accusation in 12:24 was made precisely as a criticism of Jesus' Sabbath observance, suggesting that his opponents claimed to see through his behavior as a masquerade for his basic wickedness. They too could read hearts; they could discern the essential evil in him. Although the evidence is meagre, we are warranted in postulating a scenario in which Jesus' opponents considered him as 'witch' when they accused him of demon possession in 12:24. After all, we have demonstrated amply from this text how the Christian assessment of the Pharisees is fully intelligible according to the same scenario.

As we noted earlier, in a group that sees evil disguised as good and discerns a discrepancy between external appearances and internal states, it is to be expected that some in the group will claim the ability to see beyond appearances so as to unmask the disguised evil. One would expect this skill to be highly developed in such a context, and it is. For example, John the Baptizer, the discerning prophet and hero of this group, could read hearts so as to unmask wickedness disguised as repentance. When John saw 'many of the Sadducees and Pharisees coming for baptism,' he was not fooled by this display of sincerity, but discerned hypocrisy and deception: 'You brood of vipers! Who warned you to flee from the wrath to come?' (3:7). Baptism, a mere external show of repentance, is not what they required to make them clean: 'Bear fruit that befits a change of heart' (3:8), that is, a total reform of life, inner and outer, a reform that would include acceptance of Jesus as God's designated reforming prophet.

It is in this vein that Jesus was said to be able to read hearts. On the one hand, he could 'see faith,' that is, commitment within people (9:2). But he was especially skilled in 'knowing their (evil) thoughts': 'Jesus, knowing their thoughts, said: "Why do you think evil in your hearts? . . ."'(9:4); 'Knowing their thoughts, he said: "Every kingdom divided against itself . . ."' (12:25). Jesus was so skilled at this that he could tell (1) when people merely 'honor God with their lips, but their heart is far from God' (15:8) and (2) when people are self-deceived (22:29), deceive others (24:4–5, 24) or act as false prophets (7:15; 24:11, 24). John the Baptizer and Jesus both claimed to have to a high degree this skill of reading hearts so as to unmask deception and hypocrisy.

1.4c. Function of witchcraft accusations

According to Douglas' profile, the characteristic activity of this kind of society focuses on discernment and eradication of the witch. In the world of Palestinian Jews under consideration, witchcraft concerns relativize 'righteous' behavior, for 'righteousness' was not to be sought in traditional, external behavior directed at interpersonal relationship with God. Instead focus is on behaviour directed at one's fellow, to have impact on them. Thus, acts of piety, such as prayer, fasting or sacrifice are put in the service of witch hunting and witch cleansing. Public prayer, fasting and almsgiving are protestations of innocence and prominence in a witch-ridden world.

On the other hand, the primary act in the process of coming to grips with personal, group-felt misfortune is the 'witchcraft accusation.' With this accusation, the two-faced witch is identified and the threat to the boundaries of the group is revealed. This item points up an important feature, namely, the function of witchcraft accusations in this type of social group. In a highly contentious society marked by strong rivalry and strong ambition, the accusation functions to 'denigrate rivals and, pull them down in the competition for leadership' (Douglas 1970, xviii; 1982, 114). Such accusations are, in short, 'an idiom of control.' On this point Douglas echoes the consensus of anthropologists on the social function of witchcraft accusations (Mair 1969, 203, 216; Goody 1970, 211).

As regards the situation in Matthew's early community, in the intense and disorderly contentiousness over reform of Torah, accusations of demonic possession served to denigrate the Pharisees, who were rivals of the Jesus faction, by showing that they were not reformers at all but corrupters of Torah purity. This, then, is the proper background of the extensive polemic that Matthew's gospel recorded. For example, Jesus' followers developed a polemic against the Pharisees that amounts to a complete dishonoring of their rivals. They were a 'brood of vipers,' 'an evil and adulterous generation,' 'hypocrites,' 'whitewashed tombs,' and the like. And they were accused of being demonic and in the service of Satan; they were possessed of seven demons worse than the first that once was successfully expelled from them (12:43–45//Luke 11:24–26). How can they be teachers of Torah, being evil? Christian witchcraft accusations against the Pharisees, then, served to discredit these rivals for leadership.

Alternately, the Pharisees were wont to criticize every action of Jesus in terms of his orthopraxis: he ate with sinners (11:19//Luke 7:34); he did not wash before eating (15:1–10); he violated the Sabbath (12:9–13). How could a person so lax about purity be a true reformer of Torah? And so his exorcisms served as occasions for his enemies to claim that he performed them because he was in league with the Prince of demons. According to them, Jesus only appeared to observe Torah and teach its proper observance, but in fact he was evil and in league with Satan to corrupt the synagogue. The accusation of demon possession against Jesus, then, was intended to dishonor and discredit him.

Witchcraft accusations have two possible effects. If successful, they will lead to the expulsion of the witch from the village, which action could then end the tension of this ongoing conflict. But often the political resources of the accusing party are insufficient to bring about this expulsion, and in this case the accusations might lead instead to 'fission'

(Douglas 1970, xviii; 1982, 114). The accusers themselves cannot remain in a polluted world that threatens them so acutely. Hence, they voluntarily withdraw from the conflict under the guise of maintaining their standard of purity. One thinks of the Qumran community in this regard. Expulsion or fission – in either case the group remains small and disorganized. Generally speaking, then, such groups prove unable to assimilate any lessons in conflict management from their experience.

As regards the desired effects of witchcraft accusations against rivals in Matthew, both Christians and Pharisees would expel each other if they could! But the followers of Jesus were too few in the small villages to expel the Pharisees. Furthermore, as a minority, they lacked recognized authority. On the other hand, neither could the Pharisees get rid of those Jews who followed Jesus, distributed as they were in individual households and claiming to be true members of the covenant. The reason for this was that the Pharisees' authority was not unanimously accepted in the synagogue. Of course, after the destruction of Jerusalem in 70 CE and with the spread of Judaean elites to the north, the particularistic Judaism of the Pharisaic sort would gain the ascendancy and become more successful in excommunicating Christians (see John 9:22, 34; 12:42; 16:2 as evidence of this later phenomenon).

There is some evidence to suggest that on occasion 'fission' took place in the tense situations where the followers of Jesus and the Pharisees engaged in reciprocal witchcraft accusations. The ritual of erecting boundaries and distinguishing inside from outside served in some cases to set the members of Jesus-movement groups apart from their own neighbors and households. Furthermore, their deep appreciation of their own holiness and the threats to it from all the surrounding pollutions made it finally impossible to maintain the status quo. Some of these followers of Jesus seem voluntarily to have gone into exile. We can track their footsteps in the advice given them: 'If anyone will not receive you or listen to your words, shake the dust from your feet as you leave that house or town' (10:14 // Luke 9:5). Yet, it is hard to determine whether this action was self-imposed exile or whether it represented the success of Pharisaic accusations resulting in expulsion: 'When they persecute you in one town, flee to the next' (10:23; see 5:11–12).

At least those agents commissioned to preach about the Jesus movement were able to 'shake the dust from their feet' and 'flee.' But for most of Jesus' followers in so small a society, both leaving and capitulating were alternatives as impossible as forcing their enemies to do the same. Another path seems to have been taken. We have a window on it in the parable of the wheat and the tares: tension-filled tolerance (13:24–30, 36–43). According to the parable, the polluting tares are found living in threatening proximity to the pure wheat. Jesus is credited with making clear the source of this evil in a genuine witchcraft accusation: 'The enemy who sowed them is the Devil' (13:39). The group's leaders would like to uproot (i.e. expel) the tares, but this would be as impossible as replanting the genuine wheat in a new, pure field. The final solution is a painful compromise: 'Let them both grow until the harvest,' when the evil tares will finally be expelled. If we may take this parable, especially with its allegorized interpretation, as having some bearing on the actual situation of Matthew's group, then it appears that the members of the Jesus faction were unable to expel the evil ones. Finding fission impossible, they remained in a state of acute tension with their neighbors, in disorderly conflict with their rivals for reform.

The type of interpersonal relation with God that the followers of Jesus could not construct and express in a rival synagogue went underground. These group members then prayed, fasted and gave alms 'in secret' (6:3–4, 6, 17–18). They remained protected in the few 'worthy' households where they could sustain their distinctive point of view and the behavior that followed from it (10:13). Interaction with their Pharisaic rivals remained unavoidably close and contentiousness stayed at an intense level. The group's boundaries continued to be precariously maintained by the identification of pollutants within the group and especially by witchcraft accusations against rivals outside the group. The expulsion of the Pharisees, which the Christian Jews earnestly desired, must grudgingly be put off 'until the harvest,' when God will separate them from the wheat.

1.5. Conclusion

We began by carefully noting that in the early segments of Matthew, not only do Pharisees accuse Jesus and his subsequent followers of being possessed, but that Jesus and his followers likewise accuse Pharisees of demon possession. It is surely an understatement to describe this stratum of text in Matthew's gospel as a situation of intense and disorderly conflict. The proper identification of these charges lies in appreciating them from the perspective of cultural anthropology as accusations of witchcraft in first-century Mediterranean society. Drawing upon the works of Mary Douglas, we set up a model for describing the social system of a group that engaged in witchcraft accusations. In particular, the model afforded a detailed and coherent look at the cosmology of the social group in which such accusations are made and at the function of these accusations. This produced an adequate scenario for a considerate reading of a foreign, ancient text.

Through the use of this anthropological model, our attention has been focussed not on black cats, broomsticks or sorcery, but on the social interaction in typical witchcraft societies. Witchcraft accusations function there as a medium of control where intense contentiousness over leadership exists, and where procedures for settling claims of legitimacy are absent. Yet as enlightening as this type of investigation is, it raises important questions. For many non-Mediterraneans, it will not be particularly comforting to find in a sacred text the type of religious viewpoint or posture that is described in anthropological terms as a 'witchcraft society.' Nor will it be edifying to see how early Jewish followers of Jesus, our ancestors in faith and the primary witnesses of our faith, employed accusations of witchcraft as pointed polemic to denigrate their rivals, the Pharisees (see Matt 12:43–45). While this way of imagining behavior in the gospels often disturbs U.S. readers, it does have its value, for it presents us with a typical view of first-generation, Jewish followers of Jesus. Their perception and employment of witchcraft accusation, moreover, was not distinctive, for as we noted in the introduction to this chapter, similar accusations of demon possession are found also in John's gospel, Paul's letters and other early Christian documents as well. But the witchcraft model offers significant insights into the typical social dynamics of many early Christian communities, their view of the world and their patterns of conflict with those both inside and outside the group.

One final point, the use of an anthropological model coupled with historical and linguistic perspectives, identified one level of conflict in the history of Matthew's community. But the Jesus-movement group with which we associate this gospel evidently did not always remain in this situation, for it was later able to assimilate Mark's more liberal gospel. The final form of Matthew indicates that significant changes took place in the group's cosmology as a result of new experiences. The group became somewhat less dualistic in perspective, less perfection-oriented with the inclusion of Gentiles and other peoples (22:10). Concern for radical purity lessened and maintenance of impermeable boundaries diminished as Matthew's community became gradually more heterogeneous in membership. Thus, we are encouraged to assess the history of Matthew's community from a fresh perspective. We may not have fresh archaeological or historical data, but we can more clearly plot out the ways in which the later Matthean community differed from the earlier 'witchcraft society,' a term not applicable to the final editor's audience as intensely as to the early group. The use of this anthropological model, then, generates new ideas and fresh data for a continued critical reading of the text.

FURTHER READING

Basic works by Mary Douglas, in which the grid-group model is developed and witchcraft societies are described, are Douglas 1966; 1982. On witchcraft accusations see also Douglas 1970 (ed.). Another classic anthropological study is Evans-Pritchard 1937/1976.

The models which underpin Malina and Neyrey's approach are set out in Malina 1981; 1986a (see also ch. 5 below).

For other work on the New Testament using Douglas' grid-group model see Neyrey 1986a; 1988a, 115ff; 1990; White 1986; Atkins 1991; Carter 1997; Gordon 1997.

For other work on New Testament texts employing anthropological perspectives on witchcraft and sorcery accusations, see Neyrey 1986c; 1988b; 1990; Esler 1994, 131–46; also relevant are studies of the 'evil eye' in the New Testament: see Elliott 1990b; 1992a; Derrett 1995.

On the approach developed by the Context Group, see further *Introduction* §3 above, and ch. 5 below.

For a critique of the use of Mary Douglas' grid-group model to study early Christianity see Sanders 1993, 100–14.

2

The Earliest Christian Communities as Sectarian Movement

ROBIN SCROGGS

INTRODUCTION

In this essay, published in 1975 in a *Festschrift* for Morton Smith, Robin Scroggs offered 'the first methodologically conscious and detailed attempt to apply contemporary sociological studies of sectarianism to early Christianity' (Esler 1987, 46). (One should also note, however, the earlier comments about Johannine sectarianism in Meeks' classic essay of 1972 [see esp. p. 70].) While Scroggs used the work of sociologists on sectarianism, comparable work was published at the same time by John Gager (see ch. 6) using the work of anthropologists on 'millenarian movements' (see further Holmberg 1990, 77–117). Noting the early work on the concept of the religious sect by Max Weber and Ernst Troeltsch, Scroggs derives his list of the characteristics of a religious sect from the work of a number of sociologists, especially Werner Stark. Scroggs outlines seven 'sectarian characteristics' and then seeks to show how 'the earliest church directly stemming from the mission of Jesus exhibits all of these central sect-type characteristics' (p. 76). On the whole the evidence is drawn from the synoptic gospels, though on certain points, notably 'egalitarianism', Pauline texts (Gal 3:28, etc.) are cited.

One of Scroggs' main claims is that, in contrast to the established emphasis upon theological ideas, this sociological approach offers a new perspective from which to view the situation and concerns of the early Christians (see also Scroggs 1980, 165–66). 'The church becomes from this perspective not a theological seminary but a group of people who have experienced the hurt of the world and the healing of communal acceptance' (p. 89). This may indeed be an important corrective to previous readings (Bengt Holmberg suggests that 'our middle class Christian reading glasses come off'; 1990, 113) though Stephen Barton rightly points out that Scroggs' model is in fact 'wedded to his own theological and ideological agenda' (1993, 143). For Scroggs: 'Traditional Christianity . . . has lost all feeling for the sectarian protest of the earliest church' (p. 90). Barton makes other pertinent criticisms: that Scroggs' approach oversimplifies both the concept of the sect and early Christianity itself, which are each 'described in a very general and monolithic way' (1993, 144). Moreover, the sect model draws attention to some of the textual evidence, but leads to other evidence being ignored. There is also a questionable tendency to assume that the church fits the model even where evidence is lacking (p. 82; cf. Scroggs 1980, 166; note Horrell 1996a, 14 with n. 34).

A certain bluntness in the use of the theoretical resources thus characterises Scroggs' essay. Yet it remains a ground-breaking article which pointed the way in an important direction for New Testament studies. Subsequent studies of sectarianism and the early church have generally been more nuanced. Bryan Wilson's typology of sects, based upon the nature of a sect's response to the world, has been particularly influential, allowing for more specific descriptions of the sectarian character of early Christian communities (e.g. Elliott's 1981 description of 1 Peter as reflecting the situation of a 'conversionist sect' [see ch. 13 below]; Esler 1994, 70–91, on 'introverted sectarianism at Qumran and in the Johannine community'). Dynamic models which attempt to analyse the changing character of early Christianity, especially in relation to its parent Judaism, have also been developed. For example, Philip Esler (1987, 65ff) outlines the change 'from Jewish reform movement to Christian sect' (a model taken up by Watson 1986); John Elliott (1995a) has written of the transition from 'faction' to 'sect'.

Despite the telling criticisms and cautions which Holmberg and Barton, among others, raise, the issues and perspectives introduced through the study of early Christianity as a religious sect have become well established in New Testament study. Questions about boundary definition, relationship with (and hostility to) parent Judaism, attitudes to 'the world', language about insiders and outsiders, and so on; all these and more have been brought to our attention at least partly through the study of early Christianity as a sectarian movement.

Morton Smith has consistently brought fresh insights and perspectives to the study of early Christianity and Judaism. One result has been a healthy antidote against the poison of overtheologizing which has been characteristic of so much New Testament scholarship during the neo-orthodox era. In retrospect I think it is easy to see how we were imprisoned within narrow walls and how neglected were the paths which scholars in the previous generation had begun to break.[1] It is now past time, following the lead of Morton Smith, to return to some of these paths and to continue the explorations begun and then mostly broken off. In no way will pursuing such interests militate against legitimate theologizing. They will, rather, enrich the theological enterprise, yet make it more responsible to the reality of human existence.

In this paper I want to explore the data we have about Jesus and the earliest church from the standpoint of a well-defined sociological model, the religious sect.[2] It is surprising that, as far as I know, this model has never been applied in any detail to the emergence of Christianity. Even Ernst Troeltsch steered clear of such an attempt and, indeed, would have rejected a serious identification of the Jesus movement with pure sectarianism, however much he saw certain sectarian tendencies there.[3] And while post-Troeltsch sociologists have refined and solidified the typology and done numerous case studies of specific sects, they have, for whatever reasons, not dealt with the beginnings of Christianity. It is my conviction that the community called into existence by Jesus fulfills the essential characteristics of the religious sect, as defined by recent sociological analyses.[4] Should this prove so, then the sect model provides

[1] I refer to such scholars as Troeltsch 1931, Cadoux 1925, Deissmann 1911, and especially Case (e.g. 1923; 1933). There were also reductionist socialistic portraits of early Christianity, such as that of Kautsky 1925.

[2] Foundations and popularizing of the typology of the religious sect were begun by Max Weber 1949, 93–94, and Troeltsch 1931. The typology, supported by numerous case studies, has been sharpened and refined by recent sociologists. See, e.g., Niebuhr 1929, Clark 1937, Nisbet 1953, Yinger 1946, Wilson 1967 and the especially detailed and helpful volume by Stark 1967.

[3] Troeltsch 1931, 39–69. The closest he comes to an identification is pp. 331–37, 341.

[4] Since I am not a sociologist I state at the beginning my amateur status with regard to intra-sociological discussion about the typology. There are critiques of the sectarian model, such as Berger 1954. I am impressed, however, by the consistency with which the data of recent sect investigations support the basic pattern. We should keep in mind that for Weber the type is an *ideal*-type; that is, it is an intellectual construct which has heuristic value. No concrete historical phenomenon is ever going to fit the model perfectly.

One final comment can be made at this point. Weber and Troeltsch both set out the sectarian model as over against that of the 'church', the one giving definition to the

us with a new perspective from which to view our material, one which will help gestalt the fragmentary data, and which will illumine the cares and concerns of the people who were attracted to Jesus and who formed the nucleus of the Christian communities. It will help us understand the quality of the experience in these communities. In this paper I will first describe sectarian characteristics, then attempt to show how the communities exhibit these traits. Obviously I can only give a general statement of the argument. Detailed substantiation would require a much longer paper than is possible here.

Sectarian characteristics

1. The sect begins as protest

Sect emergence is closely related to reaction against economic and societal repression within a particular class or classes of society.[5] The sects are usually populated either by folk who have been denied a share in the wealth of the society or by those to whom status is denied by the establishment. Frequently, of course, denial of wealth and status happen to the same groups of people. Werner Stark summarizes the matter very clearly.

> The chief reason for men getting together in order to form sectarian group-
> ings has been their unhappiness in, and revolt against, a social system
> within which their position – the position of their class – was, in Veblen's
> terminology, humilific, for instance because their livelihood was insecure or
> their wages low, or their status (Max Weber's 'estimation of honour') was
> unsatisfactory. (Stark 1967, 6)

While most sociologists seem to emphasize economic humiliation as primary, it is crucial to see that that is not the only cause of disvaluation and deprivation. Stark, for example, points to the presence of well-off merchants in some radical Russian sects, such as the Skoptsy. Although wealthy, in the feudal Russian society of the time they were outcasts and

---

other. Berger, however, points to a critique of van der Leeuw, that the sect really stands over against the total community (what I call in this paper, 'the world') rather than some specific religious group which might be called a 'church'. 'The correlate of the sect is therefore not the church but the community' (van der Leeuw 1938, 261, cited in Berger 1954, 471). It is this dialectic I pursue here.

[5] Stark, 1967, 5–29; Niebuhr, 1929, 19–32; Yinger 1946, 37–38; Clark 1937, 16, 218; Wilson 1967, 31.

'a despised and depressed class' (Stark 1967, 14). The issue, then, is not primarily economic, but human degradation itself, wherever establishment society humiliates and dehumanizes people (cf. Stark 1967, 37–46; Wilson 1967, 31).

By coming together the people express their desire to be rid of that humiliating situation in the world and to form a new world where they can find acceptance and value. But it is especially important to keep in mind that the protest is not always conscious to the minds of the sectarians, and in ancient times this must have been particularly true. Writing of American sects, Clark says: 'The sects themselves do not recognize the economic factor in their history. . . . In the sectarian mind the causes of divergence are theological' (1937, 18). The members may very well 'feel' the societal rejection but they may not be able to speak it and certainly not to analyze the reasons for and result of their joining the community.

Of particular interest for us is the influence of the sect leader in the question of sect emergence. Weber put great emphasis upon the charismatic prophet as the dominant cause of emergence (Weber 1963, 46–79). More recent writers seem to place the weight more on spontaneous movement within the alienated class, and Stark specifically argues against the individualism of Weber (Stark 1967, 46–47). Stark does, however, make an important exception. 'It can happen that the depressed stratum is so abject and wretched that it has not even the strength to protest and rebel. If so, we have before us a somewhat special case, and the leaders are apt to come from outside, for instance, from a stratum that is just a little less abject and wretched than the common run' (1967, 46). This will have important bearing when we turn to Jesus and his audience.

2. The sect rejects the view of reality taken for granted by the establishment

Given the protest involved in the sect, it is inevitable that it will express in various ways its rejection of that society that has humiliated it.[6] The outside society may mean primarily the political establishment, or the control of wealth and land by the upper class, or the religious establishment, or even the intellectual establishment. Usually the

---

[6] E.g. Stark 1967, 101, 110–11, 128ff, 145ff; Niebuhr 1929, 18–19; Clark 1937, 21, 220–24; Wilson 1967, 9–41.

establishment forces are seen as allied with each other. The hostility expressed takes the form of as much separation from the world as possible, more often a qualitative than geographical separation, and the laying down of strictures against it. As Stark rightly sees, the sect is counter-culture, not a sub-culture.[7] It is, of course, forced to use the language and some of the artifacts and customs of the establishment, but it intends to create a reality, in so far as is possible, totally different from that of establishment society.

This rejection is obviously reinforced by any persecution the sect may have to suffer. And the more hostility and separation the sect displays, the more likely some form of persecution will develop. The sect, however peaceful, calls into question the correctness of the establishment position, and all the power and authority the establishment possesses may not keep it from feeling threatened.

3. The sect is egalitarian

The implication of the above remarks is that there is very much a positive dimension to life within the sectarian community. Indeed, while the negative factors in society at large explain why people enter the sect, it cannot explain why they remain. Here we need to consider the quality of life the member finds within, a quality which helps him regain a self-acceptance, a new sense of his humanity, an experience of joy and love.

One key expression of this new quality of life is the egalitarianism which is usually found within sects.[8] Members are completely equal to each other, no matter how much status distinction the 'world' might assign. All the societal barriers fall, economic, class, birth, age, and sex. Peasant is equal to landowner, slave to master, woman to man, youth to age.

Consistent with this is the usual absence of a hierarchical structure of organization.[9] People become leaders by virtue of their ability, not because of personal status or official office. Or as it is usually put, the authority stems from the Spirit.

4. The sect offers love and acceptance within the community

While the world continues to humiliate the outcasts, within the society, where each is equal to the other, mutual love and acceptance are joyfully

---

[7] Stark 1967, 128ff. This is true, even if the sect is aggressively missionary in character; the conversion is out of the world into the sect, with the sharp boundary still being maintained.
[8] Stark 1967, 115ff; Wilson 1967, 10; Niebuhr 1929, 18; Clark 1937, 21.
[9] Stark 1967, 119–25; Wilson 1967, 10.

experienced. This existence is seen as that life intended and demanded by God, as salvation, as the realization of one's true worth. This quality of life is antithetical to harsh outside reality; thus the positive quality of life within makes the outside world seem even darker and more demonic than ever. In the community the member knows not only that God loves him but that other people can and do as well. The sect, in fact, is the true family of the participant.[10]

As a result of this liberating love, it is no surprise that pent-up, repressed emotions flow out. Within the sect emotional intensity may run high, and such expressions are usually highly valued.[11] The classic case of emotional intensity, at least in western sects, is ecstatic speech, glossolalia. Stark is perhaps too extreme, but nevertheless provocative, when he comments: 'This speaking with tongues, or glossolalia, a frequent accompaniment of the ecstatic condition, shows again what the essence of all these phenomena is: like dadaism, it is a rejection of the world and its rationality' (1967, 136). It may well reflect a rejection of that establishment logic and rationality so often used as instruments of repression; but glossolalia must also be allowed its positive side. The speaker knows himself to be caught up into the divine, true reality and experiences in this an encounter with God or Spirit, a transcendent reality that cannot be expressed in the words of the world. The intense emotional expression is a release *for* as well as a release *from*. One's life is somehow put back together in an integrity that had been ripped apart by the rack of the world's hostility.

5. *The sect is a voluntary association*

Members are not born, they are converted and they must make a committed decision.[12] Thus the ritual which symbolizes this decision, the initiation, is lifted up as of great moment (Stark 1967, 165–66). It 'throws' the convert out of the world and enables him to enter that community in which authentic reality can be experienced and lived.

6. *The sect commands a total commitment from its members*

This is the necessary corollary of all the above.[13] The sect *is* different from the world and must be kept so. Otherwise the world invades the

---

[10] Stark 1967, 127; Kanter 1972, 9–18, 43–49, 86–103; 1973.
[11] Stark 1967, 133, 163; Clark 1937, 220–21; Niebuhr 1929, 18, 36.
[12] Stark 1967, 120–21; Wilson 1967, 7–8.
[13] Stark 1967, 165; Wilson 1967, 10, 42–43.

sect and it loses its essential characteristics.[14] Thus each member must live out the vision of the sect completely. Wilson writes: 'Not only does the sect discipline or expel the member who entertains heretical opinions, or commits a moral misdemeanour, but it regards such defection as betrayal of the cause, unless confession of fault and appeal for forgiveness is forthcoming' (Wilson 1967, 24).

7. Some sects are adventist

A final frequent characteristic of the sect can be listed here, although it is not always present. Adventist sects are those which look forward to the final breaking in of God's kingdom. Often this point is believed to be near at hand. Such attitudes are so common that Clark can write: 'Adventism is the typical cult of the disinherited and suffering poor' (1967, 25. Cf. also Niebuhr 1929, 31; Wilson 1967, 27–28).

The earliest church as sectarian

I believe it possible to show that the earliest church directly stemming from the mission of Jesus exhibits all of these central sect-type characteristics. Obviously the problems involved in documenting such a claim are immense and cannot be more than pointed to in a sketch such as this.

1. Sociological data for New Testament times is sparse. Neither Jewish nor Christian writings are *directly* interested in offering such data. Information even about the Roman legal processes and taxes in Palestine is inadequate.

2. The book of Acts, which purports to tell the history of the church, is of little use for our purpose.[15] Paul's letters mostly reflect his own distinctive ideas and communities and thus will not be appealed to here, although there is in them some information about Hellenistic Christian churches.

3. We are thus left with the gospel traditions as our main source. Here data is plentiful, but evaluation of the data is extremely difficult. Form and redaction criticism are basic to the task, but a great deal of

---

[14] Wilson well comments: 'If the sect is to persist as an organization it must not only separate its members from the world, but also maintain the dissimilarity of its own values from those of the secular society. Its members must not normally be allowed to accept the values of the status system of the external world' (1967, 41).

[15] It is late, tendentious, and offers few traditions that can be sociologically evaluated. See Haenchen 1961.

'reading between the lines' is still necessary. It would be comforting to have a consensus about which traditions are authentically Jesus, which come from the agrarian setting of Palestinian Jewish Christianity, and which reflect the urbanization of the church, already an accomplished fact prior to Paul. Such comfort is not to be had. Here I can only lay down my methodological judgments. (*a*) This paper is interested in the historical Jesus only in so far as he was the initiator of the community. Thus most of the discussion and data will center around the community called into existence by Jesus. But since the *earliest* church and the hearers of Jesus' message are essentially the same group of folk (at least sociologically speaking), traditions which probably originated in the *earliest* church can legitimately be used to describe the reaction by the hearers to Jesus himself as well as to the societal setting of the pre-resurrection community. Concomitantly, authentic Jesus traditions passed down by the church can legitimately be used to describe attitudes in the church. (*b*) Although the judgment must be held with some caution, most of the synoptic traditions *seem* to reflect an agrarian rather than an urban setting. Thus I develop my argument in terms of peasant rather than proletariat, realizing that this puts a severe restriction on the topic.

4. The church was never a monolithic reality. Whether one takes a cross-section (synchronic) or follows a developmental line (diachronic), there were differences and even sharp clashes within the emerging communities. Certainly later traditions reflect in some cases a movement away from sect-type reality.

Despite these difficulties, I believe the worth of the project justifies an attempt to overcome them, to sort out the various strata of material, and to put them together within a sociological perspective.

1. The earliest community emerged out of protest

It is generally agreed that the economic picture of first century Jewish Palestine was one of extremes.[16] There were few wealthy and many poor. The society was largely agrarian and towns or cities of any size, few. There was, as a result, scarcely a middle class at all. Some trading, a small fishing industry, scattered artisans, and a few government officials composed the middle class. Even the largest city, Jerusalem, was reasonably small and apparently filled with many people without stable

---

[16] See Grant 1926; Hoehner 1972, 65–79; Kreissig, 1969.

means of livelihood.[17] Thus most of the people eked out their existence from the land, either in some form of agriculture or in shepherding. The average freeman had little more and sometimes less prosperity than the slave. Either he worked as a day laborer or a tenant farmer for the large landowners, or he owned a small plot of land (Kreissig 1969). Much is made of the exorbitant taxation which burdened even the small peasant farmer, especially because of the double taxation (to Rome and to Israel).[18] The peasant thus seems to have been in a marginal situation at best. The great majority were alienated from the modest wealth Judaism possessed. E. E. Urbach (1964) has recently argued, contrary to the views of many, that there were both Gentile and Jewish slaves owned by Jews before 70 CE. While it seems impossible to determine the size of this class, Urbach seems to suggest they were not a minimal group. This group would in general participate in the alienation of the free peasants (so also Kreissig 1969, 237–39).

At least as important is a second alienation; the peasant was an outcast of the establishment culture of his day. Indeed, for some he was an untouchable. Such splits are present in all societies, and by looking at our own, it would seem to be inevitably true that the peasant would have been rejected by the wealthy landowners and the establishment religious leadership at Jerusalem, the chief priests, scribes, and elders of the synoptic tradition. The hostility to these groups expressed in the Synoptics may reflect such rejection. For the rejection is not all on one side. The outcast resents his situation and, however repressed, cannot help but build up hostility toward the establishment.

What we do have evidence for is the squared off hostility between the Pharisees and the peasants, the latter being the bulk, at least, of the class called in rabbinic literature the *am ha-aretz*.[19] The Pharisees, with their fellowships and strict laws of table and ritual purity, had made the peasants into virtually an untouchable class (see Neusner 1963, 22). And since the Pharisees claimed to represent God's will, they in effect,

---

[17] See Jeremias 1969. He is inconsistent in his judgment of the size of the city in the first century CE. Usually he estimates 25,000 (e.g. p. 84), but on p. 83 he offers the much higher figure of close to 55,000. Even if the latter is correct, Jerusalem was a city of modest size.

[18] Grant estimates 30–40% (1926, 105).

[19] I use this term with caution, for it may be a more inclusive category than that of 'peasant'. Morton Smith uses it to denote 'the average Palestinian Jew,' which, of course, included the peasants (1956, 73). Furthermore, as is well known, the precise delimitation of 'Pharisee' is not completely clear either. For a recent statement of the problems here see Bowker 1973.

whatever their expressed intent, read the peasant out of the kingdom of God.[20] It is not difficult to imagine the peasant's reaction to the Pharisaic stand – pure hostility.[21] But this hostility would have ultimately been directed against God and the peasant himself. Who would tell him that the Pharisees were 'wrong'? To feel that he was violating God's decrees was an inevitable result of the Pharisaic exclusivism and the peasant could only have felt locked out of religion, resentful toward God and more than ever convinced of his own worthlessness.

Because of the recent work of Morton Smith and Jacob Neusner we are in a better position to assess the situation between Pharisee and peasant in the first century CE than ever before. In his pathbreaking work on the pre-war Pharisees, Neusner has shown that the authentic traditions show the Pharisees interested in precisely the same issues that are debated in the Gospels. These concerns center around table fellowship and ritual purity, just those matters which would have set the peasant off as an outcast (see Neusner 1971, vol. III, 301–19; 1973, 67–80). Smith has shown that Josephus' claim in Antiquities that the pre-war Pharisees were in control of the minds of the masses is tendentious. Josephus is here attempting to convince the Romans that the Pharisees should be allowed to govern the Jewish community.[22] Smith doubts the Pharisees had control over any group except themselves, and the conclusions of Neusner substantiate that doubt. Thus Josephus can no longer be used to suggest the *am ha-aretz* supported the Pharisaic platform. Almost surely the reverse is true; the peasant would have resented the Pharisee and been scorned in return.[23]

---

[20] This is, in fact, the charge in Matt 23:13; they have shut the kingdom of heaven against people.

[21] From materials from the second century CE, the mutuality of the hostility between the two groups is clear. The rabbis consider the *am ha-aretz* as subhuman and acknowledge the deep-rooted hatred of the peasants in return (Pes. 49b). There is no reason to suppose that the same feelings were not present a century earlier.

[22] Smith 1956, 75–77, followed by Neusner 1973, 64–65.

[23] The only problem is whether the Pharisees were visible and menacing enough to cause such hostility among the peasants. Josephus admits they numbered only about 6000, and Neusner describes *them* in sectarian terms. If they were a small group, without political power and influence, how could the peasant have found them a threat? The lack of political power is not important, because the issue is not what the Pharisees could or could not make the peasants *do* but how they made them *feel* about their relationship in society and with God. That the Pharisees were visible enough to cause this feeling seems to me proven from the intense hostility expressed in the *pre-seventy* materials in the Synoptics. These materials attack the Pharisees for their exclusivism, not their hostility to Christianity *per se*. Thus the attack is not from the perspective of 'Christian' so much as it is from 'outcast'.

Into this scene Jesus steps and his mission is directed toward the healing of the society of his times. On the one hand Jesus did address the alienated and hostile peasant class, although F. C. Grant's claim that 'the gospel is, in fact, the greatest agrarian protest in all history' can only be taken as unnecessary hyperbole.[24] But on the other hand Jesus also addressed the establishment, if in tones of warning and challenge. As Jeremias has so beautifully shown, Jesus' message is a description of God's loving care for the poor, dispossessed, the 'riff-raff, shunned by all respectable people' (1955, 120); yet the parables are a challenge to the establishment to change its attitude toward him and his defense of the poor. The elder brother, the grumbling workers in the vineyard, the self-righteous Pharisee all represent the establishment who in effect say as Hillel was reputed to have said, 'No *am ha-aretz* fears sin.'[25] Yet Jesus tries to keep the door open. The elder brother in the parable of the prodigal son is 'left' standing in the field. Whether he remains there or comes to the feast is still open.

Jesus' mission is also to the tax, or toll, collectors. While these were not economically dispossessed, they were as much an outcast group as were the peasants, in a way similar to the merchants who were drawn to Russian sectarianism.[26] Indeed, it is not improbable that an early bad-mouthing of the Christian communities was to say they were bands of 'toll collectors and sinners.' It is even possible that Jesus or the church was not afraid to relate his mission to prostitutes.[27]

That Jesus and some of his co-leaders were not of the peasant class does not call into question the peasant makeup of his following. It is, rather, an example of Stark's claim that sect leaders have to come from a slightly higher class when the protest-group is too abject to produce its own leadership. Jesus was a *tektōn*, probably a carpenter, but at least an artisan of some sort. Peter, Andrew, James, and John were fishermen, and

---

[24] Grant 1950, 303. For a different view, see Buchanan 1964–65, 195–209. That Jesus spent time in the villages, or may even have lived for a while at Capernaum does not call into question the essentially peasant make-up of his audiences. The villages were populated by peasants who worked in the fields in the daytime.

[25] *Abot* 2.6. Neusner disputes the authenticity of the saying (1971, vol. I, 226).

[26] See Donahue 1971, 39–61. He argues strongly that *telōnai* were not publicans, that is, tax collectors, but the collectors of indirect taxes and should be called toll collectors. They were most likely the agents who did the actual collecting and, although not themselves wealthy, still must have belonged to the middle class.

[27] The woman in the story in Luke 7:36–50 *may* be seen as a prostitute. Matt 21:32 suggests that the Baptist circle included prostitutes, and the same is likely true of the Christian communities.

the severely stylized miniature of the calling of these disciples nevertheless includes the information that the family of James and John were wealthy enough to own a boat and have hired servants. Levi was a toll collector.

Thus Jesus led a protest movement, an 'agrarian protest' if you like. Yet two features characterize the distinctiveness of the protest. First, his ultimate aim was to move beyond protest. He did attract to himself the 'riff-raff' and despised groups. In his teaching he doubtless collected and expressed their resentment far better than they could have or would have. But at the deepest level the protest is not needed because the establishment is wrong. God is here and does love and accept the outcast. Jesus' word and act are theological through and through, even when they are directed to a distraught society.[28] He speaks to the economic and societal distress only indirectly through his attack upon the establishment leaders. In no way does he think the solution depends upon their change of heart. The matter of repentance on the part of the establishment is left open, but that repentance, if it comes, is for its own good. The younger brother is already enjoying reconciliation with his father. The feast has already begun.

Secondly, and most strikingly, Jesus does not seem to have tried to create cadres of people to withdraw from the world. He has followers, some close, some much more distant, but all indications are that he attempted to found no closed organization which would further rigidify the boundaries between the establishment and the outcasts. He addresses, in the final analysis, all Israel and wishes to heal the deep breaches in his society. Although his words to the establishment are sharp, one can imagine he was as passionate in his hope for its repentance as he was for that of his peasant following.[29]

2. *The early church rejected the reality claimed by the establishment*

The earliest church shared in the same reaction against and rejection of outside society that characterizes the typical sect. The pattern is, however,

---

[28] I do not believe it permissible to drive a wedge between the *theological* and the *societal*. If theology speaks out of and to man's experience, indeed, to total humanity, then the two belong inseparably together.

[29] There is even a hint in the traditions that Jesus had positive contact with some Pharisees. The warning the Pharisees give Jesus about Herod (Luke 13:31) is striking and may be historical. In Luke 7:36–50 the scene of the banquet is set at a Pharisee's house, although interpretation of that story is difficult. Throughout the gospels Jesus and the Pharisees are in dialogue, and not all of those pericopae need be attributed to ideal scenes or church settings.

complex and not every part of the sequence is evidenced – though it can be assumed. The community lives and proclaims a reality different from that outside. The proclamation is, in part, rejected by that outside world, which may either ridicule or make more serious negations. This in turn feeds the community's already existing hostility toward the outside.

A. *The general community.* How did the well-known story of Jesus' rejection by his *patria* (Mark 6:1–6) function for the early communities? It cannot have been simply a bit of biographical reporting. The story rather symbolizes the rejection the early believers themselves experienced in their own *patria.* Just as happened with their leader, so the believers have to anticipate rejection by their home villages, including their friends and relatives.[30] Such use of Jesus as model and symbol of rejection is made explicit in Matthew 10:25. Elsewhere the tradition reports that Jesus was slandered with the title, 'Beelzebul' (Mark 3:22). This should prepare the followers for similar slanders. 'It is enough for the disciple to be like his teacher, and the servant like his master. If they called the master of the house Beelzebul, how much more will they malign those of his household' (see also Luke 13:26–28, 13:34f; Matt 12:41f, 17:24–27; Mark 9:19).

B. *The family.* Even clearer is the reality of family split-ups. Considering the strong family ties esteemed in Judaism, this posture must be considered radically extreme. Of course part of the situation is due to family quarrels about the Jesus community with the inevitable result that part of a family would reject the claims of the new community and part accept (Matt 10:34f, par Luke 12:49–53; Mark 13:12). Behind this situation, however, is the deeper issue about one's prime loyalty. For the community has taken the place of the family as the locus of primary allegiance. 'If any one comes to me and does not hate his own father and mother and wife and children and brothers and sisters, yes, even his own life, he cannot be my disciple' (Luke 14:26).[31] In Mark 3:31 Jesus' family comes to seek him. He (apparently) refuses to go to them, pointing instead to those gathered about him: 'Here are my mother and my brothers' (Mark 3:34). In what is clearly a church formulation,

---

[30] Luke 4:16–30 is a revision and expansion of the Markan story. Included here is a bit of pre-Lukan tradition, vv. 25–27 (Bultmann 1957, 31), which may reflect similar views.

[31] The stronger language in this version of 'Q' is indication of its primary status over against the Matthean, where hate has been replaced by 'to love more than' (Matt 10:37), yet Matthew's interpretation must be accurate.

Jesus, in response to Peter's claim to have given up everything, says, 'Truly, I say to you, there is no one who has left house or brothers or sisters or mother or father or children or lands, for my sake and for the gospel, who will not receive a hundredfold now in this time, houses and brothers and sisters and mothers and children and lands, with persecutions, and in the age to come eternal life' (Mark 10:28–30). The members of the community in some significant fashion have separated themselves from that part of the world which is the hardest to leave, the nuclear family itself.[32]

C. *Hostility because of the failure of the missionary enterprise.* It is not hard to imagine the courage needed to missionize for the 'Way'. Knowing already what to expect from the world outside, and being mostly unlearned and private persons, the missionaries would have needed great resoluteness of will to become public persons with a suspected message from a group founded by an executed criminal. The tradition shows that such missionaries frequently had difficult times without much success. 'Jesus' foretells this experience. 'They will deliver you up to councils; and you will be beaten in synagogues; and you will stand before governors and kings for my sake, to bear testimony before them' (Mark 13:9). In another logion specific Galilean cities are mentioned – Chorazin, Bethsaida, and Capernaum – which have apparently rejected the Christian mission. Judgment is leveled upon them: 'But I tell you that it shall be more tolerable on the day of judgment for the land of Sodom [or Tyre and Sidon] than for you' (Matt 11:22, 24; see also Matt 10:15; Luke 14:16–24).

Even more pointed is the hostility directed against the various sides of the Jewish establishment.

D. *Against the Pharisees.* That expressions of bitterness against the Pharisees are far earlier than the post-seventy era is demonstrable from their presence in 'Q'.[33] In the infamous 'woes' against the Pharisees, the intense bitterness of the community of outcasts is vividly expressed (Luke

---

[32] And yet divorce is strongly repudiated, Mark 10:2–9; Matt 5:31f. It is interesting that of the materials relevant to family division only Luke 14:26 mentions a spouse, and it is just this saying that most clearly is speaking of valuation, not of physical separation. Does the prohibition of divorce have its *Sitz-im-Leben* in the communities precisely in the split-ups within families? If so, then the answer is clear: No matter how much dissension between spouses over the gospel, it is not grounds for divorce.

[33] Since Matthew is frequently seen to be in bitter dispute with the post-seventy Pharisees, I will appeal to Luke's rendering of 'Q' as being less influenced by redactional concerns.

11:37–52). Here the Pharisees are accused of two sorts of things. On the one hand the burden of Pharisaic rules about purity and tithing are inveighed against. This charge seems further split into two sub-charges. The Pharisees want to put their rules upon everybody as a condition of entering the kingdom of God (cf. here the Matthean version in 23:13); and their own execution of these rules is viewed as self-centered and prideful action. On the other hand, the Pharisees are accused of moral turpitude (extortion and wickedness, neglect of justice and the love of God). Just what this blame consists of is difficult to imagine by any objective criterion. The accusations sound very much like blind and emotion-packed charges by outsiders against a situation they know very little about – displaced hostility – as, for example, university people are often accused of communism. The true source of the hostility is certainly the pain of being seen as sinners before God, as unworthy to enter the kingdom.[34]

E. *Against the official establishment.* In chapters 11 and 12 the author of Mark has collected several traditions that reflect the church's hostility against the leaders of the official establishment. Here, it is significant to note, the Pharisees have disappeared and the chief priests, scribes, and elders, figures in political power, are the antagonists. Central are the temple incident and the cursing of the fig tree. I think it clear that Mark takes the temple incident not as a 'cleansing' but as a doom oracle ('You have made it a den of robbers'), and the fig tree story as a curse against Israel. It is, further, my conviction that he has correctly understood the original intent of both stories, although both have undergone alteration during oral transmission which has blunted this intent. The parable of the vineyard and its tenants that immediately follows in Mark (12:1–9) is put there by the author to clarify his understanding of the previous narratives. The symbolism is crystal clear. The leaders of Israel have continually rejected God's servants, and now his son they have killed and 'cast him out of the vineyard.' As a result God 'will come and destroy the tenants, and give the vineyard to others' (see also Matt 21:28–31; Mark 12:38–40).

[34] See the parallel in Matt 23. Further, Mark 2:1–3:6, 7:1–13, 8:11f, 10:2–9, 12:13–17. Mark is very careful in his handling of the Pharisees; they appear only when a question of law is the issue (if my argument is allowed that in the redactional context the Pharisaic request for a sign in 8:11f is a challenge to Jesus to validate his just completed feeling of the *Gentile* multitude (8:1–10)). Also Matt 15:12–14; 5:20; Luke 14:1–6, 18:9–14.

F. *Against the wealthy.* The earliest traditions show unmitigating hostility against the wealthy. These materials are well known and need not be detailed here. Suffice it to point to the Lukan version of the beatitudes and woes, usually seen as more primitive than Matthew's, where the poor (not the poor in spirit) are blessed and the rich condemned (6:20–26). The mitigation in Mark added to the saying about the camel and the eye of the needle does not belong to the saying itself, but in its present form is Markan redaction (Mark 10:23–27). And the black and white extreme is carried out with due harshness in the story about the rich man and Lazarus (Luke 16:19–31).[35]

G. *Against the intellectuals.* It frequently happens that the sect is suspicious of the intellectual, because his ratiocination is believed to be used as a weapon of repression (as it frequently is). For the Christian communities, the Pharisees and the scribes would perhaps be the most visible groups whose stance could be accused as a repressing intellectualism. And, indeed, traces of such suspicion are found. A 'Q' saying has Jesus rejoice: 'I thank thee, Father, Lord of heaven and earth, that thou hast hidden these things from the wise and understanding and revealed them to babes . . . All things have been delivered to me by my Father; and no one knows who the Son is except the Father, or who the Father is except the Son and any one to whom the Son chooses to reveal him' (Luke 10:21f). The 'babes,' not the intellectuals, have the truth (see also Mark 4:11f).

The traditions discussed here are just the barest sampling. It is amply clear that the community of Jesus knows itself to be excluded and rejected by the world. The individual members doubtless 'felt' this before they were converted; perhaps it is the community (or Jesus) which has brought to consciousness the awareness and freed the convert to express his feeling of rejection and his hostility to those who, he feels, have excluded him. The community stands over against the establishment world, with its wealth, pride, ingrouped relationships, intellectualism, and repression of the outcast.

3. *The early church was egalitarian*

Protest and hostility against repressive agents can explain sect emergence, but they cannot explain sect continuation. Without strong positive elements within the community the church would not have survived.

---

[35] See further Mark 10:17–22, 12:41–44; Luke 12:13–21, 33, 19:1–10.

In fact, the positive dimensions are far more important than the negative. To continue to keep separate from the world means that a quality of life within the community is experienced such as to give fulfillment for its members. What, then, was communal life like in the early Christian groups?

Of central importance was the strong egalitarian policy within the *earliest* church. Elsewhere I have suggested that Galatians 3:28, 1 Corinthians 12:13, and Colossians 3:11 are fragments of a primitive baptismal formula, which is probably most complete in Galatians 3:28 (Scroggs 1972, 291–92). 'For as many of you as were baptized into Christ have put on Christ. There is neither Jew nor Greek, there is neither slave nor free, there is neither male nor female; for you are all one in Christ Jesus.' When a person enters the community, the roles, valuations, and burdens the outside world has laid upon him fall away, and baptism marks his entrance into a community where everyone stands equal before God. In the outside world, a person has to remain a slave or a woman; inside, the slave is equal to his master, the woman, to man.[36]

The synoptic traditions say the same thing in other words. Distinctions based on status are put down. 'Whoever would be great among you must be your servant, and whoever would be first among you must be slave of all' (Mark 10:43f).[37]

The crucial test is in church organization. Outside of the church at Jerusalem there does not seem to have been any hierarchical structures in the beginning; deacons, elders, and bishops appear only later. Synoptic data supports this judgment. In Matthew 23:8–11 the church is prohibited the honorific terms, rabbi, father, master. In the section of church discipline in Matthew 18, the procedure recommended to correct a wrong doer within the community advances from the individual to the community as a whole; no church officers are mentioned. A tradition in Luke 6:40 runs in the same direction. 'A disciple is not above his teacher, but every one when he is fully taught will be like his teacher.'[38]

---

[36] Cf. the story about Mary and Martha in Luke 10:38–42. Here Mary's participation in the intellectual life of the community is given preference over the 'woman's' role of Martha.

[37] See also Mark 3:31–35, 9:33–37, 10:42–45; Luke 22:24–27.

[38] Käsemann argues that in the early communities there were only two categories, the *prophetic* charismatic and the *righteous* member, using as evidence Matt 10:41 and 13:17 (1954–55, 258).

4. *Within the community the believer experienced joy, love, and a fulfilled existence*

The source of this fulfillment is clearly the strong sense that God does indeed care for the outcast believer. The tradition is varied in its expression here. It may retell the parables of Jesus about the workers in the vineyard or the prodigal son (Matt 20:1–16; Luke 15:11–32). Significant in the latter, as in several other stories, is the strong sense of joy and rejoicing at being sure once again of God's love (e.g. Luke 15:3–10; Matt 13:44f). The tradition may repeat those sayings of Jesus in which the presence of the kingdom is stated or implied.[39] The joy and peace can be expressed in logia such as the following. 'Are not two sparrows sold for a penny? And not one of them will fall to the ground without your Father's will. But even the hairs of your head are all numbered. Fear not, therefore; you are of more value than many sparrows' (Matt 10:29f). 'Fear not, little Flock. It is your Father's good pleasure to give you the kingdom' (Luke 12:32). The logia in the sermon on the mount (Matt 6:25–34) promising the elimination of anxiety suggest the same reality: a community of believers who so strongly feel the presence of God's care that they know themselves loved, accepted, and recreated by God himself.[40] It is thus not surprising to find evidence of glossolalia – the ecstatic release of repressed emotions – within the earliest church. Although no Synoptic materials mention the practice, its presence in the early church is secured by three references in Acts and several in Paul.[41]

This acceptance spills over into communal relations. The believer is to love his neighbor as himself. He is to be free to give up possessions for the poor. While so-called 'primitive communism' is documented only for the Jerusalem church, logia embedded in the tradition may suggest it was more widespread. 'Sell your possessions, and give alms' (Luke 12:33). As already suggested, the community functions like an extended family where all are brothers and sisters. And where love fails, reconciliation and constant forgiveness are called for (Matt 5:21–24, 6:12, 18:21f).

Thus the believer realizes a quality of existence within the community he has not found outside, apparently not even within his own family.

[39] Mark 3:26f; Luke 10:18, 23f, 11:20, 17:21; Matt 11:2–6, 11f.
[40] Also Matt 7:7–11, 11:28–30; Mark 10:13–16, 19f, 29f.
[41] Acts 2:1–4; 10:46, 19:7. 1 Cor 12–14 (where Paul says he himself speaks in tongues, 14:18), perhaps 1 Thess 5:19, and very likely Rom 8:26 (so Käsemann 1971, 131).

The tradition, of course, ascribes the source of this reality to God or Jesus, but there can be little doubt that God is trusted as he is because love and acceptance are actual realities within the community itself.

The remaining three characteristics of the sect can, since they are so obvious in the case of earliest Christianity, be dealt with briefly.

5. The early church was a voluntary association

This of necessity was the case in the early years of the church. In the face of ridicule, harassment, and persecution it required a strenuous act of will to join. Whether or not there was infant baptism at an early stage does not affect the dominant voluntaristic structure of the community.

6. The early church demanded a total commitment from its members

Again the logia from the gospels are striking and well-known. To be a disciple one must take up his cross, sell his possessions, cut off hand, pluck out eye, not look back. The ethical injunctions are equally strenuous: not to be provoked to anger, not to look lustfully, to refuse to give oaths, to go the second mile, to turn the other cheek. Total commitment to a totally different life style from that of 'the world' is possible and necessary.[42]

7. The early church was apocalyptic

As suggested above, one frequent, if not necessary, characteristic of the sect is its apocalyptic or adventist perspective. Few people will doubt that earliest Christianity was so oriented. The imminent expectation of the eschaton is consistently there. In the post-Pauline church the intensity of this feeling will become muted, or even essentially discarded. But the church prior and contemporaneous to Paul very much believed in the nearness of God's final judgment.

Conclusion

Thus, in my judgment, the earliest church meets all the essential characteristics of the religious sect. But if the conclusion is justified, what profit lies therein? What new insights does this enable us to have about the emergence of early Christianity?

---

[42] E.g. Matt 5:17–20, 27–30, 33–37, 48, 6:24, 7:13f, 21–33, 10:37–39, 19:10–12; Mark 8:34–38, 10:11f; Luke 6:27–36, 9:59, 62, 14:33.

We now have a basically different gestalt from which to view the data. The use I have made of Synoptic pericopae in this paper illustrates how the gestalt changes the way the material is viewed. The church becomes from this perspective not a theological seminary but a group of people who have experienced the hurt of the world and the healing of communal acceptance. The perspective should enable the interpreter to be more sensitive to the actual life situations within and without the community. For example, through this perspective the protest nature of the community becomes clearer. It helps us to see that the church in its own way dealt with the problems individuals faced in repressive social circumstances.[43]

In conclusion I would like to give one specific example of how the view of the church as a sectarian movement sheds new insight on the data. When we ask the question, 'how did the earliest church understand the death of Jesus?,' the answers we usually get and give are theological – a foreordained plan, an atonement for sin, a defeat of the invisible powers. But what do the Gospels say about such views? That it was foreordained by God can be substantiated at places (e.g. Mark 8:31, 14:21) but is no more dominant than satisfying. The Synoptics are virtually silent about the atoning significance of the death, and completely so where it ought to be most marked, namely in the account of the execution itself. Schreiber's attempt to see the death in Mark as the triumph over the powers is completely forced (1967, 33–40, 64–78).

The usual theological answers thus are not adequate. Based on the evidence of the Synoptics, one would almost be forced to say there was no interpretation given at all. And yet this cannot be; the execution of Jesus by the Roman government could not be ignored for any number of reasons. What, then, could it have meant to the early believers to have to confess that their hero was a duly executed criminal? Pious Christianity has so romanticized the event, or so escaped into the resurrection, that it can no longer see the starkness of the fact. But from that brute reality the early believers had no such escape.

Recent work on the redaction history of Mark, combined with awareness that the church was sectarian, open the door toward a new understanding based on the lived realities of the people, rather than in some theological slogan. John Donahue has argued that the so-called

---

[43] It seems to me this approach gets closer to an appreciation of the real societal involvement of Jesus and the communities than all the arguments about connections with the Zealotic movement.

'night trial' in Mark, i.e. that before religious authorities on religious charges, is a Markan creation (Donahue 1973, 53–102). The story of the passion in any pre-Markan form knew of no such trial. Independently, Anitra Kolenkow in her work on the 'day trial' before Pilate reached the conclusion that the earliest form of this story had no apologetic elements at all (see Kelber, Kolenkow, Scroggs 1971, 550–56). Jesus stands trial on political charges and nothing in the earliest account attempted to blunt the nature of the trial. When both of these findings are put together, an early passion account emerges in which the political nature of the charges, the trial, and execution are very clear. This means that early Christians did not flinch from admitting that their hero was a duly executed Roman prisoner, executed on charges of sedition against the government. And there is no evidence that at this early stage they were the slightest bit embarrassed about such a situation.

How can we understand such lack of embarrassment? Traditional Christianity, full of support for law and order, is incapable of such understanding; it has lost all feeling for the sectarian protest of the earliest church. From the standpoint of sectarian reality, however, the death of Jesus offers a powerful symbolism for the outcast and alienated members of the early communities. From this perspective a two-fold meaning of the death can be seen. 1. It gathers together into one symbolism the hostile and protesting feelings of the sect against the world. *Of course* the Jews and the Romans collaborated together to kill Jesus. For the sectarian there is nothing strange about that. It was, rather, to be expected. The death symbolizes the demonic quality of the world. Further, it serves to make more explicable the suffering of the believers caused by ridicule and persecution. 'If they called the master of the house Beelzebul, how much more will they malign those of his household.'

2. The same reality must also have been a symbol of liberation as well. Before, the establishment provided the norms for the outcasts, however much those norms excluded them from participation in the society. But now that those norms have led to the execution of Jesus, God's son, it reveals those norms for what they truly are, the ways of man, or Satan, not the ways of God. They no longer can be passed off as divinely ordained and thus have lost the demonic control over the believer they once had had. The death thus symbolizes the liberation of the community from the mores and claims of the world, from polite society as well as from political authority, from the sacred as well as secular establishment.

The death of Jesus was a strong and effective positive symbol for the church, precisely because he was executed by the legitimate authorities. And this is why the church was not embarrassed by it. Who knows, it may even have bragged about it. And this is why as long as the church maintained its strongly sectarian form it did not need to introduce apologetic elements into the tradition. Nor did it need to search for theological reasons other than the very basic and profound one it had from the beginning. For the symbol of the death as protest and liberation is, just because it stems out of the living experiences of the folk, theological at its heart, if one is prepared to deal with a theology that takes as its first duty the attempt to explain to man what his predicament and his promise are.

FURTHER READING

A number of the classic sociological works on sectarianism are listed by Scroggs (n. 2). Particularly influential in New Testament studies has been the work of Bryan Wilson (see e.g. Wilson 1961; 1967). A convenient extract summarising Wilson's typology of sects is Wilson 1963. For an overview of Wilson's work see Miller 1979. Also influential is the earlier work of Troeltsch 1931 (see extract in Gill 1996).

Alongside the early work of Scroggs, note should be taken of Meeks 1972, and related work using anthropological work on millenarian movements (Gager 1975; cf. ch. 6 below).

Notable works in New Testament studies which have taken up and developed a sectarian analysis of early Christianity include Elliott 1981; 1995a; Watson 1986; Esler 1987; 1994; MacDonald 1988.

For critical overviews see Holmberg 1990, 77–117; Barton 1993; and the sharp criticisms of Sanders 1993, 114–25.

3

The Wandering Radicals:
Light Shed by the Sociology of Literature on the
Early Transmission of Jesus Sayings

GERD THEISSEN

INTRODUCTION

In a series of essays published in the mid-1970s, Gerd Theissen made what remains among the most influential contributions to the sociology of early Christianity (see *Introduction* §2; also ch. 9). The essay printed here, first published in 1973, attempts to link some of the traditional concerns of form criticism – the transmission of Jesus' sayings and their setting in the life of the church – with a sociological analysis of roles within the Jesus movement. Theissen argues that the radicalism of the synoptic sayings which speak of a rootless, wandering, propertyless existence, should not be ignored or interpreted away. On the contrary, Theissen proposes, we should see that such sayings reflect the pattern of life adopted deliberately and voluntarily by the wandering radicals, who travelled around the villages of Palestine (and beyond) proclaiming the message of the kingdom. His thesis is briefly summarised: 'the ethical radicalism of the sayings transmitted to us is the radicalism of itinerants' (p. 102). These wandering radicals, who followed the example of the Son of Man with 'nowhere to lay his head', were dependent on the support of sympathisers in the villages where they stayed. Hence, in his more popular *Sociology of Early Palestinian Christianity* (1978), Theissen presents an analysis of the Jesus movement in terms of three 'roles': that of the bearer of revelation, the Son of Man; the wandering charismatics; and the local sympathisers. The wandering charismatics, Theissen suggests, bear

Reprinted by permission from *Social Reality and the Early Christians* by Gerd Theissen, copyright © 1992 Augsburg Fortress.

   Lecture held in the University of Bonn on November 25, 1972. Some of its main ideas arose out of discussion with my colleague the Rev. H. Frost. I should like to thank him here for his stimulating suggestions [– G.T.].

some analogy to the Cynic preachers who travelled around the Roman empire, and in another essay (see Theissen 1982, 27–67) he analyses one of Paul's conflicts at Corinth as a conflict between two different patterns of leadership: between 'itinerant charismatics' and 'community organisers' (see also ch. 12 below). One of Theissen's most influential (and controversial) theses is outlined in the closing pages of the essay below: that as Christianity spread from rural Palestine to the urban centres of the Roman empire, so the radical ethic preserved and practiced by the wandering itinerants became inappropriate and impractical. It was replaced by an ethos of 'love-patriarchalism' more suited to this urban, cosmopolitan setting, and which was ultimately successful in shaping an enduring form of Christianity which was eventually adopted more widely within the later Roman empire (see also Theissen 1982, 106–10; further chs 9, 10, 12 below).

Criticisms of Theissen's bold theses have come from a number of quarters (see ch. 10 for criticisms of the love-patriarchalism idea). Richard Horsley (1989) and Wolfgang Stegemann (1984), while acknowledging the importance of Theissen's work, have both raised questions concerning the 'wandering radicals' thesis. Stegemann argues that Theissen does not employ sufficient source-critical discernment in his use of the synoptic material. Moreover, one of the crucial passages, Mark 10:28–30, does not, according to Stegemann, support Theissen's thesis. On the contrary, it 'points to a *community situation*' which applies to all those who change their allegiance 'for the sake of the gospel' (1984, 158). Horsley similarly argues that 'Mark 10:28–29 . . . places those addressed in a new "home" and the broader "family" of a renewed community (with lands!) rather than in an ethos of homeless wandering' (1989, 44). Stegemann agrees with Theissen that the prophets whose activities are recorded in the Q-tradition 'were undoubtedly *wandering* prophets' (1984, 162) but rejects the idea that they took on their poverty as a voluntary and ethical decision. Rather, like most of the lowly people in Palestine at that time, they unavoidably lived in a context of poverty and hunger (see pp. 160–64). Finally, Stegemann suggests that the depiction of wandering charismatics patterned like Cynic philosophers and adopting an ethical radicalism is in fact 'the contribution of Luke himself' (p. 164), even though 'he regards this special lifestyle of the disciples as a thing of the past' (p. 165). This Lukan presentation may in itself raise important contemporary challenges, but it is not to be confused with the historical reality of the Jesus movement (pp. 164–67).

Horsley's criticisms are aimed more widely at Theissen's *Sociology of Early Palestinian Christianity* (1978) *in toto*. Horsley criticises both Theissen's handling of the evidence, and his (predominantly) functionalist theoretical framework (see also Elliott 1986a). In relation to the wandering charismatics, Horsley maintains that the evidence simply does not support Theissen's conclusions, and that the analogy Theissen draws with the Cynics is inappropriate (see 1989, 43–50). Not unlike Stegemann, he insists that 'Jesus' preachers and healers . . . worked in community bases. They were not simply supported by local communities, but were apparently engaged in attempts to revitalize community life' (1989, 47).

These various criticisms contain points of importance, but in my view Theissen's thesis needs to be amended and nuanced, not discarded (see the recent discussion in Tuckett 1996, 355–67, where questions are raised about the criticisms of Stegemann and others). There were certainly itinerant missionaries active and influential in both Palestinian and wider contexts, including members of Jesus' own family (see further Bauckham 1990, 45–133; Eusebius *EH* 1.7.14; also ch. 12 below). And, at the very least, whether one accepts his reconstruction or not, even Theissen's harshest critics agree on the importance of his work: 'He has led many of us to rethink a highly important branch of Christian origins' (Horsley 1989, 10).

The sociology of literature investigates the relations between written texts and human behavior. It studies the social behavior of the people who make the texts, pass them on, interpret them, and adopt them (see Fügen 1970). And it analyzes this behavior under two aspects: first, as typical behavior; second, as contingent behavior – behavior conditioned by outside circumstances.[1]

It was form criticism that introduced the first of these aspects into biblical studies.[2] Typical features of the texts led the critics to conclusions

---

[1] Max Scheler, for example, describes sociological inquiry under these two aspects (1960, 17).

[2] The questions asked by the sociology of literature have been part of historical-critical research from the beginning. In his *Tractatus Theologico Politicus* of 1670, Spinoza demanded a historical interpretation of the Bible, meaning by this: (1) research into the

about equally typical features in the social conduct of the people concerned. That is to say, they argued back to a *Sitz im Leben* – a real-life situation, in which a text was continually used, and where this use actually shaped the text itself. We may think of instruction, for example, or perhaps mission, or worship.

The second aspect was the question about the circumstances determining the behavior that has made the text what it is. This question goes a little way beyond form criticism. Form criticism is primarily concerned with the intentions of the transmitters of a text and of its addressees. In the case of the biblical texts, these intentions are largely religious. So explaining a text in the light of its place in early Christian congregational life was generally interpreted to mean showing how it developed out of the faith of that congregation. But of course the life of early Christian communities included aspects that were not religious at all. One of these aspects was the problem of making a living, in the quite down-to-earth, commonplace sense. Another was the different social conditions in which a Galilean farmer lived, compared with a man or woman living in the great cosmopolitan city of Corinth. Surely we should expect life in this wider sense too to have influenced the New Testament texts?

To investigate the New Testament in the light of the sociology of literature therefore means asking about the intentions and conditions determining the typical social behavior of the authors, transmitters, and addressees of the New Testament texts. Now, we can ponder long enough about how to see the relationship between spiritual intentions and their less spiritual conditions.[3] According to Max Scheler, for example, the essential content of a mental or spiritual insight can never be derived from historical and social factors; but the spread and acceptance of that

---

language; (2) the interpretation of biblical books in the light of their own presuppositions; (3) the question about the author, the situation in which the books came into being, and their reception, as well as the practices and customs of their own environment (see Theissen 1993, 89ff, esp. 91–92). This last question undoubtedly includes questions belonging to the sociology of literature.

[3] We may name only a few possible models: (1) Determination models. Intellectual or spiritual traditions are retrospectively explained, in a process of hindsight, by way of (material) factors of cause and effect or by teleological intentions (history's plan, etc.). (2) Reflection models. In intellectual and spiritual traditions, natural processes of growth arrive at an awareness of themselves. (3) Action models. Traditions are attempts to respond to historical social situations. On the one hand, the traditions are confronted by these situations. On the other hand, the conditions also have their effect on human intentions.

insight may very well be influenced by these things.[4] And here our subject is not the *birth* of a spiritual tradition. We are discussing its spread, its transmission, and its preservation. It must surely be admitted that this is a sociological problem, even if one believes that the importance of sociological research for illuminating intellectual and spiritual traditions can be as clearly limited as Max Scheler maintains.

The transmission of Jesus sayings in the early Christian community is a sociological problem particularly because Jesus gave no fixed, written form to what he said. A written tradition can survive for a time even when it has no bearing on the behavior of men and women, or even if the tradition's intention runs counter to that behavior (see Bogatyrev and Jakobson 1929). But oral tradition is at the mercy of the interests and concerns of the people who pass it on and to whom it is addressed. Its survival is dependent on specific social conditions.[5] To mention only one of these: the people who pass the tradition on must in some way or other identify with that tradition. It is improbable that ethical precepts will be passed on for long if no one takes them seriously, and if no one

---

[4] Scheler 1960, 21: 'The mind . . . determines solely and exclusively the makeup of possible cultural factors – why they are as they are and not otherwise. But the mind as such does not originally and essentially possess the least trace of "power" or "efficacy" by which to bring these factors into existence. It is certainly a "determining" factor, but not an "implementing" one in the genesis of the potential culture.' This model is undoubtedly somewhat dogmatic. That is to say, it is influenced by the desire to rescue, a priori, at least one sector from the grasp of sociological investigation. In my view, the genesis of a religious tradition cannot be understood apart from factors of social history; nor can the prevailing power of such a tradition be put down exclusively to these factors. What is true is that we always find the emergence of something new more mysterious than its later history.

[5] Social conditions for the oral traditions about Jesus may be designated as follows: (1) The Jesus tradition was rooted in recurrent, typical behavior toward other people on the part of the transmitters. This was relatively independent of individual preference or caprice. If mental or spiritual attitudes are to survive, they must be anchored in the permanent necessities of life and in the constant characteristics of a particular life-style. (2) An interest in the part of the people addressed, who are passive preservers of tradition (see von Sydow 1948). Traditions continue to be passed on only as long as they find listeners. Whatever runs counter to the concerns and attitudes of these listeners will be eliminated or modified. It will fall victim to what Bogatyrev and Jakobson call 'the preventive censorship of the community' (1929, 903). We need only think of the adaptation to congregational conditions which we can observe in the different variants of Jesus sayings. (3) A sociological continuity between Jesus and the people who passed on his sayings. Scandinavian scholars quite properly tried to show that this continuity existed, their aim in so doing being to overcome the skepticism of the form critics about the authenticity of Jesus' sayings (see Riesenfeld 1957, 43–56; Gerhardsson 1964). In my view, however, the attempt is a failure.

makes at least an attempt to practice them. Given this premise, if we ask about the *Sitz im Leben* of Jesus' ethical teachings – the real-life situation to which they belong – we soon find ourselves in difficulty. Form criticism postulates that these teachings had their situation in congregational life. But – to take one example – what about the saying in Luke 14:26: 'If anyone comes to me and does not hate his own father and mother and wife and children and brothers and sisters, yes, and even his own life, he cannot be my disciple'? We should be inclined to call in question the whole postulate about a situation in congregational life, rather than to assume that a saying like this could ever have provided the basis for the shared life of men and women. Their ethical radicalism makes Jesus' sayings absolutely impracticable for the regulation of everyday behavior. So we are faced all the more inescapably with the question: Who passed on sayings like these by word of mouth over a period of thirty years and more? Who took them seriously? This is the problem on which we shall be concentrating here.

Are there any criteria that can help us to find an answer to the question? We might start off skeptically. All we have at our disposal are texts. We have no direct knowledge about the social behavior which is involved, and which they reflect. It can only be deduced. Form criticism had three ways of making this deduction (see Bultmann 1961, 5–8):

1. *analytical deduction* from the form and content of a tradition to its situation (or *Sitz im Leben*);

2. *constructive deduction* from direct statements about the situation presumed to the traditions that were anchored there;

3. *deduction by analogy* from contemporary parallels that are similar in content.

In the course of our discussion I shall use all three methods of deduction.

The sayings tradition offers a particular wealth of material for analytical deduction. The sayings enjoin particular behavior. This is translated into reflective form in general maxims and is pictorially presented in parables and apophthegmatic scenes which illustrate the maxim in question. Of course the behavior that is commanded, thought about, and illustrated, on the one hand does not simply coincide with actual behavior on the other. But if the divergences are typical ones, they can be allowed for in our deductions: as we know, commandments are radical at points where real life inclines toward compromise.[6] Prohibitions often allow us to deduce that the forbidden behavior actually exists.[7] But in general we may assume heuristically, or as a working hypothesis, that the sayings of Jesus were practiced in some form or other. If they had been notoriously disregarded, they would hardly have survived over a period of one or two generations. It seems more likely (and there is evidence of the fact here and there) that they were *adapted* to actual behavior – so that the analytical inference, or induction, from the sayings to this behavior suggests itself even more. There should be no doubt about the fact that the sayings of Jesus are meant seriously and literally. We must not assume that the early congregations already harbored the kind of text interpreters who assure us that none of it was intended to be taken so seriously – interpreters who maintain that this saying was added later, that the other was conditioned by the time, that the third was symbolic, the fourth contradictory, and that the fifth can be relativized by other New Testament statements. On the contrary, we must assume that Jesus' sayings were consistently taken seriously and were practiced. We should not forget that one of these sayings asks: 'Why do you call me "Lord, Lord", and not do what I tell you?' (Luke 6:46).

Let us now consider why Jesus sayings were passed on, looking also at the conditions of the transmission. We shall draw on the help of the criteria I have suggested and shall proceed in two stages. First, we must start from the way the transmitters saw themselves, as this emerges from the form and content of the logia, or sayings. Our aim here is to discover the behavior that is behind them. Our findings will have to be tested by the methods of constructive deduction and analogy. In a second stage we can then go on to ask about the conditions that determined this behavior, even when the transmitters were not consciously aware of the fact.

1. The self-understanding of the transmitters and their conduct

The sayings tradition is characterized by an ethical radicalism that is shown most noticeably in the renunciation of a home, family, and

---

[6] For example, it was one of Paul's maxims not to allow himself to be kept by his congregations. This did not prevent him from gratefully accepting support from the congregation in Philippi (Phil 4:10ff), although elsewhere he almost makes his salvation depend on his making no use of an apostle's usual privileges (1 Cor 9:13–18).

[7] The staff forbidden in Matt 10:10 is conceded to the early Christian missionaries in Mark 6:8. The mission to the Gentiles is forbidden in Matt 10:5f; yet as we know, it took place.

possessions. From the precepts that have to do with these things, we can arrive analytically at some conclusions about the lifestyle that was characteristic of the people who passed on the texts.

Jesus' sayings preach an ethic that is based on homelessness. The call to discipleship means renouncing any permanent abode. The people who are called leave their boats and their fields, their customshouse and their home. Jesus tells one of his disciples: 'Foxes have holes, and birds of the air have nests; but the Son of man has nowhere to lay his head' (Matt 8:20). Homelessness belonged to the discipleship of Jesus, and not merely during his lifetime. The *Didache*, for example, is familiar with itinerant Christian charismatics and says that they practice *tropous kuriou*, the Lord's way of living (*Did.* 11.8).

The ethic of the sayings excludes family ties as well. Giving up a fixed place of abode means breaking with family relationships. To hate father and mother, wife and children, brother and sister is one of the conditions for discipleship (Luke 14:26). According to Mark 10:29, the disciples left their homes, their fields and their families. They violated even the minimum requirements of family piety. One disciple wants to bury his father, who has just died. But he is told: 'Leave the dead to bury their own dead' (Matt 8:22).[8] To have children oneself is undesirable: one saying talks about people who have deprived themselves of their procreative power for the kingdom's sake (Matt 19:12).[9] What someone with an average ethical attitude to the family thought about the early Christian wandering charismatics requires no very extensive discussion. Understandably enough, the early Christian prophet did not count for much in his home town and in his own family (Mark 6:4).[10] We could

[8] See Hengel 1968. Klemm (1969–70) rightly objects to interpretations that tone down the 'offensive' sayings of Jesus.

[9] It is hard to say how far the logion should be taken literally. Blinzler (1957) believes that it is intended to defend the disciples against the insulting term 'eunuch'. Greeven (1968–69) thinks that this is a pictorial way of talking about the people who are leading a sexually ascetic life. Quesnell (1968) even claims that what is under discussion is the sexual asceticism of someone whose wife has been unfaithful, who – although he casts the woman off for adultery – abstains from a new marriage out of faithfulness to the old one.

[10] In Mark 6:4, relatives and members of the family (*oikia*) are explicitly mentioned, although these are missing in *POxy* 1.5 and *Gospel of Thomas* 31. Either Mark 6:4 has modified a general adage (Bultmann's view in 1961, 31–32), or *POxy* 1.5 and *Gospel of Thomas* 31 are secondary developments of Mark 6:4. This is the view taken by Schrage 1964, 75, 77; also Grässer 1969–70. The saying probably once existed on its own, out of context (see Haenchen 1966, 220). In this form it would then certainly, like Matt 5:11f, have referred to early Christian prophets.

hardly expect the abandoned families to have reverenced him as a hero. It was in fact difficult to justify his behavior. There are sayings that postulate the disintegration of the family as a necessary manifestation of the end time (Luke 12:52f).[11] Others remodel the concept of the family: one's brothers, sisters, and parents are the people who do God's will (Mark 3:35). On the other hand, the breach with the family was probably hardly ever put into practice consistently. For example, many men took their wives with them on their wanderings (see 1 Cor 9:5).

A third characteristic of the sayings tradition is criticism of wealth and possessions (Degenhardt 1963). As the story of the rich young ruler shows, renunciation of possessions was considered essential for full discipleship (Mark 10:17ff). Treasure should be gathered in heaven, not on earth (Matt 6:19–21).[12] It is easier for a camel to go through the eye of a needle than for a rich man[13] to enter the kingdom of God (Mark 10:25). A person who renounces possessions is renouncing the usual way of saving himself from anxiety. That is why the saying passed down to us says:

> Do not be anxious about your life, what you shall eat or what you shall drink, nor about your body, what you shall put on. Is not life more than food, and the body more than clothing? Look at the birds of the air: they neither sow nor reap nor gather into barns, and yet your heavenly Father feeds them. Are you not of more value than they? . . . And why are you anxious about clothing? Consider the lilies of the field, how they grow, they neither toil nor spin . . . . (Matt 6:25ff)

We should not read into this saying the mood of a Sunday afternoon stroll with the family. It has nothing to do with delight in birds and

[11] This actualized a prophetic, apocalyptic tradition: Mic 7:6; Zech 13:3; *1 Enoch* 100:2; 99:5; *Jub* 23:16; *Syr Bar* 70:6; 2 Esd 6:24. It is interesting that Matthew should take up this saying in the sending of the Twelve (Matt 10:21); that is, that he lets it be addressed to wandering charismatics especially. On Luke 12:51–53, see Schulz 1972, 258–60.

[12] In Luke the command not to gather treasure on earth is missing. It has been transformed into a positive exhortation: he should use his wealth in order to give alms. According to Pesch (1960), Luke is modifying the tradition here, formulating a 'message to the Christian congregations in the Hellenistic world, and their socially difficult class structures' (p. 375). I believe that this interpretation is correct. According to Degenhardt, however, it is the version in Matthew that is secondary (1963, 88–93).

[13] There is in my view no reason for assuming that the original reading was 'man' (*anthrōpos*) instead of the present 'rich man'. This is the view of Legasse 1963–64. Similarly, Walter maintains that the saying is not asserting 'that a human being could perhaps enter the kingdom of God by casting away earthly possessions or through other ascetic endeavors' (1962, 210). This is sound Protestant dogmatics, but hardly in line with early Christian radicalism.

flowers and green fields. On the contrary: what this saying is talking about is the whole rigor of the life led by the wandering charismatics, outlawed, without any home and without protection, people who made their way through the countryside without any possessions and without any work (see Hoffmann 1972, 327–28).

We can now formulate our thesis:[14] the ethical radicalism of the sayings transmitted to us is the radicalism of itinerants. It can be practiced and passed on only under extreme living conditions. It is only the person who has severed his everyday ties with the world – the person who has left home and possessions, wife and child, who lets the dead bury their dead, and takes the birds and the lilies of the field as his model – it is only a person like this who can consistently preach renunciation of a settled home, a family, possessions, the protection of the law and his own defence. It is only in this context that the ethical precepts which match this way of life can be passed on without being unconvincing. This ethic only has a chance on the fringes of society; this is the only real-life situation it can have. Or to be more exact: it does not have a situation *in* real life at all. It has to put up with an existence *on the fringes* of normal life, an existence that from the outsider's point of view is undoubtedly questionable. It is only here that Jesus' words were saved from being reduced to allegory, from reinterpretation, from softening or repression – simply because they were taken seriously and put into practice. And that was possible only for homeless charismatics.

We can check the soundness of this thesis in a second process of thought, by means of a constructive deduction from the evidence. In the charge with which the disciples are sent out in the Synoptics[15] and in the *Didache* too,[16] direct statements about the early Christian itinerant

---

[14] This thesis is a development of Kretschmar's ideas (1964). Hoffmann takes these ideas further in a similar direction (1972, 312–34). The theory I am maintaining here grew out of a conversation with the Rev. H. Frost, who drew my attention particularly to the significance of the charge with which the disciples are sent forth, and what it tells us about the people who passed on the Jesus tradition.

[15] For modern analyses of the sending discourse, see Hahn 1965, 33–36; Hoffmann 1972, 236–334; Schulz 1972, 404–19. The interpretation I am putting forward here is especially close to Hoffmann's, but I have not tried to follow up his attempt to localize the logia traditions in the history of the time – that is, in the context of the disputes between 'the hawks' and 'the doves' before the Jewish War.

[16] On the rules in the *Didache* about the treatment and condemnation of the itinerant Christian charismatics see e.g. Kretschmar 1964, 36–37, who points to some illuminating links with the Syrian itinerant ascetics.

charismatics have been preserved for us. In the Synoptics we are told the rules given to the first Christian missionaries. The *Didache* gives the rules for dealing with these people. We now have to show that to some extent these directives point to the very behavior which we have discovered was characteristic of the people who passed on the sayings.

The obligation to dispense with home and one's familiar country is included in the charge to the disciples. In the *Didache*, the point is made even more forcibly: an apostle is to remain no more than one day, or at most two, in the same place. If he remains three days, he is a false prophet (*Did.* 11.5).

Poverty is an equally clear obligation. The missionaries are to take no money with them, no purse, only one garment, neither shoes nor staff (Matt 10:10). According to the *Didache*, the apostles should be given bread for only a single day, and never money. If anyone asks for money he is a false prophet (*Did.* 11.6).

The nonfamily character of this wandering life does not emerge so strongly. A puzzling passage in the *Didache* says that the wandering prophets practice the *musterion tēs ekklesias* 'the mystery of the church.'[17] They are not to be condemned for this. Judgment is to be left to God – provided that these prophets do not teach other people to behave in the same way (*Did.* 11.11). This is probably an allusion to women who accompanied the wandering prophets, and whose relations with them were not unequivocal. Sexual abstinence was no doubt an official requirement. However, the passage is still a *musterion* for us too.

The conduct enjoined in the transmitted sayings was therefore practiced by at least *one* group of early Christians: the itinerant charismatics, the apostles, prophets, and missionaries. That does not necessarily prove that these people were also the transmitters of the sayings themselves. But this is probable, especially since there are some clues that point in this direction.

In the passage about the sending of the Twelve in the Gospel of Matthew there is an explicit mention of the 'words' of the wandering

---

[17] Audet gives a survey of exegetical opinion (1958, 451–52). He himself argues against a sexual interpretation. But it is quite possible that what is being thought of is the practice of adoptive or spiritual brotherhood or sisterhood – that is, living together with the obligation to abstain from sexual relations. The woman's pregnancy will often have made the problematical character of this undertaking apparent, as Irenaeus makes plain when he is talking about this practice among the Valentinians (*Adv. haer.* 1.6.3).

charismatics: 'If any one will not receive you or listen to your words . . .' (Matt 10:14). Now, these do not have to have been Jesus' own words. But the only saying that Matthew quotes directly as having been proclaimed by these wandering charismatics is a saying of Jesus: 'The rule of God is at hand' (Matt 10:7; Luke 10:9). Their sayings were therefore at least partly identical with Jesus' own sayings.

The missionary charge in Luke goes even further: 'He who hears you hears me, and he who rejects you rejects me' (Luke 10:16; cf. Matt 10:40). Jesus himself is present in the words of the itinerant missionaries. This presence should not be viewed as a mystical identity. The wandering missionary is Jesus' voice because he passes on Jesus' words – because he is Jesus' messenger. This is confirmed by the form of the logia. Some of them are in the first person.[18] In some of them the Amen formula shows that they are meant as a revealed truth taken over by the speaker (see Berger 1970). The two groups complement each other. For example, the person who in the first person utters the 'But I say to you' of the Sermon on the Mount becomes Jesus' representative through what he says: 'He who hears you hears me.' This applied particularly to wandering charismatics, as a variant of this saying shows: 'He who receives you receives me, and he who receives me receives him who sent me' (Matt 10:40). This saying is a recommendation to the congregations to take the wandering charismatics in.[19]

---

[18] In Mark 13:6 early Christian prophets are characterized by the first-person style of their discourses. These people will hardly have been purporting to be the returning Messiah, for anyone who 'comes in Jesus' name' (Mark 13:6) will hardly claim identity with him. The *egō eimi* ('I am') is rather to be viewed as a stylistic device of prophetic speech. Luke's polemic at this point against early Christian itinerant prophets is even more unambiguous. Their proclamation that *ho kairos ēggiken*, 'the time is at hand' (Luke 21:8), corresponds precisely to the charge in the missionary discourse (Luke 10:9; Matt 10:7).

[19] Käsemann (1960, 162–85) already put forward this view in 'Die Anfänge christlicher Theologie'. See also the *Didachē*'s instruction that wandering charismatics are to be received as if they were the Lord (*Did.* 11.2). The wandering charismatics' awareness that they were Jesus' representatives is to be found in other logia as well. In my view it explains the change from the first person to the third in Mark 8:38, which has always been felt to be a puzzle: 'Whoever is ashamed of me and of my words . . . of him will the Son of man also be ashamed . . .' As the transmitter of Jesus' sayings, the early Christian wandering prophet could identify himself with Jesus and speak in the first person ('Whoever is ashamed of me and of my words . . .'). But he was very well able to distinguish between himself and the future judge. The closest analogy to this is to be found in the sending of the Twelve, where we read 'If any one will not receive or listen to your words . . .' (Matt 10:14). Corresponding to this is the other saying: 'Whoever is ashamed of me and my words . . .' – 'my words' meaning the words of Jesus passed on by the wandering charismatics, which could be distinguished from the person of Jesus because of this

In my view, these rules for the early Christian itinerant charismatics allow us to make a constructive deduction: these people were practicing an ethic that corresponded to the logia tradition; the tradition's eschatological theme was part of their proclamation; and they saw themselves as people who were in line with Jesus' sayings. They were the transmitters of Jesus' words, even after the Gospels had taken form. In the second century, Papias was still culling Jesus traditions from the itinerant disciples of the Lord who passed by.[20]

Finally, we can underpin our thesis by a conclusion from analogy. All wandering charismatics were not Christians. In the first and second centuries there were numerous itinerant Cynic philosophers and preachers as well. They too existed on the fringes of society (see Friedlaender 1910, IV, 315–16, 346–53; Dudley 1937 esp. 125ff). They were in opposition to the emperors Vespasian and Domitian, and the emperors in their turn joined battle with them. Other people thought that the finest of these men were patterns of human living – the philosopher Epictetus, for example. Talking about the Cynics, Epictetus asks: 'How is it possible to live happily without worldly possessions, naked and without house or home, without any care for the body, without a servant and without a country?' And he replies:

Behold, God has sent you the man who can prove through his deeds that it is possible. I have none of these things. I sleep upon the ground. I have neither wife nor children, no little palace, nothing but earth and heaven and a single great cloak. And yet what do I lack? Am I not free of anxiety? Being without fear, am I not free? (*Discourses* 20.46–48)

The ethic of the early Christian sayings that have come down to us and the ethic of Cynic philosophy resemble each other in their three

transmission through other people. A similar awareness that they were representatives comes out in the saying about the sin against the Holy Spirit, that is, against the Spirit of the early Christian prophets (Mark 3:28f par.). We already find this 'prophet' interpretation in *Did.* 11.7. In my view it is a particular sociological type of Christian faith that finds expression here – that is, the radicalism of the early Christian itinerants. Perhaps the sense of being representatives, which was cherished by the early Christian wandering charismatics, is also present in Matt 25:31–46 (see Michaelis 1965). Michaelis identifies 'the least of the brethren' with the apostles. This interpretation would in fact be in line with logia which make God's attitude to men and women at the judgment dependent on their behavior toward Jesus' messengers (Luke 10:16; Matt 10:40ff). Nevertheless, the command to be hospitable is no doubt intended to apply to everyone.

[20] Eusebius *EH* 3.39.4: 'But when anyone came who was a disciple of the elders, I asked them about the elders' words.'

most important features: they are ethics based on the renunciation of home and country, family ties, and possessions. Since the ethic of the Cynics was spread by itinerant philosophers, it will be permissible to conclude, by analogy, that the people who passed on the Jesus tradition belonged to a comparable sociological group. This conclusion by analogy is based on structural similarities, not on historical links between the two movements. All the same, links are not entirely lacking.[21] In Gadara, in east Jordan, Menippus, Meleager, and Oinomaos are evidence that Cynic ideas existed for a period of five hundred years.[22] Even more significant is the fact that in the second century, Peregrinus – the target of Lucian of Samosata's mockery – was at first an itinerant Christian charismatic who was then converted to Cynicism and continued his wandering life under different colors (Bernays 1879). Itinerant Cynic philosophers and early Christian wandering charismatics alike stepped outside normal life. But of course their inward, spiritual reason for doing so differed. The philosophers detached themselves from existing conventions and customs by way of an intellectual process in which they set *phusis* ('nature') over against *nomos* ('law') as antitheses. The early Christian wandering preachers did the same in mythical images in which the old world, doomed to destruction, was contrasted with a new one.

If the sayings of Jesus were passed on by wandering charismatics what does this tell us about their authenticity? The skepticism of the form critics is based on the recognition that the Jesus sayings were shaped by the institutions and needs of the congregations that grew up after Easter. These institutions and needs were neither established by Jesus nor envisaged by him. For, as Alfred Loisy said: 'Jesus proclaimed the kingdom of God, and what happened was the church.'[23] If by the church we understand local congregations and their institutions, then there is no sociological continuity between Jesus and Christianity in its early

---

[21] Hommel (1966) draws attention to points of intersection between the logia tradition and philosophical motifs belonging to the Socratic tradition. He sees a link especially in the theme about the priority of spiritual relationships over family ones, which is particularly relevant for the logia tradition. On the theme that the wise man accepts no money, see Betz 1972, 100–17.

[22] On these Cynically influenced writers or philosophers, see the relevant articles in PW and in Bartels and Huber 1965.

[23] See Loisy 1904, 155. On the interpretation of this famous dictum, see Hoffmann-Axthelm 1968.

form.[24] But it was different in the case of the wandering charismatics. Here Jesus' social situation and the social situation of one branch of early Christianity are comparable: Jesus was the first wandering charismatic. The people who passed on his sayings took over 'the Lord's way of life,' the *tropous kuriou* (*Did.* 11.8); thus, sayings that show the impress of their life-style are by no means necessarily 'nongenuine.' The radicalism of their wandering life goes back to Jesus himself. It is authentic. Probably more of the sayings must be 'suspected' of being genuine than many a modern skeptic would like to think.

But the Jesus tradition is authentic in a different, transferred sense as well. It is *existentially* authentic. It was practiced. Here both modernist and conservative interpreters are often equally blind. Thus an exponent of existential interpretation and the 'new hermeneutics' sees the demand to the rich young ruler to give away his possessions as a call to accept Jesus' word.[25] The hearer must hear. In this encounter, we are told, the call to discipleship must 'no longer be interpreted ethically or socio-logically'; what is being said is 'religious in the most genuine sense.'[26] Now, the new hermeneutic aims to interpret bygone texts for the present – in this case, no doubt, for a present in which it is quite coolly taken for granted that Jesus' words are not practiced. The aim itself is no cause for reproach. But no one should make it a reason for letting himself be seduced into using hermeneutical profundity as a way of setting aside the clear meaning of Jesus' sayings. This should be avoided, if only out of respect for the people who once took these sayings seriously. And even today it is worth remembering and thinking about the fact that once upon a time there were men and women who, when they passed on Jesus' sayings, could assure their listeners without the suspicion of a jarring note that 'heaven and earth will pass away, but my words will not pass away' (Mark 13:31).

---

[24] S. Schulz's extensive work (1972) is an attempt to localize the tradition of the sayings of Jesus in a Q congregation. Because of the radical ethics of the sayings, these congregations must be made highly 'unworldly' ('enthusiastic'), this being put down largely to the imminent expectation of the parousia. Skepticism about the authenticity of the Jesus sayings is inevitably intensified.

[25] Fuchs 1971, 10–20: 'Here we must not too hastily lose ourselves in sociological questions, for "sell" has a dialectical sense: discipleship consists in the acceptance of his Word' (p. 18).

[26] Fuchs 1971, 19. Even the tentative sociological approaches made by classic form criticism are rejected: 'We should not draw on sociological categories, as is the inevitable practice in the form criticism of Bultmann and, especially, American theology' (p. 82).

2. *The conduct of the transmitters and the conditions that shaped it*

We started by considering the intentions behind the sayings tradition. The premise for the inference we made about practical behavior was that mental and spiritual intentions are something to be taken seriously; that is to say, they have practical consequences for 'earthly' behavior. We shall now, in a second stage, proceed to reverse this heuristic assumption. We may also assume that entirely 'earthly' conditions can have practical consequences for mental and spiritual intentions. The different factors that go to make up these earthly conditions may be divided into three groups, and we shall consider certain aspects of them, one after another: (1) socioeconomic factors, such as the question of how to make a living, a person's occupation, and the social class to which he or she belongs; (2) socioecological factors, such as urban or rural milieu; (3) sociocultural factors, such as the language, norms and values of particular groups of people. Since religious traditions deal only very shamefacedly with their not-so-religious preconditions (or do not deal with them at all), it is, in the nature of things, very difficult to arrive at soundly based assertions here. Methodologically justified skepticism is undoubtedly called for. But there are no grounds for the opportunistic skepticism which maintains that it is methodologically impossible to know anything about this sector – the real reason being that at bottom the skeptics have no desire to know anything about it. Generally these skeptics know astonishingly well in their heart of hearts that the factors I have named have at least a subordinate importance.

One very simple socioeconomic question is treated in the sayings tradition as clearly as we could wish. That is the question of livelihood, or means of support. The missionary charge to the disciples contains one negative and one positive utterance here. The negative instruction is as follows: 'Take nothing for your journey, no staff, nor bag, nor bread, nor money; and do not have two tunics' (Luke 9:3); 'salute no one on the road' (10:4). What interests us particularly is the renunciation of bag, staff,[27] bread, and money. Cloak, bag, and staff were the

---

[27] To renounce the staff meant renouncing the most modest means of self-defense (see Hoffmann 1972, 313ff). Anyone who wandered through the country in this way had no choice other than to abide by Jesus' saying 'if any one strikes you on the right cheek, turn to him the other also . . . and if any one forces you to go one mile, go with him two miles' (Matt 5:39–41). The logion could be directly related to the situation of the

characteristic 'uniform' of the itinerant Cynic philosophers,[28] the 'mendicant friars of antiquity,' as they have been called. The prohibition of bag[29] and staff was probably intended to avoid the least shadow of an impression that the Christian missionaries were these beggars, or were like them. They were probably forbidden to greet any one on the way for the same reason.[30] Anyone who demonstratively displays his poverty and accosts another person on the road could easily be misunderstood. The command not to move from house to house in the same village or town (Mark 6:10; Luke 10:7) has a similar point.[31] It might all too easily have suggested an attempt to exploit materially a village's readiness to receive the wanderers. It is clear that the early Christian itinerant charismatics were forbidden to employ the usual beggar's practices.[32] But they were also forbidden to make any planned provision for the future.

This gives even more force to the question: What did these people live from?[33] We have a positive instruction on this point:

Whatever house you enter, first say, 'Peace be to this house!' And if a son of peace is there, your peace shall rest upon him; but if not, it shall return to

wandering charismatics. For someone who is in any case on the move, it is a matter of indifference whether he is forced to render any particular service for one mile or for five or three.

[28] Diogenes Laertius 6.13. Here cloak, bag and staff, appendages that later counted as signs of a Cynic philosopher, are probably being attributed to Antisthenes (see Dudley 1937, 6). On traveling equipment in the ancient world in general, see Hoffmann 1972, 313ff.

[29] The Cynic Crates wrote a play called *Pēra* ('bag'). Deissmann 1923, 86–88 accepts the meaning 'beggar's sack'. W. Michaelis takes a different view ('*Pēra*,' *TWNT* 6:119–21). He writes; 'Jesus will hardly have come across the type of the itinerant "religious" or philosopher with the beggar's sack, such as were to be found in the cults of Asia Minor and among the Cynics' (p. 121 n. 13; see *TDNT* 6).

[30] W. Grundmann (1969), for example, takes a different view, maintaining that this was a warning against wasting time.

[31] Haenchen puts this prohibition down to experience: jealousy and quarrels arose when different families in turn received the missionaries (1966, 230).

[32] Haenchen also believes that the demonstrative poverty of the itinerant missionaries was intended to guard against the suspicion that they wanted to line their pockets (1966, 222).

[33] Although Schulz shows marked concern for the revolutionizing of material conditions in contemporary society, where the interpretation of texts is concerned (1972, 172ff, 487ff), questions about the material conditions of their transmission do not seem to interest him. With regard to our problem he writes quite simply: 'We must be careful not to read more into this instruction than is actually said: the apocalyptic laborers in the harvest are real workers who have a claim to food and drink' (p. 417).

you. And remain in the same house, eating and drinking what they provide, for the laborer deserves his wages. Do not go from house to house. (Luke 10:5–7)

It was therefore evidently expected that there would always be people who would freely provide the necessary support. Here the appeal was not to a charitable turn of mind but to what was just and right: labor deserves its wage. What kind of labor? The charge to the disciples names two things: healings and eschatological proclamation – healings for the present, proclamation for the future. And the proclamation was not merely a matter of powerless words; it offered support at the last judgment. This emerges from the salutation of peace.[34] The greeting is conditional. If the wandering preachers are rejected, the greeting reverts to them like some magical power. But the hostile place will suffer a worse fate at the impending judgment than Sodom and Gomorrah (Matt 10:15; Luke 10:12). We may conclude from this that if the wandering preachers were received, the eschatological judgment would pass the receptive houses and villages by. Healings in the present and eschatological protection – this was 'the work performed' by the wandering preachers, and it was to be given without payment: 'You received without paying, give without pay' (Matt 10:8). Nevertheless, the work performed was worthy of its proper wage. That it should be paid for in food, drink, and shelter was really a matter of course.[35] This is certainly not begging in the normal sense. It is an elevated kind of begging, charismatic begging, for which the problem of livelihood is only marginal, since 'the beggar' is confident that this problem will solve itself, so to speak, according to the motto: 'Seek first the kingdom of God and his righteousness, and all these things shall be yours as well' (Matt 6:33). It is not just by chance that among the Jesus sayings we find what is really a piece of beggar's lore: 'Ask, and it will be given you; seek, and you will find; knock, and it will be opened to you' (Luke 11:9ff par).

Of course conditions in the real world will have seen to it that these things did *not* always take care of themselves. The story about the

---

[34] On the background of 'the peace' in the history of religion, see Hoffmann 1972, 296–302. On pp. 310ff, he interprets the salutation against the background of the time: 'the sons of peace' are gathered together in their conflict with the zealots of the resistance movements. But does the solution not have a very general connotation?

[35] Krauss 1925: 'Jesus apparently requires his disciples to live from the hospitality of the people to whom they happen to come and in whose towns or villages they preach.'

plucking of the ears of corn makes this clear. Form-critical analysis assumed that this incident transformed conditions in the early Christian congregations into an ideal scene (see Bultmann 1961, 14). But this prompted the objection that it can hardly have been a recurrent custom in these congregations to wander hungry through the fields on the Sabbath.[36] It is quite true that this could scarcely have happened in a local congregation of respectable working Christians. But for itinerant preachers, without money and without bread, it may well have been a typical situation. In the story, the breaking of the Sabbath is justified by the circumstance that in Old Testament times the priests had a right to the sacred bread. But the explanation is not logical. The priest was not breaking the Sabbath when he gave the offerings to unauthorized persons. But the logical flaw has been introduced for a practical reason, which emerges when we realize that the story has been molded by the problems of wandering charismatics; for their claim to material support was justified by Paul (1 Cor 9:13) and in the *Didache* (13.3) by the very same right to the sacrificial offerings that was conferred on the priest in the Old Testament.[37] On this occasion theological logic (or the lack of it) has been adapted to very human needs.

The wandering charismatics will often have gone hungry because no one would take them in. They were often hunted away like vagabonds without any rights. A consoling saying which many scholars have puzzled over is meant for this situation:[38] 'When they persecute you in one town, flee to the next; for truly, I say to you, you will not have gone through all the towns of Israel, before the Son of man comes' (Matt 10:23). If the people addressed here were merely single-minded missionaries, the saying could have been of little comfort; for the missionary must have despaired at not being able to reach all the different towns before the

[36] See Haenchen 1966, 118–23. He writes: 'The Christians certainly did not have any particular preference for walking through the fields on the Sabbath, eating ears of corn' (p. 122). But Beare (1960) rightly points out that conflicts about the Sabbath could spring up even about minor matters, and that plucking ears of corn was perhaps merely an example of disputes of this kind.

[37] As far as I am aware, it was Roloff who first pointed out this connection (1970, 52–62, 71–73): '1 Cor 9:14 therefore gives good grounds for considering that this logion [i.e. Mark 2:25f] was also drawn upon in the post-Easter situation, as a way of justifying the claim to material support of those who proclaimed the gospel' (p. 72). I myself consider it most improbable that the *Sitz im Leben* was a eucharistic one (Grassi's view [1964–65]). According to Kuhn (1971, 72–81) vv. 25f were added only by Mark; but this can hardly be proved.

[38] See the historical survey of research on the subject in Künzi 1970.

111

end. But for the charismatic mendicant it was consoling. Until the end of the world, he would continually find places in which he could manage to exist by preaching and healings even if he was often driven away.

From all this it must surely be clear that the early Christian wandering charismatics were outsiders. They will have had some sympathizers in the various towns and villages. But it is not difficult to imagine what the majority thought about them – men without a home or a proper job, who upset other people by preaching the imminent end of the world, and who in their mind's eye already saw the places where they were rejected and found no support go up in flames. The general opinion will not have been very different from Karl Kautsky's view; he talked in plain unvarnished terms about 'scroungers and conspirators,' and ascribed to them arsonist fantasies – though it was the Messiah who was going to kindle the blaze for them.[39] In this judgment we do not merely hear the austere tones of the (early) socialist work ethic. It surely also reflects a very generally widespread rejection of outsiders of this kind. The wandering charismatics will have been held in similar contempt in their own time. A saying of Jesus consoles them: 'Blessed are you when men revile you and persecute you and utter all kinds of evil against you falsely on my account. Rejoice and be glad, for your reward is great in heaven, for so men persecuted the prophets who were before you' (Matt 5:11f).

We may perhaps ask whether all the abuse was groundless? Were the wandering charismatics not to all intents and purposes indistinguishable from other vagabonds of dubious reputation? The *Didache* indicates that this was in fact the case. It warns people against traveling *christemporoi* – people who hawk Christ round the doors. Lucian, probably unjustly, is able to jeer at one of these Christian prophets, meaning to unmask his would-be religious conduct as the behavior of a parasite. What subjectively seemed to be religiously justified freedom from the basic social ties could from outside look like work-shy vagrancy.

---

[39] Kautsky 1921, 404–405: 'and numerous scroungers without possessions or family or home wandered incessantly from place to place. . . . The final threat which the evangelist puts into Jesus' mouth is typical of the beggar's revengeful spirit, when his expectations of alms are disappointed. He would like in return to see the whole town go up in flames as a result – but the Messiah is to play arsonist for him.' As far as the revengeful spirit is concerned, this is correct enough. But on the other hand it is just this revengeful spirit that is resisted, as Luke 9:51–56 shows. Kautsky's summing up is as follows: 'It was itinerant "scroungers and conspirators" like this who, thinking themselves full of the Holy Spirit, brought . . . the fundamental principles of the new proletarian organization, the "joyful message", the gospel' (p. 405).

As outsiders, the early Christian wandering charismatics will have found their chief support among the people who were themselves living on the fringes of society: the weary and heavy-laden, the poor and the hungry, the men and women whom in their sayings they call blessed (see also Hoffmann 1972, 326). The Jesus tradition was characterized by commitment to the people who were socially and religiously the down-and-outs, the tax collectors and the prostitutes.[40] If this remained an essential element, it was no doubt because the people who passed on Jesus' sayings belonged to the lower levels of society themselves. It is not by chance that among these sayings we find aphorisms which are definitely and specifically suited to a particular social class: for example, 'To everyone who has will more be given; but from him who has not, even what he has will be taken away'[41] (Matt 25:29). Nobody who is one of the 'haves' talks like this.[42] The Synoptic tradition is undoubtedly one of the few traditions in the ancient world where even groups that were otherwise dumb find a voice. History is written by the rulers, largely speaking; but here we see the world from a different perspective – 'from below.' What form criticism has shown to be the singularity of the Synoptic tradition is no doubt connected with this fact.

In my view, the sayings tradition can be better understood if we take into account the expressly social and economic factors – that is, the necessity of finding material support and justifying the claim to it, the

[40] Bouwman (1969) puts forward a view that is worth consideration. He supposes that the Christian preachers were occasionally hospitably received by people whose previous life was criticized by Pharisaic Christians (one may perhaps ask here whether it was only their *previous* life). He sees the *Sitz im Leben* of Luke 7:36ff in this problematical situation. Laland (1959) also sees the *Sitz im Leben* of Luke 10:38ff in the problems of itinerant missionaries. 'The women of the house are immediately so much claimed by the need to minister to the guest's external wants that it is impossible for them to listen to the Lord's word' (p. 82). The houses visited by the itinerant missionaries were certainly not homes with a large staff of servants. And the saying 'Few things are needful' (Luke 10:42; RSV alternative reading) is perhaps intended to stress the modesty of the itinerant charismatics: they will not be a burden on their hosts materially.

[41] See Derrett 1965, esp. 194–95, where the saying is interpreted as describing the relationship between capital and profit 'If a merchant possessing capital shows a profit, people eagerly offer him further capital, the trader who reports no profit loses the capital entrusted to him. From him that has not (profit to show) is taken (withdrawn) even that (capital) which he still has.' Perhaps this is somewhat too narrow an interpretation. The fact that the rich always become richer and the poor poorer is a very general experience, however conducive to pessimism it may be.

[42] We may also remember the pessimistic picture of the law, for example, in the exhortation to reconciliation: the petty debtor is thrown into prison anyway, whatever the legal position may be (Matt 5:25–26).

outsider role of the people who passed the tradition on, and the 'class' character of the tradition itself. To these social and economic factors must be added the socioecological ones. The tradition suggests a rural context. We need only think of the images in the parables. The characters in these stories are small-holders, day laborers and tenant farmers, shepherds and vineyard owners. We hear about seedtime and harvest, farmland and weeds, herds and fish.

We have to take this rural background of the early Christian wandering charismatics into account if we want to understand their claim to the support of other people. Anyone who had once made a living as a farmer or fisherman gave up his chances of gainful employment when he renounced a settled place to live. Craftsmen were in a different position here, because tools could be carried, unlike fields and lakes.[43] Consequently the *Didache* sees few difficulties for itinerant artisans who want to settle down in a local community.[44] But in the case of the Christian incomer who does not happen to be an artisan, we find the revealing exhortation that the congregation should see to it 'that no idle Christian lives among you' (*Did.* 12.4). A craftsman could move freely from place to place and earn his keep by working. If he produced 'for the market,' his geographical mobility was actually a help. What he did not sell in one place he sold in the next. The bigger the market the better. The itinerant craftsman would therefore seek out the towns and cities. So is it just by chance that Paul, the craftsman, was able to renounce his right to material support when he and Barnabas began the mission to the great Hellenistic cities, whereas Peter, the fisherman, insisted on it (see 1 Cor 9:5f)?[45]

---

[43] On the preconditions for the local mobility of artisans, see Bienert 1954, 299–313. He points out that their job alone made it impossible for the Galilean fishermen to combine work with leadership of the Jerusalem congregation (p. 304).

[44] For a different view, see Knopf 1920, 34. In his view the artisan was especially in need of help, whereas the seller of merchandise could help himself.

[45] G. Dautzenberg rightly sees that the renunciation of material support 'must be seen in the context of the situation of the early Christian itinerant missionaries in Palestine-Syria, and was pre-Matthew' (1969, 216). He takes sociological factors into account in explaining the generalized version of the claim to this support in 1 Corinthians 9. The background is the 'transition of mission to the Hellenistic settlements of the Mediterranean world, which were no longer so firmly structured by family and kinship' (p. 217). In my view we should bear in mind the recurrent theme of philosophical tradition: the sage takes no payment for his wisdom – a theme presupposing the widespread education and semi-education of urban society. See Betz 1972, 100–17. Dautzenburg also makes the urban milieu accountable for the renunciation of the claim to support: Paul and Barnabas

The wandering radicals are associated with a rural milieu for a second reason too. Urban congregations, because of their size, had to develop separate ministries and forms of organization quite early on. But itinerant charismatics could preserve their authority only where the local congregations did not confront them with unduly strong ministries or leadership forms.[46] The sayings tradition assumes that congregations will be small: 'Where two or three are gathered in my name, there am I in the midst of them' (Matt 18:20). For where two or three are gathered together, no particular authority structures are needed, but, as a tiny minority, the group is all the more dependent on the encouragement of supraregional authorities – that is, the prophets and apostles who moved about from place to place.

Finally, we must remember that villages and small towns were closer together than the cities. If, as the *Didache* says (11.6), a person was only permitted to take provisions for a single day's journey, this was hardly enough if the great distances separating the cities had to be covered.[47] This practice presupposes a rural mileu. If Paul really wanted to extend his mission to the cities of the whole world, he was well advised to dispense with the missionary's right to material support. No charismatic mendicant could have carried through a project of this scope; it required a planner and an organizer.

It is interesting that the logia tradition should have been originally rooted in a rural environment, because the Christianity of the ancient world was in fact largely an urban phenomenon. The countryman was *paganus*, a heathen. There are only two pieces of direct evidence for early rural Christianity (see Knopf 1900, esp. 326). The Bithynian

---

'had deliberately left the interior of Syria-Palestine and had turned to the Hellenistic population of the great cities' (p. 218). It is true that Paul justifies his renunciation as something divinely imposed and tailored to him personally (see Käsemann 1959). But his interpretation must be somewhat relativized, for Barnabas also renounced his right to material support. It was more than merely a personal decision on Paul's part. [On this whole issue see Theissen 1982, 27–67 – Ed.]

[46] Käsemann (1968, 92) localizes the prophets whom he assumes passed on the logia in 'little congregations along the borders of Palestine-Syria, where the small number of members meant that leadership by a charismatic was the only possible form of organization. An itinerant prophet may even have looked after a whole group of congregations of this kind.' (Trans. direct from German original.)

[47] According to Knopf, the assumption is 'that the Christian congregations [i.e. those presupposed in the *Didache*] were not too widely scattered – at most a day's journey on foot from one another' (1920, 31). Conditions of this kind are more easily conceivable in the country than in the towns.

governor Pliny reports to the emperor Trajan that 'the plague of the new superstition' (he means Christianity) has spread 'not merely throughout the cities but also in the villages and the countryside' (*Ep.* 10.96) – which confirms the mainly urban character of Christianity in its early days. The second piece of evidence is to be found in *1 Clement* (42.4). According to this, the apostles had proclaimed the *basileia tou theou* ('the kingdom of God') in country districts and cities. Now, the *basileia* is one of the themes of the sayings tradition, and the apostles are wandering charismatics. The fact that the writer should mention the country areas first of all when he is considering their influence is a point at least worth bearing in mind.

If we ask why early Christianity was a largely urban phenomenon, we come across a sociocultural factor, among other things; and that is the language. I should like to look at this briefly now. In the cities the common, everyday language was *koine* Greek, whereas in the country areas the original vernaculars survived[48] – in Asia Minor until well into the sixth century (Holl 1908). But in the Syro-Palestinian area, from the very beginning, the language of Christianity was Aramaic, which was the dialect of the country people; and it is Aramaic that clearly underlies the sayings tradition. One of Jesus' sayings points to this area: 'Go nowhere among the Gentiles, and enter no town of the Samaritans, but go rather to the lost sheep of the house of Israel' (Matt 10:5).[49] If something is forbidden it is generally because it is being practiced; so we shall probably not go far wrong if we deduce that the wandering radicals had made their way from Palestine into other areas as well. But Palestine was no doubt the center.[50]

---

[48] For example, when Irenaeus was in Lyons he tried to learn Celtic, so that he could preach to the country people (*Against the Heresies*, 1.10.2; 3.4.1f). On the language problem, see Schneemelcher 1959; Andresen 1971, 20–21.

[49] Kasting (1969, 110–14) believes that the saying is an editorial addition of Matthew's. It certainly fits in with Matthew's redactional concept, though only in the form given to it in Matt 15:24, where it applies solely to Jesus. In 15:24 Matthew has probably altered the traditional logion of Matt 10:5 during his editing process.

[50] This localization of the movement also explains the Jewish-Christian character of the logia tradition. It presupposes Christian congregations belonging within the group of Jewish synagogues and subject to their jurisdiction (Matt 10:17). The rabbis are recognized as authority (Matt 23:2f), but at the same time the scribes and Pharisees are sharply criticized. This ambivalence could be explained as follows. The local congregations distributed throughout the countryside did in fact belong to Judaism. But the main sustainers of the traditions separating Christianity from Judaism were itinerant charismatics, who did not belong to any organization. Here criticism of Judaism, and of the scribes and Pharisees, could remain very much alive, whereas their settled local

The economic, ecological, and cultural factors I have described were the social conditions under which the sayings were passed on. Without these conditions, they would neither have come down to us, nor would they have been transmitted in the form in which we now have them. Of course this does not mean that the tradition is *derived* from these conditions in any way. There are no sufficient grounds for any such postulate. The sources merely allow us to establish a connection, an interdependence between a religious tradition and particular social conditions. Anyone who maintains any more than that must believe that it is possible to make assertions about reality regardless of the data at our disposal – assertions that would be more than the necessary theoretical constructions without which it is impossible to uncover, investigate, or understand data at all. To make assertions of that kind would be to depart from the realm of critical scholarship. But even within these limits there is still enough that has to be investigated, interpreted, and comprehended. Let me in closing therefore mention some hypotheses about the transmission of the sayings in early Christianity which may take us a little further.

1. We come across very few Jesus sayings in the early Christian letters. There will be a sociological reason for this, among other things. These letters come mainly from the urban, Hellenistic congregations (see Deissmann 1923, 210–11). These congregations included people from different social classes. In Corinth and Rome (where we know most about conditions) this led to conflict.[51] The congregations that had this kind of structure were characterized by a family-like 'love patriarchalism'[52] which preserved, mitigated, and softened the social

---

sympathizers were inevitably inclined to make more or less considerable compromises. If it had not been for itinerant outsiders, Christianity would soon have lost its independent character. See Kretschmar 1964, 47: 'In the historical situation of Palestinian Christianity before it dissolved its ties with the ethnic Jewish community, it is not surprising that we should hear nothing about any offices or ministries, apart from charismatics – that is, prophets, teacher, "saints". . . . Here these charismatics will have been the only representatives of the Christian message who made any distinct impression on the outside world.'

[51] On the congregation in Rome, see especially Gülzow 1969. I hope to be able to show elsewhere that social factors also played a part in the congregational conflicts in Corinth [see Theissen 1982 – Ed.].

[52] The concept of 'love patriarchalism' derives in substance from E. Troeltsch 1912, 67–83. Troeltsch characterizes Paul's fundamental ethical attitude as follows: 'It was the type of Christian patriarchalism which was based on both a religious recognition of earthly

differences. The early Christian 'duty codes' (*Haustafeln*) are characteristic examples of this ethic. Here the nonfamily ethic of the early Christian wandering radicals had no place – simply because it was impracticable. Even if Jesus' sayings were known, it was still impossible to live accordingly. But any part of an oral tradition which a society is unable to accept will be jettisoned by way of the 'preventive censorship' enforced by that society. A sociological transmission threshold hindered Jesus' sayings from gaining access to these congregations. Here the Son of man of the synoptics was replaced by the cosmic Christ.

2. The logia tradition was able to gain ground beyond its original social setting in places where it changed its character. Where people were unable to practice its ethical radicalism, they could transform it into gnostic radicalism. So radical action became a radicalism of perception, which does not necessarily have to have any practical consequences. We find a tradition that has been modified in this direction in the *Gospel of Thomas*,[53] a collection of Jesus sayings. Relatively homogeneous groups in the church probably provided the social setting for this gnostically modified radicalism. These groups were probably often made up of men and women who were fairly prosperous.[54] A radicalism of perception without any practical consequences was not unduly costly, even for these people.

3. The fact that the original spirit of these sayings has been more or less preserved for us is due to the written form they were given in the logia source and the Gospels. It is interesting in this connection that they should have come down to us only in the framework of the Gospel

---

inequalities and a religious transcending of them. This was already prepared for in late Judaism, but it acquired a special coloring through the warmth of the Christian idea of love – through the union of all in the body of Christ' (p. 67). Troeltsch talks about 'the fundamental idea that the given inequalities should be accepted and made fruitful for the ethical values of the relationship between one person and another' (p. 68).

[53] We must, of course, remember that in the *Gospel of Thomas* we find not only a modified logia tradition but also a tempered Gnosticism. But the concrete demands have lost their edge and have been translated into the realm of the speculative – and that is the important point here. This modification is not simply part of the tradition itself (*pace* Robinson 1964). The people who have passed the tradition on have changed themselves. They now came from a different social milieu, in which the words of Jesus in their plain and manifest sense were no longer practicable.

[54] See Andresen 1971, 103. The problem is discussed in detail by Kippenberg 1970. He writes 'Sociologically, I would localize Gnosticism in the intellectual Hellenistic class of the countries on the eastern fringe of the Roman empire, which had come under the heel of the Roman legions in the second to first centuries BC' (p. 225).

form – that is, embedded in accounts of Jesus' life. These look back without exception to a past era and already view the ethical radicalism of the transmitted sayings from a historical distance.

This distance is especially evident in Luke. He sensed so great a tension between the original social world of the Jesus tradition and the world of the people he was addressing that he appended to his Gospel a history of 'the acts of the apostles.' In Acts he shows how Christianity, starting in Galilee (or, to be more precise, in the renowned city of Jerusalem), made its way into the great cities of the Hellenistic world.[55] Luke, even more clearly than the other evangelists, stresses that the period when Jesus was alive was a special era, in which special, different ethical rules applied. Because of this, he is able, on the one hand, to preserve Jesus' words most faithfully of all. Yet, on the other, he unmistakably dissociates himself from the radicalism of the early Christian itinerants. In the farewell discourse according to Luke, Jesus expressly revokes his commandments for wandering charismatics. From now on, the charge to go out without purse, bag, and shoes is no longer to apply. Now the disciples are to take with them money, bag, and even a sword. For times have changed (Luke 22:35f). In his own era Luke was fighting the successors of the first wandering charismatics. For him they were false prophets. There were in any case only twelve legitimate apostles. These were the great itinerant missionaries of the early period. And even in this period it is not so much they who provide the pattern for Christianity in its model form; the model is rather the congregation in Jerusalem, of which Luke presents a highly idealized picture. Here, he tells us, everyone put his possessions at the disposal of the whole community. Significantly enough, however, the only evidence Luke can adduce for this is Barnabas – an apostle and an itinerant charismatic. And so he too involuntarily betrays what is in any case the historical probability: consistent discipleship was to be found only among the homeless, roving charismatic mendicants.

If we trace the transmission of Jesus' sayings in early Christianity, we discover in those days the Christian faith assumed three social forms: the radicalism of the itinerant charismatics, love patriarchalism, and gnostic radicalism. Here we find the lines laid down for the three types whose annals Troeltsch traced throughout Christian history: sects,

[55] The 'town' or 'city' already has considerable importance in the Gospel: Luke makes Jesus start his ministry in an urban milieu. See Hoffmann 1972, 278–80.

institutionalized church, and what he calls 'spiritualism' (see Troeltsch 1912). The ethic of the wandering radicals has continually sprung up afresh in sectarian movements – among the Montanists, the Syrian wandering ascetics, the medieval mendicant friars, and on the left wing of the Reformation. Gnostic radicalism has again and again found expression in individualistic and mystically disposed conventicles, inside and outside the church. But it is Christian love patriarchalism to which we owe the surviving institutions of the church. Quite successfully, and not without wisdom, this love patriarchalism tempered early Christian radicalism to a degree that made it possible for the Christian faith to become a practicable form of living for men and women in general. In the disputes of the second century this love patriarchalism prevailed over other social forms of early Christian faith such as Montanism and Gnosticism. It defined what was orthodox, what was canonical, and what was exegetically legitimate. But it did not completely suppress the other traditions, so that again and again it has provided nourishment for 'heterodox' trends. This love patriarchalism has continually found a way of assimilating or excluding radical movements. As we know, the exclusion was effected with more patriarchalism than love – to put it more bluntly, through the application of physical force. This would have compromised Christianity irrevocably had it not been that the call to repentance continually made itself heard out of the traditions of early Christian radicalism.

FURTHER READING

Theissen's ideas are also developed in a number of other essays (see Theissen 1979; 1982; 1993, esp. 60–93, 141–49). His sociological analysis of the Jesus movement is presented in concise and accessible form in his popular book (1978), which is dependent on the detailed research published in the more technical essays.

Theissen's approach to deriving sociologically relevant evidence from religious traditions and texts, which underpins the approach in Theissen 1978, is outlined in detail in Theissen 1982, 175–200. Other important methodological essays are to be found in Theissen 1979, 3–76 and 1993, 1–29, 231–87.

The classic work on form criticism, with which Theissen links his work here, is Bultmann 1972.

For critiques of Theissen's work on the Jesus movement see Stegemann 1984; Elliott 1986a; Horsley 1989. Note the recent discussion in Tuckett 1996, 355–91.

The social history of Jesus and the Palestinian Jesus movement is of course a vast topic on which a huge amount has been written. Particular mention may be made of the alternative reconstructions of Schottroff and Stegemann 1986; Horsley 1993; Ebertz 1987. See also, from a very different social-scientific perspective, the work of the Context Group (e.g. Malina and Rohrbaugh 1992; Malina 1996a; Malina and Neyrey 1988 – see ch. 1; *Introduction* §3). On Q and the history of early Christianity (again from a potentially lengthy bibliography) see Catchpole 1993; Tuckett 1996.

It is neither strictly relevant nor feasible here to give bibliography relating to the ongoing quest for the historical Jesus; for a recent textbook on this subject see Theissen and Merz 1998.

4

The Socio-Redaction Criticism of Luke–Acts

PHILIP F. ESLER

INTRODUCTION

In this essay, the opening chapter of his book *Community and Gospel in Luke–Acts: The Social and Political Motivations of Lucan Theology* (1987), Philip Esler sets out the reasons why he believes a social-scientific approach should be adopted, defends it against potential criticisms, and outlines the main model which he uses in his analysis of Luke–Acts. While not wishing to reject the traditional methods of biblical criticism, Esler argues that they have failed to develop adequate ways of analysing the social context within which the theology of the texts was formed and expressed. Biblical scholars therefore need the help of the social sciences. Here Esler proposes a fusing of redaction criticism – which is important to see how Luke has edited and shaped his sources – with social-scientific methods and models, and thus labels his approach 'socio-redaction criticism' (pp. 127–30).

Esler's conception of social-scientific method is notably 'scientific' (cf. Horrell 1996a, 9–26), though he is careful to emphasise 'that there are no social laws yet known which apply trans-historically to all societies' (p. 131) and insists that models and comparative studies, while vital, must never be allowed to 'fill-in' gaps in the evidence from the New Testament period. In response to Edwin Judge's criticism of the use of social-scientific models in New Testament research (Judge 1980), Esler maintains: (*a*) that purely empirical fieldwork of the sort Judge seems to call for is impossible, since we all bring presuppositions, implicit models, etc. to the task, and (*b*) that social-science models are meant to serve as research tools, not as a fixed grid to impose upon the evidence.

The main model Esler employs is derived from the influential work of Peter Berger and Thomas Luckmann (1967), and centres on the concept of 'legitimation'. In essence, Esler argues that the author of Luke–Acts is engaged in constructing a symbolic universe which legitimates the new social institution of the Christian sect to its members: 'Luke creates a symbolic universe which orders history in such a way as to provide a past, present and future for his Christian contemporaries' (p. 145). The context in which Luke undertakes this legitimating work is understood by Esler from the perspective of social-scientific studies of sectarian movements: the Lukan community, originally a Jewish reform-movement, has become a sect which needs to legitimate its own existence in distinction from, and in opposition to, its parent body, Judaism. These theoretical resources are presented fully in chapter 3 of *Community and Gospel*. As becomes clear from a reading of that chapter, the word 'church' (contrasted with 'sect'), used in the essay below, refers not to the Christian church specifically, but to whatever established, official institution the sect is related. In the case of the Lukan community, this is, of course, Judaism (see Esler 1987, 47–70).

Esler's book has generally been well-received, and has made a major contribution to the development of social-scientific approaches to New Testament interpretation (see Barton 1993, 152–56; Holmberg 1990, 101–105). The theoretical resources he employs – from the work of Berger and Luckmann and from studies of sectarian movements – have remained prominent in social-scientific approaches to the New Testament, although some questions have been raised about these resources and their potential pitfalls (see Barton 1993; Sanders 1993, 114–25; Horrell 1993). One may also question the reliability of 'mirror-reading' from Luke's account information about the community for which he writes, and a degree of circularity is evident in Esler's approach (see Rodd 1988, 129–30; Barton 1993, 154–55). E. P. Sanders (1990, 176–80) and James Dunn (1990, 179–81) have disputed Esler's reconstruction of the nature of the dispute at Antioch (see Esler's response in 1994, 52–69). Esler's own approach has also evolved considerably in the years since the publication of *Community and Gospel*. Without in any way abandoning the methods set out in this book, he has in more recent work (see Esler 1994, esp. 19–36; 1995b) focused more upon the models of Mediterranean culture developed by Bruce Malina (1981) and central to the work of

the Context Group, of which Esler is a member (see further
Introduction §3; ch. 1 above and ch. 5 below), and, in his latest
research, on the approach to social identity pioneered by Henri Tajfel
(Esler 1998b).

❦

1. Social and political influences on Lucan theology

At one point in *The Theology of St Luke*, during a discussion of the
relationship between the church and the world, Hans Conzelmann asserts
that Luke 'lays as the foundation of his defence of the Church a comprehensive consideration of its general position in the world; he fixes
its position in respect of redemptive history and deduces from this the
rules for its attitude to the world' (Conzelmann 1960, 137; German
original 1954, 117). To hold this opinion Conzelmann must assume
both that Luke's theological position (his attitude to redemptive history)
and his views on how the church must adapt to its social and political
context are quite distinct and that the first has generated the second.
Upon just a little reflection, both of these assumptions begin to appear
highly arbitrary and unlikely. Consider what model they imply for
the manner of Luke's composition of his Gospel and Acts. Is it not
that of a glorified armchair theorist, who ponders over purely religious
questions before issuing forth from his scriptorium to enlighten his
fellow-Christians as to the correct attitude which they and their
community should adopt to their social and political environment? Not
that Conzelmann is alone in subscribing to this model of theological
activity. It has an ancestry at least as old as the pre-exilic traditions of
Moses' Torah-laden descent from Mount Sinai, and flourishes still
in much European theology, as Latin American theologians tirelessly
observe.

But now set Conzelmann's two assumptions on their head. What if
Luke did not sharply differentiate the theological realm from the social
and political, but saw them, in fact, as closely inter-related? What if
social and political exigencies played a vital role in the formation of
Luke's theology, rather than merely constituting the areas in which it
was applied? With these assumptions we are forced to envisage quite a
different role for the theological activity of the evangelist. He appears
now as a figure embedded in the life of his community at all its levels,

religious, social, political and economic. He emerges as someone stirred to take up his pen not from an interest in theologizing for its own sake, but because he fervently believes that the Gospel, properly interpreted and presented, is a message of salvation for his fellow-Christians across the whole range of their troubled existence.[1]

The dominant theme in *Community and Gospel* is that these alternative assumptions and this alternative model are correct. Accordingly, the general thesis argued is that social and political factors have been highly significant in motivating Lucan theology; in other words, that Luke has shaped the gospel traditions at his disposal in response to social and political pressures experienced by his community. It is not claimed that such factors constitute a total explanation of why Luke–Acts was written. Proper account must always be taken of specifically religious aspects of the evangelist's motivation. Nevertheless, it has become increasingly clear to the present writer in the course of this work that it is entirely unrealistic to expect to be able to appreciate the purely religious dimension of Luke–Acts apart from an understanding of the social and political realities of the community for which it was composed. It is submitted that the results obtained from the argument are a rich confirmation of Peter Berger's view that the relation between religion and society is always dialectical (Berger 1969, 48).

To demonstrate that the social and political circumstances of Luke's community have shaped his theological understanding obviously has wide ramifications in other areas of theology. By restoring the connection between a particular New Testament theology and the historical experience of the community for which it was formulated, it is to be expected that a range of possibilities and paradigms will emerge which could assist in the creation of contemporary theology similarly attuned to the struggles of other groups at this moment in human history.[2]

---

[1] In spite of its frequent use in Mark, the nominal form *euaggelion* does not appear in the Third Gospel and only occurs twice in Acts (15:7; 20:24); Luke may have thought it had acquired the connotation of a literary genre and, if so, that it was less suitable than the word *diēgēsis*, which he uses at Luke 1:1. Nevertheless, Luke's intense interest in the concept of 'gospel', of good news, in connection with the ministry of Jesus and the work of the early church, is evident in his use of the verbal form *euaggelizomai*, which occurs ten times in his Gospel and fifteen times in Acts.

[2] An approach to the use of Scripture in Christian theology similar to this has recently been advocated by Ogletree 1983, 1–14.

2. *Towards a socio-redaction criticism of Luke–Acts*

Somewhat surprisingly, amidst the battery of critical approaches to the New Testament there is none which is really suited to explicating the relationships between Luke's theology and his community. The necessary methodology must be characterized both by its capacity for isolating the evangelist's unique theological intentions and by its having some apparatus for probing deeply into his social and political setting. The first requirement can only be satisfied by some form of redaction criticism; in reaction to form criticism, this focuses upon the role of the evangelists as authors in their own right, who have each expressed a particular theological viewpoint, rather than treating them as collectors of tradi-tional material. The continuing viability of redaction criticism has recently been confirmed by the work of scholars such as E. Güttgemanns (1979) and, more notably, W. H. Kelber (1983). They have demon-strated that the transition from oral traditions to written texts, from orality to textuality, involves not a steady progression (as Bultmann and others imagined) but a sharp break in the entire mode of perceiving and presenting the Gospel.

Yet redaction criticism, as it has developed over the last thirty years, has not acquired the conceptual equipment needed to satisfy the second requirement – the analysis of social context. Some explanation is necessary for this curious phenomenon. The form critics, after all, were interested in the social setting of the individual units of tradition which they investigated. Thus Bultmann wrote:

> The proper understanding of form-criticism rests upon the judgement that the literature in which the life of a given community, even the primitive Christian community, has taken shape, springs out of quite definite conditions and wants of life from which grows up a quite definite style and quite specific forms and categories. Thus every literary category has its 'life situation' (*Sitz im Leben*: Gunkel), whether it be worship in its different forms, or work, or hunting, or war. The *Sitz im Leben* is not, however, an individual historical event, but a typical situation or occupation in the life of a community.[3]

Unfortunately, the form critics never arrived at any firm understanding of the life situations so integral to their approach. Perhaps this was not so surprising in the case of Martin Dibelius (1934), who moved

[3] Bultmann 1972, 4. It should be stressed that *Sitz im Leben* refers to a particular situation *within* the life of a community; it is not an appropriate phrase to describe the entire social setting of a community, although it is often incorrectly used in that sense.

synthetically from assumed life situations (especially the sermon) to the New Testament data, but it is certainly so in the case of Rudolf Bultmann (1972), whose procedure was analytical, proceeding from a detailed analysis of the text to postulation of the situations in which the forms had arisen. Perhaps the result would have been different if anyone at the time had heeded Oscar Cullmann's acute observation that form criticism could only be set upon a firm foundation by the development of a special branch of sociology capable of studying the norms governing the growth of popular traditions (Cullmann 1925, 573).

When redaction criticism was initiated after the Second World War, the concern of its proponents with the significance of the unique and individual contribution of each evangelist did not entirely deflect their attention from the question of social context.[4] Consider what W. Marxsen, the author of the pioneering redactional study of Mark, had to say on this matter:

> Thus we inquire into the situation of the community in which the Gospels arose. The community ought not to be unqualifiedly viewed as located in a specific place, though we shall keep in mind the possibility of defining it exactly. Our concern is much more with what is typical in this community, its views, its time, perhaps even its composition. Hence a sociological element is present throughout. But over against form history this element is joined to an 'individualistic' trait oriented to the particular interest and point of view of the evangelist concerned. (Marxsen 1969, 24)

Like the form critics, however, the redaction critics also failed to utilize or generate a method for investigating social context. Marxsen's perceptive recognition of a 'sociological element' in his task must be set against the strange fact that nowhere in his work on Mark does he avail himself of a sociological method; his approach is entirely literary-historical. Historical method, as is becoming more widely appreciated, is directed to the particular, the unique and the unusual.[5] It is rather unsuitable for recovering the usual, typical and recurrent features of a past community, upon a comprehension of which, however, hangs the possibility of appreciating its social setting. If one asks what kind of approach does hold the promise of furthering research into these features, the answer

---

[4] For a detailed treatment of the genesis and characteristics of redaction criticism, see Rohde 1968.

[5] Burke 1980, 33: 'Sociology is concerned with the establishment of general laws, while history is concerned with the particular, the unrepeatable, the unique . . .'.

can only be one which draws upon ideas and techniques from the social sciences. It is an exercise in futility to attempt social analysis and yet ignore those very disciplines which take this matter as their subject and which have a long history of grappling with it. These disciplines, especially sociology, make it their business to examine just those typical and recurrent aspects of social behaviour and institutions which we must investigate in the context of Luke's community.

This advocacy of the use of the social sciences is not breaking fresh turf in New Testament exegesis. Since the early 1970s exegetes have been turning increasingly to the social sciences in the hope of finding new ways to understand and interpret the New Testament.[6] The most original and impressive work in the field has come from Gerd Theissen, now Professor of New Testament at Heidelberg University. His first contribution was an article published in 1973 on itinerant radicalism and the tradition of the sayings of Jesus, as seen from the perspective of the sociology of literature.[7] After this he produced a string of articles and books dealing with early Palestinian Christianity (notably, Theissen 1978), the social structure of the Hellenistic communities and the tensions to which they were subject (Theissen 1982), and the theory of the application of sociology to the New Testament (Theissen 1974c). Most of these studies have now been translated into English.[8] The other major works in this area are the superb article by W. A. Meeks on the relationship between Son of Man theology and sectarian pressures in the Johannine community (1972) and his recent book *The First Urban Christians* (1983), the article by R. Scroggs on the sectarian nature of earliest Christianity (1975 – see ch. 2 above – Ed.), the book by J. G. Gager which applies such sociological concepts as millenarianism, cognitive dissonance and conflict to the New Testament (1975),[9] the

[6] There is something of a pre-history to the movement to apply the social sciences to the New Testament. Karl Kautsky's Marxist analysis (1925), first published in German in 1908, is a direct ancestor of more recent efforts at sociological exegesis. For a recent Marxist interpretation, see Belo 1981. Troeltsch also employed sociological perspectives in his work *The Social Teaching of the Christian Churches* (1931), first published in German in 1911. During this period the Chicago school of biblical critics, especially Shirley Jackson Case, were preoccupied with the social aspects of the origins of Christianity, but without investing very seriously in sociological theory – see Keck 1974, and Funk 1976.
[7] Theissen 1973 [now in Theissen 1993, 33–59 and ch. 3 above – Ed.].
[8] There is a bibliography of the major works of Gerd Theissen in Theissen 1982, 25–26. [See also Theissen 1993 – Ed.].
[9] There are reviews of this book by D. L. Bartlett, J. Z. Smith and D. Tracy in *Zygon* 13 (1978), 109–35 [see also ch. 6 below – Ed.].

book by B. Holmberg (1978) on Paul and power and that of J. Elliott on 1 Peter (1981). B. Malina (1981) has made a particularly interesting contribution from the viewpoint of cultural anthropology.

Parallel with the growth of interest in this sociological approach to New Testament exegesis has come an ever-growing concern with the social background of early Christianity.[10] Many of the scholars engaged in the latter pursuit eschew the use of ideas and techniques from the social sciences and content themselves with the traditional methods of historical analysis. For reasons explained below, however, more useful results will be obtained if these researchers do engage in some degree of sociological analysis, at least to the extent of examining their own preconceptions.

The methodology adopted in *Community and Gospel* distinguishes it from the existing literature in the field to the extent that it takes up the broad approach of redaction criticism and fuses to it a conscious application of ideas and techniques drawn from the social sciences. This approach also differentiates our methodology from that utilized in the few other attempts which have been made to explain the theology of a New Testament work in terms of the social and political pressures upon the author's community – such as the article by W. A. Meeks on John's Gospel, the last chapter of his *First Urban Christians*, and the study of 1 Peter by J. Elliott. These works are devoted to exposing the relationships between theology and its social context and functions but are unable to adopt redaction criticism, as one can in the investigation of Luke's theology. Accordingly, throughout what follows the prevailing methodology is called 'socio-redaction criticism'. This is a more exact designation than 'sociological exegesis', which is used by J. Elliott of his style of analysis of 1 Peter, because of the importance of the redactional element in our investigations.

In the remainder of this essay, we shall outline the methodology of the social sciences in order to indicate how they may be applied to New Testament exegesis, respond to objections which have been made to such an enterprise and, finally, describe the sociological model which is employed in *Community and Gospel.*

---

[10] There have been a number of articles published which offer a general survey of the renewed interest in the social implications of early Christianity. Examples are Meeks 1975; Smith 1975; Harrington 1980; and Scroggs 1980.

3. *The methodology of the social sciences*

To see what the social sciences, especially sociology, can offer to New Testament study, it is essential to understand how they operate, to observe the methods used and the kinds of results obtained by scholars working in these disciplines. The question of the extent to which sociology and anthropology, for example, are sciences as much as the physical sciences such as physics and chemistry must be left unexplored. This raises very difficult issues, such as the role of human free will and human un-predictability in the social context.[11] There is a long history of attempts by sociologists to argue that their discipline is a science, but many sociologists strongly resist this classification.[12] Nevertheless, much sociological research does attempt to use scientific method, or a fairly close approximation to it, and without some appreciation of that method, therefore, it is no easy matter to penetrate the language employed by social scientists to describe their various forms of research, or to evaluate the status of the results they produce.

The ultimate aim of science is the formulation of laws which describe constant relations between phenomena (Duverger 1964, 226). But this is not its only aim, and, in practice, the discovery of laws is possible only in the most advanced sectors of scientific research. The difficulties which are involved in demonstrating that sociology and anthropology are as genuinely scientific as, for example, physics and chemistry, are nowhere more apparent than in the fact that there are no social laws yet known which apply trans-historically to all societies (Mills 1978, 166). Nevertheless, other more modest aspects of scientific method are within the reach of sociology and anthropology. The three levels of research evident in the physical sciences – description, classification and explanation (Duverger 1964, 226) – are all present in the social sciences, with the exception of the highest form of explanation, laws.

The vital role of description (the first level of research) results from the fact that only after the scrutiny and comparison of a wide range of material is it possible to develop appropriate explanations of it. Much

---

[11] On the question of free will and the formulation of social laws, see Kaufmann 1958, 169–81. MacIntyre believes that there are a number of sources of systematic unpredictability in human affairs which preclude the possibility of the existence of social laws like those discovered by the natural sciences – see 1981, 84–102.

[12] For an introduction to this debate, see Rex 1969, 1–26. There is something of a classic attack on the dominance of scientific method in much sociology in Mills 1978, 60–86. A more positive appreciation of the scientific side of sociology is found in Willer 1967.

sociological research still locates itself largely on the descriptive level (although scarcely to the total exclusion of classification and explanation), as sociologists attempt to come to terms with the astonishing variety of social phenomena. Classification, the second level of research, is an intermediate stage between description and explanation and involves the grouping together of similar phenomena. This reduces the almost infinite variety of particular facts to a number of categories. Until categories have been determined one cannot define relations between them.

An example of the often decisive impetus a convincing classification can give to scientific progress is the effect on biology of the classificatory system elaborated by Linnaeus in the eighteenth century. It is readily apparent, however, that the social sciences do not lend themselves to systems of classification as rigid and as clearly delineated as those, for example, current among biologists. The classifications in the biological sciences are often justly called 'natural' classifications; at present, no such claim can be made for any classificatory system used by sociologists. For the present and the immediate future we must proceed on the basis that any classificatory system generated by sociologists is not 'natural', that is, it does not correspond with the inherent ordering of reality but is an abstraction, an intellectual construct devised to assist researchers in grappling with the vast diversity of social phenomena. Max Weber referred to each category in such a system as an 'ideal type':

> An ideal type is formed by the one-sided *accentuation* of one or more points of view and by the synthesis of a great many diffuse, discrete, more or less present and occasionally absent *concrete individual* phenomena, which are arranged according to those one-sidedly emphasized viewpoints into a unified analytical construct (*Gedankenbild*). In its conceptual purity, this mental construct (*Gedankenbild*) cannot be found empirically anywhere in reality. It is a *utopia*. Historical research faces the task of determining in each individual case, the extent to which this ideal construct approximates to or diverges from reality . . . (Weber 1968b, 90. See further Martindale 1959)

Howard Becker and John McKinney, two American sociologists, have devoted considerable attention to the theory and application of such types. They prefer to call them 'constructed' rather than 'ideal' types to emphasize their artificial nature and to steer clear of any suggestion that they are ideal in the Platonic sense. McKinney defines the constructed type as 'a purposive, planned selection, abstraction, combination, and (sometimes) accentuation of a set of criteria with empirical referents that serves as a basis for comparison of empirical cases' (McKinney 1966, 3). In *Community and Gospel*, the word 'type' is used for the ideal type of Weber and the constructed type of Becker and McKinney, these being essentially identical. Put simply, a 'type' is a tool 'intended to institute precise comparisons' (Martindale 1959, 88). Furthermore, where 'type' is the term used to describe one unit in a classificatory system, typology, denotes the complete system, the assemblage of such types. One well known example is Max Weber's typology of authority, in which he differentiated three relevant types: rational, traditional and charismatic authority.

To construct a typology which will have relevance in a wide range of empirical situations – that is, one which is relatively free from time and space markings – it is necessary to base it upon as many empirical cases as possible (McKinney 1966, 61–66).

Finally, it must always be remembered that a typology is an instrument, a tool of research. McKinney observes that the most widespread misuse of the typological method involves the unjustifiable reification of types (1966, 17). Once a set of characteristics has been abstracted out and formulated into a type the temptation is to forget that it is merely a tool for ordering concrete phenomena and to begin treating it as a social law.

The third level of scientific research is that of explanation, which consists of demonstrating the dependence of two phenomena. Explanation is inextricably linked with prediction, since if A and B are dependent, then one can predict that A will be present if B is present (Duverger 1964, 227–28). This level of research is only possible when enough phenomena have been described and the basic classifications in the field have been sufficiently defined. The process of explanation normally begins with a theory, which is an integrated set of relationships that has already received some degree of empirical confirmation. David Willer correctly insists upon the desirability of restricting the term 'theory' to an at least partially validated set of relationships (1967, 9). Prior to such validation it is not a theory but a set of hypotheses. We may define hypotheses as relations deduced to exist among unobserved facts (Worsley 1970, 70). Once we have a theory and an hypothesis based upon it, the next stage is to test the hypothesis empirically. This is the verification stage of explanation (see Zetterberg 1954). The hypothesis will either be confirmed, which will strengthen the claim of the theory to be a law, or it will be only partially confirmed or simply disconfirmed, in which case it may be necessary to modify or even discard the theory.[13]

Before we outline the dominant forms of verification in the social sciences, some attention must be given to the meaning of models (especially *vis-à-vis* typologies, with which they are often erroneously identified) and their role in the process of explanation in the social sciences. A model is a conceptualization of a group of phenomena, a simplified and schematized picture of reality, which is capable of generating a set of hypotheses which, once verified, may either found or substantiate a theory. One example of a model is Herbert Spencer's presentation of society as an organism evolving steadily and irreversibly (Willer 1967, 31). Models are distinguished from systems of classification such as typologies by their having what may be regarded as an inner dynamic: since they are fashioned from a set of terms in a state of inter-relatedness, the variation of one of those terms will produce a predictable response in the entire set. This dynamic built into models enables them to be used to generate a wide range of hypotheses. David Willer uses the term 'mechanism' for this dynamic (1967, 17). Typologies, on the other hand, lack a 'mechanism', they merely classify phenomena into certain accentuated categories and do not specify what may be expected of mixed cases falling in between the types (1967, 44ff). Models are explanatory and predictive, typologies, *pace* McKinney,[14] are not. The use of types can lead to the development of hypotheses about particular situations, but only *after* the typology has been applied to the situation, careful comparisons have been made and the search has commenced for an explanation of the divergences noted between fact and typology. Models, on the other hand, arm researchers in advance with hypotheses to test upon the relevant empirical data.[15] The account of the legitima-tion of a new social order presented by Peter Berger and Thomas Luckmann in their work *The Social Construction of Reality* (1967), which

---

[13] There is a revealing schematic representation of the whole process of explanation in Worsley 1970, 70.

[14] McKinney 1966, 41 and *passim*. Martindale also rejects McKinney's view that types are explanatory and provides cogent arguments for this not being the case – see Martindale 1959, 58 and *passim*.

[15] Confirmation for this view can be found in the remark by Weber 1968b, 90: 'The ideal typical concept will help to develop our skill in imputation in *research*: it is no "hypothesis" but it offers guidance to the construction of hypotheses.'

is the central sociological concept used below, is best understood as a model. The implications of this for the conduct of this study are dealt with later.

The comparative method

We now conclude this treatment of the methodology of the social sciences with a brief discussion of the uses of the comparative method: first, to assist in the verification of hypotheses (the third level of scientific method) and, secondly, as a means of generating insights and fostering the sociological imagination.[16] As to the first issue – how can social scientists verify their hypotheses? In the natural sciences experiment is the main method of verifying hypotheses; but only occasionally is experiment possible in the social sciences, for it is very difficult to isolate phenomena in order to establish reciprocal relations between them as demanded by the experimental method. In any event, experiment is only possible with contemporary social structures and institutions and can be of no help in the use of sociological approaches to historical materials. In the absence of experimental verification social scientists fall back on the comparative method (see further Vallier 1971). The process of comparison assumes similarities and differences; one does not compare things which are totally like or totally unlike. But to verify hypotheses it is necessary to make what Duverger calls 'close comparisons' (see Duverger 1964, 261–67). The aim here is to compare two items which have as many features as possible in common and then to explain the differences. This method is analogous to an experiment where all conditions are kept constant, except for the variable whose behaviour is to be observed. For such a comparison of social data to be effective it is obviously necessary that the comparison be between two or more structures or institutions from contexts which are both similar culturally and not too distant chronologically. Otherwise the comparison will be too artificial to contribute to the verification of hypotheses.

The second use of the comparative method is quite different. It involves what Duverger calls 'distant comparisons', by which social structures or institutions from widely different cultures are compared. These commonly consist of comparisons across distinct historical periods. Here one is looking for resemblances rather than the differences

---

[16] Cf. Mills 1978, 221: 'Imagination is often successfully invited by putting together hitherto isolated items, by finding unsuspected connexions.'

investigated by the use of close comparisons. Since the things compared are so far removed from one another, it is natural that they are different. The main focus of interest is the extent to which they are similar and the significance of those resemblances. With this form of comparison the researcher is not seeking to verify hypotheses but to generate them, because the insights which are produced by the comparisons will prompt a whole range of questions to put to the historical data under consideration. In other words, this is a way of fostering the sociological imagination. Duverger appropriately describes distant comparisons as one means of 'provoking the shock which produces discovery'; they are more 'an attitude of mind consisting of keeping eyes open for relationships, analogies and resemblances' when faced with phenomena than a rigorous method (Duverger 1964, 267).

One approach available under either method of comparison is the application of an existing typology to a case under consideration. It is not necessary that the comparison be made between different sets of data, as was the case, for example, with de Tocqueville's early comparisons of the social and political institutions and structures of France, Britain and the United States (Smelser 1971). As we have seen, a good typology is based upon as wide as possible a range of empirical data, and its resulting high level of generality will improve its usefulness when used in a comparative exercise upon a particular set of data. With close comparisons, of course, it will be necessary that the types have been developed from data culturally similar to the case under study or at least be stripped of temporal and spatial markings. This is not necessary with distant comparisons, since as long as there is some point of analogy to enable the comparison to be made in the first place, it does not matter if there are wide divergences between typology and data.

One other form which distant comparisons may take, apart from those involving two sets of data or a typology and one set of data, must be mentioned here. This is the comparison of the conceptualized phenomena in a model with actual cases. One must tread carefully here. As already explained, the function of a model is to generate hypotheses which, if verified, may be used to substantiate a social theory. And there is nothing in principle to prevent a particular historical case being used to test the hypotheses deriving from a model, as long as all necessary precautions have been taken to ensure that there is no cultural inconsistency between model and data which would have the effect of precluding the meaningful testing of hypotheses from the model in that particular case. In spite of this, however, the propositions of a model can plainly be utilized in a quite different way – not to generate hypotheses, but to supply material for a distant comparison with a particular historical situation. This process is very similar to the distant comparisons between fact and typology, only here the material brought to the actual case is a set of dynamically related propositions, not a mere classification. The use of Berger and Luckmann's *The Social Construction of Reality* in what follows will illustrate this process.

One fundamentally important caveat, implied throughout the preceding methodological discussion, must now be emphasized and applied to the entire task of using sociological ideas in New Testament exegesis. No social laws have been found which apply across different historical periods. When we bring to a New Testament text comparative material in the form of contemporary data, typology or model we have no justification whatever for assuming that what was the case outside New Testament society was the same within it. That is to say, comparative materials of whatever character can never be relied upon to plug holes in our knowledge of the social world of the New Testament. For it may be in just those places where we do lack information that the greatest divergences occur from our own experience. Comparison can suggest an entirely fresh way to approach this or that feature of the New Testament, may suggest an entirely new range of questions to put to it, but the comparative method cannot prove the viability of that approach or answer those questions. Such results can only flow from a painstaking examination of the text itself, and in that task the traditional types of criticism retain a great deal of their relevance.

4. Objections to the application of the social sciences to the New Testament

Resistance to the use of the social sciences in New Testament exegesis takes two broad forms. The first is an objection to the very idea of the enterprise: namely, that the social sciences are reductionist, that they purport to provide a total explanation of the biblical data and leave no scope for purely religious factors or the activity of individuals to figure in the explanatory task. The second is an objection at the practical level; its proponents do not rule out the use of the social sciences as a matter of principle, but they maintain that they are no use in exegesis because, for example, they are too dependent upon contemporary cultural patterns to assist in understanding first-century texts. These two objections must now be considered in turn.

There is little to be said for the reductionist criticism. Certainly some of the founders of sociology, such as Émile Durkheim (1964), believed that social factors could totally explain religion. And K. Kautsky (1925) did write a reductionist account of Christianity from a Marxist viewpoint. Today, however, sociologists are far more humble about the possibilities of their discipline. They realize that, although the investigation of a given phenomenon using sociological concepts and techniques will result in an explanation of that phenomenon, such an explanation will be inevitably partial, in that the phenomenon will almost certainly be susceptible to other forms of explanation, such as economic or political or even purely religious ones. Bruce Malina has described this process as follows:

> . . . to explain sets of data – and not models – from the perspectives of biology, sociology, political science, economics, and the like is not reductionistic. Rather, such varied explanations pushed to their limit simply reveal how much can be known and explained by using a given model. The data set, the range of information, remains intact. (Malina 1982, 237)

Moreover, by pointing out the recurrent and typical features of a social phenomenon, sociology establishes the necessary context within which, and only within which, its unique features can be appreciated (Malina 1982, 238). Throughout the course of *Community and Gospel*, for example, the sociological approach adopted continually serves to throw the creative activity of the Third Evangelist into sharp relief.

Perhaps the most noteworthy example of the second line of objection to the use of the social sciences in the study of early Christianity – that it is impractical – is to be found in an article by E. A. Judge,[17] an ancient historian who appears to have pioneered the prosopographical approach to the New Testament which has been fruitfully employed by W. A. Meeks in *The First Urban Christians* (see Judge 1960a). In one section of his article, Judge begins by referring to B. Holmberg's claim in *Paul and Power* that much New Testament scholarship is affected by the 'idealistic fallacy', which consists of interpreting historical phenomena

---

[17] Judge 1980. Another article containing a negative attitude to sociological interpretation is that of Rodd 1981.

as being directly formed by underlying theological structures and of ignoring the continuous dialectic between ideas and social structures. He then goes on to question whether Holmberg has balanced his dialectic between ideas and facts, theology and social structure:

> His methodological stance does not bestride ideas and facts in an equally secure manner. In particular he does not have his foot on firm ground on the factual side. The extensive reading list conceals a dangerous gap. It couples with New Testament studies a strong admixture of modern sociology, as though social theories can be safely transposed across the centuries without verification. The basic question remains unasked: What are the social facts of life characteristic of the world to which the New Testament belongs? Until the painstaking field work is better done, the importation of social models that have been defined in terms of other cultures is methodologically no improvement on the 'idealistic fallacy'. We may fairly call it the 'sociological fallacy'. (Judge 1980, 210)

A little later in this section, in commenting on the approach of Gerd Theissen, Judge writes:

> I should have thought there was no hope of securing historically valid conclusions from sociological exercises except by first thoroughly testing the models themselves for historical validity. (Judge 1980, 212)

From these statements it is possible to summarize the chief features of Judge's understanding of sociological models and their role in historical research:

1. Sociological models must be historically tested or 'verified' before they can be applied. Presumably, this means that they must closely fit the historical data to which they are to be applied, otherwise they will be discarded.

2. Sociological models are 'defined' with respect to particular cultures. This hinders their being applied to first-century society.

3. It is possible to carry out historical 'field work' prior to the use of models. In other words, Judge is espousing an empirical hunt for 'the social facts of life characteristic' of the New Testament world, free from theoretical presuppositions.

None of these propositions, however, is consistent with the methodology of the social sciences, as just described. The first of them, the notion that typologies and models must first be subjected to historical verification or validation before they can be applied involves the error of viewing them not as mental constructs, as research tools, but as something akin to social laws. As long as the comparative material has some analogy to the situation it is quite unnecessary that it correspond exactly. Reading between the lines of Judge's article, one senses that his real worry with sociological exegesis is that its exponents will attempt to plug holes in first-century data by drawing upon relevant features of the comparative materials they apply to the New Testament text. As we have seen, this would be a serious misuse of the comparative method, one which must be avoided. The answer to the second feature of Judge's attitude is that sociologists are well aware of the desirability of producing models and typologies which, as far as possible, have been stripped of temporal and spatial markings. In developing his well-known typology of sects, Bryan Wilson has consciously aimed at achieving this result (Wilson 1973, 9–30). But, in any event, distant comparisons can be made even where the model does show signs of its cultural context.

The case for using the social sciences in biblical exegesis is most thoroughly established by demonstrating not merely that this is a useful additional approach to the text, but also that the traditional historical mode of analysis is defective precisely in as much as it fails to utilize concepts and perspectives from sociology and anthropology. Consider the third aspect of Judge's attitude, his espousal of historical 'field work', of a hunt for 'characteristic' social facts *prior* to the use of models. Here Judge is advocating what amounts to a fairly pure form of empiricism, and this exposes his position to the same objection which can be made to such empiricism in any field: namely, that it is quite impossible for a researcher to collect facts without his or her already subscribing to a whole range of theoretical presuppositions. To define a field of enquiry and to make decisions as to which are the significant facts within that field, an historian must have already made a number of decisions at the theoretical level. In such a case, those decisions usually take the form of intuitive hunches. By not consciously and deliberately acknowledging and reflecting upon his or her preconceptions, the historian runs the risk of imposing modern notions of categorization and significance upon data from a period where they may be quite inappropriate. When Judge speaks of 'characteristic' social facts, for example, he is employing a term of comparison – to say a fact is characteristic, distinctive, of one society only makes sense in the context of other societies where it is not. Yet until Judge acknowledges, conceptualizes and justifies the implicit comparison he is making with other societies we can have no confidence in any claim that a particular fact is characteristic of the society in question. This is where a theoretical input from the social sciences, especially in the use of models and types, is needed. As T. F. Carney has accurately put it: 'Models bring values – in the subject matter and in its analyst – out into the open' (Carney 1975, xiv).

This failure to sort out the conceptual basis of their craft is quite common among historians and New Testament exegetes applying historical-critical methods. It is reflected not just in pretensions to purely empiricist methodologies but also in the non-reflective use of models and typologies. Historians and theologians who express antipathy to these heuristic devices unwittingly employ them whenever they speak, for example, of city-states, patronage, class and status, feudalism and capitalism, sect and denomination. A greater awareness of the logical status of such terms would improve the clarity of their application and would also serve to remind historians and historical theologians of the inevitability of a sociological perspective in their work. There is an elegant expression of a view similar to this in the first chapter of Peter Brown's *Religion and Society in the Age of Saint Augustine* (1972, 18–20). Here Brown suggests that historians have much to learn from psychoanalysis, from 'the disciplined and erudite study of living societies by the social anthropologist' and from 'the sense of perspective and of unexpected combinations in much sociological literature'. For Brown, what the social sciences have to offer is assistance in understanding the present and then the past; they remove 'the patina of the obvious that encrusts human actions', they allow us to pierce the stereotypes and conventional formulae of human action in the present, so that we can obtain a far more clear-sighted view of the past.

5. Legitimation and Luke–Acts

The primary contention of *Community and Gospel* is that much of what is unique in the theology of Luke–Acts should be attribututed to Luke's desire to explain and justify, to 'legitimate', Christianity to his Christian contemporaries; in other words, that his main objective is one of 'legitimation' (a concept considered immediately below). I argue that Luke wrote in a context where the members of his community, who were mainly Jews and Gentiles (including some Romans) who had been associated with synagogues before becoming Christians, some of whom were rich and some poor, needed strong assurance that their decision to convert and to adopt a different lifestyle had been the correct one. To substantiate this approach extensive use will be made of sociological perspectives, and it is now necessary to introduce the most significant of these – 'legitimation'.

My approach to legitimation is derived, with some modifications, from *The Social Construction of Reality*, by P. L. Berger and T. Luckmann, which was first published in 1966. Subtitled *A Treatise in the Sociology Of Knowledge*, this work has acquired something of a classic status among sociologists and other scholars working in the social sciences, although it has not escaped criticism.[18] Its authors describe the book as an 'enquiry' (1967, 30) into the manner in which social reality is constructed, but it may perhaps most usefully be regarded as a model of the genesis and maintenance of society and social institutions.

According to Berger and Luckmann, legitimation is a process which is carried out after a social institution has originated in the first place. In essence, legitimation is the collection of ways in which an institution is explained and justified to its members. Berger and Luckmann focus almost exclusively upon the form of legitimation which is necessary in the second and subsequent generations of the existence of such an institution.

But legitimation should not be thought of as applicable solely to those who are raised in the second generation. Even in the first generation adult members of the new order will need to have it explained and justified to them, especially where they have some residual allegiance to the old order, or where their new position exposes them to pressures which might make their loyalty waver. The creators and subsequent leaders of new movements might be unshakeable in their convictions, but many of the rank and file will profit by, or even require, careful legitimation of their new beliefs and practices. Berger himself recognizes the importance of legitimating a new social order to its adult members in a later work, *The Social Reality of Religion* (1969, 48). Although Berger and Luckmann do not burden *The Social Construction of Reality* with examples of specific historical data from which they have developed their model, it is a simple task to cite numerous cases where the leaders

18 Thomason 1982 and Gill 1977, 18–20. Neither the criticism of Thomason nor that of Gill, which essentially relates to epistemological aspects of *The Social Construction of Reality*, affects the use of ideas in that work for instituting comparisons with the data in Luke–Acts.

of new movements have thought it necessary or desirable to legitimate those movements to their members. Assistance in where to look for such legitimatory processes is available in an article by A. F. C. Wallace (1956), in which the author attempts a broad taxonomy of what he calls 'revitalization movements'. He uses the term 'revitalization' to describe the whole range of attempted, and sometimes successful, innovation of entire cultural systems, or at least substantial portions of those systems. The main phenomena he includes within this classification are revolutions, religious revivals, charismatic movements, sects and cargo cults, and reform, mass and social movements generally. It is clear that legitimation plays a vital role in nearly all of these movements, and in many cases there exists documentation, produced by their instigators and leaders, which fulfils a plainly legitimatory function. With respect to revolutions, for example, J. Baechler has accurately written that 'there is no revolutionary phenomenon without at least the germ of an ideology, to give it meaning and to serve as its justification' (1975, 106). Very often such ideologies have been distilled in the form of revolutionary manifestos, which tend to become legitimatory documents for the new order if the revolution succeeds. In recent times this flourishing genre was inaugurated by the American Declaration of Independence (4 July 1776) and the French *Declaration of the Rights of Man and the Citizen* (26 August 1789). A document close to the time of Luke–Acts, yet performing much the same task, is the *Res Gestae Divi Augusti*, in which Octavian left a permanent record of his achievements in such a way as to legitimate the new political order he had bestowed on Rome. Religious sects (see *Community and Gospel*, ch. 2) have also been a source of legitimating documents. Some of the writings emanating from the medieval millennarian sects discussed by Norman Cohn in *The Pursuit of the Millennium* (1970), for example, have a legitimatory function.

Having shown that the function of legitimation is, as Berger and Luckmann put it, to make 'objectively available and subjectively plausible' (1967, 110) the meaning of a social institution, we may now examine some of the particular aspects of the process. One purpose which frequently motivates a legitimating process is that of integration. The institution will only make sense as a totality to the participants in diverse institutional processes if it is integrated, if it is characterized by its parts intermeshing into a whole. This may be referred to as the 'horizontal' level of integration and plausibility. But there is also a vertical dimension to the need for integration and plausibility: namely, that each individual in the institutional order must feel that his life, in its various stages, is meaningful, that his biography makes sense in this institution. Through this aspect of legitimation, therefore, the history of the institution and the biography of its individual members are united (1967, 110–11).

The integrative purpose and function of legitimation is most clearly seen in what Berger and Luckmann called the 'symbolic universe' fashioned for a new social order by its legitimators. A symbolic universe is a body of theoretical tradition which integrates different provinces of meaning and encompasses the institutional order in a symbolic totality (1967, 114). By 'symbolic' is denoted reference to realities other than those of everyday experience (1967, 113). Within such a universe, the members of the institution have an experience of everything being in its right place and also of the various phases of their biography as ordered; as they look back into their past or forward into the future, they conceive of their life unfolding within a universe whose ultimate coordinates are known. Over the institutional level as well, symbolic universes operate as sheltering canopies. The symbolic universe also orders history; it locates all collective acts in a cohesive unity that includes past, present and future. Thus individuals are linked with their predecessors and successors in a meaningful totality, so that they can conceive of themselves as belonging to a universe which was there before they were born and will be there after they die.

A little reflection quickly discloses the *prima facie* applicability of this model to Luke–Acts. For the elaborate historical framework of Luke–Acts provides many resemblances to the model and offers a rich selection of data for detailed comparison. First of all, more than any other New Testament writer, Luke takes great pains to present Christianity as a faith with a past. His Gospel begins with a number of incidents involving pious Jewish men and women who are firmly located in the ancestral beliefs and practices of Judaism while all the time looking forward in hope to the redemption of Israel. Throughout Luke–Acts the author continually emphasizes the loyalty of Jesus and his followers, especially Paul, to Jewish tradition and the way in which the Christian event is the fulfilment of that tradition. Secondly, there are many places in the work where one senses the present for Luke's audience, but perhaps the most prominent of these is Acts 20:28–32, where Paul addresses the elders of Ephesus and warns them to be on their guard against 'fierce wolves' who will invade the flock of God. It is impossible not to feel that Luke is writing for his Christian contemporaries, for whom this prophecy has become a harsh reality. Finally, Luke establishes a future for the Christian faith, both by providing in Acts a sequel to his Gospel – a fact which, as C. K. Barrett (1961, 57) has observed, itself has definite implications for an understanding of Lucan eschatology – and by presenting the parousia as delayed and not imminent, as demonstrated by H. Conzelmann (1960, 95–136). Thus, along the lines of the model of legitimation outlined immediately above, Luke creates a symbolic universe which orders history in such a way as to provide a past, present and future for his Christian contemporaries. He links them with their predecessors and successors in a meaningful totality.

At this point we must introduce a particularly common characteristic of the symbolic universe erected to legitimate a new social order – the claim that it is not novel, but is actually old and traditional. Berger has nicely explained this process in *The Social Reality of Religion*. Imagine yourself, he says, a fully aware creator of a society, 'a kind of combination of Moses and Machiavelli', faced with the problem of best ensuring the continuation of your institutional order which has just been established *ex nihilo*. Even when the means of power have been employed, for example, in checking one's opponents and ensuring the succession of power to one's designated successors, there still remains the problem of legitimation – which is all the more urgent because of 'the novelty and thus highly conscious precariousness of the new order'. The problem, Berger suggests, is best solved by applying the following recipe:

> Let the institutional order be so interpreted as to hide, as much as possible, its *constructed* character. Let that which has been stamped out of the ground *ex nihilo* appear as the manifestation of something that has been existent from the beginning of time, or at least from the beginning of this group . . . (Berger 1969, 33)

Movements which include in their legitimatory apparatus the claim to be old and traditional are extremely common, especially in societies at a pre-industrial stage of development. Rebellions and revolutions often espouse 'the revival or reintroduction of an idealized society that allegedly existed in the society's own past' (Johnson 1968, 138). Examples include the counter-revolution in the Vendée in 1793, the ideology of the Confederate rebels in the American Civil War and the ideology of the Franco forces in the Spanish Civil War (Johnson 1968, 137). A fine example from the first century CE is the *Res Gestae Divi Augusti*.

Many new religious movements also legitimate themselves as reassertions of pristine beliefs and practices long dormant. The writings of Luther and many of the other Reformers are obvious cases in point. With respect to the New Testament itself, W. A. Meeks has recently argued that in his letter to the Galatians Paul defines and defends the radically new Christian order in terms drawn from the old, Jewish order which gave it birth (1983, 172–76). Much of the theology of Luke–Acts is also informed by this particular legitimatory strategy.

So far our analysis of legitimation has not taken into account the effect of any forces which may impede the creation of a symbolic universe. But a social world is rarely constructed *in vacuo*; the experience of a Prospero or a Robinson Crusoe is not common. Often a new world can only be created in the teeth of opposition from the upholders and defenders of one already in existence. In *The Social Construction of Reality* Berger and Luckmann note that the maintainers of a society often fail in their attempts to socialize and keep socialized all the inhabitants of that society. The problem becomes particularly acute when one group comes to share a version of the symbolic universe different from that adhered to by society at large. In such a case, 'the deviant version congeals into a reality in its own right, which, by its existence within the society, challenges the reality status of the symbolic universe as originally constituted' (1967, 124). This poses a threat to the dominant institution, which then commences repressive measures against the new group. The new group must counter these and confrontation results. Each group will develop a theory to justify itself *vis-à-vis* the other, or, as Berger and Luckmann put it: 'Two societies confronting each other with conflicting universes will both develop conceptual machineries designed to maintain their respective universes' (1967, 126).

Once again, Berger and Luckmann do not supply examples of this phenomenon. On the political level, however, it can be illustrated from the propaganda battles which occur in revolutions, with the revolutionaries and the threatened establishment each attempting to have its view of reality prevail with the populace. When the model is applied to religion, on the other hand, it is obvious that the archetypal example of the process is the confrontation between an existing church and a sect which has broken, or is attempting to break, away from it. In such a case the conceptual machinery which the sect develops to maintain and justify itself as against the church from which it split will be reflected in the theology of the sect.[19] It is very important to remember that the opposition which a sect encounters from the church from which it arose is not based solely upon doctrinal differences, for a sect threatens the position and status of the persons responsible for maintaining and servicing the church. Inasmuch as the sect raises the possibility of drawing further members out of the church and even, eventually, threatening its continued separate existence altogether, it poses a risk to the privileged position which the leaders of the church enjoy. This aspect of the antagonism a church will feel towards a breakaway group is far too often forgotten. Peter Richardson, for example, when he is discussing the persecution of Christians by Jews in the first few decades of the existence of Christianity, remarks that in 'this situation it would beg the question to apportion "blame": Christian teaching (rightly) gave offence to orthodox Jews, and the inevitable result was opposition aimed at stamping out Christianity' (Richardson 1969, 46). Once a sociological imagination is exercised on the New Testament texts, it becomes impossible to impute such a simple motive to Jewish opposition. The clash between the old faith and the new was to a large degree a struggle for power, although this is not to deny that strong feelings over doctrinal matters also played a part. We must, accordingly, be continually open to the political implications of the New Testament texts.

But in addition to its leaders feeling their positions threatened by a sect, there is another essentially non-doctrinal issue which may provoke in a church massive hostility towards the sectarians: namely, an identity of membership and even of interest as between a church and a particular ethnic group, so that the sectarian threat to the church is also perceived as endangering the ethnic group. Such a threat might arise, for example, where the sect begins recruiting outside its own ethnic group and even establishes liturgical practices, involving outsiders, which imperil the boundaries erected to maintain the integrity of that ethnic group against foreign invasion. This fact was highly significant in the development of that form of Christianity subscribed to by Luke's community.[20]

One final matter remains in a consideration of the confrontation of church and sect. The differences between the two are rarely settled by a

[19] For a detailed explanation of the differences between 'church' and 'sect' from a sociological point of view see *Community and Gospel*, ch. 3.
[20] See *Community and Gospel*, ch. 4.

process of rational discussion leading to a peaceful resolution. Even at the level of doctrine – and we have seen that they are likely to be at loggerheads on political and sometimes also ethnic issues – the nature of the disputes between church and sect is not likely to allow their easy resolution. As Berger and Luckmann put it: 'From the point of view of intrinsic plausibility the two forms of conceptualization may seem to the outside observer to offer little choice' (1967, 126). In such a situation, rather than relying merely upon the theoretical ingenuity of their respective legitimators, church or sect or both may attempt to apply force directly to reach a solution. The one with the bigger stick, normally the church, has the better chance of imposing its view of reality. Naked power will supplant discussion. Often the power which the church uses in its attempt to restrain or even eliminate a sect will be provided by the police or judicial powers of the state. The state will tend to be amenable to such a course of action because of a coincidence of interest between itself and the church in suppressing the sect. This coincidence will occur where the church enjoys something of a religious monopoly in that society; this has been explained by Berger and Luckmann as follows:

> Traditional definitions of reality inhibit social change. Conversely, breakdown in the taken-for-granted acceptance of the monopoly accelerates social change. It should not surprise us, then, that a profound affinity exists between those with an interest in maintaining established power positions and the personnel administering monopolistic traditions of universe-maintenance. In other words, conservative political forces tend to support the monopolistic claims of the universal experts, whose monopolistic organizations in turn tend to be politically conservative. Historically, of course, most of these monopolies have been religious. It is thus possible to say that Churches, understood as monopolistic combinations of fulltime experts in a religious definition of reality, are inherently conservative once they have succeeded in establishing their monopoly in a given society. Conversely, ruling groups with a stake in the maintenance of the political status quo are inherently churchly in their religious orientation and, by the same token, suspicious of all innovations in the religious tradition. (Berger and Luckmann 1967, 140)

One could cite many examples of this process, but two will suffice for the present. First, Luther's *Letter to the Princes of Saxony*, written in July 1524, and pointing out to them the dangers inherent in Thomas Müntzer's millennial agitation, and his subsequent pamphlet *Against the Thievish, Murderous Gangs of the Peasants* (1525), which did much to rouse the princes of central Germany against the rising Müntzer had so helped to foment (Cohn 1970, 241, 248), exemplify the tendency for a church leader to enlist the state against what is perceived to be a common threat. Secondly, a very large number of the African religious leaders who broke away from European mission churches in Africa in the last three centuries to found independent sects were imprisoned, banished or even executed by colonial administrations, often at the behest of the missionaries (Barrett 1968, 220).

The suitability of this aspect of the model to Luke–Acts is quite apparent. Although there were many religions competing for attention in the eastern parts of the Roman empire in the first century CE, Judaism did enjoy something very close to a monopoly within the separate Jewish enclaves, some of which were recognized and sanctioned by the Romans as *politeumata*,[21] in the Greek cities of the East. Throughout Luke–Acts there are many occasions in which the Jews attempt to enlist the support of the Roman authorities against Jesus and his followers in a fashion richly consonant with the model. Luke's response to this forms a vital part of the symbolic universe he constructs in the work.

We have now completed our outline of the model of legitimation – specifically, the legitimation of a sect with a history of staunch opposition from the church from which it arose; in *Community and Gospel* this is applied in a comparative way to particular aspects of Lucan theology.

FURTHER READING

Among the theoretical resources which Esler adopts, prominent and influential works are those by Berger and Luckmann 1967; Berger 1969; Wilson 1963; 1967; 1973. Esler also draws comparative material on religious reform and sectarian movements in Africa from Barrett 1968.

On the use of sect models in New Testament studies see ch. 2 above and suggestions for further reading there.

Esler's study was originally presented as an Oxford DPhil thesis, and his sociological approach was taken up and applied in different ways to Pauline texts in two other Oxford theses, produced very soon after Esler's and also published in the Society for New Testament Studies Monograph Series: Watson 1986 and MacDonald 1988 (see ch. 8 below).

[21] For Diaspora *politeumata*, see Smallwood 1976, 139, 141, 247, 285, 359–61, 369–70.

For critical overviews of Esler's book, see Rodd 1988; Holmberg 1990, 101–105; Barton 1993, 152–56. A critique of Berger and Luckmann's theory in relation to New Testament studies may be found in Horrell 1993; 1996a, 39–45; note the response by Esler 1998a. There is continuing debate concerning appropriate ways to conceive of a social-scientific approach to the New Testament, and over the place of models and scientific method within such an approach: see *Introduction* §6.1.

5

'Despising the Shame of the Cross': Honor and Shame in the Johannine Passion Narrative

JEROME H. NEYREY

INTRODUCTION

In this essay Jerome Neyrey presents a study of the Johannine Passion narrative read through the lens of a model of honour and shame which, he suggests, encapsulates the pivotal values of ancient Mediterranean culture. According to this model, developed in various publications by Malina, Neyrey and others, the society in which Jesus and the early Christians lived was one in which the quest for honour dominated public encounters of all kinds (see *Introduction* §3). In these public settings, challenges to one's honour had to be countered, unless one was to be openly shamed, for shame is the counterpart of honour. On the other hand, a successful riposte to an opponent's challenge increased one's own honour and lessened theirs. Thus these encounters may be seen as 'games' of 'challenge–riposte'.

Neyrey therefore reads the Johannine Passion narrative as an extended contest for honour, involving Pilate, Jesus, Jewish leaders and the crowd. In the eyes of outsiders and enemies, the crucifixion of Jesus is 'unqualified shame' (p. 159); on the other hand, from the perspective of the disciples of Jesus, and the narrator of the account, his death, albeit ironically, conveys honour. 'In short, the gospel inculcates an ironic point of view that death and shame mean glory and honor' (p. 167). By adopting this model, Neyrey argues, we can avoid imposing on biblical characters 'modern notions of the self or motivations and strategies typical of the modern world'. Appreciating the typical honour–shame dynamics of the ancient world leads to a 'more authentic cultural and historical reading' (p. 175).

Originally published in *Semeia* 68 (1994), pp. 113–37. Copyright © 1996 by the Society of Biblical Literature. Reproduced with permission.

Underpinning this reading of the Johannine Passion narrative, as is the case with much of the work by the Context Group, is a set of models outlining the pivotal values of ancient Mediterranean culture which is particularly indebted to the early study by Malina (1981), who in turn drew on the work of cultural anthropologists (see *Introduction* §3). Certainly this set of models serves to illuminate some of the ways in which the ancient culture works, and to help modern readers to avoid implicitly imposing the values and assumptions of their own cultural context onto texts which reflect a very different world. However, there is perhaps a danger that a somewhat generalised picture of Mediterranean culture is constructed (see *Introduction* §3; §6.1), which may not sufficiently allow the subtleties and varieties within various situations and in various texts to emerge. Anthropologists tend now to stress how cultures vary over space and time (see Chance 1994, 140–43). Studies of a specific context must therefore seek to appreciate the particularities of that situation, not least the possible divergence between values 'in theory' and actual social practice (does John's 'ironic' approach in any way subvert or reject the dominant culture of honour?). Anthropologist John Chance raises the question as to whether in Neyrey's case there is a risk that 'the author' may be 'perhaps unwittingly projecting his analytical model onto the data' (Chance 1994, 146). Is it right to assume, for example, that power, knowledge, and so on, should all be seen as facets of honour? Is the tortuous process culminating in the crucifixion really fundamentally about a contest for honour and a concern not to be shamed? Neyrey claims that: 'Whenever Jesus appears in public, the scene is generally described as a challenge to his claims of honor. The same perspective can profitably be applied to the conflicts between Paul and his opponents. Always honor is at stake, either as claimed or challenged.' (p. 175) Perhaps Chance's cautions should be heeded: 'blanket applications of a monolithic model of honor and shame should be avoided'; 'there is more to Mediterranean culture than honor and shame' (1994, 148; see further *Introduction* §3). Nevertheless, we should certainly be wary not to throw any babies out with the bathwater: work like that of Neyrey has undoubtedly brought our attention to social dynamics recorded in our texts but all too often ignored by modern readers whose cultural assumptions are very different. However, biblical scholars working with the methods and resources of other disciplines need constantly and critically to appraise and revise their approach in the light of ongoing developments in those disciplines.

❦

1. *Introduction*

New Testament authors reflect the general perception of crucifixion in the Greco-Roman world as 'shame' (Heb 12:2). Various classical authors give us a sense of the typical process of crucifixion, which at every step entailed progressive humiliation of the victim and loss of honor (Hengel 1977, 22–32):

1. Crucifixion was considered the appropriate punishment for slaves (Cicero, *In Verrem* 2.5.168), bandits (Josephus, *War* 2.253), prisoners of war (Josephus, *War* 5.451) and revolutionaries (Josephus, *Ant.* 17.295; see Hengel 1977, 46–63).

2. Public trials ('misera est ignominia iudicorum publicorum,' Cicero, *Pro Rabinio* 9–17) served as status degradation rituals, which labelled the accused as a shameful person.

3. Flogging and torture, especially the blinding of eyes and the shedding of blood, generally accompanied the sentence (Josephus, *War* 5.449–51 & 3.321; Livy 22.13.19; 28.37.3; Seneca, *On Anger* 3.6; Philo, *Flac.* 72; Diod. Sic. 33.15.1; Plato, *Gorgias* 473bc & *Republic* 2.362e). Since, according to *m. Mak* 3.12, scourging was done both to the front and back of the body, the victims were nude; often they befouled themselves with urine or excrement (3.14).

4. The condemned were forced to carry the cross beam (Plutarch, *Delay* 554B).

5. The victim's property, normally clothing, was confiscated; hence they were further shamed by being denuded (see Diod. Sic. 33.15.1).

6. The victim lost power and thus honor through pinioning of hands and arms, especially the mutilation of being nailed to the cross (Philo, *Post.* 61; *Somn.* 2.213).

7. Executions served as crude forms of public entertainment, where the crowds ridiculed and mocked the victims (Philo, *Spec. Leg.* 3.160), who were sometimes affixed to crosses in an odd and whimsical manner, including impalement (Seneca, *Consol. ad Marciam* 20.3; Josephus, *War* 5.451).

8. Death by crucifixion was often slow and protracted. The powerless victim suffered bodily distortions, loss of bodily control, and enlargement of the penis (Steinberg 1983, 82–108). Ultimately they were deprived of life and thus the possibility of gaining satisfaction or vengeance.

9. In many cases, victims were denied honorable burial; corpses were left on display and devoured by carrion birds and scavenger animals (Pliny, *H.N.* 36.107–108).

Victims would thus experience themselves as progressively humiliated and stripped entirely of public respect or honor.

The issue, however, lies not in the brutal pain endured. For among the warrior elite, at least, the endurance of pain and suffering were marks of *andreia* or manly courage (e.g., Hercules' labors; Paul's hardship catalogues, e.g., 2 Cor 6:3–10; 11:23–33). Silence of the victim during torture was a mark of honor (see Isa 53:7; Cicero, *In Verrem* 2.5.162; Josephus, *War* 6.304). But mockery, loss of respect, and humiliation were the bitter parts; the loss of honor, the worst fate. Although the gospels record in varying degrees the physical torture of Jesus, they focus on the various attempts to dishonor him by spitting on him (Mark 14:65//Matt 26:67; see Mark 10:33–34), striking him in the face and head (Mark 14:65//Matt 26:67), ridiculing him (*empaizein*: Mark 15:20, 31; Matt 27:29, 31, 41), heaping insults upon him (*oneidizein*: Mark 15:32, 34; Matt 27:44), and treating him as though he were nothing (*exouthenein*, Luke 23: 11; see Acts 4:11).

This study of the Johannine passion narrative views it precisely through the lenses of honor and shame. We suggest that despite all the shameful treatment of Jesus, he is portrayed, not only as maintaining his honor, but even gaining glory and prestige (Malina and Neyrey 1988, 95–131). Far from being a status degradation ritual, his passion is seen as a status elevation ritual. This hypothesis entails a larger consideration, namely, the importance of honor and shame as pivotal values of the Mediterranean world (Malina 1981, 25). We presume that the original audience would have perceived Jesus' passion in these terms.

Modern readers, however, are not cognizant of these pivotal cultural values. We neither understand the grammar of honor nor appreciate the social dynamics in which they play so important a part. If we would interpret the narrative of Jesus' death from the appropriate cultural point of view, we must attempt to see things through the lenses of ancient Mediterranean culture, which were those of honor and shame. In the cultural world of the New Testament, Jesus' death by crucifixion was acknowledged as a most shameful experience. Paul merely expressed what others perceived when he labelled the crucified Christ as a *skandalon* to Jews and *mōria* to Greeks (1 Cor 1:23). The author of Hebrews explicitly calls the cross 'shame' (*aischunes*, 12:2).

The gospels acknowledge that prophets are denied honor in their own villages (*atimos*, Mark 6:4//Matt 13:57). They tell of messengers sent to a vineyard, who are wounded in the head and treated shamefully (*etimasan*, Mark 12:4). But the early Christians counted this type of public shame as honor: '. . . rejoicing that they were counted worthy to suffer dishonor (*atimasthēnai*) for the name' (Acts 5:41). Honor and shame, then, are not only integral parts of the language patterns which describe the fate of Jesus and his disciples, but a basic element in the way the Christian story perceives and deals with suffering, rejection, and death.

2. A brief grammar of honor and shame

Greeks, Romans, and Judeans all considered honor and shame to be pivotal values in their cultures (Adkins 1960; Malina 1981; Gilmore 1987). From Homer to Herodotus and from Pindar to Paul (Nagy 1979, 222–42; Friedrich 1977, 290), men lived and died in quest of honor, reputation, fame, approval, and respect. Lexical definitions offer a wide range of overlapping meanings for honor/ *timē*: (1) the price or value of something, (2) respect paid to someone, (3) honorary office, (4) dignity or status, (5) honors or awards given someone (Schneider 1968, 169–71). Paul Friedrich offers a social grammar of honor based on Greek epic poetry: 'The structure of Iliadic honor can be stated in part as a larger network that includes propositions about honor and nine honor-linked values: power, wealth, magnanimity, personal loyalty, "precedence," sense of shame, fame or "reputation," courage, and excellence' (1977, 290).

A detailed grammar of honor can be found in Malina's *New Testament World*, and in our co-authored essay of 1991(a) but a summary of it may aid readers unfamiliar with the topic. Honor comes to someone either by *ascription* by another (birth, adoption, appointment) or by one's own *achievement*. Achieved honor derives from benefaction (Luke 7:5; Diod. Sic. 6.1.2), military prowess, success at athletic games, and the like. In the warrior culture of Greece and Rome, honor accrues with prowess in battle (see David and Goliath) or endurance in labors (Heracles; see 2 Tim 4:7–8). Yet most commonly honor is acquired in the face-to-face game of challenge and riposte which makes up much of the daily life of individuals in villages and cities.

Honor resides in one's name, always an inherited name. Sons enjoy the honor of their father's name and membership in his clan. Hence, they are regularly identified as 'the son of so-and-so' (e.g., 1 Sam 9:1–2; Ezra 7:1–6). Yet individuals might be called by honorific names such as 'Rabbi' (Matt 23:7) or 'Prophet' (John 9:17) or 'Christ' (John 7:26). These labels, which are claims to precedence and honor, are likely to be bitterly contested.

Honor resides in certain public roles, statuses, and offices. Fathers enjoy great honor in their households, honor which is sanctioned in the Ten Commandments. Most notably, honor was attached to offices such as king and high priest, as well as governor, proconsul, and other civic or imperial offices. In the great tradition of the aristocrats, the hierarchical ranking of honor was clearly known (Garnsey 1970, 221–71). But in the little tradition of peasants and artisans, such ranking was a matter of considerable debate and controversy, which we can observe in the squabbles over the seating at dinner tables (Luke 14:7–11).

Honor has 'a strong material orientation' (Schneider 1968, 170). That is, honor is expressed and measured by one's possessions which must be on display. Wealth in general denotes honor – not simply the possession of wealth, but its consumption and display: e.g. banquets, fine clothes, weapons, houses, etc. Hence it is not surprising to hear Josephus describing as 'honor' the benefactions Vespasian bestowed on him: 'raiment and other precious gifts' (*War* 3.408). Similarly he describes the honors given Daniel: '(The king) gave him purple to wear and put a chain of linked gold about his neck' (*Ant.* 10.240). Finally Josephus records Haman's suggestion to the Persian king concerning how to honor a friend: 'If you wish to cover with glory the man whom you say you love, let him ride on horseback wearing the same dress as yourself, with a necklace of gold, and let one of your close friends precede him and proclaim throughout the whole city that this is the honor shown to him whom the king honors' (*Ant.* 11.254).

Anthropologists describe the physical body as a microcosm of the social body (Douglas 1966, 115). The values and rules pertinent to the macrocosm are replicated in the way the physical body is perceived and treated. Let us examine how the body replicates honor.

1. *The head and face* are particular loci of personal honor and respect. A head is honored when crowned or anointed. Servants and courtiers honor a monarch by avoiding looking them in the face, that is, by the deep bow. Comparably, to slap someone in the mouth, spit in their face, box their ears or strike their heads shames this

member and so gives 'affront' (Matt 26:67; Luke 22:63–64; Mark 15:17–20).

2. *Clothing* covers the dishonorable or shameful parts of the body (1 Cor 12:23–24), namely the genitals and the buttocks. Clothing, moreover, symbolizes honor: 'Men are the glory of God and their clothes are the glory of men' (*Derek Eretz Zuta*). Elites signal their status by their clothing and adornment (Luke 7:25; see *m. Yoma* 7.5). Purple clothing was a particular mark of honor, worn by kings (Judg 8:26), priests (Exod 28:4–6; 39:1, 28–29; 1 Macc 10:20; 11:58), and nobles at court (Ezek 23:6; Esth 8:6; Dan 5:7; see Reinhold 1970, 7–21, 48–61). Uniforms signal rank or office. Philo provides a striking example of the way clothing replicates honor in his description of Pharaoh's investiture of Joseph with symbols of status giving him a '. . . royal seat, sacred robe, golden necklace, setting him on his second chariot, bade him go the round of the city with a crier walking in front who proclaimed the appointment' (*Jos.* 120). The costuming of Jesus in a purple robe and a crown of thorns mocks him with the normal trappings of honor. Being stripped of clothing, moreover, eliminates all marks of honor and status; it also indicates a loss of power to cover and defend one's 'shameful parts.'

3. *Bodily postures* express honor. Masters sit at table, while servants stand and wait upon them (Luke 17:7–8; see 13:29). Twenty-four elders stand around the throne where God is seated; they fall down before him in worship (Rev 4:10). *Proskunein* describes a posture whereby someone bends low to kiss another, either on the hand or the foot; thus it comes to mean bowing before or showing respect for someone (Josephus, *Ant.* 11.209).

Yet in the perception of the ancients, honor, like all other goods, existed in quite limited supply (Foster 1967, 304–5). There was only so much gold, so much strength, so much honor available. When someone achieved honor, it was thought to be at the expense of others. Philo, for example, condemns polytheism, because in honoring others as deities, the honor due to the true God is diminished: 'God's honour is set at naught by those who deify mortals' (*Ebr.* 110; see Josephus, *Ant.* 4.32; *War* 1.559). When John's disciples lament to their master that Jesus is gaining more disciples and honor, they understand that Jesus' gain must be John's loss. John confirms this, 'He must increase, but I must decrease' (John 3:30). Thus, claims to honor by one person will tend to be perceived as threats to the honor of others, and consequently need to be challenged, not acknowledged. In fact, two Gospels state that it was out of envy that Jesus' enemies handed him over (Mark 15:10//Matt 27:18; cf. John 11:47–48).

Philotimia or love of honor was a powerful driving force in antiquity. We are particularly interested in how this was played out in the rather ordinary circumstances of life. Honor must be both claimed and acknowledged. After all, it is the respect one has in the eyes of others. But honor claims are vulnerable to challenge. Challenges must be met with an appropriate riposte or honor is lost. All such claims, challenges, and ripostes take place in the public domain, and their verdict of success or failure determines the outcome of these games (Malina 1981, 30–33; Malina and Neyrey 1991a, 36–38, 49–51). Claim, challenge, riposte and verdict, then, constitute the formal elements in the endless contests for honor and respect.

Thus far we have discussed 'honor,' but we must be equally aware of 'shame.' Contempt, loss of face, defeat, and ridicule all describe shame, the loss of honor. The grammar of honor presented above can be reversed to describe 'shame.' Shame can be *ascribed* or *achieved*. A magistrate may ascribe shame by declaring one guilty and so worthy of public flogging (2 Cor 11:23–25); a king may mock and treat one with contempt (Luke 23:11). God may declare one a 'Fool!' (Luke 12:20). Thus the elite and those in power may declare one honorless and worthy of contempt: '. . . exclude, revile, and cast out your name as evil' (Luke 6:22). Yet shame may be *achieved* by one's folly or by cowardice and failure to respond to a challenge. One may refuse to participate in the honor-gaining games characteristic of males, and thus bring contempt on oneself.

The bodily grammar for honor works also for shame. If the honorable parts of the body, the head and face, are struck, spat upon, slapped, blindfolded, or otherwise maltreated, shame ensues. If the right arm, symbol of male power and strength, is bound, tied, or nailed, the resulting powerlessness denotes shame. If one is publicly stripped naked, flogged, paraded before the crowds, and led through the streets, one is shamed. Shame results when one's blood is intentionally spilled, but especially when one is killed by another.

3. Irony: turning shame into honor

Since there are two parties competing in the passion narrative, there are two perceptions of what is occurring. The enemies of Jesus bind, slap,

spit upon, blindfold, flog, strip, and kill Jesus; their actions are all
calculated to 'mock' and 'revile' him. In their eyes they have shamed
Jesus. But the gospel, while it records these actions and gestures of shame,
tells quite a different story. In the evangelist's eyes, Jesus' shame and
humiliation is truly the account of his glory: 'Ought not the Christ
suffer and so enter into his glory?' (Luke 24:26; see Acts 14:22; Heb
2:10). Indeed, in the Fourth Gospel, his death is regularly described as
glory and glorification (John 7:39; 12:28; 17:5; see 21:19). Or, to
paraphrase Paul, foolishness, weakness, and shame in human eyes are
wisdom, strength, and honor in God's eyes (1 Cor 1:20, 25). Thus the
story of Jesus' shame is ironically understood by his disciples as his 'lifting
up,' his exaltation, his enthronement, in short, his honor. The issue
might be rephrased: Who gets to judge whether the crucifixion is honor
or shame? If the public verdict rests with the Judeans, then Jesus is
shamed. But if the community of believers renders the verdict on the
basis of God's riposte or Jesus' demonstration of power in death, then
the verdict is of honor.

This ironic perspective is part and parcel of the principle that
Jesus constantly narrates: that last is first, least is greatest, dead is alive,
shame is honor (Duke 1985, 95–116, 126–38). Hence, two perspectives
need to be distinguished as we read the account of Jesus' crucifixion: in
the eyes of outsiders and enemies, his crucifixion is unqualified shame!
But in the eyes of his disciples, it is ironic honor. Let us now take these
abstract notions of honor (and shame) and use them as an exciting and
illuminating lens for perceiving the passion narrative of Jesus, the
honorable one.

4. Honor and shame in John 18–19

4.1. Arrest (18:1–11)

Although capture and arrest normally denote dishonor, this narrative
presents a scene of honor displayed and maintained. First of all, honor
means power and control (de la Potterie 1989, 29). In this regard, when
the cohort approaches Jesus, he steps forward to take charge of the
situation. By claiming that 'Jesus knew all that was to befall him' (18:4),
the narrator signals Jesus' control of the situation (see 19:28). Moreover,
he questions the powerful forces gathered against him: 'Whom do you
seek?' In the cultural scenario of honor and shame, the questioner

generally acts in the challenging or commanding position (see Mark 11:27–33).

At his remark, 'I am he,' the soldiers 'drew back and fell to the ground' (18:6), leaving Jesus standing. Honor is thus signalled by bodily posture. Commentators regularly note that Jesus' 'I AM' can be read as the divine name which he is granted to use (Neyrey 1988a, 213–20). Falling to the ground characterizes human reactions in the presence of the glory of God (Ezek 1:28; 44:4) or at least an honor-bestowing posture in the presence of a superior person (Dan 2:46; Rev 1:17). At a minimum, Jesus enjoys such a prominent and honorable status that armies fall at his feet. Even if Dodd is correct that the narrator is drawing on psalms describing how one's foes stumble and fall when attacking (Dodd 1963, 76–77), nevertheless some vindication or riposte to a challenge is evident. If this language describes Jesus' heavenly status, then he enjoys the same honor as God, an honor that God commands (5:23). To use God's name, 'I AM,' might be considered an act of power; and honor is always attached to power.

The narrator repeats the sequence of events in 18:7–8, which doubles the impression of Jesus' strength and honor. His control of the situation extends even to his command about the safe departure of his disciples: 'Let these others go' (18:8). Weak people do not tell a cohort of Roman soldiers what to do. This proves, moreover, that his word of honor is true and trustworthy: 'This was to fulfil the word which he had spoken, "I did not lose a single one of those you gave me"' (18:9). Thus the narrator presents Jesus firmly in control: knowing all that will happen, asking questions, controlling the events, giving commands, and receiving profound respect from his would-be assailants. He is without doubt the most honorable person in the situation.

Jesus' commanding posture reminds the reader of the Noble Shepherd discourse, where he disavowed that he was a victim and claimed power even over death: 'No one takes my life from me, but I lay it down of my own accord. I have power to lay it down, and I have power to take it again' (10:18). Since power is one of the public faces of honor, Jesus' power to protect his sheep as well as his power to lay down his life indicate that he suffers no shame whatever here. Nothing happens against his will, so he is in no way diminished.

Yet others in the narrative see the scene differently. Simon Peter drew his sword and struck at one of the arresting crowd, which we must interpret as his riposte to the perceived challenge to Jesus' honor. In other circumstances, his action would be labelled an honorable thing, namely, the defense of one's leader against an honor challenge. Jesus himself states this: 'If my kingdom were of this world, my servants would fight, that I not be handed over to the Jews' (18:36). Normally failure to respond to a challenge is shameful, but here Jesus explains that it is precisely out of honor that he refuses to resist, that is, out of respect for the will of his Father: 'Shall I not drink the cup which the Father has given me?' (18:11). Peter's riposte, then, is unnecessary, for Jesus' honor is not threatened. Indeed, it belongs to the virtue of *andreia* or courage to endure what must be endured (Seeley 1990, 117–41). And courage of this sort is an honorable thing.

4.2. Jewish investigation (18:12–14, 19–24)

Outsiders see only that Jesus has lost power: 'The cohort seized Jesus and bound him' (18:12). His captors take him to the private chambers of Annas, a very powerful enemy, who questions Jesus. Recall that questions are generally challenges. Here Jesus delivers a bold response: 'I have spoken openly to the world; I have always taught in the synagogues and in the temple, where all Jews come together' (18:20). Jesus claims that he has acted as an honorable man, always appearing in the appropriate male space, the public arena, and speaking boldly and clearly. His *parrēsia* (bold speech) denotes courageous and honorable public behavior (see 1 Thess 2:2). In contrast, this Gospel declares as shameful people who are afraid to speak openly about the Christ (9:22–23; 12:42; see Phil 1:20).

The narrative interprets Jesus' bold speech as a riposte to Annas' challenging questions. Jesus commands his interrogator, 'Ask those who have heard me. They know what I said' (18:21). This occasions a severe counter-challenge from one of the officers standing by, who 'struck Jesus with his hand' (v. 22; see 19:3). The gesture was surely a slap in the face, thus giving an 'affront' to Jesus. It is similar to the blows given Jesus according to the synoptic accounts (Matt 26:67; Mark 14:65; Luke 22:63–64; see Matt 5:39). But Jesus is not silenced or humbled as was Paul, when he was struck by Annas' servant (Acts 23:4–5). He gives an appropriate riposte, 'If I have spoken wrongly, bear witness to the wrong; but if I have spoken rightly, why do you strike me?' (18:23). Thus he withstands the insult and continues to speak boldly; he has the last word.

4.3. Roman trial (18:28–19:16)

The very fact of being put on trial is itself an honor challenge, simply because the one who is publicly accused experiences his claims to honor (name, worth, reputation) to be publicly questioned. Modern people have idealized trials as occasions not only to clear one's name, but to put the system itself on trial, that is, to challenge the challenger. Our judicial process, moreover, functions on the presumption of innocence. Not so the ancients, where guilt was presumed. It was inherently shameful to be seized and publicly charged with wrongdoing, 'If this man were not an evildoer, we would not have handed him over to you' (18:30).

The trial episode (18:28–19:16) can be described as an extended game of charge and refutation or challenge and riposte. This occurs on several levels. First, those who deliver Jesus engage in their own challenge–riposte game with Pilate. Pilate *claims* the honor of procurator and magistrate as he questions them ('What accusation?' 18:29); they *challenge him* by asserting their own power ('If this man were not an evildoer . . .' v. 30); and this leads to Pilate's *riposte* ('Take him yourselves . . .' v. 31). For the moment Pilate wins, as they are forced to admit that they have no power: 'It is not lawful for us . . .' (v. 31). This challenge–riposte game between Pilate and the Judeans will be continued in 18:39–40 and 19:6, 12–16. But the main contest focusses on the formal process of Jesus before Pilate, which also is an elaborate game of challenge and riposte.

Commentators note the alternation of scenes in the trial from outside to inside, and even the chiastic shape of the narrative. Raymond Brown (1970, 859) provides the following arrangement (for minor variations, see Giblin 1986, 223).

1. *Outside* (xviii 28–32)
   Jews demand death

2. *Inside* (xviii 33–38a)
   Pilate questions Jesus
   about kingship

3. *Outside* (xviii 38b–40)
   Pilate finds Jesus not guilty;
   choice of Barabbas

4. *Inside* (xix 1–3)
   Soldiers scourge Jesus

7. *Outside* (xix 12–16a)
   Jews obtain death

6. *Inside* (xix 9–11)
   Pilate talks with Jesus about
   power

5. *Outside* (xix 4–8)
   Pilate finds Jesus not guilty;
   'Behold the man'

Commentators are wont to contrast these scenes as 'public' (outside) and 'private' (inside). Yet the designation 'private/inside' is misleading here, for we should not imagine Pilate and Jesus having a *tête-à-tête*. And even if the narrative action occurs 'within' the Roman compound, it is still a 'public' place occupied by Roman soldiers, and not the 'private' world of the household (see 12:1–8; 13:3–5). Dodd's remark that there are two stages, 'a front stage and a back' (1963, 96), seems more accurate. Yet the narrative distinction between 'going within' and 'going out' serves to mark the various scenes and different audiences. The 'outside' public scenes are the honor contests between Pilate and the Judeans. The so-called 'inside' scenes, which comprise the *cognitio* of the trial between judge and the accused, are also public in that they occur in the public forum of the Roman courtyard or praetorium, whether this be the fortress Antonia (Josephus, *Ant.* 15.292) or the new palace of Herod (Benoit 1952, 545–49). The 'outside' crowds are informed of the results of the 'inside' contest, which affects their challenge–riposte game with Pilate. The honor–shame dynamic, then, occurs on both stages, but between different sets of contestants.

Trials under Roman jurisdiction have a formal structure which is helpful to note (Sherwin-White 1963, 12–20; Neyrey 1987, 509–11):

Formal Elements of a Roman Trial	1st	2nd
1. arrest	18:1–11	——
2. charges	18:28–32	19:7
3. judge's cognitio	18:33–38a	19:8–11
4. verdict	18:38b	19:12
5. judicial warning	19:1–6	——
6. sentence	——	19:13–16

This structure indicates that Jesus' trial went through two forensic cycles; it helps, moreover, to clarify the roles of Pilate, Jesus, and the crowds, especially in terms of the four formal elements of an honor contest. The crowds, who function as the witnesses or accusers in the forensic process, *challenge* Jesus' *claims*. Pilate, the judge, examines these challenges and determines whether Jesus' claims are honorable or not. Jesus, who is on trial, is challenged precisely as to his honorable status. Let us now view in greater detail these forensic elements and roles in terms of honor and shame.

Charges (18:29–33). This gospel mentions that Roman soldiers partici-pated in the seizure of Jesus (18:3); their presence indicates that Jesus was in some sense arrested. The charges against him which Pilate investigates are formal challenges to his claims to honor and status: 'Are you the *King of the Jews*?' (18:33; see also 19:7, 14, 19). From the beginning, Jesus has been acclaimed as a most honorable person, and so enjoys a singular portion of ascribed honor. On the basis of God's own prompting, John the Baptizer acclaimed him 'Son of God' (1:34). Disciples acknowledge him as 'the Messiah' (1:41) and 'Son of God and King of Israel' (1:49). Even a leader of the Judeans accepts him as 'a teacher come from God' (3:2). According to the story, various people acclaim him 'savior of the world' (4:42), 'prophet' (6:14; 9:17), 'king' (6:15; 12:13–15), and 'Christ' (7:26). In the game of honor and shame, all of this constitutes a claim of honor, the public identity and reputation of Jesus, which is now being challenged in this trial.

Cognitio (18:33–38). The judge's *cognitio* of Jesus in his judicial quarters serves as the forum where Jesus' honor claims are both *challenged* and *defended*. On the level of rhetoric, Pilate asks questions which challenge Jesus, whose riposte is initially the clever strategy of answering a question with a question (see Mark 11:28–33; 12:14–16). Pilate challenges with a question: 'Are you the King of the Jews?' Jesus parries with his own question: 'Do you say this of your own accord . . . ?' Pilate asks more questions: 'Am I a Jew? . . . What have you done? . . . So you are a king then? . . . What is truth?' On the narrative level, then, Pilate is perceived as asserting his own honor claims as the embodiment of Roman authority by his rhetorical posture as the figure whose duty it is to ask questions and so challenge others. This initial exchange sparkles with honor challenges. Pilate asks a question, presumably concerning the charge against Jesus. By questioning Pilate, Jesus might be said to be giving a riposte: 'Do you say this of your own accord . . .' (v. 34). Pilate's response is not only scorn ('Am I a Jew?'), but a mockery of Jesus. How shameful, he points out, that 'Your own nation and the chief priests have handed you over' (v. 35).

This sparring game quickly fades, for the narrator wishes to portray Jesus giving a solemn *riposte* to the challenge to his identity and authority. 'Kingship' is Pilate's challenge, a very noble and honorable status, which Jesus defends. Twice he proclaims, 'My kingship is not of this world' (18:36, 37). If his kingship is not of this world, it must belong to another world (8:23), that is, God's world, which is eternal, unchanging, and truly honorable. Although this 'world' was once a worthy recipient of divine favor (3:16; 4:42; 10:36; 12:47), it quickly proved hostile to Jesus. He became an alien here in this world and met only challenge and opposition (1:9–10; Meeks 1972, 67–70). The world's hostility, then, constitutes an ongoing challenge to Jesus' honor. But the assertion that his kingdom is not of this world implies that he belongs to a better kingdom, which must triumph over the hostility experienced here. Although challenged, Jesus belongs to a kingdom where he is honored as he should be (5:23; 17:5, 24).

This Gospel speaks of a ruler of this world, who will be Jesus' chief challenger. But even this powerful figure 'has no power over me' (14:30); he will be cast out (12:31) and judged (16:11). Thus Jesus boasted to his disciples, 'I have overcome the world' (16:30). This powerful challenger appears to be Satan (Schnackenburg 1982, II, 391). But as the passion narrative progresses, even the Roman emperor will qualify as a rival of God (19:12, 15). Yet if Jesus' kingship were of this world, his followers would do the honorable thing and 'fight, that I not be handed over to the Jews' (18:36). The vindicator of his kingship, then, must be a most powerful person also 'not of this world,' namely God. He will give the riposte for King Jesus (12:28; 17:1). But the claim that Jesus is a king remains unassailable: 'You say that I am a king; for this I was born, and for this I have come into the world' (18:37). Jesus makes another *claim* that pertains to his kingship, 'Every one who is of the truth hears my voice' (v. 37). This directly echoes the remarks about the shepherd in 10:3–4, 26–27 (Meeks 1967, 66–67). If 'shepherd' is a metaphor for king (i.e., David, the Royal Shepherd), then Jesus reaffirms his honor as king. Good and honorable people, he says, acknowledge this honor claim by 'hearing my voice.' Whether scornful or cynical (Brown 1970, 869), Pilate's retort, 'What is truth?' indicates that he rejects this claim.

Verdict (18:38b). The source of Jesus' honor, while not made explicit here, will shortly be made clear to the court (19:8–11). Yet the reader knows that Jesus enjoys maximum ascribed honor from the most honorable being in the universe, namely, God (see 5:36–38; 12:27–28). All that Jesus is, has, and does comes from God (5:19–29). The reader knows that he comes from God and is returning to God (13:1–3; 17:1–5), where he will be glorified with the glory he had before the creation of the world. At this point in the trial, Jesus has given an adequate riposte to the challenge to his honor; he is a king and defends that claim. On the narrative level, Pilate's forensic verdict of innocence tells the reader, at least, that Jesus' claims are publicly judged to be honorable: 'I find no crime in him' (18:38). Honor defended is honor maintained. Yet the public verdict in this honor contest remains unclear.

In acknowledging a custom, Pilate offers to those who have just challenged Jesus' honor the release of this same 'King of the Jews' (18:39). This should be interpreted as Pilate's personal challenge to the crowd (Rensberger 1988, 92–94). Their challenge to Jesus had just been rejected (v. 38), and now Pilate taunts them by inviting them to accept Jesus in the fullness of his honor claim, 'Will you have me release to you the "King of the Jews"?' (v. 39). Pilate asks Jesus' challengers publicly to accept a riposte to their challenge, and so admit defeat in this game. His question, then, continues the honor–shame contest between him and the crowds (see 18:29–31). Yet, the crowds give a counter-challenge to Jesus' honor claim and Pilate's gambit: 'Not this man!' The shame of being disowned by one's own occurs again (v. 35); Jesus' enemies prefer the release of Barabbas, a thief or social bandit, to him (18:40). The contest between Pilate and the crowd continues as a stalemate.

Judicial warning (19:1–5). Pilate gives Jesus a 'judicial warning,' such as Paul received when five times lashed and three times beaten with rods (2 Cor 11:24–25; cf. Acts 5:41). Judicial warnings were intended to inflict pain but especially to humiliate and so discredit troublemakers. In essence, Jesus is beaten and mocked. Even if the technical terms 'mock' and 'mockery' do not occur here (cf. *empaizein*, Matt 27:29; Mark 15:20; Meeks 1967, 69), native readers whose world is structured around honor and shame know what is going on. In the honor culture of ancient warriors, stoic endurance of physical pain denotes courage and honor (*andreia*). But to be mocked is by far more painful than the physical beating because it produces the most dreaded of all experiences, shame.

As regards his body, Jesus is shamed by being stripped naked, bound, and beaten in the public forum of the Roman soldiers. His head, the most honorable member of his body, is mocked with a 'plaited crown of thorns.' His body is dressed in purple, the royal color. Many of the soldiers 'struck him with their hands,' surely on the face or head, and sarcastically acclaimed his honor, 'Hail, King of the Jews' (19:3). Each of these ritual gestures has been shown to be a characteristic element in the honoring of Persian and Roman rulers (Alföldi 1970: *proskunēsis*/ bending the knee: 11–16, 45–70; acclamation, especially as *dominus*: 38–45, 209–10; crown: 17–18, 128–29, 263–67; clothing: 143–56, 175–84, 268–70; scepter: 156–57, 228–35; throne: 140–41, 159–61). Thus a mock coronation ritual occurs (Blank 1959, 62; Meeks 1967, 69–72), whose primary function is to shame Jesus, the alleged King of the Judeans.

But if the actors in the drama are portrayed as shaming Jesus, it does not follow that readers of this gospel must concur. On the contrary, insiders have been repeatedly schooled in irony to see Jesus' death as his 'being lifted' to heaven (3:14; 8:23; 12:32) or his 'glorification' (12:23; 13:31–32; 17:1, 5). The grain of wheat dies and falls into the ground, but thereby lives and bears fruit. In short, the gospel inculcates an ironic point of view that death and shame mean glory and honor. The mock coronation of Jesus, which in the eyes of outsiders means shame, truly betokens honor from the viewpoint of insiders. In terms of Jesus' honor, it truly is a status elevation ritual. Although ironically invested with imperial honors, Jesus nonetheless is acclaimed as honorable, especially in his shame (Duke 1985, 132–33). Rensberger describes this scene as Pilate's humiliation of the Judeans by the sarcastic presentation of a Roman's interpretation of Jewish messianic hopes (1988, 93–94).

New charges/new cognitio (19:7, 9–11). Pilate then brings forth this Jesus who has been mocked and dishonored. I do not know when modern readers started thinking that such a presentation was supposed to inspire sympathy for Jesus, because in the culture of the time such a scene would surely provoke laughter and derision. Crowds regularly gathered at public executions to participate in the mockery (see Matt 27:38, 39, 41). The crowds react here in culturally predictable ways by continuing their dishonoring of Jesus: 'Crucify him! crucify him!' (19:6). Rejection by one's *ethnos* and delivery to the Romans would be shame enough; now his own people call for his shameful death.

With Pilate's verdict of Jesus' innocence, the trial should be over ('I find no crime in him,' 19:5, 6). But a new charge is made, which constitutes a new *challenge* to Jesus' honor: 'By our law he ought to die, for he made himself the Son of God' (19:7). The crowds consider this 'claim' to be so serious a charge as to warrant the death sentence. And so a new trial ensues to deal with the new charge.

Let us view this new charge from the perspective of honor and shame. In antiquity people were constantly 'making themselves' something, that is, claiming a new and higher status or role (Acts 5:36). Hence the public accusation that Jesus *makes himself* something functions as a *challenge* to a perceived empty claim, a common phenomenon in antiquity (*kenodoxos* and *alazōn*; see Acts 8:9; 12:22–23; Josephus, *War* 2.55, 60; *Ant.* 17.272, 278). This sort of challenge to Jesus occurred regularly throughout the narrative (1) '. . . *making himself* equal to God' (5:18); (2) 'Who do you *make yourself to be?*' (8:53); (3) 'You, a mortal, *make yourself God*' (10:33); (4) 'He *made himself* the Son of God' (19:7); (5) 'every one who *makes himself* a king . . .' (19:12). In the course of this narrative, the author has consistently dealt with this charge by dividing the charge/challenge: (1) it is *denied* that Jesus 'makes himself' anything, but (2) it is *defended* that he is such-and-such (Neyrey 1988a, 20–23). For example, Jesus claims in 5:19–29 that he is 'equal to God.' This is no empty claim, for he insists that God has granted him both creative and eschatological powers and the honor attached to them. The Father (1) *shows* him all that God is doing (5:20), (2) *has given* all judgment to the Son (5:22), (3) *has granted* the Son also to have life in himself (5:26), and (4) *has given* him authority to execute judgment (5:27; Neyrey, 1988a, 20–25). Thus, Jesus does *not* 'make himself' anything, for that would be a vainglorious claim and thus false honor. But he truly is 'equal to God,' 'King,' and 'Son of God' because these honors, roles, and statuses are ascribed to him by God (see the ascribed honor of being 'made king' in 6:15).

It is not, moreover, accidental in the Gospel traditions that Jesus himself rarely claims to be prophet, king, son of God, etc. These tend to be ascribed to him either by God (13:31; 17:5, 24; see Mark 1:11; 9:7) or by others: (Son of God, 1:34, 49; Christ, 1:41; 10:24; King, 1:49; 6:15; 12:13; Savior, 4:42; and Prophet, 4:19; 6:14). Thus the tradition steadfastly maintains that Jesus is an honorable person in two respects: he does not seek honor by making vain claims to such-and-such a status, but he is regularly ascribed great honor by others. The reader, then, has been schooled how to interpret this new charge against Jesus, rejecting any sense of a vain glorious claim and affirming the truth of the honor ascribed to Jesus.

The new forensic charge requires a new *cognitio* by the judge (19:8–11). Pilate asks the appropriate question in terms of honor and shame: 'Where are you from (*pothen*)?' (19:9). True honor is ascribed honor;

and ascribed honor is a function of one's father and clan or one's place of origin (Malina and Neyrey 1991a, 32–34, 39–40; 1991b, 85–87). Concerning place of origin, honor was earlier denied Jesus because he is from Nazareth, from which no good comes (1:46; see Titus 1:12). Paul claims honor by coming from Tarsus, 'no mean city' (Acts 21:39), and Jerusalemites claim honor from being born there (Ps 87:5–6). Concerning father and clan, it is almost a universal phenomenon in the Bible that when characters are introduced or described, they are always identified as the 'son of so-and-so' or the 'daughter of so-and-so.' For an individual's honor is bound with that of his or her father. The rules in the *progymnasmata* for writing an encomium all stress that writers begin their praise of someone by noting that person's family and place of origin (Lee 1986, 188–206). All of the extant texts of the *progymnasmata* on writing an encomium start with praise for *eugeneia*, which consists in noting (1) origin (*genos*), (2) race (*ethnos*), (3) country (*patris*), (4) ancestors (*progonoi*), and (5) parents (*pateres*). Hence Pilate tests Jesus with the appropriate question, *pothen ei su*, which may refer either to his 'place of origin' (8:23) or his parents (6:41–42). But the question directly touches Jesus' honor.

Jesus now remains silent (19:9). He neither defends himself nor offers a riposte to the challenge. Silence in the face of accusation is very difficult to assess; but in an honor and shame context it would probably be read as a shameful thing (see Neh 6:8). To fail to give a riposte to a challenge is to accept defeat and so loss of honor.

Yet readers have already been socialized in just this aspect of Jesus' honor, and so the riposte has been given in advance. Knowledge of whence Jesus comes (*pothen*) and whither he goes (*pou*) has been a major issue throughout the narrative. Outsiders either do not know (3:8; 8:14; 9:29) or falsely think they know (6:41–42; 7:27–28). Many times Jesus proclaims the correct answer, namely, that he descends from heaven (6:38), or that he descends from heaven and ascends back there (3:13; 6:62). Insiders like the blind man accurately deduce the true 'whence' of Jesus because of his power to heal (9:30). And finally the reader is told that Jesus comes from God and returns to heaven (13:1–2). Thus readers can answer Pilate's question; they know 'whence he is,' namely, a person whose parent is none other than God and whose 'country of origin' is no less than heaven. His honor, then, is secure in their eyes.

The narrative suggests that Jesus' silence *challenges* Pilate's power, for he responds with new questions: 'Will you not speak to me? Do you not know that I have power to release you and I have power to crucify you?' (19:10). 'Power' (*exousia*) is at stake; and power is an expression of honor. Although Jesus gives no riposte to this new challenge concerning his origin, he does in turn offer a counter-challenge to Pilate's claim of power: 'You would have no power over me unless it were given you from above' (19:11). Hence Pilate's power is a relative thing. The truly powerful figure is not Caesar, from whom Pilate enjoys ascribed honor, but none other than God, from whom all power flows (John 10:29). Emperors, kings, and governors all owe their power and honor to God (Rom 13:1; 1 Tim 2:2; 1 Pet 2:13–17). This narrative, moreover, asserts that it is God's will and purpose that Jesus undergo this trial (John 12:27). God commanded that he 'lay down his life and take it up again' (10:17–18). Inasmuch as sons are commanded 'Honor your father' (Exod 20:12; Deut 5:16; Mark 10:19), the presentation of Jesus as the obedient one (Heb 5:8; see Mark 14:36//Matt 26:39//Luke 22:42) marks his actions here as honoring his Father and thus warranting the honor of an obedient son.

In fact, Jesus ironically states that even Pilate is behaving honorably because he acts in accord with the power given him from above. The dishonorable people are those 'who have delivered me over to you' (19:11); they are the sinners. Thus in the confrontation between him and Pilate, Jesus remains successful; he suffers no loss of honor. In fact, he seems to have gained an ally of sorts in Pilate, his judge, 'who sought to release him' (19:12).

Final verdict and sentence (19:12–16). In the next scene, the grand public tableau of the trial, the two sets of contestants play another episode of challenge and riposte. In terms of the Pilate-vs-Jesus contest, Pilate's move 'to release him' functions as a definitive riposte to the crowds' various challenges to Jesus' claims to honor. Pilate thrice declares Jesus innocent, and so Jesus cannot be shown to be 'making himself' anything. But in terms of the Pilate-vs-crowd contest, the latter issues one final challenge, not so much to Jesus' claims, but to the honor and status of Pilate himself. 'If you release this man, you are not Caesar's friend; anyone who makes himself a king sets himself against Caesar' (19:12b).

As historians remind us, a 'friend' is often described as the object of political patronage (Bammel 1952, 205–210; Brunt 1965, 1–20). Thus Josephus, when speaking of a circle of aristocrats, calls them 'persons of power among the Friends of the King' (*Ant.* 12.298); Antiochus wrote to his 'governors and Friends' (*Ant.* 12.134). Philo records how Flaccus acted harshly against those who 'insult a king, a Friend of Caesar's, a person who had received Pretorian honours from the Roman Senate' (*Flac.* 40; cf. 1 Macc 2:18; 3:38; 10:65). Thus Pilate owes Caesar a debt of loyalty for his ascribed honor as procurator. Whatever honorable status he enjoys depends on his being the faithful client of an imperial patron. But Pilate's status as 'Caesar's *friend*' (and client) is directly challenged by the crowds, who accuse him of shaming Caesar by supporting a rival king. Pilate answers this challenge in a scene in which all of the various challenges and ripostes are resolved.

Pilate's riposte takes the form of a solemn judicial verdict and sentence. But the scene as narrated contains a fundamental ambiguity. The text states that 'he (Pilate) brought Jesus out and sat down at the judgment seat' (19:13). Controversy surrounds the verb 'sat down' (*ekathisen*), which may be read transitively (i.e., Pilate *sat* Jesus *down* on the judgment seat) or intransitively (i.e., Pilate himself *sat down* on the seat). Grammatical studies support both readings. Those who argue that Jesus was seated point to the irony of the powerless Jesus assuming the role of judge, a role ascribed to him by God according to John 5:22, 27; and 12:31. This reading would follow the gospel axiom that last is first, weakest is greatest, the judged one is the judge. Indeed it would be an extraordinary piece of irony for the dishonored Jesus to assume this position of great honor (see Luke 24:26).

But the literal reading of the passage portrays Pilate's riposte to the crowd's challenge to him. As judge and magistrate in charge of these affairs, including the exercise of the *jus gladii*, Pilate now assumes all of the trappings of his office. Honor is replicated in bodily posture as Pilate seats himself on his official seat, the *bēma*, while the other participants stand (19:13). Exercising his authority, he issues a proclamation to the crowds: 'Behold your king!' Rhetorically, this remark is a command ('Behold!') and an insult ('your king,' see 18:39). It ostensibly upholds the original claims of Jesus by dismissing the challenges of the crowd. Thus the judge has rendered a third verdict of innocence (18:38; 19:4, 12), which functions as a riposte to the challenges to Jesus' honor. But the claim that Jesus is a king is no more acceptable to the crowds now than it was earlier.

Finally the two strands of the honor contests coincide. The crowds challenge Pilate's verdict, even as they shame Jesus: 'Away with him . . . crucify him' (19:15a). Pilate had previously noted the shame of being disowned by one's own *ethnos* (18:35), which shameful action is now repeated. Ostensibly, Pilate has lost the game, and his honor has been diminished. But he makes one last move, a final riposte to the power of the crowd.

Inasmuch as 'king' has been the contested claim throughout the trial, Pilate demands of the crowd a formal judgment in the case: 'Shall I crucify your "king"?' (19:15b). Questions, of course, are challenging, and the response to this question brings maximum shame on Jesus' antagonists: 'We have no king but Caesar' (19:15c). Their remark is an act of supreme dishonor to their heavenly Patron and Sovereign. At the conclusion of the Greater Hallel we find the following prayer:

> From everlasting to everlasting thou art God;
> Beside thee we have no king, redeemer, or savior;
> No liberator, deliverer, provider;
> None who takes pity in every time of distress or trouble.
> We have no king but thee. (Meeks 1967, 77)

It is they who prove to be the 'friend of Caesar,' thus shaming God and God's anointed king. Rensberger notes that Pilate has once more humiliated his opponents by having them publicly deny their claims to a political messiah (1988, 96). Yet no reader would fail to note that God is now mocked and must vindicate his divine honor. The advantage seems to lie with the crowd who bends Pilate to its will and succeeds in dishonoring Jesus ('Crucify him!' 19:15).

A judicial sentence is pronounced, but one which is fraught with irony. The official judge, Pilate, apparently yields in this game of push and shove; his sentence is hardly honorable or just. Jesus' accusers, who earlier claimed that they had no legitimate authority to put a man to death (18:31), finally succeed in a plot that began in 5:18 and was solemnized at a rump trial in 11:50–53. Their success in having Jesus killed would be a mark of honor for them in the eyes of observers, but readers of the narrative know that this 'sentence' is fully within the control of Jesus (12:32–33; 10:17–18) and the will of God. The sentence of a shameful death, then, is but an apparent loss of honor.

4.4. Title (19:19–22)

The game of push and shove continues over the public title attached to Jesus' cross. Pilate's inscription, 'Jesus of Nazareth, King of the Jews,' may be read as a final ironic riposte by the narrator in defense of Jesus' honor, comparable to Caiaphas's 'prophecy' about Jesus' death (11:51). It is also Pilate's act of authority in defense of his own embattled status. The title, which may be construed as another honor claim, is once again challenged by the Jerusalem elite, who urge a more shameful version: '"This man said, I am King of the Jews."' Again, they charge that Jesus vaingloriously assumes honors not rightfully his (19:7, 12). This time Pilate wins: 'What I have written, I have written' (19:22).

4.5. Crucifixion (19:17–37)

The normal sequence of events which accompanies crucifixion was listed at the beginning of this study. In view of that, the shameful elements narrated in the crucifixion of Jesus in the Fourth Gospel are the crucifixion itself, with Jesus' position as the middle figure in a triptych of criminals, themselves shameful persons (19:18). The mocking title over the cross publicly challenges Jesus' claim to honor and status. He is apparently stripped naked, for his clothing is confiscated by his executioners (19:23–24). The synoptics all record various persons, 'mocking' him (Mark 15:27–32; Matt 27:38–43; Luke 23:35–36), which is absent from the Fourth Gospel's account. Yet the very scene is a public humiliation (John 19:20); spectators would give public witness to the shame of Jesus' death (see Philo, *Spec. Leg.* 3.160). Thus to them he dies a brutal death, apparently a victim whose life was taken from him in violent fashion. His blood is spilled, without hope of vengeance or satisfaction. This is what outsiders see and count as shameful.

The narrator, however, instructs insiders to perceive this scene in terms of honor. First, Jesus does the honorable thing by his mother. She is presumably a widow, and now her only son is dying. In that culture, she has no male (husband or son) to defend her; she will suffer a tragic loss of honor with this death. But Jesus defends her honor by adopting as 'brother' the Beloved Disciple, and by ensuring that his new kinsman will defend his mother's honor by 'taking her into his own house' (19:27; see Acts 1:14).

Shame lies both in being a victim and more especially in the exercise of power by another over one's life. That may be what the eye sees in Jesus' death, but not what the ear hears in the narrative. Jesus is honorably presented as the figure in control of events. He *knows* that all is now completed (v. 28) and he *chooses* to die, 'It is finished' (v. 30). Because the narrative has prepared us for this scene, we are not reading these honorable ideas into the text. Back in the exposition of the role of the Noble Shepherd in John 10, Jesus explicitly described the honorable character of his death. First, he knows it, and so manifests control over his life: 'I lay down my life' (10:17); 'I lay it down of my own accord' (10:18). Second, he is no victim; no one shames him by taking his life: 'No one takes it from me' (10:18); no one shames him by having power over him: 'I have power to lay it down and I have power to take it again' (10:18b). Just as he manifested control and power at his arrest, so he is presented here as doing the same thing. Honor is thus maintained.

Finally, his body was mutilated, a shameful act (recall the treatment of Hector's body by Achilles; see 1 Sam 31:9–10; 2 Sam 4:12; Josephus *Ant.* 20.99). The soldiers intended to break his legs and thus hasten death. Yet Jesus is spared this humiliation because he had already died. Moreover, the text puts an honorable interpretation on this by comparing Jesus' body to the paschal lamb, none of whose bones were broken (Exod 12:46; John 19:36). He dies, then, 'unblemished.' Nevertheless his chest is pierced, the wanton mutilation of a corpse. Yet as Josephine Ford has shown, the piercing of Jesus' side yields both blood and water, which in rabbinic lore constitutes a kosher object (1969, 337–38). And so the narrator rescues Jesus' honor by indicating that this mutilation was controlled by God's prophecy through Zech 12:10.

4.6. *Jesus' burial (19:38–42)*

Under other circumstances, the bodies of the crucified might be left to rot on the cross and become food for scavengers (see Rev 19:17–18). This final shame precluded reverential burial by kin, both a mark of honor and a religious duty. Yet in our narrative, purity concerns demand some rapid disposal of the corpses; and so the body of Jesus is buried.

This gospel narrates that Jesus' body received quite an honorable burial, despite the shame of his death. Joseph and Nicodemus bring a prodigious quantity of spices, 'a mixture of myrrh and aloes, about a hundred pounds,' enough spices for a royal burial (see 2 Chron 16:14 and Josephus, *Ant.* 17.199). They perform the honorable burial ritual, 'binding the body in linen cloths with the spices, as is the burial custom of the Jews' (19:40). A new tomb is at hand, wherein they honorably lay Jesus. Despite the shame of crucifixion, some honor is maintained by this burial.

5. Summary and conclusions

As we learn more about the pivotal values of honor and shame in their cultural setting, we come to appreciate how the narrative of Jesus' passion is perceived and articulated in this perspective. Honor and shame are not foreign categories imposed by an alien culture, but values rooted in the very cultural world of Jesus and his disciples, whether Roman, Greek, or Judean. We have observed what these ancient people value, how they strive either to gain or maintain their reputation, and how honor is replicated in the presentation and treatment of the physical body. When we appreciate the typical form of a challenge / riposte encounter, we gain greater clarity into the common social dynamics of the male world of the first century in all its agonistic flavor. It is always tempting for modern readers to psychologize biblical characters, often imposing on them modern notions of the self or motivations and strategies typical of the modern world. Appreciation of the ancient psychology of honor and shame offers more authentic cultural and historical reading of those social dynamics.

Our understanding, moreover, of the cultural dynamics of honor and shame is a necessary and welcome addition to the standard tools of historical criticism. Our use of them greatly aids in the fundamental task of interpreting documents from a culture quite different from our own. And our appreciation of these cultural phenomena can only aid in our sympathetic understanding of other biblical and ancient documents, which share the same cultural values.

As a result of this study, readers of biblical documents should be able to apply the understanding of honor and shame to other texts. Using honor and shame as a template, readers can then bring to light the social dynamics operative, for example, in most of the public scenes of Jesus and his opponents. Whenever Jesus appears in public, the scene is generally described as a challenge to his claims of honor. The same perspective can profitably be applied to the conflicts between Paul and his opponents. Always honor is at stake, either as claimed or challenged. Thus no study of conflict in the biblical texts would be complete without its assessment in terms of the cultural dynamics of honor and shame.

FURTHER READING

Classic works by anthropologists on the theme of honour and shame include Peristiany 1965; Pitt-Rivers 1977. For more recent discussion see Herzfeld 1980; Gilmore 1987; Peristiany and Pitt-Rivers 1992.

Basic works setting out the approach which underpins the work of the Context Group are Malina 1981; Neyrey 1991a; Rohrbaugh 1996; all of which include chapters on the subject of honour and shame. Moxnes 1996 (in Rohrbaugh 1996) offers a recent overview and concise bibliography. See further *Introduction* §3.

There are now many publications which use the 'honour–shame' model as a perspective from which to interpret New Testament texts. Some recent examples are: Moxnes 1988a; 1988b; Malina and Rohrbaugh 1992; Elliott 1995b; Rohrbaugh 1995. The whole issue of *Semeia* in which Neyrey's essay first appeared is devoted to essays exploring the theme of 'Honor and Shame in the World of the Bible' (vol. 68, 1994). Also in that issue are responses by two anthropologists (Chance 1994; Kressel 1994); that by Chance is particularly useful. For further critical responses see *Introduction* §3; §6.2.

6

Christian Missions and the Theory of Cognitive Dissonance

JOHN G. GAGER

INTRODUCTION

Among the most creative and stimulating early studies applying social-scientific perspectives to early Christianity was John Gager's book *Kingdom and Community*. In this work Gager sketches various aspects of 'The Social World of Early Christianity' (the subtitle of the book). He begins by outlining the inadequacies of existing methods in biblical study, where theological assumptions often shape historical enquiry, and suggests that the incorporation of insights from the social sciences into the study of early Christianity offers a new 'paradigm' for the subject. Gager then proceeds to consider early Christianity as a 'millenarian movement', to analyse its patterns of leadership and authority from a Weberian perspective, to assess the social status of the early Christians in the context of the social structure of the Roman empire, and to consider reasons for Christianity's ultimate success within that empire. The extract below, in which Gager employs the theory of cognitive dissonance to understand the enthusiastic evangelistic activity of the early Christians, forms one of the most controversial and debated sections of the book. In essence the theory explains this zealous evangelism as a response to the disconfirmation of early Christian beliefs, specifically the non-appearance of the promised kingdom (see below). The 'dissonance' between reality and conviction was resolved through enthusiastic proselytisation. Gager suggests that the theory may also shed light on the post-conversion behaviour of some early Christians, notably Paul (see further Gager 1981; Segal 1990; Taylor 1992, 63–74; 1997a; 1997b).

Gager is careful not to import the theory, which was developed from the observation of certain religious groups in North America, uncritically or wholesale. Rather, he suggests certain modifications and additions which arise from the study of early Christianity (pp. 190–92 below). Nevertheless, his approach has attracted some criticism. Cyril Rodd (1981), criticising the use of cognitive dissonance theory by both Gager and Robert Carroll (1979), argues that the nature of the biblical evidence and the cultural differences between 'then' and 'now' render the application of such modern sociological models inappropriate. Bruce Malina (1986b) argues that most peoples, including the ancient Mediterraneans, live constantly with a range of beliefs and attitudes which are to some degree 'dissonant' – what he terms 'normative dissonance'. The notion of dissonance cannot therefore explain the rise of Christian missions. John Elliott too suggests that the theory is anachronistic for the New Testament period, deriving from 'modern social experience with no ancient counterpart' (Elliott 1993, 97; note also the criticisms in Maier 1991, 9–10). Others, however, notably Nicholas Taylor, have defended the usefulness of cognitive dissonance theory 'as an heuristic paradigm if not as a prescriptive model for the study of early Christianity' (Taylor 1998, 150).

What is indisputable, it seems to me, is that Gager's work offers an interesting and provocative new perspective from which to view the persistence and growth of early Christianity. Instead of explaining the phenomenon theologically, with reference to the early Christians' convictions about the gospel, the theory of cognitive dissonance explains their activity by appealing to features of human behaviour that have been observed in other contexts too, and for which there are psychological and sociological explanations. But do these features of human psychology and society characterise the ancient Mediterranean context, and is the available evidence sufficient to make such deductions? Does the New Testament evidence support the idea of a specifically disconfirmed belief causing dissonance in the way the theory suggests? These and other questions certainly need to be considered, but in view of Gager's arguments against the frequent though generally implicit influence of theological commitments upon the answers to historical questions (1975, 4–9), it is equally important to ask: If this theory is rejected, is it because it does not fit the evidence or is itself implausible, or because it is felt to be theologically unacceptable (cf. Scroggs 1980, 174)?

※

Despite uncertainty about numerous aspects of primitive Christianity, the sources are unanimous in reporting certain basic traits. Among these is an enthusiastic dedication to missionary activity.[1] There was, to be sure, a protracted and often bitter debate about whether the mission should focus exclusively on Jews ('Go nowhere among the Gentiles, and enter no town of the Samaritans, but go rather to the lost sheep of the house of Israel' – Matt 10:5f; cf. also the story of the Syrophoenician woman in Matt 15:21–28) or should include Gentiles as well ('Go therefore and make disciples of all nations . . .' – Matt 28:19!). Even among those who advocated a universal calling, there was disagreement about the conditions under which Gentiles could embrace the faith. Should they assume the full burden of the Mosaic Law ('But some believers who belonged to the party of the Pharisees rose up, and said, "It is necessary to circumcise them, and to charge them to keep the law of Moses."' – Acts 15:5) or just a partial burden (Acts 15:19f)? Still others, like Paul, maintained that allegiance to the Christ meant freedom from the Law altogether (Galatians, *passim*). But transcending these disagreements was a consensus that a primary obligation of the community as a whole was to proclaim the gospel of Christ in the world. More than any other cult in the Roman Empire, Christianity was a missionary faith and, of course, owed its ultimate status in the empire to the success of its mission.

The fact of Christian mission is plain enough, but the underlying issue of what motivated it is far from clear. Indeed, the issue has seldom even been raised. In his classic work on *The Mission and Expansion of Christianity in the First Three Centuries*, Adolf Harnack deals systematically with every issue *except* that of motivation. Almost in passing, he remarks that the churches inherited their missionary zeal from Judaism.[2] Just a few pages later he strikes a somewhat different note in suggesting that missions arose as a response to the death of Jesus

---

[1] In addition to the works of Harnack, Hahn, and Cullmann, noted below, see also Jeremias 1958; Georgi 1964, esp. 83–281; and Green 1970.

[2] Harnack 1908, vol. I, 9, see also, pp. 15–16. The missionary character of Judaism is also emphasized by Georgi (1964, 83–187), although both Harnack and Georgi recognize the differences between Jewish and Christian missions. I am rather inclined to agree with the observation of A. D. Nock that 'we should be cautious in inferring widespread efforts by Jews to convert Gentiles. Individual Jews did undoubtedly try to "draw men to the Law", but in the main the proselyte was the man who came to the Law, and the duty of the Jew was to commend the Law by his example (see Deut 4:6) rather than by missionary endeavor' (Nock 1961, 582).

and as an expression of their hope in the coming of the kingdom in the near future (Harnack 1908, vol. I, 44). But why, one is tempted to ask, should the death of Jesus and the expectation of the kingdom have led to mission? More recent studies have also taken up the matter of motivation but have succeeded merely in proliferating the number of explanations: words of Jesus, a sense of responsibility for the un-evangelized world, the experience of Jesus' resurrection, etc. Of these perhaps the most common explanation is that the enthusiastic antici-pation of the End was the fundamental motivation for early Christian missions. F. Hahn locates the initial impetus in Jesus' own command to proclaim the message of the kingdom (Mark 6:7–13; Luke 9:1–6, etc.), and adds that the events of Jesus' death and resurrection 'awoke in the whole of the primitive Church a white-hot expectation of its [the kingdom's] imminence, and now [it] had to be made known afresh to men' (Hahn 1965, 51). Similarly, O. Cullmann has argued that early Christian eschatology, rather than paralyzing the communities, turned them outward toward the world (Cullmann 1956). In particular, he points to Mark 13:10 ('And the gospel must first be preached to all nations') as evidence for the connection between mission and eschatology (Cullmann 1956, 415).

Undeniably the missionary zeal of the early churches was related to their eschatological consciousness. But this statement alone hardly settles the matter, for it still leaves the basic questions unanswered. Why, for instance, did the churches ignore those sayings in the Gospels that limited the mission to Israel? Why did they attach such importance precisely to missionary commands? Or, to put the matter somewhat differently, why did the communities that eventually produced the Gospels choose to represent and emphasize Jesus' role as initiator of missions? What precisely is the connection between missionary action and eschatological awareness? Why did missions persist long after most Christians had ceased regarding the kingdom as imminent? Why is it that certain Jewish communities in this period (e.g. the Essenes at Qumran), who also understood themselves to be living in the last days, did not undertake vigorous missions? Or, on a more general level, why is it that in the case of early Christianity expectation of the End did not lead, as often happens, to an isolationist or quietist stance toward the outside world? In short, explanations that appeal to eschatology as the basic motivation for missions are not really causal explanations at all. They simply note that the early communities were both eschatological and missionary and then proceed to assume that the one must have caused the other. *Post hoc ergo propter hoc* ['After this therefore on account of this' – Ed.].

Rather than abandon the connection between eschatology and missions, I would contend that the precise nature of their connection can be understood by appealing to the theory of cognitive dissonance, as developed by L. Festinger and others. As presented in *When Prophecy Fails. A Social and Psychological Study of a Modern Group That Predicted the Destruction of the World*,[3] the theory states that under certain conditions a religious community whose fundamental beliefs are disconfirmed by events in the world will not necessarily collapse and disband. Instead it may undertake zealous missionary activity as a response to its sense of cognitive dissonance, i.e. a condition of distress and doubt stemming from the disconfirmation of an important belief. The critical element of the theory is that 'the presence of dissonance gives rise to pressures to reduce, or eliminate the dissonance. The strength of the pressures to reduce the dissonance is a function of the magnitude of the dissonance' (Festinger 1957, 18). Among the various techniques for reducing dissonance, Festinger *et al.* argue that proselytism is one of the most common and effective. Rationalization, i.e. revisions of the original belief or of views about the disconfirming event, will also operate, but proselytism almost always occurs. The assumption, often unconscious, is that '*if more and more people can be persuaded that the system of belief is correct, then clearly it must, after all, be correct*' (Festinger *et al.* 1956, 28, emphasis original). Thus, the authors argue, we find the apparent paradox that an increase in proselytizing normally follows disconfirmation.

To support and illustrate the theory of cognitive dissonance, the authors devote the bulk of *When Prophecy Fails* to a group (Lake City) in the 1950s that had predicted the destruction of the world on a given December 21 and that had made extensive preparations for the occasion. The most striking feature of the group is that when December 21 had come and gone, i.e. when the central belief of the group had been unequivocally disconfirmed, the members responded not by disbanding but by intensifying their previous low level of proselytizing. Eventually the group broke up as the result of a number of factors (legal action and ineffective proselytism), but its initial response to disconfirmation aptly

---

[3] Jointly authored by L. Festinger, H. W. Riecken, and S. Schachter (1956). See also Festinger's further elaboration of the theory in Festinger (1957).

substantiates the basic theory. Other examples illustrate the same sequence: the Millerite movement in the North-eastern United States of the 1840s; the messianic fervor surrounding Sabbatai Zevi in the Near East between 1640 and 1670; and finally the origins of Christianity. Although the authors regard early Christianity as the best historical illustration, they finally conclude that it cannot, because of uncertainty on one or two issues, serve by itself to validate the theory. But once the theory has been established through other, more controlled movements, should we not re-examine its relevance as a tool for investigating the source of missionary activities in earliest Christianity?

At the outset, *When Prophecy Fails* stipulates five conditions that must be present before one can expect disconfirmation to produce increased proselytism (Festinger *et al.* 1956, 4):

1. A belief must be held with deep conviction and it must have some relevance to action, that is, to what the believer does or how he behaves.

2. The person holding the belief must have committed himself to it; that is, for the sake of his belief, he must have taken some important action that is difficult to undo. In general, the more important such actions are, and the more difficult they are to undo, the greater is the individual's commitment to the belief.

3. The belief must be sufficiently specific and sufficiently concerned with the real world so that events may unequivocally refute the belief.

4. Such undeniable disconfirmatory evidence must occur and must be recognized by the individual holding the belief. . . .

5. The believer must have social support. . . . If [however] the believer is a member of a group of convinced persons who can support one another, we would expect the belief to be maintained and the believers to attempt to proselytize or to persuade nonmembers that the belief is correct.

There is little need to argue that early Christianity meets the first, second, and fifth conditions. The conviction with which early Christians held to their beliefs was greeted by many pagans with a mixture of admiration (for their remarkable tenacity) and contempt (for the unworthiness of the beliefs themselves; see Dodds 1965, 120–21). The decision to embrace the faith in the first decades often entailed the irrevocable loss of family, friends, and social status. And it is clear that missionary activities flourished primarily after the death of Jesus. Questions do arise, however, concerning the third and fourth conditions. Can we locate important beliefs that were specific enough to be disconfirmed by events in the world, and is there any evidence that believers regarded such events as having occurred? To answer these questions I propose to consider two critical moments in the early history of the movement, in fact the same two moments mentioned earlier by Harnack – the death of Jesus and the expectation of the kingdom.[4]

The event of Jesus' death

On the matter of Jesus' death, we must be able to demonstrate that it was regarded by his followers as in some sense disconfirming beliefs and hopes that they had attached to him during his lifetime. And as a subsidiary issue, our case will be strengthened if there are also indications that his death continued to disconfirm belief for a period of time thereafter.

There is no doubt that the crucifixion of Jesus constituted a major obstacle to the conversion of many Jews. Paul says as much in 1 Cor 1:23 ('but we preach Christ crucified, a stumbling block to Jews and folly to Gentiles'), and his assertion is supported by an examination of Jewish messianic expectations prior to the time of Jesus. There are no signs that any group of Jews awaited a suffering Messiah, let alone one who would be crucified by Rome (see Cullmann 1959, 60). In other words, insofar as the followers of Jesus shared the messianic views of their time, they were unprepared for the death of the one whom they believed to be the fulfillment of their messianic dreams. But a problem arises precisely at this point: how far did Jesus' followers adhere to traditional messianic formulations? Jesus himself is portrayed in the Gospels as predicting his future suffering and death (Matt 16:21 – 'From that time on Jesus began to show his disciples that he must go to Jerusalem and suffer many things from the elders and chief priests and scribes, and be killed, and on the third day be raised').[5] 'If this view is maintained,' comment the authors of *When Prophecy Fails*, 'then the crucifixion, far from being a disconfirmation, was indeed a confirmation of a prediction

---

[4] It should be noted that *When Prophecy Fails* deals only with Jesus' death and that it ignores recent critical literature on the New Testament.

[5] Mark's version (8:31) reads 'And he began to teach them that the Son of man must suffer many things . . .'. Mark's text can be interpreted to mean that Jesus is speaking of a person *other than himself*. In clarifying this ambiguity, by substituting 'he' for 'the Son of man', Matthew no doubt reflects the universal belief of early Christianity that Jesus was and understood himself to be the Son of man.

and the subsequent proselytizing of the apostles would stand as a counterexample to our hypotheses' (Festinger *et al.* 1956, 24). But the difficulties raised by this text are actually less severe than the authors recognize. There are two possible views about the origin of these predictions. Either they were created after the event in order to lend supportive meaning to the otherwise disconfirmatory event of the crucifixion[6] – in which case the text must be, read as *sustaining* the theory – or they originated with Jesus himself. Even in the second case, however, there is firm evidence that the prediction was not accepted or understood by the disciples and that Jesus' death still came as a rude shock to them.

The passages in question (Mark 8:27–33; 9:30–32; 10:33–34), when read as a whole, tend to support rather than contradict the theory of dissonance. The first section (Mark 8:27–29) culminates in Peter's confession, 'You are the Christ [i.e. the Messiah],' in which Peter clearly represents the universal belief of early Christians. The confession is then followed by Jesus' command to remain silent about this (8:30) and by his teaching that he (Matt 16:21), or the Son of man (Mark 8:31), must suffer and die. To this Peter responds with dismay, presumably at the prediction of suffering and death – Matt 16:22 makes this explicit: 'God forbid, Lord! This shall never happen to you' – thus expressing his inability to comprehend or accept the notion of a suffering Messiah. And finally, Jesus turns on Peter angrily, calling him Satan and questioning even his loyalty to God, again presumably for his failure to understand the need for suffering and death. Here again, Peter must be seen as representing more than his own personal views. To summarize: Whether or not this scene actually occurred in Jesus' lifetime, it conveys the clear sense that the death of Jesus was a problem for his followers from the beginning and that its problematic character persisted thereafter, no doubt reinforced by Jews who maintained that a crucified Messiah was a contradiction in terms.

The relevance of this passage for the theory of dissonance is twofold. In the first place, it obviously springs from a sense of doubt and distress about Jesus' death, and in the second place, it represents the process of rationalization that, according to Festinger *et al.*, normally accompanies proselytism. And on this particular issue, it is still possible to trace the

---

[6] This is the view of most contemporary critics; see, for example, Conzelmann 1969a: 'These [sayings about the suffering Son of man] are all *vaticinia ex eventu*: not prognoses for the further development of the situation, but dogmatic assertions' (p. 133).

process of rationalization whereby the early church sought to persuade others and itself that Jesus' death was both necessary and beneficial. The Gospel of Luke records a rather striking conversation between two disciples and the resurrected Jesus, whom the disciples do not recognize: 'But we had hoped that he was the one to redeem Israel. Yes, and besides all this, it is now the third day since this [the crucifixion] happened' (Luke 24:21). To this expression of disappointment, Jesus replies, 'O foolish men, and slow of heart to believe all that the prophets have spoken! Was it not necessary that the Christ should suffer these things and enter into his glory?' (Luke 24:25). In what we may call the first stage, we find the risen Jesus himself claiming that his death was both necessary and in accordance with the Scriptures as properly, i.e. in a Christian context, interpreted. Much the same view is expressed by Paul when he affirms that 'Christ died for our sins in accordance with the scriptures . . . that he was raised on the third day in accordance with the scriptures . . .' (1 Cor 15:3f). Although neither Luke nor Paul cites a specific passage from Scripture, both reflect a situation in which an effort has been made to turn the disconfirmatory evidence of Scripture (traditional interpretations had not produced the idea of a suffering Messiah) into supporting evidence (correct interpretation showed that such was precisely what had been intended from the beginning).[7] A final stage appears in those Gospel passages in which Jesus predicts, before the event and in detail, the necessity of his suffering and death (Mark 8:3, etc.).

It would appear, then, that we are justified in maintaining that the death of Jesus created a sense of cognitive dissonance, in that it seemed to disconfirm the belief that Jesus was the Messiah. Even the event of the resurrection, which the Gospels present as having surprised the disciples every bit as much as the death, seems not to have eradicated these doubts. Thus according to the theory, we may understand the zeal with which Jesus' followers pursued their mission as part of an effort to reduce dissonance, not just in the early years but for a considerable time thereafter. Initially, it might seem reasonable to suppose that Jesus' death was most problematic for converts from Judaism, but there is good reason to believe Paul when he reports that the crucified Christ was 'a stumbling block to Jews and folly to Gentiles' (1 Cor 1:23). Long after

---

[7] For a thorough discussion of the manner in which Christians used the Old Testament to support their views, see Lindars 1961.

Paul's time, Lucian (*Death of Peregrinus* 13) and Celsus (Origen, *Against Celsus* 2.39f) continued to mock Christians for their faith in a crucified Savior, whereas Justin Martyr raises the question, surely not a rhetorical one, 'Why should we believe that a crucified man is the firstborn of the unbegotten god . . . ?' (*First Apology* 53:2).

The non-event of the kingdom

We may now return to the issue raised at the start of our discussion, that is, the connection between mission and eschatology. Specifically, can we now envisage the continuing mission as deriving, at least in part, from disappointment and despair over the delay of the kingdom? In different terms, were the eschatological hopes of early Christians 'sufficiently specific and concerned with the real world so that unequivocal disproof or disconfirmation is possible,' and are there intimations that believers sensed such disconfirmation 'in the form of the nonoccurrence of a predicted event within the time limits set for its occurrence'? (Festinger 1957, 248).

Recent scholarship has given affirmative answers to both questions.[8] The earliest Christian communities stood in the mainstream of Jewish apocalyptic thinking. With but one possible exception (the Gospel of John), the earliest ascertainable traditions, i.e. the Gospel sources and the letters of Paul, present a unified picture. The kingdom would happen in the near future; and it would happen as an event in history, indeed as the final event of history in its present mode. The resurrection, the act of divine judgment, and the transformation of the physical and political orders – all were understood to be specific and unmistakable events in the real world. In this respect, Paul's description of the eschatological drama in 1 Thess 4:16f ('For the Lord himself will descend from heaven with a cry of command, with the archangel's call, and with the sound of the trumpet of God . . .') may be taken as typical expressions of widely shared beliefs. Whether or not Jesus himself first announced the imminent arrival of the kingdom has been a much debated matter. I am inclined to the view that Jesus shared and thus prompted the belief that the kingdom was imminent,[9] but I am even more certain that our picture of primitive Christian eschatology does not hinge on an answer to the

---

[8] See Perrin 1967, for a discussion of the central issues and a survey of recent literature.
[9] For the contrary view that Jesus' sayings about the kingdom were intensified eschatologically by his followers after his death see Stauffer 1956.

question of Jesus' predictions about his death. As with these predictions, the texts that portray the kingdom as an event in the near future (Mark 1:15; 14:25; 11:12–14, etc.) can have only two possible sources – Jesus or the earliest Christians. Thus even if it should prove methodologically impossible to assign them with certitude to Jesus, the only alternative is the early community.[10] And from that point on, they were transmitted and received *as words of Jesus*. In either case, the structure of the problem remains unchanged: a specific and important prediction that is liable to disconfirmation.

In the final analysis, however, the surest testimony on this issue is expression of concern about the delay of the kingdom in Christian texts themselves. In 1 Clement 23:3–5 (written around 96 CE), the author speaks openly of such concern:[11]

> Let that Scripture be far from us which says: 'Wretched are the double-minded, those who doubt in their soul and say, "We have heard these things even in our fathers' times, and see, we have grown old and none of this has happened."' (translation from Richardson 1953, 55)

2 Peter 3:3–9 (probably written around 125 CE) reflects a similar situation:

> First of all you must understand this, that scoffers will come in the last days . . . saying, 'Where is the promise of his coming? For ever since the fathers fell asleep, all things have continued as they were from the beginning of creation.' . . . But do not ignore this one fact, beloved, that with the Lord one day is as a thousand years, and a thousand years as one day. The Lord is not slow about his promise as some count slowness. . . .

Both passages reveal that the traditional chronology of the kingdom was under attack, whether by outsiders (i.e. Jewish antagonists) or by Christian revisionists (e.g. Hymenaeus and Philetus who are anathematized by the author of 2 Tim 2:18 for 'holding that the resurrection

---

[10] In the second edition of his important work on responses to the delay of the kingdom (Grässer 1960, 220–26), E. Grässer responds to his critics' charge that his false premise (Jesus expected the kingdom immediately) leads inevitably to false conclusions (the delay created difficulties because Jesus' words were disconfirmed). By insisting on his interpretation of Jesus, however, he fails to see that the results of his study would remain valid for Christian believers even if his reconstruction of Jesus cannot be sustained.

[11] Compare also 2 Clement 11:2 (usually dated between 100 and 150 CE), which cites the same (unidentified) passage from Scripture ('Wretched are the double-minded . . .'), but concludes on a different note: 'If we have done what is right before God's eyes, we shall enter his kingdom. . . .'.

is past already'). Paul, too, confronts the issue in 1 Thess 4:13–5:11, where the concern appears to have arisen quite apart from any outside instigation:

> But we would not have you ignorant, brethren, concerning those who are asleep [i.e. have died], that you may not grieve as others do who have no hope. . . . For this we declare to you by the word of the Lord, that we who are alive, who are left until the coming of the Lord, shall not precede those who have fallen asleep. . . .

This passage is especially revealing because it points to the specific occasion for the concern, namely, the death of some believers. In other words, the kingdom had been expected before any believers, or at least the first generation, would die, and Paul is forced to remind his readers that the coming event of the resurrection was the positive assurance that those who had died would not miss 'the coming of the Lord.' Finally, of the many passages in the synoptic Gospels, one will serve to complete our survey.[12] The prediction in Matt 10:23 ('Truly, I say to you, you will not have gone through all the towns of Israel, before the Son of man comes.') has been variously interpreted as an authentic saying of Jesus and thus a primary *source* of later concern about the delay, or as a product of the early tradition, a word of consolation spoken in the name of Jesus, and thus a *response* to the delay.[13] Both, of course, are possible. But once again either view leads to the same consequences, for the saying entered the tradition *as a word of Jesus* at an early stage. As those who had known Jesus began to die, this saying and others like it (esp. Mark 9:1 – '. . . There are some standing here who will not taste death before

---

[12] Grässer (1960) notes four types of material in the synoptics that reflect concern about the delay: first, expressions of uncertainty about precise chronology (Mark 13:32); second, commands and parables urging constant alertness in view of this uncertainty (Mark 13:33; Luke 12:25, 36–38); third, prayers and petitions that the kingdom come (Matt 6:9–15; cf. Rev 22:17; 1 Cor 16:22); and fourth, direct expressions of concern (Matt 24:45–51; 25:14–30; Luke 20:9). In addition, he details a series of texts that represent more far-reaching attempts to resolve the concern: statements of outright consolation (Luke 18:7–8; Mark 9:1; 13:30; Matt 10:23); the so-called parables of contrast (e.g., Mark 4:30–32); and finally, actual changes in the timetable (Mark 13:10).

[13] This verse is the key to Albert Schweitzer's interpretation of Jesus' ministry. In *The Quest of the Historical Jesus* he argues that Jesus was distressed when his words remained unfulfilled and thus he turned toward Jerusalem in an effort to force God's hand (1959, 358–60). Thus Jesus himself becomes the first to express concern about the delay of the kingdom. Schweitzer's views were later taken up and expanded by Werner 1957. Werner argues that the delay was the single most important force in shaping the development of Christian doctrine.

they see the kingdom of God come with power.') become a source for concern rather than an attempt to assuage it. In fact, it seems quite likely that the anxiety reflected in later texts (e.g., 2 Peter and 1 Clement), arose from the fact that specific prophecies like that of Mark 9:1 had been unequivocally disconfirmed. Thus we should probably conceive of the response to the delay in at least two stages: an initial disappointment among the earliest believers who had expected the end in the immediate future, a disappointment that evoked consolation in the form of sayings like Mark 9:1; and a subsequent disappointment among those who had expected the end within the first generation of the faithful, a disappointment that produced consolatory sayings (e.g. Mark 13:10 – 'And the gospel must first be preached to all nations') as well as more systematic efforts to de-eschatologize the Christian message.[14] The success of these efforts may be seen in the fact that by the year 150 CE not only was Christianity no longer an eschatological community, but, as the reaction to the apocalyptic fervor of Montanism clearly reveals, that it had come to regard eschatological movements as a serious threat. Toward the end of the first century Christians could still pray, 'Thy kingdom come' (Matt 6:10). But at the end of the second century, Tertullian tells us that Christians prayed 'for the emperors, for their deputies and all in authority, for the welfare of the world, *and for the delay of the final consummation*' (*Apol.* 39.2; cf. 32.1)!

At this point it is obvious that Festinger and his colleagues' discreet glance at early Christianity is far more significant than they have recognized.[15] We may now formulate their position as follows: Rationalization in connection with important beliefs, specifically the death of Jesus and the delay of the kingdom, represents an effort to reduce doubt and despair and thus is evidence of cognitive dissonance. When, in addition, missionary activity is regularly associated with the same beliefs, it can and must be interpreted as a further attempt to reduce dissonance. In contrast to O. Cullmann, who rejects the notion that mission was 'something which has been substituted for the unrealized hope of the kingdom' and who insists that 'if this were true, then the Church has carried on its mission because it has been obliged to renounce eschatology' (Cullmann 1956, 409), it now becomes possible to reverse Cullmann's

---

[14] One outstanding example is the Gospel of Luke; see Conzelmann 1960, 95–136.
[15] See the comment of P. Berger 1969, 195, n. 30: 'The similarity of the phenomena analysed in the case study [*When Prophecy Fails*] with what New Testament scholars have called *Parousieverzögerung* is astonishing and highly instructive.'

terms and to conclude that the church initially carried on its mission *in an effort to maintain* its eschatology. The strength of this factor in relation to other motivating forces is beyond final determination. Here we must rest content with the general principle that as other factors, such as commands of Jesus or influence from Judaism, are minimized, the factor of cognitive dissonance must be maximized.

One final question: Does our discussion suggest the need for any modification in the theory itself? Festinger *et al.* set out from the observation that disconfirmation of important beliefs produces a sense of disappointment, ranging from doubt to despair, as well as pressures to reduce this disappointment. One method for reducing it is to give up the belief; but in other circumstances, as they say, 'it may even be less painful to tolerate the dissonance than to discard the belief' (Festinger *et al.* 1956, 27). In other words, individuals find it easier to maintain a disconfirmed belief when there is group reinforcement. Thus 'the other circumstances' must include loyalty to the group itself, so that it becomes less painful to maintain a disconfirmed belief than to abandon one's loyalty to the group. The authors point in this direction when they admit that 'there is a limit beyond which belief will not stand disconfirmation' (Festinger *et al.* 1956, 23). Our examination of early Christianity suggests that this outer limit is not absolute but is rather a function of (1) the extent to which individual members have transferred former loyalties and identities (family, friends, religion, profession) to the new group; and (2) the extent to which the group itself succeeds in retaining and sustaining these new loyalties.

This last point is of particular importance because it has been questioned in a follow-up study to *When Prophecy Fails*, entitled 'Prophecy Fails Again: A Report of a Failure to Replicate.'[16] The authors examined a Pentecostal community (True Word) that appeared to meet the five conditions. But the group did not turn to proselytism following its prediction of nuclear destruction on a given date. This result led the authors to propose two revisions in the theory itself: first, 'that the more social support an individual receives above the minimum he needs to maintain his belief, the less he will have to proselytize' (Hardyck and

---

[16] Hardyck and Braden 1962. For a more general critique of dissonance theory see Brown 1965, 601–608. It should be noted that on one particular issue, our analysis has endeavored to meet Brown's criticism. He notes that investigators have rarely made an effort, at the beginning of their studies, to determine whether a specific combination of ideas, beliefs, or actions is in fact dissonant for their subjects (p. 597). Throughout this section I have argued that the texts reveal just this awareness of dissonance.

Braden 1962, 139) and, second, 'that if a group is receiving considerable ridicule from nonmembers, one way of reducing dissonance that would be apparent to them would be to convince these "unbelievers" that the group is right' (Hardyck and Braden 1962, 140). The second proposal obviously reinforces our own analysis of early Christianity and requires no further analysis. As for the first proposal it would appear that either the theory itself needs modification or that the type of social support was different in the two cases (Lake City and True Word). There is, in fact, one significant and perhaps decisive difference between early Christian communities and the Lake City group on the one hand and the True Word group on the other. Hardyck and Braden note that 'many members of the True Word group had worked together for several years' (Hardyck and Braden 1962, 140) and that their prophet, Mrs. Shepard, had been proclaiming her prophecy for nearly four years before the final deadline was set (Hardyck and Braden 1962, 136). In other words, the fact that the identity of individuals with the group as well as their breaking of old loyalties had long been established suggests that the prophecy was less important to the members than the existence of the group itself. For the earliest Christians, however, as well as for the Lake City group, the prophet and the message were recent, the movement was new, and between them prophet and prophecy were the basic occasion for the coalescence of the groups. This situation, in which the creation of the group and the subsequently disconfirmed belief are inseparable, seems a likely explanation for the presence of proselytism in the one case and its absence in the other.

Thus we may summarize the proposed modifications in the theory of dissonance as follows:

1. Proselytism as a means of reducing cognitive dissonance will appear primarily in new groups, like early Christianity, whose existence has been occasioned by or associated with a belief that is subsequently disconfirmed.

2. Public ridicule at the time of disconfirmation may play an important role in turning such a group toward missionary activity.

3. The limit beyond which belief will not withstand disconfirmation is a function of the degree to which identification with the group supplants the original belief as the basic motivation for adherence to the group.

To these we may add one further point. Festinger mentions, though he does not emphasize the fact that rationalization always accompanies proselytism in the period following disconfirmation – the timetable was wrong; the event really did occur in some unexpected and imperceptible fashion; the disconfirming event, when properly understood, turns out to be confirmatory after all, etc. Thus the total process of adjustment includes a social (proselytism) as well as an intellectual (rationalization) component. And insofar as rationalization occurs, it will inevitably alter the shape of the original belief, whether by setting a new deadline, by recasting it in more general terms, or by relegating it to a lower rank within the total nexus of the group's beliefs and practices. In other words, what at first appeared to be a paradox in our explanation of early Christianity – that its status as a millenarian movement enables us to understand both its failure, in the sense that all such movements fail, and its success, in the sense that its very failure became the occasion for the intense missionary activity that ensured its ultimate survival – turns out not to be a paradox at all.

Conversion and dissonance[17]

In the preceding discussion I have attempted to reinforce Festinger's proposal that cognitive dissonance associated with the disconfirmation of important beliefs was one among several factors behind missionary activity. Beyond this, there is a quite different area, not considered by Festinger, in which dissonance theory can be related to missions. In *A Theory of Cognitive Dissonance*, Festinger deals with dissonance in relation to the general question of decisions and their consequences (Festinger 1957, 32–83). Briefly, he notes that dissonance is an inevitable consequence of decisions and that the magnitude of dissonance, and thus of pressures to reduce it, depends on two elements – the importance of the decision and the initial attractiveness of the unchosen or rejected alternative. Successful reduction of dissonance, he maintains, will tend to increase confidence in the decision taken and to intensify the attractiveness of the chosen alternative in contrast to the rejected one (Festinger 1957, 83). These are familiar stages in the process of rationalization. What Festinger does not consider is the further possibility that attempts to diminish postdecision dissonance may also, as in the case of disconfirmed beliefs, lead to or reinforce an inclination to proselytism.

---

[17] I am indebted to my colleague, Alan Segal, for calling this further application to my attention.

The relevance of these propositions for the question of conversion is readily apparent. Without pursuing the matter in detail, let me suggest several ways in which efforts to reduce postconversion dissonance may have influenced the experience of early Christians. In the case of Paul, for instance, one is tempted to say that his effort to play down the status and significance of the Mosaic Law (e.g., Gal 3–4) is an attempt to diminish the attractiveness of the rejected alternative. More generally, the recurrent polemic against pagan cults may express the need of pagan converts to reduce dissonance by emphasizing the discrepancy between rejected and chosen alternatives. The intensive commitment which so often characterizes new converts should also be seen in the same light. Finally, proselytism itself, again among recent converts, would serve to reduce dissonance, not only by stressing the incompatibility of the two alternatives but also by assuming, in Festinger's words, that 'if more and more people can be persuaded that the system of belief is correct, then clearly it must, after all, be correct' (Festinger *et al.* 1956, 28).

Two words of caution are in order before completing this brief aside. First, I do not wish to claim that cognitive dissonance is the single explanation for either missionary activity or polemic against Judaism and paganism. Several factors were involved, and dissonance must be counted among them. Second, dissonance theory will apply only in those cases that involve conversion as defined above, i.e., a decision between incompatible and attractive alternatives. *In this sense*, not all early believers would qualify as converts. Paul would, of course, and he behaves accordingly. But for those who did not see Christianity as a choice between incommensurables, e.g., for those 'Jewish Christians' who disagreed violently with Paul as to the status of the Law, one would have to speak of conversion, if at all, in a different manner. The same would be true of 'pagan Christians' who saw in Christianity the fulfillment of Greek wisdom rather than its antithesis. This particular result points forward to the discussion of orthodoxy and heresy. The harsh attitude of emergent orthodoxy toward both 'Jewish Christianity' and syncretistic Gnosticism can thus be viewed as a process of emphasizing the discrepancy between chosen and rejected alternatives. These movements were threatening precisely because they diminished this discrepancy and thereby increased dissonance for those who had made the decision to convert.

FURTHER READING

The works in which the theory of cognitive dissonance is first set out are Festinger, Riecken and Schachter 1956; Festinger 1957. For further developments see Festinger *et al.* 1964; Brehm and Cohen 1962. Some cautions are raised in the work of Hardyck and Braden 1962 and Snow and Machalek 1982. Criticisms are also made by Mills 1983.

Critical reactions to Gager's book as a whole were presented in an issue of the journal *Zygon*: see Bartlett 1978, Smith 1978, Tracy 1978. See also the critical overview in Holmberg 1990, 78–81.

For further applications of the theory in New Testament studies, see the studies of Paul by Gager 1981; Segal 1990; Taylor 1992; 1997a; 1997b. An important work applying the theory to the prophetic traditions of the Hebrew Bible is Carroll 1979. (The same extract as here from Gager's book and an extract from the work of Carroll may be found in Gill 1996.)

The most sustained critique of the use of cognitive dissonance in New Testament studies is Malina 1986b, who draws particularly on the work of Mills 1983. See also Rodd 1981.

In defence of the theory's value as a useful tool in the study of early Christianity, see Taylor 1998.

7

The Social Level of Pauline Christians

WAYNE A. MEEKS

INTRODUCTION

One question of obvious relevance to the social history of early Christianity concerns the social level of the first Christians. Indeed, this has been a matter for discussion since the very earliest times. Not only do New Testament writers occasionally make comments which seem to indicate something about the social composition of the churches (e.g. 1 Cor 1:26–28), but pagan authors too make reference to the kind of people who joined this new movement. Some, like Celsus, writing in the second century (see Meeks' opening paragraph below), criticised Christianity as a religion which attracted only the lowly and uneducated; others, such as Pliny, writing in Asia Minor earlier in the second century, noted that Christians were drawn from 'every age, every estate [*ordo*], and both sexes' (*Ep.* 10.96).

In this essay, a chapter from his wide-ranging investigation into the social world of the Pauline churches, *The First Urban Christians* (1983), Wayne Meeks offers a survey of both direct, prosopographic evidence and indirect evidence concerning the social level of the Pauline Christians. His findings add weight to what he refers to as a 'new consensus' (p. 198) – namely, that the Pauline churches encompassed 'a fair cross-section of urban society' (p. 230). This stands in contrast to an 'old consensus' which generally assumed that the members of the Pauline congregations 'came from the poor and dispossessed of the Roman provinces' (p. 198).

Having argued that status is the most appropriate measure of social level for the early Christians, Meeks notes, following the work of a number of sociologists, that a person's status is a composite of a number of factors; it is 'multidimensional'. If someone's rankings

Reprinted by permission from *The First Urban Christians: The Social World of the Apostle Paul*, by Wayne A. Meeks, London and New Haven: Yale University Press; copyright © 1983 Yale University.

on the various measures of status are broadly consistent, then they may be said to have a high degree of 'status consistency, status congruence, or status crystallization' (p. 202). On the other hand, if there is wide variation among the various factors, a person may be said to experience 'status inconsistency'. Meeks' original proposal, based on the results of his survey of the Pauline Christians, is that a large number of those about whom we have information seem to be, to some extent, 'status inconsistent' and that this may have been a major factor in their being attracted to Christianity. Meeks makes this suggestion tentatively, aware of the limitations in the available evidence, but reiterates it in the closing pages of the book, which have been added to the end of the essay below.

Meeks' proposals about the high number of 'status inconsistents' in the Pauline congregations and the influence of status inconsistency upon conversion have been criticised. Some have noted the lack of sufficient evidence to make such generalised claims, since we only have information about a few named individuals and much of the relevant material relates to the church at Corinth (Schöllgen 1988, 78–80; see also Pleket 1985). Others have wondered about the proportion of 'status inconsistents' in the Roman empire as a whole, and especially in a recently re-founded colony like Corinth: the majority of status inconsistents in a Pauline congregation (even if this conclusion were verifiable) might simply reflect their frequency in the wider social context (Horrell 1996a, 100). Furthermore, while the 'new consensus' which Meeks supports remains at present quite firmly in place, questions have begun to be raised, notably by Justin Meggitt (1996; 1998b). Future debate will be interesting and important.

Meeks' book as a whole has drawn a certain amount of criticism. Some have questioned the soundness of the historical conclusions (Schöllgen 1988; Pleket 1985); others have queried the lack of consistent theoretical foundations (Malina 1985b; Elliott 1985; Stowers 1985). Nevertheless it has generally been welcomed as an impressive and creative achievement which offers considerable insight into the social world of the early Pauline congregations. Gerd Theissen, for example, is forthright in his praise: 'Social history has here reached a high level of maturity. I am deeply impressed' (1985, 113).

'Proletarians' or 'middle class'?

Celsus, the first pagan author we know of who took Christianity seriously enough to write a book against it, alleged that the church deliberately excluded educated people because the religion was attractive only to 'the foolish, dishonourable and stupid, and only slaves, women, and little children' (Origen *C. Cels.* 3.44, trans. Chadwick 1965, 158). The Christian evangelists, he said, were 'wool-workers, cobblers, laundry-workers, and the most illiterate and bucolic yokels,' who enticed 'children . . . and stupid women' to come along 'to the wooldresser's shop, or to the cobbler's or the washerwoman's shop, that they may learn perfection' (*C. Cels.* 3.55, Chadwick 1965, 165–66). Celsus lived in the second century, but he was sure that Christianity had always been a movement of the lowest classes, for Jesus himself had only been able to win disciples among 'tax-collectors and sailors,' people 'who had not even a primary education' (*C. Cels.* 1.62, Chadwick 1965, 56–57). This was the sort of jeer to which the second-century apologists for Christianity had frequently to respond,[1] and modern authors have more often than not assumed that the early critics were right. Did not Luke's Jesus pronounce a woe against the rich (Luke 6:24), James warn against kowtowing to 'the rich who oppress you' (James 2:1–7), and Paul himself writes that God had chosen 'what is foolish in the world . . . what is weak . . . what is low and despised' (1 Cor 1:27)? The notion of early Christianity as a proletarian movement was equally congenial, though for quite different reasons, to Marxist historians and to those bourgeois writers who tended to romanticize poverty.[2]

Of particular importance in shaping this century's common view of Paul and his congregations was the opinion of Adolf Deissmann, professor of the New Testament at Heidelberg, then at Berlin. Deissmann saw that the hundreds of newly discovered documents written on papyrus or ostraca – letters, contracts, school lessons, bills of sale, magical spells – had revolutionary implications for understanding not only the

---

[1] E.g., Minucius Felix, *Octav.* 36.3–7; *Actus Petri c. Simone* 23 (Lipsius-Bonnet 1891, 1:71.24–25); cf. Justin *2 Apol.* 10.8; Tatian *Orat. ad Gr.* 32. As late as the last quarter of the fourth century, Libanius could chide those of his own class who had become Christians with having received their doctrines from 'your mother, your wife, your housekeeper, your cook' (*Or.* 16.47, trans. A. F. Norman in the Loeb ed.). But contrast Tertullian, *Apol.* 1.7, cf. *Apol.* 37.4; *Ad Scap.* 5.2. Tertullian's claims recall what Pliny had written to Trajan even earlier: 'many of every age, of every estate [*ordo*], of both sexes' (*Ep.* 10.96.9). See also Vogt 1975.

[2] See the brief but vivid sketch by Kreissig 1967, 93–96.

SOCIAL-SCIENTIFIC APPROACHES TO NEW TESTAMENT INTERPRETATION

vocabulary and grammar but also the social setting of the New Testament. He had a genius for popularizing the results of his own and others' research, and two extended trips through the Middle East enabled him to reconstruct 'the world of St. Paul' in terms of a vivid, thoroughly romantic travelogue (Deissmann 1911, esp. 27–52). In general his identification of the language of the New Testament with the vulgar *koinē* of the nonliterary papyri supported the view that the writers had belonged to the lower classes, but Deissmann had some difficulty in situating Paul himself. His occupation would have placed him among the lowest of the free poor, like the weaver whom Deissmann had watched in Tarsus in 1909, 'making a coarse cloth on his poverty-stricken primitive loom,' yet 'the very fact that he was born a Roman citizen shows that his family cannot have lived in absolutely humble circumstances' (1911, 49, 50). Paul wrote unliterary Greek, yet 'not vulgar to the degree that finds expression in many contemporary papyri. On the ground of his language rather Paul should be assigned to a higher class' (1911, 50). Still, Deissmann was confident that Paul's closest ties were to the 'middle and lower classes . . . As a missionary chiefly working amongst the unliterary masses of the great cities Paul did not patronizingly descend into a world strange to him: he remained in his own social world' (1911, 51). Until recently most scholars who troubled to ask Deissmann's question at all ignored the ambiguities of the evidence that Deissmann had at least mentioned. The prevailing viewpoint has been that the constituency of early Christianity, the Pauline congregations included, came from the poor and dispossessed of the Roman provinces.

Within the past two decades, however, a number of scholars have looked at the evidence afresh and come to conclusions very different from Deissmann's about the social level of the first-century Christians. The convergence of these inquiries, which have been undertaken from diverse viewpoints, has led Abraham Malherbe to suggest that 'a new consensus may be emerging' which would approve Floyd Filson's dictum of more than forty years ago, 'The apostolic church was more nearly a cross section of society than we have sometimes thought.'[3] The role of

[3] Malherbe 1977a, 31. Filson 1939, quotation from p. 111. Compare Eck 1971, 381: 'If one takes account of the whole body of sources relevant to this set of questions, and avoids arbitrary generalizations from a few of them, the inference is unavoidable that the adherents to the Christian religion present a virtually exact mirror-image of the general social stratification in the Roman empire. And that was so from the beginnings depicted in the NT documents.'

the upper classes is particularly emphasized by E. A. Judge, who points to the pervasive but seldom-mentioned importance of *amicitia* and *clientela* in Roman society to support his conviction that 'Christianity was a movement sponsored by local patrons to their social dependents' (Judge 1960b, 8; cf. 1960a). Robert M. Grant, looking primarily at evidence from the second through the fourth centuries, concurs: 'The triumph of Christianity in a hierarchically organized society necessarily took place from the top down.' He infers that, also in the earlier period, Christianity should be viewed 'not as a proletarian mass movement but as a relatively small cluster of more or less intense groups, largely middle class in origin.'[4] Malherbe has drawn significant clues for the social level of the New Testament writers and their audiences from recent studies of language, style, and genre, which have the effect of refuting Deissmann in the area of the latter's central contributions. Malherbe emphasizes the ambiguities of the linguistic data that Deissmann noted but chose to set aside in his general conclusions (Malherbe 1977a, 29–59). These studies, too, suggest that the educational and therefore probably the social level of Paul and at least some members of his congregations was a good bit higher than has commonly been assumed. The most careful, consciously sociological analysis of social stratification in the Pauline communities, however, is found in the series of articles published by Gerd Theissen, which discuss the situation in Corinth. He, too, finds leading figures in the Christian groups of that city who belong to a relatively high economic and social level, but Theissen emphasizes the evidence that the church, like the larger society is stratified. The conflicts in the congregation are in large part conflicts between people of different strata and, within individuals, between the expectations of a hierarchical society and those of an egalitarian community (Theissen 1974a, 1974b, 1975c [all now in 1982]).

If these studies and others like them are indeed moving toward a consensus, it is still not clear just what this consensus will tell us about the social characteristics of the Pauline groups. Some of the scholars just mentioned emphasize the status of the leading figures; others, the social distance between those figures and the majority of the members. To

---

[4] Grant 1977, 11. Grant's judgment is not far from the conclusion reached by the Marxist church historian Heinz Kreissig 1967, 99, 'that Christianity spread in the first century of our era not so much among the "proletarians" or solitary handworkers of the smallest scale or yet small peasants, but rather in the urban circles of well-situated artisans, merchants, and members of the liberal professions.'

one observer the mixture of classes in the church simply shows that the Christian movement inevitably conforms to the social structure of the society as a whole; to another, it reveals a fundamental conflict between the values of the Christian group and those of the larger society.[5]

Measuring social stratification

Something more is at stake here than merely deciding whether we shall count only the highest, only the lowest, or the average members of the Christian congregation. There is also a more fundamental question, what we mean by 'high' or 'low.' We will do well to follow the lead of M. I. Finley (who in turn was adapting the views of Max Weber) in distinguishing in ancient society three different kinds of ranking: class, *ordo*, and status (Finley 1973, 35–61). Of these, class is not very helpful. In the everyday speech of popular sociology (such as 'lower middle class'), it refers almost exclusively to income level, with perhaps the added qualification of the way in which income is obtained. ('Middle class,' for example, usually implies not only an intermediate level of income, but also earned income rather than inherited wealth.) For Marx, class was determined by relation to the means of production, yielding only three: landlords, capitalists, and workers. For Weber, too, class was determined by economic factors, but defined by the market rather than by production. It represented 'life chances in the market' for a specifiable group of people (Lipset 1968, 296–301). None of these definitions is very helpful in describing ancient society, for they lump together groups who clearly were regarded in antiquity as different (Finley 1973, 491–50).

The 'orders' (*ordines*) or 'estates' of imperial Roman society, on the other hand, were clear-cut, legally established categories. The two most important and enduring ones were the senators and the knights: the *ordo senatorius* and the *ordo equester*. In addition, the families whose members had served or were eligible to serve in the councils or senates of the provincial cities constituted a local order in those places. These

---

[5] Scroggs 1980, 169–71, raises several critical questions about this 'new consensus,' three of which are particularly relevant to an inquiry into the Pauline groups. First, directed especially, I presume, to Judge: 'Is the Acts material as historically trustworthy as the proponents assume?' Second, '. . . should the presence of a few . . . wealthier members be allowed to change, in effect, the social location of the community as a whole? Is this not an elitist definition?' And third, 'Should economic alienation be the only alienation considered?' See the response by Judge 1980, 207–209.

orders, and the steps that led to them, the cursus honorum, were of tremendous importance to the ambitious elite of the Roman empire. Yet, given that these three top *ordines* comprised considerably less than 1 percent of the population (MacMullen 1974, 88–91), the category does not have much discriminating power for the sorts of groups we are investigating. To include as formal *ordines* also the *plebs* (in Rome) and the *ordo libertinorum* would be only slightly more useful than adding 'and everybody else.'[6]

That leaves us with the category of status as the most generally useful one for forming a picture of stratification in the Greco-Roman cities. Here some of the discussion of social stratification by modern sociologists may help us toward greater conceptual clarity. All the writers reviewed in the first part of this chapter seem to regard an individual's status as a single thing. One is high or low or middle or perhaps somewhere in between, but still measured along a single scale. In recent years, however, most sociologists have come to see social stratification as a multi-dimensional phenomenon; to describe the social level of an individual or a group, one must attempt to measure their rank along each of the relevant dimensions. For example, one might discover that, in a given society, the following variables affect how an individual is ranked: power (defined as 'the capacity for achieving goals in social systems'), occupational prestige, income or wealth, education and knowledge, religious and ritual purity, family and ethnic-group position, and local-community status (evaluation within some subgroup, independent of

---

[6] Consequently I do not entirely understand John Gager's remarks in his review of Robert M. Grant, Malherbe, and Theissen (Gager 1979, 180). Gager appropriately chides Grant and Malherbe for not distinguishing social class from social status, but then he identifies class with *ordo* and proceeds to argue that 'some persons of relatively high social status, but few of high social class were attracted to Christianity in the first two centuries.' If I understand his concluding comment correctly, he then infers that such high-status-but-low-class (*ordo*) persons would perceive themselves as *relatively* deprived. That would depend, I think, on their reference group. I am not likely to feel oppressed nor are the people who matter to me likely to snub me because I shall not ever receive a peerage in the British realm. Similarly, I wonder whether Erastus, proudly displaying his new status as aedile of Corinth on the theater pavement, was secretly seething because he could not be a Roman senator as well – though had he lived a century or two later he might well have felt so. Gager is on the right track, and the concept of relative deprivation, which figures largely in his *Kingdom and Community* (1975), is closely related to status inconsistency. But greater precision is needed. We obtain a more useful picture if we treat *ordo* not as the all-important index of prestige, but only as one of the specific dimensions of status – the most formal one, but not the most pervasive. See Cohen 1975.

SOCIAL-SCIENTIFIC APPROACHES TO NEW TESTAMENT INTERPRETATION

the larger society but perhaps interacting with it; Barber 1968). It would
be a rare individual who occupied exactly the same rank, in either his
own view or that of others, in terms of all these factors. The generalized
status of a person is a composite of his or her ranks in all the relevant
dimensions.

Moreover, the resultant status is not just the average of one's ranks in
the several dimensions. Several other considerations are involved. First,
not all the dimensions have the same weight. Wealth, especially if
displayed in conspicuously stylish ways, might count more heavily than
religious purity, but being the scion of an old and famous family might
bring even more prestige than wealth would. Second, the weight of each
dimension depends upon who is doing the weighing. For example,
Seymour Martin Lipset distinguishes three perspectives: 'objective' status,
that is, 'aspects of stratification that structure environments differently
enough to evoke differences in behavior'; accorded status, or 'prestige
accorded to individuals and groups by others'; and subjective status, or
'personal sense of location within the social hierarchy felt by various
individuals' (Lipset 1968, 310; cf. Malewski 1966). Most individuals
tend to measure themselves by the standards of some group that is very
important to them – their reference group, whether or not they belong
to it – rather than by the standards of the whole society.[7] Third, the
degree of correlation among one's various rankings constitutes another
kind of variable that affects how one is evaluated by others and how one
evaluates oneself. This is the dimension of status consistency, status
congruence, or status crystallization.[8]

If prestige was distributed in some analogous ways in antiquity, then
to describe the early Christians' social status by some single, general
category – say, 'of the middle class' – is not only vague but misleading.
It is vague because it ignores the multidimensionality of stratification. It
is misleading because it tacitly assumes that there was something in the
ancient Greek city corresponding to the middle class of modern industrial
society.

There is a further reason for being alert to the multiple dimensions of
status. A series of studies has demonstrated that, in present-day American

[7] Lipset 1968, 312; Pettigrew 1967; Merton and Rossi 1950.
[8] [Meeks explains the term 'status inconsistency' in the following way: 'In every society the
status of a person, family, or other group is determined by the composite of many different
clues, status indicators.' Where there is a high degree of disparity, or 'criss-crossing',
between these various indicators in relation to a particular person, they may be said to
experience 'status inconsistency' or 'status dissonance' (see Meeks 1983, 22–23) – Ed.].

202

society, persons of low status crystallization, that is, those who are ranked high in some important dimensions but low in others, tend to behave in certain predictable ways. Some may take political action favoring change in the society. Some may withdraw from groups and tend to become unsocial. Others may develop psychophysiological symptoms of stress. All these kinds of behavior, some sociologists believe, show that a high degree of status inconsistency produces unpleasant experiences that lead people to try to remove the inconsistency by changing the society, themselves, or perceptions of themselves.[9]

We must, of course, be cautious in applying to ancient society a theory that has been empirically generated from observations about a modern society. The hierarchies among voters of Detroit are not the same as those among citizens of ancient Corinth. The explanations and predictions incorporated in the theories of status consistency may include latent assumptions about motivation and perception – such as an exaggerated individualism and post-Freudian or at least post-Augustinian introspection – that are culturally determined. Nevertheless, these theories can have great heuristic power. They can help to keep us from oversimplifying the indexes of status, and they can suggest the sorts of connections to look for in our sources. We have already seen how Tony Reekmans (1971) could employ the concept of status inconsistency in analyzing Juvenal's attitudes toward social change, or P. R. C. Weaver (1967) in describing the upward mobility of imperial slaves and freedmen [see Meeks 1983, 22 – Ed.]. The 'criss-crossing categories' described by Finley are another term for the same phenomenon. The 'dictionary of snobbery' compiled by Ramsey MacMullen (1974, 138–41; see also ch. 4) provides valuable material for defining the dimensions of hierarchy, as seen from above.

When we consider individuals and groups who joined the Pauline congregations, then, we should not too quickly assign them to some general level. Rather, we should ask what clues we have that would indicate ranking in the several hierarchies which were relevant in that

---

[9] Lenski 1954 stimulated a series of responses and further investigations which has probably still not come to an end. Among the many publications the following seem to an outsider representative: Goffman 1957, Lenski 1956, Anderson and Zelditch 1964, Blalock 1967. E. F. Jackson 1962, Jackson and Burke 1965, H. F. Taylor 1973, Hornung 1977. For a recent attempt at quantitative measurement of correlations between status inconsistency and religious commitment, and for some important methodological cautions, see Sasaki 1979.

time and place. For example, in adapting to the provincial situation Reekmans' (1971) categories, which apply only to Rome, we should look for rankings in such categories as ethnic origins, *ordo*, citizenship, personal liberty, wealth, occupation, age, sex, and public offices or honors. We must ask, too, about the context within which each of these rankings is valid; for example, to be a freedman in the early years in Roman Corinth, a colony whose first settlers were mostly freedmen, would surely have been less of a social disability than it would have been in Rome or in Antioch.

Prosopographic evidence

In the letters of Paul and his disciples written in the first century (that is, leaving aside the Pastorals) sixty-five individuals besides Paul are named or otherwise identified as persons active in local congregations, as traveling companions or agents of Paul, or as both. Some of these are also mentioned in Acts, which adds thirteen other names and an anonymous household. Thus it is possible to draw up a prosopography of Pauline Christianity containing nearly eighty names. About most of them little information is to be found besides the name, and of some not even that. A close look at the whole list, however, does yield some clues about the social texture of the Pauline circle.

The long list of persons to whom Paul sends greetings in Romans 16 poses a problem. Paul may know some of these individuals or groups only by reputation; others he may have met only as individuals traveling in the East. Hence we should count only those whom the text specifically calls Paul's 'fellow workers' or the equivalent, or who had earlier belonged to one of the Pauline congregations.[10] That eliminates Apelles (v. 10); the members of the household of Aristobulus, probably including Herodion (vv. 10–11); the members of the household represented by Asyncritus, Phlegon, Hermes, Patrobas, and Hernias (v. 14); Mary (v. 6); the members of the household of Narcissus (v. 11); Persis, Tryphaena, and Tryphosa (v. 12); the members of the household represented by Philologus and Julia, Nereus and his sister, and Olympas (v. 15); and Stachys (v. 9).

Of the remaining persons mentioned in the letters, sixteen probably or certainly belong to the Pauline groups but lack any clear indicator of

---

[10] The problem would be simpler if, as many commentators have suggested, Romans 16 had not been originally part of the letter. Against that hypothesis, however, see Gamble 1977.

their social standing. These are Archippus of Colossae (Phlm 1; Col 4:17); Aristarchus (Phlm 24; Col 4:10f; Acts 19:29; 20:4; 27:2); Demas (Phlm 24; Col 4:14); Epaphras (Phlm 23; Col 1:7; 4:12); Epaphroditus of Philippi (Phil 2:25; 4:18); Jason (Rom 16:21; not the Jason of Thessalonica in Acts 17:5, 9); Jesus Justus (Col 4:11); Sosipater (Rom 16:21; Acts 20:4?); Sosthenes (1 Cor 1:1);[11] Timothy (1 Thess 1:1; 3:2, 6; 1 Cor 4:17; 16:10; 2 Cor 1:1, 19; Phil 1:1; 2:19; 2 Thess 1:1; Col 1:1; Rom 16:21; Phlm 1; Acts 16:1–17:14; 18:5; 19:22; 20:4);[12] Titus (2 Cor 2:13; 7:6–16; 8:6, 16–24; 12:18; Gal 2:1–3); Tychicus (Col 4:7f; Eph. 6:21f; Acts 20:4); Urbanus (Rom 16:9); the anonymous 'true yokefellow' (Phil 4:3); and the two anonymous (in the extant text) 'brothers' and 'delegates of the churches' connected with the collection (2 Cor 8:18f, 22f)

We are left with thirty individuals about whose status we have at least a clue. For several the clue is nothing more than the name itself, which in the particular context may be significant. Thus Achaicus (1 Cor 16:17), Fortunatus (ibid.), Quartus (Rom 16:23), and Lucius (Rom 16:21) in Corinth and Clement in Philippi (Phil 4:3) have Latin names in the two Roman colonies where Latin was the dominant official language. This *may* indicate that their families belonged to the original stock of colonists, who tended to get ahead. One of these, Lucius, is a Jew besides.[13] The case of Achaicus is interesting, for a resident of Corinth would hardly receive *there* the geographical nickname (it was not on Crete but in Toledo that Domenikos Theotokopoulos was named 'El Greco'). The man or his father must have lived for a time in Italy, received the name there, and then returned to Corinth, probably as one of the freedmen colonists. If so, we would have an example of the phenomenon suggested by Bowersock, Italians of Greek ancestry

---

[11] If this Sosthenes, joint author of 1 Corinthians, were the *archisunagōgos* of Corinth (Acts 18:17, apparently successor to Crispus, v. 8, who had earlier converted to Christianity), we could say something about his wealth, ethnic group, and standing in the Jewish community. However, the name is too common to justify this identification without other evidence.

[12] Also the important figure in the Pastorals. If the information in 2 Tim 1:5 comes from good tradition, we have the additional clue that not only his father was Greek, but also two generations on his mother's, Jewish, side had had Greek names.

[13] With Jason and Sosipater, in Corinth, and Andronicus, Junia(s), and Herodion, in Rome, he is called Paul's *suggenēs*, which may mean only 'fellow Jew' or more narrowly 'relative.' There is no good reason to identify him with either Lucius of Cyrene (Acts 13:1) or with the person known by the short form of the same name, Lukas (Phlm 24; Col 4:14; 2 Tim. 4:11).

returning as Roman colonists to Greece.[14] On the other hand, the Greek names of Euodia and Syntyche (Phil 4:2f) may hint that they were among the merchant groups who were metics in Philippi. It is to be noted besides that they were women who had sufficient independence to be recognized in their own right as activists in the Pauline mission. Tertius is another Latin name among the Corinthian Christians (Rom 16:22); in his case we have the further hint of a profession, or at least training, as a scribe.[15] Another professional with a Latin name is Luke (Phlm 24), a physician (Col 4:14) with Paul, probably in Ephesus. Doctors were often slaves; we might speculate that Luke had been a *medicus* in some Roman *familia*, receiving the name of his master (Lucius, of which Lukas is a hypocorism) on his manumission.

The ability to travel bespeaks some financial means (Theissen 1974b), but not necessarily the traveler's own. Many slaves and freedmen traveled as agents of their masters or mistresses, like the members of Chloe's household who told Paul in Ephesus about Corinthian troubles (1 Cor 1:11). Ampliatus (Rom 16:8), who is in Rome after Paul knew him in the East, may be a similar case, for his is a common Latin slave name (Lietzmann 1933, 125–26). Andronicus and Junia(s) (Rom 16:7) have also moved from the East, where they were imprisoned with Paul somewhere, sometime,[16] to Rome. Eck assumes that Andronicus' name marks him as a freedman and that therefore Junia, too, must be a freedwoman of the *gens Iunia* (Eck 1971, 392), but not every Jew with a Greek name in Rome was a former slave. If, with John Chrysostom, we are to take *Iounian* as the accusative of the feminine *Iounia* rather than the masculine *Iounias*, then very likely Andronicus and Junia are husband and wife, like Prisca and Aquila (v. 3) and Philologus and Julia (v. 15).[17]

---

[14] Bowersock 1965, 71. The use of a place name as a cognomen probably indicates servile origins, although that depends on circumstances under which the nickname was given. After all, L. Mummius acquired the honorific 'Achaicus' after his destruction of Corinth (Velleius Paterculus 1.13.2; Pliny *Hist. nat.* 35.4.8, § 24).

[15] Theissen 1974b, 253–54, points out that he could be a slave or, on the contrary, could hold a position in the provincial bureaucracy.

[16] That is the most likely meaning of *sunaichmalōtos*; cf. Philemon 23 (Epaphras) and Col 4:10 (Aristarchus).

[17] That a woman should be called, along with her husband, 'prominent among the apostles' has seemed unthinkable to most modern commentators, but to Chrysostom only grounds for high praise: 'How great is the *philosophia* of this woman that she is held to be worthy of the name of apostle' (*Hom. 31 Rom 2*; PG 60:669–70, quoted by Clark 1979, 20). Clark points out elsewhere (16–17) that Chrysostom often uses *philosophia* to refer to the celibate life, and that may be his implication here, too. On Junia see also Brooten 1977; Pagels 1979, 61.

Epaenetus (Rom 16:5), honored as the first Christian convert in Asia, has also traveled to Rome. His name, like that of Ampliatus, suggests but does not prove servile origins. Silvanus (1 Thess 1:1; 2 Cor 1:19; 2 Thess 1:1; cf. 1 Pet 5:12 and often in Acts), who bears the name of a Latin deity,[18] traveled widely with Paul but perhaps not at his own expense. Acts reports that he had been one of the leaders of the Jerusalem church (15:22) as well as a prophet (15:32), but neither necessarily implies anything about status in the larger society.

We can be slightly more definite about the status of the remaining individuals. Gaius (1 Cor 1:14; Rom 16:23) has a good Roman praenomen, thus resembling several Corinthian Christians already mentioned, but in addition he has a house ample enough not only to put up Paul, but also to accommodate all the Christian groups in Corinth meeting together (Rom 16:23). He is evidently a man of some wealth (cf. Theissen 1974b, 256). The same is true of Crispus, whose office as *archisynagōgos* shows that he not only has high prestige in the Jewish community but is also probably well to do.[19] It is noteworthy that these two are singled out by Paul as people whom he personally baptized at the beginning of Christianity in Corinth (1 Cor 1:14). It is tempting to assume that the third person mentioned in the same context, Stephanas, the members of whose household were the very first converts (*aparchē*) in Achaia (1 Cor 16:15), was also a person of wealth. That would be too hasty an inference, however.[20] His Greek name might indicate that his family was not part of the original colony, but either indigenous Greek or immigrant, in either case not of the highest social stratum. His having traveled with Achaicus and Fortunatus to see Paul in Ephesus suggests some independence, but they seem to be a more or less official delegation, so their expenses may have been paid by the Corinthian congregations. On the other hand, he heads a household important enough for Paul to mention twice. And the services he has rendered to the Corinthian Christians (16:15b) seem from the context to be of the sort rendered by patrons rather than by charismatic gifts (*charismata*). It is precisely in

---

[18] The most popular deity among the Italian colonists at Philippi; Collart 1937, 402–409. Acts gives him the shortened name Silas, which could represent the Aramaic form of Saul (so BAGD, s.v., and BDF, § 125 [2]), but it may just as well be simply the Greek shortened form of Silvanus, like Epaphras for Epaphroditus, or Lukas for Lucius.

[19] Theissen 1974b, 235–36; cf. Judge 1960b, 129–30; Meeks and Wilken 1978, 53–54, 56.

[20] See Malherbe's criticism of Theissen for too easily granting this status by association (1977a, 73, n. 27).

contrast to the sometimes disruptive roles of the *pneumatikoi* that Paul urges recognition due to 'people like those' (*toioutoi*), namely Stephanas, Achaicus, and Fortunatus. We are probably safe, then, in placing Stephanas fairly high on the scale of wealth, though probably not so high as Gaius and Crispus. In prestige within the Christian group he was their equal, but probably not in Corinth at large, and not so high in civic recognition as our next figure, Erastus.

Alone among the persons mentioned by Paul, Erastus is named with an official title that refers not to his role in the Christian group but to his role in the city: *oikonomos tēs poleōs*. There has been a long debate, however, over the precise meaning of that title or its equivalent in the official Latin titulature of Corinth. The Greek title is rather widely attested by inscriptions, especially in Asia Minor, in both the Hellenistic and Roman periods.[21] However, although many of these inscriptions refer to high officials charged with administering public funds or property, the title is also applied in some cases (in Chalcedon and Cos, for example) to persons who apparently were public slaves (Magie 1950, 2:850; Theissen 1974b, 239). One might argue that Paul would not have mentioned the title if it were not a public office of some consequence, but that would fail to take account of the *philotimia* which was so constant a factor in the life of the Greco-Roman world. We may be sure that if Erastus had been a city slave charged with keeping the municipal accounts, that would have been quite ample occasion for pride and congratulation within his own circle, and his children would have been glad to record *oikonomos tēs poleōs* on his tombstone.

The debate took a new turn with the discovery of a Latin inscription naming an Erastus as donor of the paving of the courtyard east of the theater in Corinth.[22] This Erastus announced his gift 'in return for his aedileship.'[23] Two aediles were elected annually in a colony; together with the two duoviri they constituted the four highest offices in the city's administration. Against the identification of aedile with *oikonomos tēs poleōs* stood the objection that the normal Greek translation is

---

[21] Landvogt 1908. See the convenient summaries in Magie 1950, 2:850–51, n. 34; and Theissen 1974b, 238–40.

[22] The inscription had been in metal letters; only the cuttings for them in the limestone survive. It extended over two paving blocks. A fragment of the left one was found *in situ* in 1929 and matched with another piece found elsewhere the year before. Not until 1947 did part of the right block turn up (Kent 1966, 99–100).

[23] [praenomen nomen] ERASTUS PRO AEDILIT[AT]E/(vac) S(ua) P(ecunia) STRAVIT (Kent 1966, no. 232 and plate 21).

agoranomos. However, the editor of the Corinthian inscriptions was persuaded that, because one of the main tasks of aediles in most colonies, management of public games, was taken over in Corinth by a special officer in charge of the famous Isthmian Games, *oikonomos* would be appropriate to the actual functions of a Corinthian aedile (Kent 1966, 100). Theissen, however, challenges that argument on the grounds that because separate officials for games are widely attested, Corinth's situation was not unique (Theissen 1974b, 243). Instead, Theissen proposes a new solution, in which *oikonomos tēs poleōs* is not the same office as aedile but a lesser one, perhaps equivalent to quaestor, but still part of the municipal *cursus honorum*. The Erastus mentioned in Romans, in that case, would have been an important official and the same person who soon thereafter was elected aedile (Theissen 1974b, 243–45). This conclusion, though far from certain, is persuasive. If it is correct, the Christian Erastus was a person of both wealth and high civic status, and we can add one further deduction made by Kent from the fact that there was no room in the broken part of the inscription for a patronymic before Erastus' (Greek) name: 'Like his contemporary, Cn. Babbius Philinus,[24] Erastus was probably a Corinthian freedman who had acquired considerable wealth in commercial activities' (Kent 1966, 100).

It was also in Corinth, according to Acts 18:2f, that Paul met Prisca and Aquila. Two letters mention a Christian community in their house: 1 Corinthians, when Paul sends greetings from Ephesus (16:19); and Romans, when he sends greetings from Corinth (16:3–5). Moreover, we hear that they have 'risked their necks' for Paul (Rom 16:4). The author of Acts has other information about them: that Aquila's family came from Pontus, that he was a Jew, that they lived in Rome until forced to leave by Claudius' expulsion of the Jews, and that they were tentmakers (18:2–3). Both have good Roman names, but in Rome that was quite common for Jews, Greek- as well as Latin-speaking, especially for women.[25] We may summarize their known indicators of status as follows: wealth: relatively high. They have been able to move from place to place, and in three cities to establish a sizable household; they have acted as patrons for Paul and for Christian congregations. Occupation: low, but

---

[24] See Meeks 1983, 48.

[25] Leon 1960, 93–121. It is not apparent why the author of Acts consistently uses the diminutive Priscilla, whereas Paul never does; we encountered the same phenomenon with Silas/Silvanus.

not at the bottom.[26] They are artisans, but independent, and by ancient standards they operate on a fairly large scale. Extraction: middling to low. They are eastern provincials and Jews besides, but assimilated to Greco-Roman culture. One thing more: the fact that Prisca's name is mentioned before her husband's once by Paul and two out of three times in Acts suggests that she has higher status than her husband.[27]

'Chloe's people' (*hoi Chloēs*, 1 Cor 1:11) are slaves or freedmen or both (Theissen 1974b, 245–49) who have brought news from Corinth to Ephesus. Whether the *familia* was situated in Corinth, with business in Ephesus, or vice versa, is not certain, but the fact that Paul expects the name to be recognized by the Corinthian Christians suggests that Chloe lived there. Whether she herself was a Christian is not stated and cannot be inferred with any confidence.[28] The case of Onesimus and his owners is clearer. Onesimus of Colossae (Phlm 10 and *passim*; Col 4:9) was not only a slave but a runaway. There is no indication what his particular task had been in Philemon's service, but Paul's eagerness to have him help in the mission suggests, despite the pun on his former uselessness (Phlm 11), that he may have had some education or special skills.[29] Philemon himself ranks high at least on the dimension of wealth and on evaluation within the sect: he has a house large enough to accommodate a meeting of Christians (Phlm 2) and guests (v. 22) and has been a patron of Christians in other ways as well (vv. 5–7). He owns at least one slave, probably a number of them, for Paul's strongly implied request to send the slave Onesimus back to work with him (vv. 8–14) evidently is not expected to be a great hardship for Philemon or the household. Apphia is usually taken to be Philemon's wife, but she is mentioned in her own right as 'the sister,' as Philemon is 'beloved' and Timothy 'the brother.' Otherwise there is no separate indicator of her status.

---

[26] Ollrog 1979 attributes 'einen gehobenen Sozialstatus' to Aquila because of his being 'Handwerker und damit Geschäftsmann' (26 and n. 105), but that betrays a misconception of ancient society.

[27] Judge 1960b, 129, reinforced by analogous examples described by Flory 1975, 8–9, 59–79, 81–85.

[28] It may be, though, that the absence of the partitive *ek* (contrast *hoi ek tōn Aristobolou, hoi ek tōn Narkissou hoi ontes en Kuriōi*, Rom 16:10f) implies that the whole of Chloe's household is Christian. In that case Chloe herself would most likely be Christian and thus among the *ou polloi . . . dunatoi* of the Corinthian Church.

[29] This would be borne out if, as Stuhlmacher 1975, 53–54, suggests, Col 4:9 reflects a later, local tradition in Colossae about Onesimus's activity in church service. That hypothesis would require, however, that Colossians be not only pseudonymous but also written considerably later than Philemon. The latter is hard to demonstrate.

Another 'sister' is particularly interesting: Phoebe, who is recommended to the Roman Christians as *diakonos* of the church in Cenchreae and '*prostatis* of many [others][30] and myself as well' (Rom 16:1–2). The two titles (if that is what they are) have evoked endless discussion. Whether *diakonos* represents an office, as perhaps in Phil 1:1, or whether it means 'missionary' (see Georgi 1964, 31–38) or more generally 'helper' (e.g., Leenhardt 1948, 11) is of considerable interest for questions of the internal governance of the early Christian groups and for questions about the role of women. It cannot, however, tell us anything directly about Phoebe's status in the macrosociety. Nor could *prostatis* if, as some commentators have recently urged, it is to be translated as 'president' or the like.[31] The term was used in that official sense in some Hellenistic cities, in the place of the more usual *prytaneis* ('executive officers'),[32] and as a title, or in the general sense of 'leader,' of officers of clubs or guilds (Poland 1909, 363–64). If it were a title in Rom 16:2, it would be in this latter sense, which is the way Paul uses the cognate participle in 1 Thess 5:12: 'those who labor among you and preside [*proistamenoi*] over you in the Lord and admonish you.' That meaning, however, is rendered impossible by the context, for it is difficult to imagine what Paul could have meant by describing Phoebe as 'also presiding over me.' The sensible solution is to follow E. A. Judge in taking *prostatis* in the sense that it often has where Roman influence is strong, as an equivalent of *euergetēs* and the Latin *patrona* (Judge 1960b, 128–29; cf. Poland 1909, 364). Paul says that Phoebe has been the protector or patroness of many Christians, including himself, and 'for that reason' (*gar*) he asks that the Roman Christians provide her with whatever she needs during her stay in Rome. We may then infer that Phoebe is an independent woman (she is probably traveling to Rome on business of her own, not solely to carry Paul's letter) who has some wealth and is also one of the leaders of the Christian group in the harbor town of Cenchreae.

Another woman, then living in Rome, may have served as a patroness of Paul in the same loose sense. This is the mother of Rufus (Rom

---

[30] 'Others' is added in several mss., including p46.
[31] E.g., Swidler 1979, 310, who observes correctly that 'the word . . . always means ruler, leader, *or protector* in all Greek literature' (my emphasis), but insists that it must mean 'ruler' here.
[32] Magie 1950, 1:59 and 2:842–43, n. 28, where a number of examples are given. See also Schaefer 1962.

16:13). If what Paul means by calling her 'my mother, too,' is that she was his benefactress, then she, too, had traveled or resided for a time in the East and had some wealth. We obviously cannot put much weight on this possibility, however. We are in only a slightly more secure position to assess the status of Mark, sometime fellow worker of Paul and of Mark's cousin, Barnabas (Phlm 24; Col 4:10). Mark's mother, according to Acts 12:12, had a house in Jerusalem that accommodated a meeting of the Christians. If that report is trustworthy, the family had some means, and the Latin surname, in a Jerusalem Jew, may imply some social ambition.

The last two persons to be considered from the letters can be reckoned as part of the Pauline circle only with some injustice to them, for they were missionaries in their own right before they met Paul. Barnabas was a leader of the Antioch group before Paul's conversion; there is good reason to call Paul his fellow worker, in the early years, rather than the reverse.[33] There is not much in the letters to indicate Barnabas' social standing, but 1 Cor 9:6 says that he and Paul were alone among the apostles in their policy of working with their own hands rather than receiving regular support. Hock (1978) has argued that Paul's manner of talking about his own work resembles that found in rhetoricians and philosophers who come from higher social levels and thus think their decision to do menial work something worthy of comment. The parallel between Paul and Barnabas suggests that they might have determined this policy jointly in the earliest stage of their mission, in Antioch and its environs. The picture of Barnabas as a reasonably well-to-do man who deliberately chose the life of an itinerant artisan to support his mission is reinforced by the report in Acts that he was the owner of a farm that he sold, the proceeds going to the Jerusalem Christians (4:36f). He is also described there as a Levite, of a family that had settled in Cyprus.

Apollos seems to have been more or less a free agent who was drawn into the Pauline orbit – according to Acts, through the good offices of Prisca. Despite a certain competitiveness among their partisans in Corinth (1 Cor 1:12; 3:1–4:6), there seem to have been good relations between Paul and Apollos (16:12). Again we are dependent on the account in Acts for any clues about status. Acts describes him as an Alexandrian Jew, *logios* and 'powerful in the scriptures' (18:24). *Logios* here implies

---

[33] A point well made by Ollrog 1979, 10–13.

at least rhetorical ability, perhaps also rhetorical training. There is some support for that claim in 1 Corinthians 1–4, where Paul contrasts the 'wisdom of God' with, among other things, a human wisdom exhibited in rhetoric.[34] Apollos' apparent ability to travel independently may further indicate some wealth.

The reports of the Pauline associates and converts in Acts must be treated with somewhat more caution, for the account is written a generation later than Paul's letters and depends on traditions that may have been distorted by time and the accidents of transmission. In addition, we must remember that the author of Luke–Acts evidently was interested in portraying the Christian sect as one that obtained favor from well-placed, substantial citizens. A number of women, including Joanna, the wife of Herod's *epitropos* Chuza, support Jesus and his companions from their own possessions (Luke 8:2f). The proconsul of Cyprus, Sergius Paulus, summons Barnabas and Paul, is impressed by their miracle as well as by their teaching, and 'believes' (Acts 13:7–12). 'Not a few Greek women of high standing as well as men' become believers in Thessalonica (17:12, RSV); an Areopagite is converted in Athens (17:34); the procurator Felix converses with Paul often, if not for the highest of motives (24:26); King Agrippa is impressed by Paul's arguments (26:2–31); the 'first man' of Malta entertains him, and he heals the official's father (28:7–10). Some or even all of these episodes may be true, but it is well to remember that the author of Luke–Acts is a sophisticated writer who is also capable of inventing typical occasions to make his points.

The list of early leaders of the Antioch congregation (Acts 13:1) is probably a reliable piece of tradition, but because Symeon Niger, Lucius of Cyrene, and Manaen, the *syntrophos* of Herod Agrippa, were most likely active there before Paul's arrival, I include only Barnabas among the Pauline associates. The asiarchs of Ephesus who were 'friends' of Paul (Acts 19:31) had best be left out of account as sounding a bit too much like a Lucan invention; besides, the story does not hint that they became Christians. It would be precarious, too, to draw inferences from the story of the Philippian jailer and his household, converted in response to a familiar sort of miracle (Acts 16:23–34; cf. also Acts 12:6–11, Euripides *Bacchae* 443–48; Philostratus *V. Ap.* 7.38; 8.5). It is true that this legend might still preserve some local tradition about early converts,

[34] See Meeks 1983, 117–18.

but in that case we would expect a name to be remembered. A name we have, and a very prominent one, in Acts 13:7–12, which reports the impression made by yet another miracle on Sergius Paulus, proconsul of Cyprus. Still, we do not hear of his being baptized, nor anything else about him or Christianity in Cyprus – although Barnabas goes there later, 15:39 – and again we should err on the side of caution by omitting him. The same is true of Dionysius of Athens, whose position as a member of the court of the Areopagus would otherwise have supplied good material for speculation,[35] and with him Damaris, about whom we know nothing anyway (Acts 17:34).

Erastus, associated with Timothy as an assistant of Paul (19:22) and surely not the *oikonomos* of Corinth; Sopater of Beroea (20:4); and Trophimus of Ephesus (20:4; 21:29; 2 Tim. 4:20) all certainly belonged to the Pauline circle, but we know too little about them to make judgments about their social level. Eutychus of Troas, famous forever as the first recorded Christian to fall asleep during a long-winded sermon (20:9–12), does not seriously warrant inclusion. Of Gaius of Macedonia (19:29) we have only the Latin name and the fact that he was free to travel with Paul. The same is true of Secundus of Thessalonica and Gaius of Derbe (20:4).

The three remaining persons named in Acts are all reported to have served as hosts or patrons of Paul and his associates. The most interesting is Lydia, the Thyatiran dealer in purple fabrics, who, as a gentile worshipper of the Jewish God, encounters Paul in Philippi and converts forthwith, with her *oikos* (Acts 16:14f; see Meeks 1983, 9ff). She persuades Paul, Silas, and their other companions to move into her house (vv. 15, 40). We have several indicators of her status. First, as a *porphyropōlis* she must have had some wealth, for purple was a luxury item (Haenchen 1959 *ad loc.*; Judge 1960b, 128); she also has a household in which several guests can be accommodated. Second, her name, occupation, and place of origin show that she belongs to the Greek-speaking merchants who have settled in Philippi alongside the Italian, agrarian colonists. Third, she is a

---

[35] Haenchen 1959, 527, n. 1, suggests that the author may be using a report about the later Athenian congregation (about which we have very little information), for as it stands the scene is contradicted by 1 Cor 16:16. The first convert in Achaia was not an Athenian but Stephanas's household in Corinth. Haenchen also suspects that 'Areopagite' may be the author's invention, to connect Dionysus with the scene just described.

pagan adherent of the Jewish synagogue.[36] Finally, she is the female head of a household.

A certain Jason (not to be identified with the Jason of Rom 16:21) is the host of the missionaries in Thessalonica, and consequently is held responsible for their conduct and forced to post bond for them (Acts 17:5–9, Malherbe 1977b, 224 and n. 15). He is evidently a gentile, with a good Greek name. He has a house and some wealth. Titius Justus, like Lydia a 'worshipper of God,' has a house adjacent to the synagogue in Corinth which becomes the temporary domicile of Paul, Silas, and Timothy after their rebuff by the Jews. His name indicates that he may be a Roman citizen; he belongs to the dominant Latin group of the colony. Unfortunately, Acts does not say explicitly whether either Jason or Titius Justus became a Christian.

Our survey of the names mentioned in the Pauline letters and in Acts has yielded few data about the social level of typical Pauline Christians. A statistical analysis of the sort so important in modern, empirical sociology would be entirely unjustified. Yet some patterns have emerged that are not insignificant. Even though many inferences must remain tentative, we can form a cumulative impression of certain types of people who were prominent in the Pauline groups and mission. Before summarizing the results, however, it will be well to look at other, less direct evidence that can be gleaned from the letters. The prosopography may tend to give skewed evidence, for it is after all the leaders, the prominent, and the unusual who would be mentioned by name, and they may very well have stood out in part because their social rankings were different from those of the majority. The letters must be searched for evidence about the social level of anonymous groups within the congregations.

Indirect evidence

Of the anonymous Christians mentioned in the Pauline letters, there is one group for which the text supplies a rather specific social location: the 'saints' who belong to 'the household of Caesar' and who join Paul in sending greetings from the place of his imprisonment to the Philippians

---

[36] It is often asserted, usually citing Kuhn and Stegemann 1962, cols. 1266–67, that 'God-fearers' tended to be of higher status than were full converts to Judaism. The evidence is not very strong, however, and even if the generalizations were valid, it could not be imposed on an individual instance apart from other information.

(Phil 4:22). Paul does not name any of them, nor does he say how many they are. We do not even know with certainty what city they were in, for some commentators have urged Ephesus or Caesarea as the place of writing, although Rome still seems the most likely.[37] We also do not know whether the Christians in the *familia* were slaves, freedmen, or both, nor where they stood in the internal hierarchy of the *familia* which ranged from menial domestics to heads of important state bureaus. Nevertheless, the imperial slaves and freedmen as a group had greater real opportunities for upward social mobility than did any other nonelite segment of Roman society,[38] and it is a precious bit of information that some members of this group had found reason to be initiated into Christianity at so early a date.

Apart from the imperial household, we have already seen that there were both slaves and slaveowners among the Pauline Christians. Philemon and Apphia represent the latter category, as does probably Chloe; 'Chloe's people' are slaves or former slaves, and Onesimus a slave who, though not a Christian in his master's house, became one as a runaway. How many or what proportion of each category may have been found in each congregation, we have no way of knowing.[39] In 1 Cor 7:20–24 Paul addresses a slave rhetorically. Although the slave, like the circumcised Jew of verse 18, is introduced *exempli gratia*, since the topic has to do with marriage, divorce, and celibacy, it would be a strange example if there were in fact no slaves among the addressees. On the other hand, it would be a mistake to infer from this passage that the majority of Corinthian Christians were slaves. There are no other admonitions in the authentic letters of Paul addressed explicitly to slaves,

---

[37] For the options, see Kümmel 1973, 324–32.

[38] See Meeks 1983, 16–23. There is also a bare possibility that Paul hints in Phil 1:13 of a penetration of the Christian faith into the military establishment, for if his imprisonment is in Rome, then *en holōi tōi praitōriōi* must refer to the imperial guards, the praetorians (see Lightfoot 1913, 99–103). If it is in Ephesus or another provincial city, the reference may be either to a group of the guards stationed there or to the governor's palace or court (Dibelius 1937, 64–65). Paul makes no claim that any of these people or of 'all the rest' have become Christians, for 'the brothers in the Lord' are mentioned separately (v. 14; see Dibelius, ibid.). He clearly does believe, however, that the witness of his imprisonment 'in Christ' (v. 13) has produced a favorable impression that creates the possibility of conversions among the personnel of the praetorium.

[39] For an exhaustive discussion of the question and of the attitudes toward slavery in early Christianity, see Gülzow 1969. Bartchy 1973 has much useful information. Among the rather extensive literature on the subject, two others may be singled out: Ste Croix 1975 and Gayer 1976.

but in the later letters written in Paul's name (as in the similar one written in the name of Peter) the common Hellenistic moral topic on the duties of household members appears, the so-called *Haustafel*.[40] In Colossians 3:22–25 the admonition to the slaves is much longer than the sentence addressed to masters (4:1), but this does not necessarily imply, as has sometimes been suggested, that the slaves were a majority of the congregation. The content of the admonitions would certainly be more readily approved by owners than by slaves.[41] The parallel in the letter that later came to be known as Ephesians is more significant; the fact that that letter seems to have been designed as an encyclical addressed to several congregations of the Pauline mission area in western Asia Minor (see esp. Dahl 1951) confirms the impression that the admonitions represent general expectations about Christian behavior rather than the situation in one particular congregation. In Ephesians 6:5–9 again the directives to the slaves are more extensive than those to the masters, but there is somewhat greater balance than in Colossians. Clearly the expectation is that a typical Pauline congregation would include both slave owners and slaves, and the ethos of the leaders is rather more that of the owners than of the slaves. It is also important to notice that these admonitions are within the context of advice for maintaining the proper – hierarchical – structure of a household.

Among the collections of moral advice, or *paraenesis*, in the letters there are a number of passages addressed to free handworkers or crafts-men. Since our prosopography includes several leaders of the Pauline mission – not least Paul himself – who belong to that category, these passages may repay a closer look. In what is usually taken to be the oldest of the extant letters, to the Christians in Thessalonica, Paul appeals to them 'to strive to lead a quiet life, to mind your own business, and to work with your own hands, according to the instructions we gave you, that your behavior may be decent in the view of the outsiders and that you may not be in need' (4:11f). This instruction probably implies, as

[40] See Weidinger 1928; Schroeder 1959; Crouch 1973; Balch 1981; Lührmann 1980.
[41] I doubt that the stress on obligations of the slaves justifies an inference that Christian eschatological hopes had inspired among them an expectation of improvement of their status, though Bassler 1979, 269–71, has recently argued for that possibility with some acuteness. She points out that the appeal to the impartiality of God – which in the *Haustafel* of Ephesians is, as we would expect, addressed to the master – is in Col 3:25 addressed to the slaves. The case of Onesimus, however, can hardly be taken as 'historical evidence of actual unrest among the slaves at Colossae.' He may be simply one slave who got fed up.

Ernest Best says, 'that the great majority of the Thessalonian Christians were manual workers, whether skilled or unskilled' (1972, 176). It is also important to notice that this is a paraenetic reminder of instruction given the Thessalonian converts when the church was first organized there. It is not a unique admonition fitted to special needs of the Thessalonians, then, but represents the kind of instruction that Paul and his associates generally gave to new converts.[42] That is confirmed by the appearance of a similar sentence in the paraenesis of the later deutero-Pauline encyclical, Eph 4:28: 'Let the thief no longer steal, but rather let him labor, working the good with his (own) hands, that he may have (the means) to share with anyone in need.' On the other hand, 2 Thess 3:6–13 (assuming that 2 Thessalonians is a real letter, whether or not Paul wrote it) presupposes the general teaching but applies it to a particular situation in which some Christians are behaving in a disorderly fashion (*ataktōs*) by refusing to work. This behavior, the author says explicitly, violates the 'tradition' which they received from Paul (v. 6). Further, the example of Paul's own manual labor, which was implicitly a model to be imitated in 1 Thess 2:9 (*mnēmoneuete*), here becomes that explicitly (vv. 7–9).[43] The admonition is pointedly renewed: 'That by working in quietness[44] they should eat their own bread' (v. 12). It is taken for granted that people work in order to eat, even though the prohibition of verse 10 may refer to the Eucharist or other communal meals.

There are a few passages in which the letters directly mention money. Several have to do with the collection for Jerusalem Christians. In 1 Cor 16:1–4, Paul gives instructions which he says he also gave to the Galatians. Each person, on the first day of the week, is to 'set aside and keep whatever he has succeeded in, so there need be no collections when I come' (v. 2). I have translated as literally as possible, for the phrase *ho ti ean euodōtai* is rather awkward, but it perhaps provides a clue to the economic situation of the Corinthian Christians. The translation suggested by Bauer's Lexicon, 'as much as he gains' (BAGD, s.v. *euodoō*) is a bit overspecific. The verb *euodoun* has taken on a very general

---

[42] Van Unnik 1964, 227–28; Dibelius 1937, 23. See the important discussion in Hock 1980, 42–47, who shows that these rules are very similar to those found in Greco-Roman moralists, especially Dio Chrysostom.

[43] In quite a different way, Paul's work is made a paradigm in 1 Cor 9; it is interesting that the principal theme of that passage, the renunciation of *exousia* to provide a model for the community, is summed up in 2 Thess 3:9.

[44] *meta hēsuchias*; cf. *hēsuchazein* 1 Thess 4:11.

metaphoric sense from its original 'have a good trip'; it can hardly refer to each individual's whole profit for the previous week, for which Paul's verb would be *kerdainein*. On the other hand, Conzelmann's 'whatever he can spare' ('was er wohl erübrigen kann'; Conzelmann 1969b *ad loc.*), is too loose. Most translators assume, rather reasonably, that the meaning is the same as in Acts 11:29, 'each, as he had prospered,' hence the Revised Standard Version here, 'as he may prosper.'[45] The phrase is in fact quite general, and we should avoid reading very much into it. What we do see clearly is that the collection is to be assembled little by little, week by week. This bespeaks the economy of small people, not destitute, but not commanding capital either. This, too, would fit the picture of fairly well-off artisans and tradespeople as the typical Christians.

The gift for the Jerusalem poor was intended to be quite substantial, as the term *hadrotēs* ('plenty, lavish gift'; 2 Cor 8:20) suggests, and as the elaborate plans for collecting it confirm. The extant second letter to the Corinthians contains two appeals for participation in the collection, which may have stood originally in separate letters. In chapter 8, Paul uses the Macedonian Christians' generosity in the project to chide and encourage the Corinthians to do better. The size of the collection in Macedonia is the more remarkable, he says, because of their 'abysmal poverty' (*hē kata bathous ptōcheia autōn*, vv. 2–3). He implicitly contrasts the economic situation of the addressees. The phrase *ek tou echein*, 'from what one has,' in verses 11–12, implies that the Corinthians have the means to 'complete' that which was begun the year before. Verse 14 speaks of their abundance (*perisseuma*) in contrast with the Jerusalem Christians' lack (*hysterēma*). The cognate verb in verse 7, which speaks of the Corinthians' abounding in spiritual things, may be a double-entendre, and so may be even the christological formula in verse 9: 'For our sakes he, though rich, became poor, that you through his poverty might grow rich.' The same word, *charis*, is used for the 'grace' of Christ's sacrifice in this verse and for the gift to Jerusalem in verse 7.[46]

---

[45] It will not do to interpolate the *kathōs* of Acts 11:29, however, as do NEB, '*in proportion to his gains*,' and Orr and Walther 1976, 356, '*commensurate with* the financial gain of the previous week' (my emphasis). These introduce a concept of proportional giving not in the text and anachronistically assume some kind of capitalistic enterprise.

[46] These motifs are more reminiscent of 1 Corinthians than of the rest of 2 Corinthians. E.g., compare 2 Cor 8:7 with 1 Cor 1:5 and 7. And the teleological pattern statement of 2 Cor 8:9 recalls the ironic *ēdē eploutēsate* of 1 Cor 4:8. On the size of the collection, see Georgi 1965, 88, who points out that the cost of travel for the large delegation bearing the gift would be sensible only if the gift was substantial.

On the other hand, we should not take the 'abysmal poverty' of the Macedonian Christians too literally, for 2 Cor 9:2–4 suggests that Paul used the same sort of argument with the Macedonians, in reverse. He has bragged to them of the eagerness of the Corinthians. Moreover, we must remember that whereas Paul had been careful not to accept monetary support from the Corinthians, he had done so more than once from the Macedonians (2 Cor 11:9; Phil 4:14–19). Their 'poverty' may be partly hyperbole occasioned by the structure of Paul's rhetoric in 2 Cor 8, which depends upon the antithesis of 'poverty' and 'wealth,' 'abundance' and 'lack,' leading on to the goal, beloved also by Hellenistic moralists, of 'equity' (*isotēs*, v. 14; see Stählin 1938, esp. 354–55).

Incidentally, Paul's refusal of support from the Corinthians is not absolute, for there are indications that he expected them routinely to help with travel expenses. In 1 Cor 16:6 he tells of his plans to stay a time with them, perhaps over the winter, 'that you may send me on my way [*propempsēte*] wherever I may go.' The same expectation is voiced in 2 Cor 1:16 for his journey to Judea, and he requests the same service in the meantime for Timothy (1 Cor 16: 11). Malherbe has argued that in such a context *propempein* generally 'means to equip him with all things necessary for the journey' (1977b, 230, n. 11), which would involve some financial outlay.

The fact that some members of the Corinthian groups conduct lawsuits against other members also implies some financial or mercantile transactions (1 Cor 6:1–11). Paul's discussion gives no information about the kind of disputes involved, except that they involve *biōtika*, matters of everyday life. Nor can we infer the level of affluence of the parties, for, as the papyri show, it was a litigious age, when even small traders or village farmers could and did appear before magistrates to complain about the encroachments of their neighbors.

It may or may not be significant that the Pauline letters occasionally use commercial language both directly, to describe aspects of the relationship between the apostle and local congregations, and also metaphorically, to make theological statements. Paul makes a very direct promise to reimburse Philemon for any damages incurred by the defection of his slave Onesimus (Phlm 18), but he also uses the formal language of partnership to reinforce the epistolary form of recommendation: 'if you hold me as your partner, receive him as myself' (v. 17). The language associated with commercial partnerships is especially evident in the letter to Philippi, both in the elaborate and carefully nuanced 'receipt' that Paul gives for the gift the Philippian Christians have sent to help him in prison (4:15–19), and also, doubtless with that gift and the relationship it represented in view, in the general statements of the opening thanksgiving (1:5, 7).[47] In the same letter Paul can speak of his conversion in terms of gain and loss (3:7f), and his disciple writing to Colossae could speak of Christ's sacrifice as 'canceling the note that was against us' (Col 2:14). By themselves, these passages would prove nothing about the occupations or wealth of Christians, but they may add one small increment to the cumulative impression that many were artisans and merchants with a modest income. The same is true of the proverb Paul quotes in 2 Cor 12:14b, 'Children ought not save up for their parents, but the parents for their children.' That does not sound like the ethos of people at the lowest end of the economic scale, who generally regarded their children, at least their sons, as economic assets, added hands in the workshop, and sometimes direct means for escape from financial straits by sale into slavery. It is wealthy misers whom Plutarch castigates for keeping and storing up their wealth for children and heirs (*De amore divit.* 526A).

It is also possible to infer something about social stratification from several of the conflicts that occurred in the Pauline communities (see Theissen 1975b, esp. 40–41). That is clearest in the case of the divisions which appeared when the Corinthian Christians gathered for the Lord's Supper, which Paul rebukes in 1 Cor 11:17–34. These divisions, about which Paul 'hears' (v. 18), may be connected in some way with the incipient factions reported by Chloe's people (1:10f), but nothing that is said here hints that either the jealousy between followers of Apollos and partisans of Paul or the 'realized eschatology' of the *pneumatikoi* is involved. It is true that Paul introduces an eschatological element, for he combines here, as often elsewhere, the notion of testing by difficult circumstances, so popular with pagan moralists as well, with the eschatological notion that the Day of the Lord alone reveals one's true worth.[48] Thus the divisions 'must' come – this sounds like apocalyptic determinism – 'in order to show who are the ones who meet the test' (*hoi dokimoi*, v. 19). The notion of testing is resumed in verses 28–32. Each person must test himself before eating and drinking, lest by failing to 'distinguish [*diakrinein*] the body' his behavior may be liable to God's

---

[47] For a thorough study of partnership language in the Pauline letters, see Sampley 1980 and 1977.
[48] E.g., 1 Cor 9:27; 2 Cor 10:18; 13:5–7; but not always explicitly eschatological: 2 Cor 2:9.

judgment (*krima*), which already manifests itself in magical punishments (v. 30). Even these, however, are 'discipline' (*paideia*) intended to save the erring from the far worse fate of being 'condemned along with the world' (v. 32). But just what is the unacceptable behavior that Paul attacks with these heavy warnings and taboos? Instead of the Lord's Supper (*kyriakon deipnon*), 'each proceeds with his private supper [*to idion deipnon*], and one goes hungry and another gets drunk' (v. 21). These private suppers ought to be eaten 'at home' (22a, 34). But what specific behavior is it that in Paul's view breaks up the communal Lord's meal? The nub of the problem seems to be stated in verse 22, a series of rhetorical questions. This form, of course, is used when the speaker wants to force his audience to draw conclusions for themselves, here, to acknowledge certain unacceptable inferences from their own behavior. Their actions imply that they 'despise the congregation of God,' because[49] they 'humiliate those who do not have.' The last phrase, *hoi mē echontes*, could be read quite concretely as continuing the *oikias ouk echete* of the preceding question; that is, those who have houses are blamed for humiliating those who do not. More likely, the phrase is to be taken absolutely, 'the have-nots,' that is, the poor. Either way, this verse makes it clear that the basic division is between the (relatively) rich and the (relatively) poor.

We can go a bit further, thanks to a very illuminating study of this passage by Gerd Theissen (1974a [see ch. 9 below – Ed.]). Theissen compares the divisions in the Corinthian Eucharist with two situations familiar in Roman society and therefore, he surmises, also in a Roman colony like Corinth. One was in collegia, where officers were sometimes assigned larger quantities of food than ordinary members. Theissen points out that most clubs and guilds were more socially homogeneous than the Corinthian congregation seems to have been, and therefore conflicting expectations might arise in the latter that would have no occasion in the former (Theissen 1974a, 291–92). The other situation was a banquet held by a patron, to which his freedmen clients as well as friends of his own social rank were invited. In the society of the principate it was apparently not uncommon for these to become occasions for conspicuous display of social distance and even for humiliation of the clients of the rich, by means of the quality and quantity of food provided to different tables. Theissen cites both Martial and Juvenal, who presented the viewpoint of the inferiors, and Pliny's letter of advice to a young

---

[49] The *kai* here is epexegetic; that is, the second clause explicates the first.

friend, advocating a less offensive policy for the patronal class. The latter is worth quoting at length:

> . . . I happened to be dining with a man – though no particular friend of his – whose elegant economy, as he called it, seemed to me a sort of stingy extravagance. The best dishes were set in front of himself and a select few, and cheap scraps of food before the rest of the company. He had even put the wine into tiny little flasks, divided into three categories, not with the idea of giving his guests the opportunity of choosing, but to make it impossible for them to refuse what they were given. One lot was intended for himself and for us, another for his lesser friends (all his friends are graded) and the third for his and our freedmen. My neighbor at table noticed this and asked me if I approved. I said I did not. 'So what do you do?' he asked. 'I serve the same to everyone, for when I invite guests it is for a meal, not to make class distinctions; I have brought them as equals to the same table, so I give them the same treatment in everything.' 'Even the freedmen?' 'Of course, for then they are my fellow-diners, not freedmen.' 'That must cost you a lot.' 'On the contrary.' 'How is that?' 'Because my freedmen do not drink the sort of wine I do, but I drink theirs.'[50]

If a person like Gaius, who opened his house for gatherings of the whole *ekklēsia* of Corinthian Christians, regarded himself very much in the way that the wealthy patron of a private association or a pagan cultic society might do, that would not be surprising. If at the common meals of the Christian community, held in his dining room, he moreover made distinctions in the food he provided for those of his own social level and those who were of lower rank, that would not have been at all out of the ordinary, even though there were some voices even in pagan society who protested the practice. It was precisely the humiliation of the have-nots to which Pliny and the satirists objected. Paul objects on quite different grounds, but Theissen has given good reason for seeking the roots of the denounced behavior in the 'status-specific expectations' of a sharply stratified society.

Theissen has argued that differing perspectives of people of different social levels were involved also in another of the conflicts that perturbed Christians at Corinth, the issue of 'meat offered to idols,' addressed in 1 Corinthians 8–10 (Theissen 1975c).[51] What is relevant here is the

---

[50] *Ep.* 2.6, trans. Radice 1969, 63–64. From Martial Theissen cites 3.60; 1.20; 4.85; 6.11; 10.49; from Juvenal, *Sat.* 5. On Juvenal's satire, see also Sebesta 1976 and Reekmans 1971.

[51] Several aspects of this issue are discussed in Meeks 1983, 97–103, 157–62.

identity of the two factions. On one side are 'the strong,'[52] who have 'knowledge' (*gnōsis*) that 'there is [really] no idol in the world' (8:1, 4) and who therefore insist upon their 'right' (*exousia*: 8:9; 9:4, 5, 6, 12, 18; 10:23, 24) and 'freedom' (*eleutheria*: 10:29; cf. 9:1, 19) to eat what they please. They are the ones to whom Paul directs his reply to the inquiry the Corinthians have sent, and with whom to some extent he identifies (note Rom 15:1, 'we the strong'). On the other side are 'the weak' (8:10f; cf. 9:22), further specified as having 'weak consciences' (8:7, 12), who lack this *gnōsis* and, because of their previous customs in paganism, regard the eating of sacrificed meat as a real and dangerous matter (8:7). Many attempts have been made to define these positions in terms of their theological beliefs or ideologies. Theissen does not dismiss all these efforts, but undertakes to show that there is also a social dimension of the conflict, to which the ideological factors would have to be related. In his reading, the 'strong' are the socially powerful also referred to in 1 Cor 1:26f. It is indeed plausible that those who, after conversion to Christianity, may still have had reason to accept invitations to dinner where meat would be served (10:27), perhaps in the shrine of a pagan deity (8:10), are likely to have been the more affluent members of the group, who would still have had some social or business obligations that were more important to their roles in the larger society than were comparable connections among people of lower status. The difference is not absolute, however, for Christian clients of non-Christian patrons would surely also sometimes have found themselves in this position. Theissen also argues, though, that the whole perception of what it meant to eat meat would have been different for people of different economic levels. The poor in fact rarely ate meat; the occasions when they did tended to be cultic, whether public or private. For wealthy people, who could have meat as a more or less regular item in their diet, it would have had far fewer numinous associations. For the poor, moreover, the Christian community provided a more than adequate substitute for the sort of friendly association, including common meals, that one might otherwise have sought in clubs, guilds, or cultic associations. For an Erastus, if indeed he was the rising public servant who in a few years would be aedile in charge of all the Corinthian meat-markets, a restriction of his social intercourse to

---

[52] Not called that explicitly here, but cf. Rom 15:1, where Paul draws a general rule from the Corinthian experience.

fellow Christians would mean a drastic reduction of his horizons and a disruption of his career.

On the whole Theissen's case, which is more elaborate than can be conveniently summarized here, is convincing, and makes the conflict between the 'weak' and the 'strong' further evidence for the presence within the Corinthian congregation of persons of significantly different strata (see also Theissen 1974b). There is one problem with his construction, however, that may warrant a refinement in the concept of social stratification that he has employed. Theissen moves directly from his demonstration that the 'strong' are relatively higher in economic status than the 'weak' to the assumption that they are consequently better integrated socially into the larger society. John Schütz has pointed out difficulties with this inference (Schütz 1977, now also 1982). First, Theissen compares the 'strong' with later Christian gnostics. 'It is plainly difficult,' as Schütz says, 'to think of gnostics, with their dour cosmologies and clannish sense of separate identity, as paradigms of social integration.' Second, in Theissen's view, the high-status Christians in Corinth include former 'god-fearers.' This, too, is surprising, if high status entails high social integration, for why would well-integrated gentiles 'forsake common civic and religious traditions in favor of Judaism'? (Schütz 1977, 7). There are two orders of problems at issue here. One has to do with adequacy of evidence and argument: Are there adequate grounds for extrapolating from second-century Gnostics to the 'gnostics' of Corinth? Because some god-fearers are known to have been of higher status than most proselytes, is it valid to assume that all god-fearers had high general status? What is relevant to our immediate concern, however, is another sort of question, which we have raised before: Is social status best understood as a single dimension or as the resultant of several different dimensions? Because Theissen has assumed a single dimension, or an average of several dimensions, he concludes that high status entails a high degree of integration, an assumption which other evidence seems to contradict. We would avoid these contradictions if we recognized that the 'strong' of the Corinthian congregation are inconsistent in status. They may enjoy a high rank in some dimensions, such as wealth, identification with the Latin element in the colony, support by dependents and clients, and in one or two cases perhaps also civic office, but they may be ranked lower in others, such as origin, occupation, or sex. Such people would share many of the attitudes, values, and sentiments of unambiguously higher social levels yet still lack status crystallization. Other persons in the Corinthian congregation who were much lower on all these scales than the 'strong' might suffer a much lower degree of inconsistency among their dimensions of status, and thus, within their own social circles, might be better integrated than those who were more mobile and more exposed.

Also in Corinth the status of women became a matter of controversy, as we see in 1 Cor 11:2–16 and 14:33b–36. These are not the most lucid passages in the Pauline letters, and a small mountain of literature about them has by no means relieved their obscurity. Fortunately we do not have to solve all their problems in order to make the few observations that are germane to our present question. We have already seen that there were a number of women prominently involved in the Pauline circle who exhibited the sorts of status inconsistency that would inspire a Juvenal to eloquent indignation. There were women who headed households, who ran businesses and had independent wealth, who traveled with their own slaves and helpers. Some who are married have become converts to this exclusive religious cult without the consent of their husbands (1 Cor 7:13), and they may, though Paul advises against it, initiate divorce (ibid.). Moreover, women have taken on some of the same roles as men's within the sect itself. Some exercise charismatic functions like prayer and prophecy in the congregation (1 Cor 11:2–16); others, as we have seen in our prosopography, are Paul's fellow workers as evangelists and teachers. Both in terms of their position in the larger society and in terms of their participation in the Christian communities, then, a number of women broke through the normal expectations of female roles.

It is not surprising that this produced tensions within the groups, and that the tortuous theological compromise stated by Paul in 1 Cor 11:2–16[53] would not settle the issue. Later in the received form of the same letter, a discussion of ecstatic speech and prophecy in the assemblies is interrupted by an absolute prohibition of women from speaking in the meetings, requiring them to be 'subordinate' and to 'ask their own husbands at home if they want to learn something'

---

[53] In brief, he leaves unquestioned the right of women, led by the Spirit, to exercise the same leadership roles in the assembly as men, but insists only that the conventional symbols of sexual difference, in clothing and hair styles, be retained. I discussed this at some length in Meeks 1974. Recent attempts to excise these verses as an interpolation are not persuasive (Walker 1975; Murphy-O'Connor 1976).

(14:33b–36).[54] The subordination of women within the household order was taught in the paraenesis of the Pauline congregations, and reinforced in the letters to Asian churches written by disciples of Paul (Col 3:18; Eph. 5:22–24; see n. 40 above). In the second century the roles of women were still controversial among people who wrote fictional accounts claiming the authority of Paul. In the Acts of Paul and Thecla a virgin of Iconium on the eve of her marriage is won to celibate Christianity by Paul's preaching. After miraculously confounding the (male) authorities who try to silence her, but supported by the women of the city and saved on one occasion by a lioness, she baptizes herself. Then she cuts her hair short, dresses like a man, and goes off to follow Paul as an itinerant apostle.[55] On the other hand, the author of the Pastoral Epistles rejects the sort of asceticism represented by Thecla and all teaching by women (1 Tim 2:9–15; 4:3), except that older women should become 'good teachers' by instructing younger women to be good wives and mothers, always subordinate to their husbands (Titus 2:3–5).[56] These second-century documents furnish no direct evidence that can help to describe the social constituency of Pauline Christianity as I have defined it, but they do illustrate the variety and the strength of reactions to status inconsistency (and violation of conventions) of one kind.

The other conflicts which are addressed in the letters of Paul and his immediate disciples did not, so far as the evidence permits us to judge, have anything directly to do with different social levels in the groups. There is one possible exception: the rivalry in Corinth between Paul and the people whom he called sarcastically the 'superapostles' (*hyperlian apostoloi*: 2 Cor 11:5; 12:11). In the invidious comparisons which were made in Corinth between them, certain signs of status seem to have

[54] Because this interrupts the discussion of glossolalia and prophecy, and because it would make nonsense not only of the directives about female prophets and leaders of prayer in 11:2–16 but also of the positive role accorded to single women in chapter 7, a number of scholars have suggested that these verses were added to the letter after Paul's time, by someone of the same views that find even more radical expression in 1 Tim 2:9–15. That is an attractive solution, although the interpolation would have had to occur before wide circulation of the Pauline letters, for there is no direct manuscript evidence. Some mss. do have vv. 34f in a different place, after v. 40, but that more likely indicates that some ancient copyist sensed the break in topic than that he had a ms. in which they were absent. Verse 36 would not follow smoothly on v. 33.

[55] Text in Lipsius-Bonnet 1891, 1:235–72; translated in Hennecke 1959–64, 2:353–64.

[56] MacDonald 1979 has argued ingeniously that the Pastoral Epistles were a direct response to the Acts of Paul and Thecla, and to the more widespread movement in Asia Minor which that document represented.

figured. That is, there were members of the Corinthian church sufficiently numerous or persuasive that Paul could address his complaints to the whole congregation, who accorded greater prestige to the recent arrivals than to Paul. Since we have only Paul's description of the situation, and that heavily laden with sarcasm and hostile interpretation, we cannot hope to reconstruct an accurate picture of the superapostles or of their reception by the Corinthians,[57] but it may be useful to note quickly those status factors to which the text alludes. First, rhetorical ability and imposing physical presence are valued. Some Corinthians have complained that, while Paul's letters are 'weighty and strong,' his 'bodily presence is weak and [his] speech despicable' (2 Cor 10:10). The claims which Paul makes just before this (10:1–6) are themselves claims about rhetorical ability, the ability 'to take every thought captive.' In 11:6 he admits to nonprofessional status (*idiōtēs*) as an orator, but claims to possess *gnōsis*. That is an argument of the same order: Paul rhetorically boasts that he is no mere sophist.[58] Second, wealth and income appear only in a curiously inverted way: not the amount of wealth or income possessed by Paul and the rivals, but the manner of self-support. The superapostles receive support from the Corinthians, which Paul interprets in a negative way (11:20); the Corinthians now are unhappy with Paul because he did *not* take money from them (11:7–12; 12:13–15). The situation is further complicated by the fact that someone has apparently suggested that the Jerusalem collection is really a fraudulent scheme by which in fact Paul is going to enrich himself while piously declining support (12:16–18). But that is a secondary calumny; the primary issue is the qualification of an apostle by the way he is supported. We may take it, to simplify a complex situation, that expecting to be paid for one's eloquence is seen by the Corinthians as a mark of professional eminence; in contrast Paul is depicted as an amateur or worse.[59] Third

[57] The most notable attempt to do so is Georgi 1964. For a sober criticism of the method, see Hickling 1975. See also Barrett 1971b and Holladay 1977, 34–40 and *passim*.
[58] On this ploy, familiar in such speakers as Dio of Prusa, see Judge 1968.
[59] Dungan 1971, 3–80, and, more carefully and ingeniously, Theissen 1975a have argued that what is at stake is the conflict between two normative styles of missionary support, with the opponents of Paul representing the intrusion into the urban areas of the mendicant, itinerant apostolate described in some of the early sayings of Jesus. The latter was originally at home in Palestinian village culture. I find neither quite convincing. Theissen's suggestion that both styles might have analogies in the contemporary idealized portraits of Cynic philosophers points rather to a different kind of analysis, which has been developed by Hock 1980.

and finally, peculiar religious qualifications play a major role: visions and revelations (12:1–10), miracles (12:12), specific divine commissioning (10:13–18), pure Jewish background (11:22f). Paul argues, first, that if these things really counted, he could claim them, too, and, second, that they are devalued by the surpassing and novel criterion of a life in conformity with the crucifixion / resurrection pattern, which he but not his opponents exemplifies. All this tells us little about the status dimensions of typical Corinthian Christians, except that they share certain measures of status that are generally recognized in the larger society, especially those having to do with rhetorical ability, and that they have superimposed on these some specifically religious qualifications. Whether this implies that a number of Corinthian Christians themselves possessed the signs of prestige that they held in esteem is far from obvious.

Mixed strata, ambiguous status

The evidence we have surveyed is fragmentary, random, and often unclear. We cannot draw up a statistical profile of the constituency of the Pauline communities nor fully describe the social level of a single Pauline Christian. We have found a number of converging clues, however, that permit an impressionistic sketch of these groups. It is a picture in which people of several social levels are brought together. The extreme top and bottom of the Greco-Roman social scale are missing from the picture. It is hardly surprising that we meet no landed aristocrats, no senators, *equites*, nor (unless Erastus might qualify) decurions. But there is also no specific evidence of people who are destitute – such as the hired menials and dependent handworkers; the poorest of the poor, peasants, agricultural slaves, and hired agricultural day laborers, are absent because of the urban setting of the Pauline groups (see Lee 1971, 132). There may well have been members of the Pauline communities who lived at the subsistence level, but we hear nothing of them.

The levels in between, however, are well represented. There are slaves, although we cannot tell how many. The 'typical' Christian, however, the one who most often signals his presence in the letters by one or another small clue, is a free artisan or small trader. Some even in those occupational categories had houses, slaves, the ability to travel, and other signs of wealth. Some of the wealthy provided housing, meeting places, and other services for individual Christians and for whole groups. In effect, they filled the roles of patrons.

Not only was there a mixture of social levels in each congregation; but also, in each individual or category that we are able to identify there is evidence of divergent rankings in the different dimensions of status. Thus we find Christians in the *familia caesaris*, whose members were so often among the few upwardly mobile people in the Roman Empire. We find, too, other probable freedmen or descendents of freedmen who have advanced in wealth and position, especially in the Roman colonies of Corinth and Philippi. We find wealthy artisans and traders: high in income, low in occupational prestige. We find wealthy, independent women. We find wealthy Jews. And, if we are to believe Acts, we find gentiles whose adherence to the synagogue testifies to some kind of dissonance in their relation to their society.

The 'emerging consensus' that Malherbe reports seems to be valid: a Pauline congregation generally reflected a fair cross-section of urban society. Moreover, those persons prominent enough in the mission or in the local community for their names to be mentioned or to be identifiable in some other way usually – when we have evidence to make any judgment at all about them – exhibit signs of a high ranking in one or more dimensions of status. But that is typically accompanied by low rankings in other dimensions. Although the evidence is not abundant, we may venture the generalization that the most active and prominent members of Paul's circle (including Paul himself) are people of high status inconsistency (low status crystallization). They are upwardly mobile; their achieved status is higher than their attributed status. Is that more than accidental? Are there some specific characteristics of early Christianity that would be attractive to status-inconsistents? Or is it only that people with the sorts of drive, abilities, and opportunities that produced such mixed status would tend to stand out in any group they joined, and thus to be noticed for the record? It may not be possible to answer these questions, but they suggest some possible considerations to be explored.

[The following paragraphs are adapted from pp. 191–92 in Meeks' book]

In this essay we have tried to sketch a profile of the social level of the typical convert to Pauline Christianty and of the mix of levels in the group. The former turned out to be in effect the profile of the most prominent members, for they were the ones likely to be mentioned by name or otherwise identified. We found that their dominant characteristic was status inconsistency or social mobility. Does it seem plausible that the powerful symbols of change grounded in tradition, symbols of personal and communal transformation, symbols of an evil world encompassed by God's judgement and grace would be particularly attractive to people who had experienced the hopes and fears of occupying an ambiguous position in society? Or, contrariwise, would such experiences among so many leaders of the community tend to reinforce just those paradoxical and dialectical symbols that are so characteristic of Pauline beliefs?

May we further guess that the sorts of status inconsistency we observed – independent women with moderate wealth, Jews with wealth in a pagan society, freedmen with skill and money but stigmatized by origin, and so on – brought with them not only anxiety but also loneliness, in a society in which social position was important and usually rigid? Would, then, the intimacy of the Christian groups become a welcome refuge, the emotion-charged language of family and affection and the image of a caring, personal God powerful antidotes, while the master symbol of the crucified savior crystallized a believable picture of the way the world seemed really to work?

On the other hand, the sorts of social and physical mobility we observed in the Pauline prosopography also imply some daring, some self-confidence, some willingness to break out of the ordinary social structures. And in the language of Paul and his associates we have vivid images of the new and the unexpected, of risk and miraculous survival, of a powerful, freedom-giving Spirit, of a world on the brink of transformation.

The churches, too, were mixtures of social statuses. The kinds of relationships that the members had previously had to one another, and still had in other settings – between master and slave, rich and poor, freedman and patron, male and female, and the like – stood in tension with the *communitas* celebrated in the rituals of baptism and the Lord's Supper. There was tension, too, between the familiar hierarchy of those roles and the freedom of the Spirit to confer distinction, by means of some charisma, upon the person of inferior status. So, too, we find in the letters, a stress on symbols of unity, equality, and love, but also correlative symbols of fluidity, diversity, individuation.

Those odd little groups in a dozen or so cities of the Roman East were engaged, though they would not have put it quite this way, in constructing a new world. In time, more time that they thought was left, their ideas, their images of God, their ways of organizing life, their rituals, would become part of a massive transformation, in ways they could not have foreseen, of the culture of the Mediterranean basin and of Europe.

FURTHER READING

A number of social-scientific publications relevant to the discussion of status and status inconsistency are listed in n. 9 above. On status in the ancient world, see Reekmans 1971; Weaver 1967; Finley 1973. But for a powerful argument in favour of a class-based analysis of the ancient society see de Ste Croix 1981 (and further discussion in Martin 1991; Rohrbaugh 1984). On the social structure of the Roman empire see MacMullen 1974; Alföldy 1985; 1986; Garnsey and Saller 1987.

An important influence on the 'old consensus' was the work of Deissmann 1911; 1927. Note also Engels (in Marx and Engels 1957, 330–32). An early challenge, influential upon the formation of the new consensus, is found in Judge 1960a (note also Filson 1939; Kreissig 1967). Particularly important for the new consensus is the detailed study of social stratification in the Corinthian community by Theissen 1974b (=1982, 69–119). See also Malherbe 1977a/1983; Kyrtatas 1987, 21–24; Clarke 1993; Horrell 1996a, 91–101 (with further bibliography there). Overviews of the discussion up to the end of the 1980s may be found in Holmberg 1990, 21–76; Kidd 1990, 35–75.

Critical reactions to the new consensus include Gager 1979; Schottroff 1985 (see ch. 10 below); Meggitt 1996; and esp. 1998b. For critical reactions to Meeks' book as a whole see Malina 1985b; Elliott 1985; Pleket 1985; Stowers 1985; Schöllgen 1988. An overview of Meeks' argument, introducing the thesis about status inconsistency, is provided in Meeks 1982.

8

Ritual in the Pauline Churches

MARGARET Y. MACDONALD

INTRODUCTION

Margaret MacDonald's book *The Pauline Churches* (1988), from
which this extract is taken, is a study of the process and patterns of
'institutionalisation' in the Pauline communities. Taking up theoretical
resources similar to those used by Philip Esler (1987; see ch. 4 above)
MacDonald considers the Pauline letters in terms derived from the
work of Peter Berger and Thomas Luckmann (1967): the letters
represent attempts to construct and maintain a symbolic universe
which shapes and orders the belief and practice of the Pauline communities. MacDonald takes the genuine Pauline letters as reflecting a
time of 'community-building institutionalisation'. Colossians and
Ephesians, regarded as deutero-Pauline, written shortly after Paul's
death, then mark a stage of 'community-stabilising institutionalisation'. Finally, the Pastoral Epistles, written near the end of the first
century, reveal a phase of 'community-protecting institutionalisation'.
In this process of institutionalisation, MacDonald suggests, there are
indications that the Pauline churches are beginning to move away
from the 'sect' type – specifically, the 'conversionist sect' type outlined
by Bryan Wilson (see chs. 2 and 4 above, ch. 13 below) – towards
the model of 'church', as described in Ernst Troeltsch's typology of
church and sect (see MacDonald 1988, 32–42, 163–66, etc.). With
her overall focus set on the process of institutionalisation, MacDonald
examines patterns of ministry, belief, ritual, and attitudes to the world/
ethics in each of the phases she identifies.

The extract printed below explores the nature and practice of ritual
in the worship of the Pauline communities (in the time of Paul himself
– the phase of community-building institutionalisation). As
MacDonald remarks, the adoption of the term 'ritual', as opposed to

'sacrament', indicates a social-scientific perspective on these religious practices, with a focus upon what they do – how they function in the formation and maintenance of community – and how they mediate the encounter with the sacred.

The two major rituals in the early Christian communities are of course baptism and Lord's supper. MacDonald examines each of these in turn, showing how baptism serves as the rite of initiation which takes believers from the sphere of the 'dirty', sinful world into the pure community of the sect. The Lord's supper, on the other hand, reinforces the central beliefs of the community members, 'regenerates' the experience of the sacred, and reaffirms their integration into the community which is, or should be, united as 'one in Christ'.

Like Wayne Meeks, whose discussion of ritual she draws upon, MacDonald uses the term 'ritual' as an overall label for the whole range of activities which take place in the worship of the Pauline communities (Meeks 1983, 140–63; also Horrell 1996a, 80–88). She also uses the terms 'initiatory rite' and 'memorial rite' to describe baptism and Lord's supper respectively (see below). Bruce Malina and Jerome Neyrey, on the other hand, adopt the term 'rite' as the overall label, and, drawing on the work of the anthropologist Victor Turner, make various distinctions between 'rituals' on the one hand, and 'ceremonies' on the other, both of which are a type of rite (Malina 1986a, 139–43; Neyrey 1990, 75–81; 1995, 200). Most fundamental is that the purpose of a ritual is status reversal or transformation (e.g. baptism), whereas a ceremony serves essentially to confirm roles or status (e.g. Lord's supper). Drawing attention to this distinction is, I think, valuable.

MacDonald's work, like much which uses social-scientific methods and terminology, offers a new perspective, a new viewpoint, from which to examine the nature of worship – specifically baptism and Lord's supper – within the early Pauline communities. She does not thereby wish to exclude more theologically orientated perspectives, nor to deny that an experience of the sacred may genuinely underlie the rituals of the Pauline churches (see MacDonald 1988, 27–28). But a social-scientific approach asks different questions, and offers fresh insights into the relationship between ritual forms and the construction of community.

The following study examines the worship of the Pauline communities. The function of ritual forms in the articulation and the preservation of the sect's identity is considered. The investigation analyses the connection between baptism and the assertion of communal identity. The role of the Lord's supper in the maintenance of boundaries separating the Pauline Christians from outsiders is investigated. The relationship between what is experienced in ritual and the process of symbolization is discussed.

1. A ritual context

As in the case of ministry structures, there has been a tendency in New Testament scholarship to contrast Paul's attitude to the 'sacraments' with the later developments of a more highly structured church. For example, both Bultmann and Käsemann have argued that Paul consciously disavowed himself of the idea that the Lord's supper had the magical effects of the 'medicine of immortality' – quoting the well-known Ignatian phrase.[1] Similar, though less extreme, comparisons are found in Conzelmann's work:

> Paul shows particularly clearly in 1 Cor 10f that the sacrament does not change a man in a mysterious way, but brings him into the historical fellowship of the faithful in the church; it is not a magical protection, but leads to life in community. Of course, it must be granted that ideas from the mysteries appear in the Hellenistic milieu. In Ignatius, the sacramental food has become the '*pharmakon athanasias*' (medicine of immortality). In that case, the cult no longer serves to establish 'everyday' faith in the world, but to mark out a holy realm from the world. (Conzelmann 1969a, 59)

In the interest of differentiating Paul's attitude to 'sacraments' from later catholic concepts, these interpreters have played down or ignored the more 'mystical' attributes of ritual forms in the early communities. They have not paid enough attention to the relation between the mysterious experiences of worship and the formation of communities, including the development of beliefs and norms. In this investigation, connections are made between what is experienced by the Pauline Christians through participation in ritual forms and the entry and continued membership within the sect. Moreover, instead of simply

---

[1] Bultmann 1965, I, 313–14; see his remarks on baptism, pp. 311–12; Käsemann 1964, 116; 1969, 246.

drawing a contrast between the earliest and later understandings, Paul's attitude to rituals is related to the social situation of a sect engaged in community-building institutionalization.[2]

The choice of the word 'ritual' rather than 'sacrament' is deliberate; it enables one to include more in the definition than what the later church identified as sacraments. The term 'ritual' is part of the vocabulary of the social scientist; when applied to Pauline communities, it implies comparison with the rites of other social groups. The discipline of cultural anthropology is particularly useful for an investigation of ritual in the ancient world. However, in order for an approach to the study of the New Testament texts which incorporates insights from cultural anthropology to be fruitful, one must be open to the discovery of contacts between aspects of the early Christian experience and those from other cultural milieus (see Douglas 1982, 6). The uniqueness of the early Christian movement is not being denied here, nor is the religious experience being reduced to the purely magical (with all its negative modern connotations).[3] Rather, what is being advocated is the willingness to locate Pauline communities within a societal context. If, for example, ritual can repeatedly be shown to reinforce the identity of a variety of social groups, one must ask if ritual functions to reinforce the identity of the Pauline sect.

In this study, Clifford Geertz's definition of ritual as 'consecrated behaviour' will be employed (Geertz 1966, 28). According to Geertz, it is in acting out the roles involved in ritual that the conviction of religious conceptions as truthful, and religious directives as sound, is somehow generated. Religious belief, Geertz argues, involves a prior acceptance of an authority which transforms human experience – experience marked by the problem of meaning (Geertz 1966, 25). This authority is discovered at some point in the world where one worships – in the midst of ritual – where one accepts the lordship of something other than oneself (Geertz 1966, 34).

Ritual action is distinctive in that it involves behaviour which is set apart for contact with the sacred. Unlike the detached observer, the participant experiences a simultaneous transformation and ordering of his or her sense of reality. For the participant in a religious performance,

---

[2] A more realistic approach to the contrast between worship in Paul's churches and that characteristic of later communities appears in Rowland 1985, 237–44.

[3] There is value in comparing the practices of Pauline Christians to the magical activities of the Greco-Roman world, as is evident in Smith 1980, 241–49.

the ritual becomes the realization of a particular religious perspective – a model of what is believed and a model for believing it. In these dramas, individuals attain their faith as they portray it (Geertz 1966, 29).

We come to the Pauline communities, by necessity, as 'detached observers'. We are aware of the incompleteness of our dissection of Pauline statements removed from their ritual context. We cannot share exactly in the experience of these early Christians. Yet, in the text we find evidence suggesting what ritual forms may have looked like. We read statements of belief obviously connected to the enactment of rituals. We know enough to make suggestions about the significance of ritual for the members of the Pauline sect. Speaking of a ritual context enables us to include more than baptism and the Lord's supper. The community gathering, the act of prophecy, the reading of scripture, the singing of a hymn, the gestures of intimacy, the preaching of the gospel and even the reading of a letter are all part of a ritual context. The Pauline correspondence itself grows out of, and is rooted in, what is experienced in the midst of ritual.

Noting both the communicative and performative functions of ritual, Wayne Meeks argues that an appropriate question with which to undertake a study of ritual in the early church is: 'What do they do?' (Meeks 1983, 142). In this investigation, a more motive-orientated question will be added to Meeks' functionalist one: 'Where do the members of the Pauline sect believe the sacred may be encountered?' The most obvious answer to this latter question is in the gathering of the ekklesia. Although it is not certain how often the group met, whether there was a central meeting place for all members in one region or whether a variety of meetings took place for various reasons, it is clear that the Pauline Christians did come together (1 Cor 11:17, 18, 20, 33, 34; 14:23, 26; 1 Cor 5:4).[4] It is in these ritual contexts that individuals discovered for the first time, or renewed their acceptance of, the authority that transformed their experience. The Pauline Christians discovered the Lordship of Christ. 1 Cor 14:23–5 indicates that when the whole church came together, there was a possibility that outsiders witnessing the ritual might become 'converted'. They would acknowledge the presence of authority, proclaiming the lordship of something other than themselves. They would declare that God is truly present among the gathering of the ekklesia (v. 25).

---

[4] Meeks 1983, 142; see Rowland 1985, 240–41.

There is not much information in the Pauline correspondence about what actually occurred during the gathering of the ekklesia. In 1 Cor 14:26, Paul writes that when the Corinthians come together each has a hymn, a teaching, a revelation, a tongue, an interpretation. This statement, coupled with the fact that Paul's letters contain citations from scripture, elements of Christian tradition and numerous exhortations, leads to the following suggestions about what was going on. If one were to enter the crowded meeting held in the room of a generous Corinthian householder, one would expect to hear the exposition of scripture and preaching, including statements explaining the significance of the Christ event. One might be reminded of the old life before baptism and be told about the shape one's new life should have now. Difficulties associated with a new life in the Lord might be discussed: Should one remain married to a non-believer? How should one relate to non-believers with whom one was forced to mingle during daily tasks? Revelations of 'words of the Lord' might break the sombre atmosphere. Prophecies about things to come would bring encouragement in the face of difficulties. The cruel treatment of the unbelieving master can be endured in the face of the promise of universal salvation. The jubilant sound of tongues might fill the room with the most elevated prayer.[5]

In 1 Cor 14:13–15, Paul states that one can pray either by 'tongue' or 'rationally'. Tongues suggests, at least to the modern reader, the most novel and spontaneous type of consecrated behaviour in the early church. However, it is important to remember that tongues and other manifestations of the Spirit, such as spontaneous prayer or prophecy, are not completely formless; there exists a framework where the individual carries out actions (Meeks 1983, 149). In order for ritual either to communicate an experience of the sacred, or to bring the participant in contact with the sacred, a pattern must exist. Evidence of a framework for even the most spontaneous of rituals is found in 1 Cor 14:26–33 where Paul gives explicit instructions concerning the number of glossolalists allowed and the time when they should be permitted to speak (Meeks 1983, 149). Paul calls for order and control; there is a time for tongues, a time for revelation, a time for interpretation, a time for prophecy. All things should be done for edification, in an orderly fashion, not with confusion, but with peace.

---

[5] See Meeks 1983, 147; on the relation between ritual in the Pauline sect and the practices of Judaism, see Meeks 1983, 147–48, 150–53; Rowland 1985, 238–44.

As a modern onlooker at the gathering in the crowded room of the generous Corinthian, one might understand the ritual behaviour to be a mixture of the familiar and the novel – a blend of the spontaneous and the customary (see Meeks 1983, 147). The patterns which determine the structure of ritual have not as yet become very solidified; the institutionalization of ritual behaviour is free to develop in various directions. However, even at this early stage, Paul's concern for decency and order is beginning to guide institutionalization in one particular direction. As time passes and patterns become more and more established, we can expect that there will be less room for the more spontaneous rituals. At any rate, from the time of the earliest church, the novel must be interpreted in terms of the familiar, the spontaneous in terms of the customary.

The ritual of the Pauline Christians is at the heart of the process of community-building; it acts to stimulate group solidarity (see Douglas 1982, 78). Members of the Pauline sect become members and remain members by sharing patterns of symbolic action. In Geertz's language, rituals both induce an ethos and define a world view (Geertz 1966, 34). This is perhaps related to what Paul points to as the most important function of consecrated behaviour, upbuilding (*oikodomē*). Paul evidently prefers the clear speech of prophecy to glossolalia; the test is whether words build up the assembly (1 Cor 14:1ff). Hymns, teachings, revelations, interpretations and even tongues are for upbuilding; they are vehicles for teaching and admonition (1 Cor 14:26). Faced with newly formed communities, Paul must deal with the problem of education. By participating in upbuilding rituals, the sect's knowledge will grow. This knowledge includes attitudes and beliefs which are appropriate for those who are now in Christ. When Paul appeals to the sect to admonish or exhort each other, he is calling for the participation in certain ritual actions. Instruction and consolation appear to be especially expected of those who prophesy (1 Cor 14:3, 19). 1 Thess 5:12 suggests that local leadership is linked to the practice of admonishing. Whether one is giving this special instruction or receiving it, one is participating in ritual. Ritual involves learning, and learning shapes the way one will behave in the future. Geertz writes: 'Even within the same society, what one "learns" about the essential pattern of life from a sorcery rite and from a commensual meal will have rather diverse effects on social and psychological functioning' (Geertz 1966, 39).

2. Baptism: purification and sect formation

The 'learning' function of ritual is especially visible in the Pauline sect's practice of baptism. Baptism was probably only possible after one had acknowledged a specific authority (the Lordship of Christ) and had acquired a certain knowledge; it might be described as a celebration of learning. Because baptism was connected with entrance into the sect, it provides a good example of how ritual functioned in sect formation.

Gal 4:6 and Rom 8:15 are most likely rooted in a baptismal setting. The newly baptized person may have come out of the water crying 'Abba!' (Father!). The Spirit was understood as speaking through the individual. He or she was being adopted as God's child (Meeks 1983, 152). Baptism appears to be recalled in the Pauline communities as a fundamental experience of transformation. Moreover, Paul's instructions indicate that this experience is understood as having implications for community life. In Rom 8:16–18 Paul provides encouragement in the face of suffering by arguing that being children of God means being heirs of God. The members of the community are joint heirs with Christ. They suffer with him in order that they may be glorified with him (cf. Gal 4:6–7). In Rom 6:2ff Paul articulates the implications of having been buried with Christ by baptism into his death. Community members have died to sin (v. 2); they should not yield their members to sin as instruments of unrighteousness (v. 13). In Gal 3:26–8 baptism is recalled by Paul in relation to his argument that circumcision should not be a requirement for the entry of Gentile converts into the community. Baptism into Christ is described as putting on Christ (v. 27). Unity in Christ is associated with transformation of relations between groups (v. 28). With respect to the relations between Gentiles and Jews in Christ, the primary concern underlying the argument of Galatians, Paul views this unity in Christ to have revolutionizing consequences in the social realm.

The close connection between the Christ event and the experience of baptism implied in the language about being buried with Christ and adopted as a joint-heir underlines the significance of the 'mystical' baptismal experience in the Pauline sect. The language about the abolition of differences of Gal 3:28 may provide some insight into the breaking down of barriers that was experienced during the rite. It is important, however, to realize that ambiguity surrounds the transition from participation in a formative entrance rite to life in a group of people whose lives have been shaped by a similar experience of the sacred. To come out of the water crying 'Jesus is Lord!' (cf. Rom 10:9; Phil 2:11) and to experience a divine adoption and unity with one's fellow initiates in Christ is a transforming experience which must come to an end, but which demands articulation with respect to everyday reality (see Geertz 1966, 38). Individuals who partake in the ritual of baptism form community with fellow children of God. There is need for group cohesion.

Adoption as a child of God necessarily means separation from those who are not the same kind of children. Baptism functions as a cleansing rite; a water bath symbolizes a transition from a 'dirty' world into a 'clean' sect. The members of the Pauline sect can be distinguished from those in the outside world because they have been cleansed and sanctified; they have been justified in the name of Jesus Christ in the Spirit of God (1 Cor 6:11). This washing is connected with the image of dying and rising with Christ (Rom 6:3–11). The participation in a symbolic death and resurrection even has a purifying effect on the dark world of the dead, as the peculiar practice of being baptized on behalf of the dead implies (1 Cor 15:29).[6] The drama is heightened by the taking off and putting on of clothes, as is suggested by the description of putting on Christ (Gal 3:26–7; Meeks 1983, 151). Having undergone baptism, the participant leaves the world inhabited by demonic powers and enters the domain of a new universe.

In his book *The New Testament World*, Bruce Malina employs insights from cultural anthropology in his discussion on Christian purity arrangements. He defines purity in terms of boundaries separating inside from outside that are necessary in order to perceive 'set-apartness'.[7] Malina describes the sacred as that which is set apart. The Pauline Christians might be seen as drawing a line around where they expect the sacred to be found. The sect – sometimes perceived as the body of Christ – becomes sacred space. This space must be kept pure, which means that categorization is necessary. The construction of a classification system implies that certain things will be kept on the outside (Malina 1981, 129).

---

[6] On this passage and its connections with the practices of Greco-Roman society, see Smith 1980, 243.

[7] Malina 1981, 125. Malina draws many of his insights from another valuable book for a sociological approach to studying the New Testament by Douglas 1966; see especially pp. 41–57.

The centrality of interaction in Christ for determining purity in the Pauline communities is suggested by the use of temple language to describe the sacred space of the sect.[8] The group itself is called the 'temple of God' (1 Cor 3:16–17; 2 Cor 6:16) or the 'temple of the Holy Spirit' (1 Cor 6:19). Sacrifice also takes on a new meaning in the sect; it refers specifically to Christ and the actions of individuals in Christ (e.g. 1 Thess 5:19–24; Rom 12:1, 15:16; 1 Cor 5:7).[9]

The zone of interaction between existence in Christ and the world of Jews and Gentiles is somewhat problematic for group members; the means of preserving the purity of the group is uncertain. This ambiguity is especially visible in Galatians where the issue of how to deal with the entrance of Gentiles into the community comes to the fore. How much heed should be given to previous biblical injunctions?

With respect to food, Paul is persuaded that nothing is unclean of itself (Rom 14:14; cf. Gal 2:11ff). Yet, leaving room for much uncertainty, Paul instructs members that they should weigh individual situations accordingly. In his instructions to the Corinthians, Paul reveals his concern for the unity of the community and for relations with outsiders (perhaps reflecting his hope that they too might be won for Christ, cf. 1 Cor 10:32ff). Paul states that food, which may or may not have been offered to idols, is intrinsically harmless (1 Cor 10:25f). This statement, however, receives important qualifications. On the one hand, no unnecessary offence should be given to outsiders (1 Cor 10:24–7, 32). On the other hand, perceptions of members who believe in divisions between clean and unclean must be given primary consideration (1 Cor 8:7–13; 1 Cor 10:28–30). Paul's concern for harmony in the community that comes from respecting individual opinions is even more strongly expressed in Romans (Rom 14:1–6, 13–15, 19–21). His desire to promote unity is especially visible in his statement that eating, abstaining, observing days and esteeming all days the same, are all good when they are done for the honour of the Lord (Rom 14:5–9; cf. Gal 4:10).

A concern for purity is also visible in 1 Cor 5–6 where the question of how to deal with transgression within the group arises. Paul instructs

[8] Malina 1981, 146. Malina compares purity rules in Judaism with the boundaries that separated the Christian community from the outside world (pp. 131–43). On the relation between purity in the Pauline community and purity at Qumran, see Gärtner 1965; Newton 1985.
[9] Malina 1981, 147–50; for detailed discussion of this topic, see Newton 1985, 52–78.

the Corinthians to cleanse out the old leaven so that they might be a new lump (1 Cor 5:7). The wicked person whose immorality corrupts the purity of the sect should be driven away (1 Cor 5:13). It is not the immorality of the outside world that is in danger of polluting the body, but the immorality that has somehow been allowed to penetrate the sacred space (1 Cor 5:9–13). Paul forbids the community members to eat with the believer who is guilty of immorality (1 Cor 5:11), while apparently legitimating eating with unbelievers, irrespective of their lifestyles (1 Cor 10:27). The believer who is guilty of immorality can corrupt the group in a way that is impossible for a non-believer, for the believer alone is subject to the requirements that membership in the church entails (Newton 1985, 99). The importance of the disputes being settled within the boundaries of the pure sect and according to the judgments of those on the inside is evident in Paul's angry response to the fact that members have gone to the courts of unbelievers (1 Cor 6:1–11). Once again, one gains the impression that ambiguity surrounds the dealings of the Pauline sect with the outside world.

A discussion of Christian purity arrangements sheds light on the connection between ritual experience and the separation of the Pauline sect from the outside world. The individual who is initiated into the community through the ritual of baptism has entered sacred space. This entry, however, leads to new questions: How are the members of the Pauline sect to interpret what they have experienced in ritual in relation to life in the everyday world? How are the boundaries surrounding the community to be maintained?

Perhaps the most obvious aspect of the language used to denote baptism by Paul is that it involves some kind of change. Geertz observes:

> Having ritually 'lept' (the image is perhaps a bit too athletic for the actual facts – 'slipped' might be more accurate) into the framework of meaning which religious conceptions define and, the ritual ended, returned again to the common-sense world, a man is – unless, as sometimes happens, the experience fails to register – changed. (Geertz 1966, 38)

Having ritually 'lept' from baptism to the everyday world, the Pauline sectarian sees the everyday world as part of a wider order-giving reality – the symbolic universe. However, in order for the new convert to maintain the boundaries between the new universe and everything outside it, it will be necessary for the individual to renew his or her own experience of the sacred. Baptism marks the beginning – but only the beginning –

of an experience that must be nurtured and rekindled if membership in the sect is to continue.

3. The Lord's supper: conviviality and continuance

While baptism enables the individual to be initiated within the community, the ritual of the Lord's supper integrates the member into the community time and time again. Like the initiatory rite, the memorial rite retells the story of the death and resurrection of Jesus and enables the believer to become personally identified with the events by participating in consecrated behaviour.[10] In Paul's letters there are only two explicit references to the Lord's supper: 1 Cor 11:17–34, 10:14–22. It is clear from these passages that the Lord's supper is a locus for the articulation of beliefs. The traditional language surrounding the events of Jesus, the mention of a new covenant, the commemorative phrase 'this is my body which is for you', and the eschatological phrase 'until he comes' underline the connection between the participation in this common meal and the process of self-definition (1 Cor 11:23–6).[11] Traditional forms and language act as a means of reinforcing the central beliefs of the community members, but also as a means of regenerating the experience of the sacred that called the community into being.

Related to the fact that the Lord's supper enhances the internal coherence of the Pauline sect, is its function in the maintenance of purity boundaries. This is especially visible in the contrast drawn by Paul between the Lord's supper and idolatrous pagan sacrifices (1 Cor 10:14–22). The activity of the Pauline sect is distinguished from that of other cultic associations. One cannot partake of the table of the Lord and of the table of demons (Meeks 1983, 160).

Although the Lord's supper generates unity in the sect, it can also become a subject of controversy. Paul cites the eucharistic traditions of 1 Cor 11:23–6 in order to address the conflicts that have arisen in the Corinthian congregation. In his analysis of 1 Cor 11:17–34, Gerd Theissen has argued that the divisions in the group (11:18) are primarily between rich and poor.[12] He suggests that the relatively well-to-do host

---

[10] On the connection between baptism and the Lord's supper, see Meeks 1983, 158. On the Lord's supper in Paul, cf. Higgins 1952, 63–73; Wainwright 1971, 80–83; Lietzmann 1979, 182–87.

[11] On the eschatological dimensions of the common meal and the connections it may have had with meals in Judaism, see Rowland 1985, 241–42.

[12] See Theissen 1982, 145–74. [Reprinted as ch. 9 below.]

of the gathering, in keeping with the practices of the day, provided greater quantities of food and better quality food for those of higher status (Theissen 1982, 160). The behaviour of the wealthier Christians during the group gathering elicited criticism. According to Theissen, Paul suggests a compromise where the wealthier are to have their private meals at home, while at the Lord's supper everyone should begin to eat together, sharing the bread and wine equally (1 Cor 11:33–4; Theissen 1982, 164).

In the conflict over the Lord's supper more evidence is discovered for the lack of clarity surrounding the relationship between the community and the outside world. Social stratification is a real characteristic of the social world in which the Corinthians live. But how is this situation to be reconciled with the unity that is experienced in Christ? Paul believes that the divisions that have occurred in Corinth contradict the deepest meaning of the ritual of the Lord's supper. In 1 Cor 10:16–17 Paul speaks of the bread and wine in terms of the community's identification with the body and blood of Christ and its unity as a group gathered around Christ (Theissen 1982, 165). Such an association recalls the unifying baptismal experience where the divisions of role and status are replaced by a communion in Christ (Gal 3:26–8; Meeks 1983, 159). Like baptism, the Lord's supper involves activity which is set apart for contact with the sacred. Behaviour during the rite can act as a basis for future judgment (Theissen 1982, 164). Corruption can be dangerous. Sickness and death can be blamed on such violations (1 Cor 11:27–32).

There is a peculiar tension between what appears to have been experienced in ritual in the Pauline communities and the position of the sect within its Greco-Roman environment. The social realities of the everyday word could be transcended and given new interpretation in sacred dramas. At the same time, however, what was experienced could not be disconnected from the realities of the society of the day: 'There is neither slave nor free' is a more cogent statement in first-century Galatia than in the advanced societies of today. Moreover, the social consequences of what was experienced during ritual performances had to be interpreted in terms of existing values and beliefs. Having 'ritually slipped' from the gathering for the Lord's supper to the crowded streets lined with households, how should one relate to the fellow sectarian of a different sex and/or social status?

4. Conclusion

It is useful to envision the worship of Pauline communities in terms of a ritual context encompassing many different forms of consecrated behaviour. As a means of bringing individuals in contact with the sacred for the first time or of renewing crucial experiences, as a means of reinforcing existing beliefs and as a powerful educational medium, ritual plays a central role in building up the ekklesia. Ritual in the Pauline sect is a combination of the spontaneous and the customary. However, even the most spontaneous sacred acts are given a framework within the ritual context. Moreover, as institutionalization progresses and the body of tradition increases, we can expect that there will be less room for spontaneous acts in the Pauline communities.

Baptism and the Lord's supper play an important role in the con- solidation and continued existence of the Pauline sect. The definition of a world view and ethos is clearly related to what is experienced in these rituals. In addition, both baptism and the Lord's supper function in the drawing and maintaining of boundaries separating the Pauline sect from the outside world, hence enabling it to remain 'pure'. The ritual experiences of the Pauline sect cannot be disconnected from the realities of Greco-Roman society. Moreover, the social consequences of the experience, which must be articulated with a view to existing social structures, are often ambiguous.

FURTHER READING

One of the most influential classic contributions to the sociology of religion is the work of Émile Durkheim (1964; first published in 1912), who emphasised the centrality of collective ritual and ceremony (see Giddens 1993, 458–59, 465–66).

Influential on MacDonald's approach is the work of anthro- pologist Clifford Geertz 1966. Also important are the anthropological studies of Turner 1969; 1974 and Douglas 1982 (see further ch. 1 above).

Studies of rituals/rites in New Testament texts include Meeks 1983, 140–63, Neyrey 1990, 75–101 and Horrell 1996a, 80–88, on the Pauline churches; McVann 1991 and Neyrey 1991b on Luke–Acts; Neyrey 1995 on John 13.6–11. The model of rituals and ceremonies employed by McVann and Neyrey is set out in Malina 1986a, 139–43.

On baptism in the New Testament see Hartman 1997; on the Lord's supper, Marshall 1980 and see further ch. 9 below.

For reactions to MacDonald's book as a whole see Garrett 1990; Watson 1990; specifically on MacDonald's use of Berger and Luckmann in connection with the interpretation of the Pastoral Epistles, see Horrell 1993.

9

Social Integration and Sacramental Activity:
An Analysis of 1 Cor 11:17–34

GERD THEISSEN

INTRODUCTION

Gerd Theissen's influential and ground-breaking essays on the sociology of early Christianity, covering both the Jesus movement and the Pauline churches (see *Introduction* §2 and ch. 3 above), combine a creative and eclectic use of sociological perspectives (cf. Theissen 1993, 231–56) with a careful analysis of historical evidence. In this essay on the conflict over the Lord's supper at Corinth Theissen explores the social aspects of this situation, arguing that the basic division was between rich and poor and suggesting specifically that the richer members of the congregation began eating their meal before others, and that they consumed food of greater quality, quantity, and variety than that which was shared by all. Through both detailed exegesis of the text, and exploration of relevant evidence from other sources for the period, Theissen outlines how this situation may have arisen and may reflect quite 'normal' patterns of social interaction at the time. He also considers the 'social intentions' of Paul's response to this conflict, a response which reflects to some extent the conflict between the social realities of a socially-mixed congregation (see Theissen 1982, 69–119; ch. 7 above) and the Christian vision of a unified community of love. Paul's response, according to Theissen, is 'a good example of the ethos of early Christian love-patriarchalism which arose in the Pauline communities' (p. 269; see further chs 3, 10; Horrell 1996a). However, the Lord's supper itself, for profoundly *theological* reasons, is for Paul, Theissen suggests, about the 'transformation of social relationships': 'The sacramental act of the Lord's Supper is a symbolic accomplishment of social integration.

From many people emerges a single entity' (p. 272). Furthermore, Theissen hints, this model of sacramental integration may have played a significant part in creating a notion of community which was of profound importance in the development of Western culture.

Theissen was by no means the first to recognise that the division at the Lord's supper in Corinth was essentially one between rich and poor (see e.g. Barrett 1971a, 261), but his detailed attention to the social dimensions of the conflict, as well as his consideration of the *social* intentions of Paul's response, marks his essay as a groundbreaking contribution to the study of the Corinthian church. Theissen's proposals have been broadly accepted by many scholars since, though questions have been raised about his reconstruction of the character of the sacramental meal (Lampe 1991) and about whether the evidence really supports the model of the Corinthian congregation as socially-stratified with rich in conflict with poor (Meggitt 1994; 1998b, 97–154; see further on ch. 7 above).

❀

From time to time in recent years a certain uneasiness with the humanistic interpretation of 'traditional' texts has become evident. This dissatisfaction is aimed not at specific results but at the basic hermeneutical stance of interpreting the past as it understood itself. In various ways a demand has been expressed not only that the meaning of what has been transmitted be developed, but that this also be confronted with its own empirical realities – in other words, that the conflict between the past's interpretation of itself and a critical analysis of that interpretation be made clear (cf. Ricoeur 1970). Not least of all it is hoped that we might thereby achieve a greater freedom from the self-interpretations of the present.

Contemporary interest about the place of sociological questions in interpreting such traditional texts should be seen in this light. In New Testament exegesis this interest can be connected with the central insight of classical form criticism, that texts have a 'setting in life' (*Sitz im Leben*), that their forms have been shaped by social relations. That insight can be further elaborated. At the outset it must be kept in mind that the social relations which have shaped transmitted texts have only in a fragmentary way made their mark on what we understand the text to mean, and that these relations may have been different from the way they are interpreted within the texts themselves. With this possibility in mind we will analyze the controversy surrounding the Lord's Supper, about which Paul expresses his opinion in 1 Cor 11:17ff.

Exegetical attention has largely concentrated on the theological dimensions of the dissension in Corinth. Concerning a number of issues there is no agreement. Was the Lord's Supper profaned by being allowed to become an ordinary meal?[1] Did spiritualizing gnostics wish to demonstrate their independence from external forms? (Schmithals 1971, 250–56, esp. 257). Did crude sacramentalists suspend its obligatory character? (von Soden 1951, Bornkamm 1969). It remains to be explained why Paul is silent about these theological motives and leaves exegesis groping in the dark on this matter. Only the social causes of the conflict emerge more clearly. Therefore it may be suggestive to put forward the thesis that this conflict has a social background and becomes more comprehensible when we correlate its social conditions with the theological arguments of 1 Cor 11:17ff.

Early Hellenistic Christian congregations were not only of a different legal structure than the associations of the surrounding world; they also differed in regard to their social composition. These associations of the ancient world were, to a great extent, socially homogeneous. Religious associations give evidence of expressing class-specific forms of sociability to an even greater degree than do professional groups of persons bound together by common occupation, where members of different social strata, such as more and less wealthy merchants,[2] could meet. By contrast, the Hellenistic congregations of early Christianity, as we find them in Corinth and Rome, display a marked internal stratification.[3] In Corinth only a few are 'wise,' 'powerful,' and 'of noble birth' (1 Cor 1:26), but they seem to dominate and stand in contrast with the majority of members who come from the lower strata. A congregation so structured

---

[1] So, for example, Weiss 1910, 283: the Corinthians were indifferent 'toward the religious character of the meal.' Von Dobschütz 1904, 21: 'The Corinthians treated the Supper as a common meal.'

[2] See Bömer 1963, 236–41: 'Especially in commercially organized groups advancement as a result of economic success was frequently easier than in religious groups, which in their very nature were more rooted in tradition and where – in antiquity – the pattern of state cults also exercised a conservative effect' (240).

[3] Judge 1960a, 60: 'The interests brought together in this way probably marked the Christians off from the other unofficial associations, which were generally socially and economically as homogeneous as possible. Certainly the phenomenon led to constant differences among the Christians themselves . . .'. I have analyzed the social structure of the Corinthian community in Theissen 1982, 69–119.

faces a difficult task in balancing differing expectations, interests, and self-understandings that are class-specific.

Therefore, the possibility cannot be excluded that in theological quarrels as well this inner social stratification is a factor which needs to be taken into consideration, that various conflicts within the congregation also have been socially conditioned. By the same token it is to be expected that many of the theological ideas of those who are party to these conflicts express an interest in shaping social relationships or have social functions extending beyond their more immediate intention. Thus we may approach our analysis of 1 Cor 11:17ff from two directions: first, from that of the social conditions which can still be discerned; and second, from that of social intentions. Both perspectives are legitimate; even when taken together they analyze the text from only one particular perspective and do not make a claim to definitive interpretation.

The social conditions of the conflict in 1 Cor 11:17–34

Analysis of the social conditions surrounding human behavior presupposes that this behavior will be described with the greatest precision, but in our case a great deal remains unclear. Four questions require an answer: (1) Were there different groupings at the celebration of the Lord's Supper, or is it a matter of a conflict between the congregation and some of its individual members? (2) Were there various points at which the meal began, and what is the sequence of the various actions mentioned in 1 Cor 11:17ff? (3) Were there quantitative differences in the portions served at the meal, or (4) qualitatively different meals for different groups? To answer these questions we must also draw on other contemporary texts to understand better what kinds of behavior were possible at this time.

Different groups at the Lord's Supper

The conflict at the Lord's Supper is revealed in the fact that 'it is not the Lord's supper that you eat. For in eating, each one goes ahead with his own meal' (1 Cor 11:20–21). That statement could be taken to mean that an exaggerated individualism is the cause of the strife, as if each person had eaten independently of the others. Paul, however, speaks not only of individual Christians but also of divisions (*schismata*) and factions (*haireseis*), which sounds as if he thinks not in terms of a string of individuals but of groups. He has already used the same term *schisma* in 1 Cor 1:10 to refer to such groups. The plural form, *schismata*, how-ever, leaves open the question of how many groups are involved in the contention surrounding the Lord's Supper. It is only from 1 Cor 11:22 that we learn that there are two groups opposed to one another, those who have no food, the *mē echontes*, and those who can avail themselves of their own meal, *idion deipnon*. This does not, however, absolutely exclude a more 'individualistic' interpretation[4] which might find support in the words *hekastos* and *idion*.

The idea that every person (*hekastos*) individually has his own meal should not be pressed. Apparently this does not mean 'every' one, for there are some who 'have nothing.' Similarly, 1 Cor 14:26 does not mean that each (*hekastos*) individual member of the congregation contributes a hymn, a lesson, a revelation, or a tongue, or it would be superfluous to include a word for those who possess no such manifest pneumatic gift (1 Cor 12:4ff).[5] Nevertheless, Paul speaks about 'every' Christian. The same is true in 1 Cor 1:12, where it is by no means certain that every member (*hekastos*) of the Corinthian congregation is to be considered a member of one of the parties mentioned there. Thus, even if the phrase *hekastos gar to idion deipnon prolambanei en tōi phagein* ('for in eating each one goes ahead with his own meal') leads to the conclusion that Paul is describing individual behavior, it is a behavior which in the circumstances is confined to a certain group.

The idea of *idion deipnon* ('one's own supper') can first of all be defined in contrast with its opposite, *kuriakon deipnon* ('the Lord's supper'). *Idios* and *kuriakos* refer to questions of ownership, as in the phrases *kuriakos logos* and *idios logos*, specifying, respectively, imperial and private treasuries (*OGIS* 669).[6] *Idion* recalls in particular the stereotyped inscriptional phrase *ek tōn idiōn* ('from one's own'; cf. Frey, *CIJ*, nos. 548, 766), indicating that the object furnished with this inscription was paid for by a donor. Thus the *idion deipnon* is most likely the meal which individual Christians bring with them. If some Christians have no *idion deipnon*, that suggests that not all contributed to the Lord's Supper but that the wealthier Christians provided for all

---

[4] Cf. for example, Conzelmann 1975, 194: Behind the various groups there is a 'theological attitude . . . an individual pneumatism, which leads to rallying around party leaders.'

[5] Similarly, *pantes* in 1 Cor 14:23 may not be taken literally.

[6] Cf. Deissmann 1927, 357ff. In Ptolemaic Egypt there was a special office of the *idiologos* who administered the private royal funds. The Roman administration took over this office.

ek tōn idiōn.[7] In this connection the words of institution have the added function of converting a private contribution into community property. For the words 'this is my body for you,' spoken over the contribution of bread, have the practical meaning: This bread is here for all of you. Bread which has its origin *ek tōn idiōn* is thus publicly declared to be the Lord's own, to be *kuriakon deipnon*.[8] It would thus be understandable that Paul here once again expressly quotes the Lord's words.

The adjective *idios* carries a second nuance as well. Not only does it characterize the food as a private possession; it also suggests something about the way it is consumed. Eratosthenes (*FGH* 241, fgm. 16) criticizes a public feast (*sunoikia*) because each participant drank privately, from his own cup brought along for that purpose, what had been provided for all: *kai ex idias hekastos lagunou par' autōn pherontes pinousin* ('each one drinks from his own flask which he has brought along'). Plutarch takes up the same problem in his table talk: Should each person be given an individual portion, or should all drink from one cup and eat from one joint of meat?

> When I was holding the eponymous archonship at home, most of the dinners (*tōn deipnōn*) were portion-banquets, and each man at the sacrifices was allotted his share of the meal. This was wonderfully pleasing to some, but others blamed the practice as unsociable (*akoinōnētōn*) and vulgar and thought the dinners ought to be restored again to the customary style when my term as archon was over. 'For in my opinion,' said Hagias, 'we invite each other not for the sake of eating and drinking, but for drinking together and eating together, and this division of meat into shares kills sociability (*koinōnia*) and makes many dinners and many diners with nobody anybody's dinner-

[7] Von Dobschütz 1904, 61–62: 'Every man brought his own portion – in distinction from the custom of the Greek guilds, where the cost of the meal was defrayed out of the guild's treasury or by individual members – but the idea was that all the contributions should be put together and then equally divided. In this way the Lord Himself, to whom the gifts were brought, was made to appear the host (*kuriakon deipnon*, I, 11:20).' But certainly not all were able to contribute to the meal, as Weiss 1910, 293, emphasizes: 'Well-to-do members brought along more ample provisions, intended as a contribution so that also the poor who had nothing could take part.'

[8] In Hellenistic sacrificial meals, too, a transfer of the offering takes place; see Aelius Aristides' hymn to Sarapis, 45, 27: 'They call him [Sarapis] to the sanctuary and install him as both guest of honor and host . . . So he is at once both sharer of the offering and the one who receives the offering.' On that Höfler 1935, 96 writes: 'The devotee of Sarapis invites his friends to the meal. He brings the food as a sacrifice to the temple, dedicates it to the god, and receives it back again as a gift from the god, perhaps after a portion has been allotted to Sarapis and his priest. Then the meal takes place, and Sarapis is thus both the guest and host in one.'

companion when each takes his share by weight as from a butcher's counter and puts it before himself. Again, how does placing a cup before each guest and a pitcher full of wine and his own (*idian*) table (as the Demophontidae are said to have done for Orestes) and bidding him drink without heed to the others, differ from entertaining him in the manner which now prevails, serving him meat and bread as though from his individual manger, except that no compulsion to silence lies upon us as upon those who entertained Orestes?' [*Quaestiones Convivales* II, 10, 1]

Hagias's point of view is summed up later in one sentence (II, 10, 2): *All' hopou to idion estin, apollutai to koinon* ('But where each guest has his own private portion, companionship fails').

We find that the relationship between *idion deipnon* and *koinon deipnon* is also discussed in other places. It would fit with good Greek tradition to put the idea of community at the head of the list of debatable issues. Plato's phrase *koina ta tōn philōn* ('friends have all things in common,' Plato, *Phaedrus*, 279c) comes to mind. But Greek banquets presuppose a certain homogeneity – not to mention the fact that the Roman colony of Corinth had been culturally very much influenced by non-Greek traditions. The problems of Greek dinner parties, as discussed by Plutarch, are at heart problems in the relationship of the individual to a community. What is problematic is thus the conduct of the individual, not the relationship of groups. In Corinth it is otherwise.

The two nuances of *idion* should be taken together: a portion of the Corinthian community brings food *ek tōn idiōn* for the congregational gathering and eats it, at least in part, as *idion deipnon*. If this behavior has certain 'individualistic' traits it is nonetheless the individualistic behavior of a particular group which as such, under some circumstances, is class-specific. Those Christians who eat a private meal probably have a high social status not only because they, in contrast with other Christians, can bring food both for themselves and for others. Their social position also is apparent in Paul's question 'Do you not have houses to eat and drink in?' That certainly sounds as though some Christians in Corinth owned houses. Had Paul merely wished to say that each should eat alone, a phrase like *en oikōi* (1 Cor 11:34; 14:35) or *par heautou* (16:2) would be more likely. As it stands his question can be addressed to only a certain portion of the Christian community, and his advice to eat and drink at home (11:34) applies only to those who have something to eat and drink. It would be cynicism of scarcely imaginable proportions to advise those who have nothing to eat at home.

One might as well Hunger at home.[9] If when they read the letter it is supposed to be clear to the Corinthians to whom the question in v. 22 is addressed, then the question itself must entail a characteristic of the group for which it is intended, namely that the group is at least to some degree well-off. Only the phrase *oikias echein* answers to that. Thus it is probable, if not entirely certain, that in this phrase there echoes the notion of house ownership. Apart from this we know that some Corinthians had houses at their disposal. Gaius is *xenos mou kai holēs tēs ekklēsias* ('host to me and to the whole church,' Rom 16:23), and Titius Justus entertained Paul as a guest (Acts 18:7).

It can be assumed that the conflict over the Lord's Supper is a conflict between poor and rich Christians. The cause of this conflict was a particular habit of the rich. They took part in the congregational meal which they themselves had made possible, but they did so by themselves – possibly physically separated from the others and at their own table.[10] Yet we learn but little about the ways and means of their 'private meal.'

Variable beginnings for the meal

Apparently there were problems with the inception of the meal. Paul admonishes them to wait for one another (1 Cor 11:33). Moreover, v. 21 could be taken to mean that each begins to eat 'right away' (*prolambanein*). However, these two passages cannot immediately be squared with each other. While according to v. 33 it seems as if the corporate meal has begun prematurely so that those who come later get less than their fair share,[11] v. 21 strongly hints that some Christians had already begun earlier with their private meal, the congregational meal

[9] A low social status has often been inferred for the *mē echontes* from 1 Cor 11:33: Because they come late to the meal, they cannot have had much control over their own time. So Lietzmann 1949, 59; Bornkamm 1969, 126; and Conzelmann 1975, 195 n. 26.

[10] Cf. Weiss 1910, 293: 'That members sat in groups, some together at separate tables, would have been unavoidable. Any injurious separation, however, into cliques or between well-off and poor, was to be avoided.' Any such division according to groups can, naturally, only be surmised. Two things speak for it: (1) The Corinthian community was very large (Acts 18:10). (2) We have a picture of the celebration of the Lord's Supper from the ancient church according to which various groups eat together. See plate 9 in Lietzmann 1927. It is not certain, however, that the picture does not actually depict a miraculous feeding.

[11] Ehrhardt 1947/48 and Bartsch 1962, 169–83, esp. 182, offer a quite different interpretation of 1 Cor 11:33–34, according to which v. 33 does not concern congregational gatherings but individuals' private meals to which the poorer Christians will have been invited. The advice, then, is to wait for these people. But it is quite improbable that 'coming together' and 'eating' in vv. 20 and 33 have different meanings. Meals in private houses are mentioned for the first time in the following verse (34).

then following later. In this case, those who came later would be less disadvantaged. We notice that 1 Cor 11:21 is a statement, v. 33 an exhortation. For that reason, in the case of a conflict v. 21 gets the nod for reconstructing the situation, especially as v. 33 would then become a meaningful warning if addressed to those who went ahead first with their private meal. In any case, the inception of the Lord's Supper was not 'regulated.'

The Lord's Supper begins with the word spoken over the bread, by means of which 'private' contributions were extended to the group. So long as the words of institution were not spoken the food which was brought remained a 'private possession.' Up to this point there could be only private meals. An external reason for the conflict over the Lord's Supper could also be the absence of any fixed order in the Corinthian service of worship, or the fact that nobody was able to impose an order.[12] There was too much *akatastasia* ('disorder'; 1 Cor 14:33).

It is frequently assumed that in Corinth a regular meal, designed to satisfy hunger, was eaten prior to the cultic meal. The fixed sequence in the words of institution (the word over the bread, the *deipnon*, the word over the cup) would then recall a practice no longer in use.[13] According to this view, quarrels resulted from the fact that some Christians came too late for the regular meal so that nothing was left for them. But the presumed sequence, a real meal followed by the Lord's Supper, is improbable.

In my opinion it is unthinkable that Paul would quote a sacred, cultic formula, expressly state that he received it in just this and no other form, yet at the same time tacitly suppose that its order is not to be followed. The formula presumes that there is a meal *between* the word over the bread and that spoken over the cup. One gets to the cup *meta to deipnēsai* ('after supper'; 1 Cor 11:25). If there were already disorder in the Corinthian worship, Paul would simply be abetting it. If he wants to bring about some order, he cannot possibly repeat obsolete instructions lest the *akatastasia* (1 Cor 14:33) be complete.

The arguments assembled by P. Neuenzeit (1960, 71–72) for a regular meal prior to the Eucharist in Corinth are scarcely persuasive:

[12] Von Dobschütz 1904, 61–62, traces the problem of the Lord's Supper back to the fact that in the gathering of the congregation there is no figure of authority in charge. Paul and Apollos, each of whom could have exercised such authority, were absent.

[13] Bornkamm 1969, 142, believes that *meta to deipnēsai* was for Paul 'only an ancient oral liturgical formula.' So also Neuenzeit 1960, 71–72, and Conzelmann 1975, 199.

1. Although the cup and bread are closely linked in 1 Cor 10:16, it by no means follows that they were administered together after the meal. Moreover, in 1 Cor 10:16 Paul reverses the customary order (bread/cup) so that we can hardly learn from this passage anything about the sequence used in actual practice.

2. Nor does anything in 1 Cor 11:21 suggest a communal meal prior to the Lord's Supper. Only anticipatory *idia deipna* are mentioned, not a *koinon deipnon*. Neuenzeit argues: 'If breaking the bread had taken place at the beginning of the celebration, then those who came later could have shared in only the Eucharist of the cup. Paul would have severely criticized any such exclusion of the poor from the Eucharist of the bread' (1960, 71). This argument is correct. This bread-Eucharist did not come at the beginning of the ceremony. However, neither did it come after some ordinary, general meal of which Paul approved. It came after the private meal of which he did not approve.

3. Neuenzeit further argues that 1 Cor 11:34 'smooths the way for a complete separation of the regular meal from the Eucharist.' But only the private meals have been separated off from the community's meals.

4. Conclusions about the sequence of the supper celebration in Corinth cannot be drawn from Acts 20:7ff; Mark 14:17–21; and John 6:52, even if one could find in these passages a sequence which goes from an ordinary community meal to a cultic Eucharist.

The wealthy Christians not only ate separately that food which they themselves had provided, but it appears that they began doing so before the commencement of the congregational meal.[14] But that alone does not adequately describe their odd behavior. The private meal seems not to be just a preliminary meal, which leads to the next point.

Different amounts of food and drink

There are some indications that the *idia deipna* extended into the Lord's Supper itself. Paul says, 'For in *eating*, each one goes ahead with his own meal' (emphasis added). The word *prolambanein* need not mean

---

[14] Bornkamm 1969, 128, very clearly describes the possible grounds for going ahead with the meal. Until the poor came, 'they could confidently spend the time eating and drinking in table fellowship with family, friends and peers. Everyone can imagine the very understandable reasons which may have played a role there: the very human tendency to a sociability among one's own; antipathy for the embarrassment that comes when rich and poor, free and slave, sit bodily at one table – real table fellowship is something quite different from charity at a distance; the worry that the "atmosphere" for receiving the sacrament may be spoiled by such an embarrassing rubbing of elbows with the poor. All that had led to the "taking beforehand" of their own meal.'

'anticipate' but can simply mean 'eat'.[15] The doubling of the terms 'meals' and 'eating,' *deipnon* and *phagein*, is hardly mere pleonasm. Rather, *phagein* refers back to the phrase *kuriakon deipnon phagein* of the preceding clause, while corresponding to the phrase *eis to phagein* in v. 33. In both instances it is the Lord's Supper to which the verb refers. The proper meal occurs *en tōi phagein*, 'during the Lord's Supper,' and not only prior to its inception. At the very least v. 21 does not exclude that possibility.

So it may be that with the words of institution, not all the food on hand was shared with the congregation, but a certain portion was claimed as 'private.' Under such circumstances, those who are wealthier would get larger portions than the others. Paul's warning in 1 Cor 11:29 also points to such a 'supplementary' meal in addition to the Lord's Supper: 'For anyone who eats and drinks without discerning the body (*mē diakrinōn to sōma*) eats and drinks judgment upon himself.' In all probability this should be interpreted to mean that some do not distinguish in the Lord's Supper between the food which belongs to the supper and their *idion deipnon*. Some have more than others.

It is not inconceivable that there was a larger portion of food for those whose contribution made the meal possible in the first place. Various associations or clubs in antiquity observed such distinctions in allotment and officially recognized 'material gifts to certain members, primarily in the form of larger shares in feasts for officials and staff members. These shares ranged from between one and one-half to two and three times the normal, giving rise to the terms *sesquiplicarii*, *duplicarii*, *triplicarii* for the various categories of officials.'[16] The *collegium* in Lanuvium (136 CE), which included slaves, might be cited as an example since it had an established rule (*CIL* XIV 2112 = Dessau 7212) that read '*ut quisquis quinquennalitatem gesserit integre, ei ob honorem partes sesquiplas ex omni re dari,*' that is, 'any member who has administered the office of the *quinquennalis* honestly shall receive a share and a half of everything as a mark of honor' (see Lietzmann 1949, 91–93). There were also special allotments, for example, for those officials who rendered lifelong service in some capacity such as secretary or messenger. A normal portion at feasts consisted of some bread, four small sardines, and an amphora of wine.

[15] *prolambanein* occurs on the stele of Apellas (ca. 160 CE) without a discernible temporal sense (*IG* IV² 126, *SIG*³ 1170). Cf. Moulton and Milligan 1963, 542.
[16] Kornemann 1900, cols 380–480, esp. 441.

We certainly should not think that in the Corinthian congregation there was a similar rule. On the contrary, in distinction from other kinds of associations in antiquity, there were in this case apparently no formal regulations, no bylaws or procedure by means of which conflicts could be avoided. It had never been determined who might merit special consideration. The existence of such regulations within other associations is significant here only in this one respect: apparently nobody was in the least offended if certain deserving members of the community received larger allotments than others. Such discrepancies were, in fact, considered fair and proper.

Had not the wealthy Christians in Corinth rendered incontrovertible service to the congregation?[17] They made rooms available for the common meal. Only through their contribution was the common meal available to everybody. If they had their own *idion deipnon* in addition to the general meal, perhaps they simply adopted a pattern of behavior customary at that time. The regulations characteristic of other associations at least enjoyed this advantage over the 'charismatic,' unregulated life of the Corinthian congregation – that it gave even those who performed only service chores the opportunity to distinguish themselves by rendering special assistance. When, by contrast, everything is left to the free sway of the 'Spirit,' those who are of privileged status are much more likely to have things their way.

Thus the wealthy Christians not only ate by themselves and began before the regular Lord's Supper, but also had more to eat. Paul alludes to the greater quantity of the *idion deipnon* when he writes, 'one is hungry and another is drunk' (1 Cor 11:21). Yet even this assumption, that there were unequal portions of food and drink, does not make wholly comprehensible the conflict connected with the Lord's Supper. For in that case Paul would only have to admonish all to share equally. But in fact he recommends that they celebrate the 'private meal' at home. One ought not to be too hasty in imputing sarcasm to Paul, as if he were saying that those who have enough to eat should eat at home; that it is not so bad if at the Lord's Supper some are hungry so long as

---

[17] That service for the community led to some people's having special authority in early Christianity as well is shown by Paul's recommendation of Stephanas in 1 Cor 16:15–16: 'We observe here a frequent phenomenon of life, that people who do something for the community thereby naturally come into a position of authority' (Weiss 1910, xxvi). The idea that holders of Christian offices enjoy even material privileges is also present in primitive Christianity: 1 Cor 9; 1 Tim. 5:17; *Did.* 13.3.

these people are not made inordinately conscious of how much better off other members are. Yet as long as it is assumed that it is a matter merely of different quantities of food for the rich and the poor Christians, Paul's suggested solution must seem odd.

Meals of different quality

Paul's instruction to eat the 'private meal' (*idion deipnon*) at home becomes more readily comprehensible if it is assumed that something better than mere bread and wine was involved, some further delicacy as was sometimes customary: *esthiousi men gar dē pantes epi tōi sitōi opson, hotan parēi* ('for all, I presume, eat meat with their bread when they get the chance,' Xenophon, *Memorabilia* III, 14, 2). Even the modest collegium of Lanuvium, comprised of members from the lower classes, provided fish in addition to bread and wine. It seems reasonable that in the Corinthian congregation some Christians were not satisfied with just bread and wine. If this were the case, however, Paul could not simply demand that this additional dish also be shared, for the very good reason that nothing was said about it in the words of institution. These words of institution are for him without doubt holy and irrevocable. But they provide only for bread and wine.

These words were also holy and irrevocable for the Corinthian congregation. In their letter they expressly declare that they have followed the traditions received from Paul. Paul takes note of this in 1 Cor 11:2 and praises the congregation for doing so. Later, in the passage we are examining, he returns to this idea and asks ironically: 'Shall I commend you in this [scilicet, that you distinguish a private meal from the Lord's Supper]? No, I will not' (11:22). From this it might be inferred that even in the matter of the Lord's Supper the Corinthians could maintain that they had remained true to the Pauline traditions. One could even argue that since the words of institution provide only for the distribution of bread and wine, everything else can be regarded as a 'private meal.' Thus the tradition is being strictly adhered to. Should Paul have praised them for that?

Such an 'ingenious' interpretation of the tradition of the Lord's Supper is not at all ingenious when seen in the framework of what was widespread and customary at that time. For some Corinthians it would not be at all strange to think that common meals, involving people of varied social status, should include food of varying quality. Such practice is well attested for the period (cf. Carcopino 1940, 270–71). If in our sources we hear only criticism of this custom, that is not surprising. Those who were in agreement with a practice had little reason to express themselves on the subject. More interesting for our purposes is the fact that the criticism comes from different perspectives. The humane tactfulness of a member of the upper classes leads Pliny the Younger to criticize the practice, while Martial and Juvenal, by contrast, express the wounded self-esteem of those who have been snubbed at such a meal. Pliny writes:

> It would be a long story, and of no importance, were I to recount too particularly by what accident I (who am not at all fond of society) supped lately with a person, who in his own opinion lives in splendour combined with economy; but according to mine, in a sordid but expensive manner. Some very elegant dishes were served up to himself and few more of the company; while those which were placed before the rest were cheap and paltry. He had apportioned in small flagons three different sorts of wine; but you are not to suppose it was that the guests might take their choice: on the contrary, that they might not choose at all. One was for himself and me; the next for his friends of a lower order (for, you must know, he measures out his friendship according to the degrees of quality); and the third for his own freed-men and mine. One who sat next to me took notice of this, and asked me if I approved of it. 'Not at all,' I told him. 'Pray, then,' said he, 'what is your method on such occasions?' 'Mine,' I returned, 'is to give all my company the same fare; for when I make an invitation, it is to sup, not to be censoring. Every man whom I have placed on an equality with myself by admitting him to my table, I treat as an equal in all particulars.' 'Even freed-men?' he asked. 'Even them,' I said; 'for on these occasions I regard them not as freed-men, but boon companions.' 'This must put you to great expense,' says he. I assured him not at all; and on his asking how that could be, I said, 'Why you must know my freed-men don't drink the same wine I do – but *I* drink what *they* do'. (*Epistulae* II, 6)

It is interesting to notice that in one matter Pliny's suggested solution is comparable to Paul's: In a common meal, one of higher social status should adjust his eating habits to those appropriate to one of a lower social class. On the other hand, when we read the criticism 'from below' in Martial and Juvenal, it is obvious that here the intention, understandably, is to put those of a lower station on the same plane as those of higher status:

> Since I am asked to dinner, no longer, as before, a purchased guest, why is not the same dinner served to me as to you? You take oysters fattened in the Lucrine lake, I suck a mussel through a hole in the shell; you get mushrooms,

I take hog funguses; you tackle turbot, but I brill. Golden with fat, a turtledove
gorges you with its bloated rump; there is set before me a magpie that has
died in its cage. Why do I dine without you although, Ponticus, I am dining
with you? The dole has gone: let us have the benefit of that; let us eat the
same fare. [Martial, *Epigrammata* III, 60]

In another passage Martial can express himself even more bitterly and
curse his 'host,' who is demonstrating before all eyes his social superiority:

Tell me, what madness is this? While the throng of invited guests looks on,
you, Caecilianus, alone devour the mushrooms! What prayer shall I make
suitable to such a belly and gorge? May you eat such a mushroom as Claudius
ate! (*Epigrammata* I, 20; cf. further IV, 85; VI, 11; X, 49)

Juvenal has described in detail Virro's banquet (*Satura* V). While the
host helps himself to good and old wine, fresh bread, plump liver, and
all kinds of delicacies, the guests must be content with bitter wine,
moldy bread, cabbage which smells like lamp oil, suspicious-looking
mushrooms, an old hen, and rotten apples. The result is a violent squabble
among those invited.

The most detailed evidence all comes from Latin authors, but for
that very reason it is valuable for throwing light on the Corinthian
situation. For Corinth of the first century CE was a new Roman foundation. The official language was Latin, and most of the inscriptions from
this period are written in Latin. Even if in many instances contact
was sought with the older Greek tradition – the resumption of the
Isthmian games, for example – the construction of an amphitheater
nevertheless demonstrates how strong was the Roman, non-Greek
influence.[18] Furthermore, the Corinthian congregation in all likelihood included people of Latin origin. Among the seventeen names of
Corinthian Christians recorded, eight are Latin: Aquila, Fortunatus,
Gaius, Lucius, Priscilla, Quartus, Titius Iustus, Tertius. One of them,
Gaius, is the host of the entire congregation according to Rom 16:23,
suggesting, among other things, that the communal meal took place in
his house.

Again, it should not be supposed that the Roman (bad) manners
just described were widespread in the Corinthian congregation. The
passages only provide evidence for contemporary patterns of behavior
allowing a host at a common meal to treat his guests differently depending

---

[18] On the cultural situation see Kent 1966, 17–31; de Waele, 1961; and Broneer 1951.

upon their social status. Freedmen and clients served as the background against which he could demonstrate his power as patron. Of course the banquets described by Pliny, Martial, and Juvenal are private banquets, but so may have appeared the common meals of the Corinthian congregation. Gaius would serve as host to the congregation, as if, so to speak, he had invited them to his house. Those who through their contribution made the common meal possible were in fact acting like private hosts, like patrons, supporting their dependent clients.

Thus we may conclude with some confidence that when the community in Corinth came together for the common *kuriakon deipnon* there was for some, in addition, an *idion deipnon* containing something in addition to bread and wine. Baked goods, fish, and meat would be candidates for such a supplementary dish. In my opinion it is quite possible that among other things meat was also eaten. Meat was apparently a food served to invited guests in Corinth, as we learn from 1 Corinthians itself. One accepts an invitation assuming that the host will serve meat (1 Cor 10:28). Plutarch also assumed that in communal meals meat is eaten (*Quaest. conv.* II, 10, 1). From 1 Cor 11:17ff only this much is clear, that the *idion deipnon* is solid food. 'For any one who eats and drinks [scilicet, bread and wine] without discerning the body eats and drinks judgment upon himself' (1 Cor 11:29). Interestingly, Paul does not say 'without discerning the body and blood,' but only *mē diakrinōn to sōma*, indicating that the problem is with the 'body of Jesus,' the bread, that is, with solid food.[19] The danger is that this food will not be distinguished from another kind of *sōma*. It does not seem to me impossible that we have here an allusion to the *sōmata* of animals (cf. James 3:3).

If it be conceded that some Corinthians now and then also ate meat as their *idion deipnon*, then a further hypothesis seems probable, one that can only be briefly sketched here. It is possible that 1 Cor 10:14–22 and 11:17ff deal with the same problem – the problem of eating meat in the congregational gatherings – from different perspectives.[20]

[19] A concrete interpretation based in distinguishing among foods is still most probable. So also Lietzmann 1949, 59. Differently, Moffatt 1918/19; Kümmel, in the supplement to Lietzmann 1949, 186; and Ehrhardt 1947/48. Certainly Paul also associates with *sōma* the meaning 'Body of Christ,' but since the sentence speaks of 'eating and drinking,' the object of eating is most likely what is meant.

[20] Bartsch 1962 is perhaps correct when he sees the same problem in 1 Cor 8–10 and 11:17ff. The common element, however, is scarcely the idea of abstinence.

In both passages the issue is whether the Lord's Supper is incompatible with any additional meal. There it is a matter of *eidōlothuton* ('food offered to idols'; 10:19), here of *idion deipnon*. It is possible that the two issues are in part identical, that in Corinth one could never absolutely exclude the possibility that a piece of meat was already ritually 'implicated.' Every piece of meat purchased could be meat sacrificed to idols, possibly even that which was consumed by some Christians at the Lord's Supper. The plausibility of this hypothesis depends on the exegesis of 1 Cor 8–10, which would exceed the boundaries of this essay [but see Theissen 1982, 121–43 – Ed.]. Accordingly, the hypothesis can only be noted as a possibility but will not be presupposed in what follows.

It is worth summarizing once again our reconstruction of the behavior of those Christians who consume their 'own meal' in the congregational gathering. Some wealthier Christians have made the meal itself possible through their generosity, providing bread and wine for all. What was distributed is declared by means of the words of institution to be the Lord's and given to the congregation. Thus, in conjunction with this common meal there could take place a private meal because the starting point of the Lord's Supper was not regulated, and up to this starting point (that is, until the words of institution) what had been brought and provided was private property. More importantly, this distinction was possible because the wealthier Christians ate other food in addition to the bread and wine, and the words of institution made no provision for sharing this with the fellowship.

This behavior elicited criticism. The core of the problem was that the wealthier Christians made it plain to all just how much the rest were dependent on them, dependent on the generosity of those who were better off. Differences in menu are a relatively timeless symbol of status and wealth, and those not so well off came face to face with their own social inferiority at a most basic level. It is made plain to them that they stand on the lower rungs of the social ladder. This in turn elicits a feeling of rejection which threatens the sense of community. One need only think of the verbal aggressiveness of Martial who, as his host's client, was only a second-class guest. Paul rightly raises his voice in protest against the wealthy Christians: 'You despise the church of God and humiliate those who have nothing' (1 Cor 11:22). Thus the bases for the conflict at the Lord's Supper are neither purely material nor purely theological. Above all, they are social, the problems of a socially stratified community in which the community's *kuriakon deipnon* threatens to become an *idion deipnon* betokening social standing, and the Lord's Supper, instead of providing a basis for the unity of the body of Christ, is in danger of becoming the occasion for demonstrating social differences.

We ought not to make the mistake of raising moralistic objections against the wealthy, as historical and sociological analysis makes possible a more measured evaluation. Before sweeping judgment is rendered on the wealthy Christians, several things should be remembered:

(*a*) Congregational meetings probably took place in the private homes of the wealthier Christians (cf. Filson 1939) and were made possible by their contributions. Under these circumstances such people would demonstrate their social status even if they had not wished to, and this quite independently of the specific content of the Lord's Supper.

(*b*) The wealthier Christians were not simply inviting the whole congregation, but in doing so were also at the same time inviting some of their peers who belonged to it. Within the framework of social intercourse among Christians of equal standing, those ordinary standards for solicitousness and hospitality, which applied socially apart from the congregational life, could not suddenly be suspended. It was part of such expectations, for example, that there would be meat to eat (1 Cor 10:27–28). Expectations closely linked to social status have their own force, regardless of personal attitudes. When Gaius, to fashion an example, plays host to the congregation at his house, he is also playing host at the same time to those who belong to the few Corinthians who are 'wise,' 'powerful,' and 'of noble birth' (1 Cor 1:26). It is natural that such people would extend special privileges to one another.

(*c*) To justify the exclusion of other Christians from their 'own meal,' the wealthier Christians could formally appeal to the *paradosis* of the Lord's Supper itself, which applied only to bread and wine. Whatever went beyond that could be declared part of a 'private meal.'

(*d*) Furthermore, the behavior of such people could take its orientation from the surrounding culture, where a lack of regard for others of those invited to the common meal was not simply outrageous. We have seen that some associations built into their regulations preferential treatment at festival meals for those who had rendered particular service, while influential Roman patrons treated clients and freedmen at their banquets as second-class guests.

In all likelihood wealthy Christians probably did not suffer from a guilty conscience in this entire matter. It is more likely that they thought of themselves as having supported the poorer Christians in generous fashion by providing a meal. The conflict thus has its roots in the collision between a consistent theory of community on the one hand and, on the other, behavior produced by social differences, something which existed not only in the Christian tradition but in Greek traditions as well. One thinks of Plutarch's discussion about the nature of community in the meal (*Quaest. conv.* II, 10); of Pliny's criticism of the way in which guests are snubbed, a criticism argued on the basis of a certain ideal of community (*Epist.* II, 6); of the *koina ta tōn philōn* (Plato, *Phaedrus*, 279c; cf. *Diodorus Siculus* 5, 9, 4; Iamblichus, *Vita Pythagorae* 30, 168; Porphyry, *Vita Pythagorae* 20). The close link between early Christian and Greek tradition on this point is demonstrated by the idealized representation of the primitive community in Luke (Acts 2:44). Thus the conflict is to be understood as a conflict between two different patterns of conduct, both of which could be expressed by the wealthier Christians as an expectation rooted in social reality. The conflict is one between class-specific expectations on the one hand and on the other the norms of a community of love which encompasses men of different social strata. Even if we cannot reconstruct in every detail the form which this role-conflict assumed, at least this much is clear: the conflict itself is rooted in the structure of the Christian congregation. In a group showing internal stratification, which supports itself through mutual generosity, those who are able to contribute the most come to achieve a certain position of superiority – even if that does not correspond to the group's self-understanding.

One final observation helps to illuminate the social side of this conflict. Those members of the congregation who come from the upper strata appear in a less advantageous light in Paul's statements. The conflict is not seen from their perspective. It is instructive, then, that Paul does not derive his information from the congregational letter.[21] It can be assumed that this letter was written by those from the upper strata. Some *topoi* of popular philosophy, which in all probability

---

[21] The relation between oral and written information is rightly accounted as being of fundamental importance for exegesis by Hurd 1965, and Dahl 1967, 313–35, esp. 323ff. They argue that the letter contained favorable news concerning the Corinthian community while the oral reports put the Corinthians in a much worse light.

had their origin in that letter, so indicate.[22] One would hardly expect that the authors divulged anything unfavorable about themselves. Others must have done that. Paul has heard by word of mouth about 'divisions' at the Lord's Supper (1 Cor 11:18). He carefully puts some distance between himself and his informants, as if only partly willing to credit what he has heard, but perhaps that is mere diplomacy. It is consistent with this that he immediately goes on to emphasize the basic legitimacy of divisions, as if he would believe these reports only to the extent that they tell of legitimate conflicts, and those of a sort unavoidable if the congregation is to be tested (11:19).

In fact Paul must have been fairly clear about the matter. Naturally, we do not know who informed him. Possibly it was Chloe's people, who perhaps were 'dependent' persons bearing their mistress's name.[23] These could then have reported not only about the partisan strife among followers of different apostles but also about the conflicts at the Lord's Supper. The repetition of the term *schisma* in both contexts would thus be understandable. So too would be the fact that Paul takes a perspective 'from below' on the Corinthian problems in both 1 Cor 1:18ff and 11:17ff. Stephanas is less likely to have been the informant. One cannot recommend somebody wholeheartedly (1 Cor 16:15ff) and at the same time suggest that one only 'partly' believes his reports. And of course there could have been others to whom Paul was indebted for his information. In any event, the problems were described to him from the perspective of those 'below.' And quite possibly the letter from the congregation touches on the same problems when it comes to the meat sacrificed to idols – now however, from a quite different perspective.

The social intentions of 1 Cor 11:17–34

Paul's ideas in 1 Cor 11:17ff do not simply presuppose certain social relationships within the Corinthian community. Above all they express social intentions, the desire to influence interpersonal relationships in a

---

[22] Hurd 1965, 65–74, gives a detailed account of the community letter. A table showing all passages containing what are generally assumed to be citations or *topoi* of the lost community letter is found on pp. 67–68. Conzelmann 1975, 15, accepts the following as community *topoi*: 'The wise man is king'; 'To the wise man all things belong'; and 'Knowledge makes free.'

[23] Family members would retain the name of their father even after he had died. See further Theissen 1982, 92–95.

certain direction. It is not accidental that Paul's statements issue in a very concrete suggestion for the Corinthian congregation's behavior. Paul wants to settle the problem of the 'private meal' by confining it to private homes. At home everybody may eat and drink in whatever way seems proper. The final result would be a lessening of the role conflict in which the wealthier Christians find themselves. Within their own four walls they are to behave according to the norms of their social class, while at the Lord's Supper the norms of the congregation have absolute priority. Clearly this is a compromise. It would be much more consistent with the idea of community to demand that this 'private meal' be shared. Paul's compromise, which simply acknowledges the class-specific differences within the community while minimizing their manifestations, corresponds to the realities of a socially stratified congregation which must yield a certain pre-eminence to the rich – even contrary to their own intentions. Within such a community the compromise suggested by Paul is realistic and practical. It offers a good example of the ethos of early Christian love-patriarchalism which arose in the Pauline communities and which we encounter most clearly in the household codes (*Haustafeln*) of the deutero-Pauline letters (Col 3:18ff; Eph 5:22ff).

This compromise, however, is the result of ideas which come from two quite different spheres (cf. Weiss 1937, 648–89). Paul's own analysis of the conflict is informed by 'sociological' perceptions, but at heart is derived from the *theological* sphere. For him, the Corinthian conflicts are part of the eschatological testing of the congregation (11:19). The social tensions between rich and poor Christians have been transposed to a symbolic world transcending the everyday reality. They become part of an eschatological drama and belong to the separation of the righteous from the unrighteous in a world which is coming to its end. By the same token, what stands at the heart of Paul's suggested solution is not simply a pragmatic suggestion to eat at home but an appeal to the real meaning of the Lord's Supper: the covenantal sacrificial victim (*Bundesopfer*) of the community is here proclaimed as the future ruler of the world. Behavior at the meal commemorating his death becomes the basis for a future judgment. Whoever partakes of the meal in an unworthy manner risks death. The sacrament is treated as being in a taboo zone, where violating the norm brings with it incalculable disaster. Paul cites as proof the incidence of sickness and death in the congregation. The sociological analysis of the circumstances of the conflict as these are presupposed in 1 Cor 11:17ff, and his interpretation of the conflict within the self-understanding of those directly or indirectly involved, contradict each other.

We have here a hermeneutical conflict. And it is better to make this clear than to mask it. Otherwise one would fail to recognize that Paul's intention in no way (or at best only marginally) lay in regulating social conflicts. His intentions are to be found on another level. Social realities are interpretively transformed into a symbolic world[24] in which rich and poor Christians play a role, but within the framework of a drama whose chief actors are God, the cultic sacrifice, the sacrament, and a world which is passing away. The social realities are interpreted, intensified, transcended. Nevertheless, all these interpretations and intensifications stand – even beyond their own intentions – in a functional relationship with this social reality. That is made clear by the example of the Lord's Supper which is at the heart of Paul's remarks.

The meaning of the Lord's Supper cannot be reduced to a single formula, but discrete sectors of meaning can nonetheless be distinguished from one another: the idea of the elements, of sacrifice, and of judgment. Each of these has a social function.

The elements are, for Paul, more than graphic representations. Bread and wine become something special in the Lord's Supper. They must be distinguished from other food. They have a numinous quality. If this is ignored, illness and death threaten.[25] In 1 Cor 10:17 Paul links a social goal with this notion of numinously charged elements: 'Because there is one bread, we who are many are one body.' That means, quite realistically: Because all have eaten portions of the same element, they have become a unity in which they have come as close to one another as members of the same body, as if the bodily boundaries between and among people had been transcended. Dogmatically one may speculate in various ways about how bread and wine are transformed into the designated elements, but in any case a transformation of social relationships takes place. From a plurality of people emerges a unity. This transformation is also represented at the

---

[24] On the idea of 'symbolic world' see Mühlmann 1962, 107–29, reprinted in Mühlmann and Müller 1966, 15–49. See further Berger and Luckmann 1967.

[25] Catholic exegesis can – for understandable reasons – render far less prejudiced opinions about the sacramental thought of Paul than can Protestant exegesis. Cf. Kuss 1971, 416: 'The food – eating and drinking – is a miraculous food, a food charged with power and having its effect everywhere in this concrete life. And over against the salvation, won by whoever eats "worthily," stands the threatening destruction (*Unheil*) which unfailingly overtakes whoever eats "unworthily."'

level of the elements: bread becomes the body of Christ, wine the blood of the new covenant.

The idea of sacrifice also represents a social dynamic. It does so, however, not on the level of inert elements but of a living being. The propitiatory sacrifice surmounts social tensions; the scapegoat takes away unresolved conflicts. There is scarcely a community that does not exist at the expense of the scapegoat. The union of human beings is strengthened when their aggressions can be focused on a common external object. It is not otherwise with the 'new covenant in my blood' (1 Cor 11:25). The sins of all are transferred to one. The latent human desire to murder is actualized in one person – representative for others. What is new in the Christian idea of sacrifice is that the scapegoat is not driven from the community and sent off into the desert but instead is made the Lord of the world and recognized as its ultimate ruler.[26]

At the heart of the idea of judgment[27] is to be found neither the 'elemental' nor the 'organic' metaphor, but a social metaphor. The one sacrificed becomes the judge, the powerless one the ruler of the world. Here too one could ponder endlessly what is really meant by the expectation of the eschatological judge, but independently of that it is easy to see that a posture of obligation appropriate for the new social relationships is being inculcated. Eschatological punishments correspond to violation of the norm. In the symbolically interpreted and transformed social world, the sanctions also appear in intensified form. Even incidences of death and illness which have already occurred are integrated into this interpreted world.

These different 'images' (the elements, sacrifice, judgment) cannot be rigorously separated from one another. They overlap, giving expression to a social dynamic which they represent on an empirical 'organic,' or social plane. For Paul, of course, these are more than images. They are realities. We must free ourselves from that 'philological cultural Protestantism' which finds Paul's weighty sacramentalism too 'primitive.' If something primitive is at work here, it is less Paul's weighty sacramentalism than the even weightier human tendency for individuals to find within the community an outlet for their need to dominate.

[26] This has obviously not prevented the church from searching again and again for scapegoats. Nevertheless, the possibility should not be ruled out that early Christian thought concerning sacrifice implies an effort to overcome the 'scapegoat complex.' The meaning of the New Testament transcends what was made of it.

[27] This idea has been particularly explored by Käsemann 1964.

Sacramental actions are dramatic representations of social processes, whatever else they may be. 'The bread which we break, is it not the fellowship of Christ's body [RSV "a participation in the body of Christ"]?' The sacramental act of the Lord's Supper is a symbolic accomplishment of social integration. From many people emerges a single entity. Interpersonal tensions are represented, and overcome, in the sacrifice. Sanctions are inculcated. This social dynamic is expressed in palpably perceptible actions. The fellowship here achieves embodiment (*Aussenhalt*).

It is not our task to evaluate the socio-historical significance of sacramental integration. According to W. E. Mühlmann, it was an important element in the rise of a sense of solidarity which transcends social stratification.

> In Europe the bourgeoisie arose from the tradition of the ancient polis, combined with the Christian sense of communal religiousness which, in turn, had its roots in the idea of the community of the Eucharist. Such a concept, for example, is wholly foreign to a true Hindu, because to him the idea of meal fellowship with someone of a different caste is abhorrent. Even a man as enlightened as Ghandi declared that free opportunities for association in matters of table fellowship and in institutions like marriage were not essential for the furtherance of the democratic spirit; that eating and drinking had no social significance whatsoever but were simply physical matters. Ghandi thereby proved that he did not understand the historical significance of the Lord's Supper for integrating in Western culture a sense of community which transcends every boundary established by caste and ritual. (Mühlmann 1962, 411)

Whether or not this far-reaching thesis is correct cannot be decided here, but it fits the Corinthian congregation. In the face of class-specific social conflicts, Paul moves the sacrament to the center to achieve a greater social integration. Even if the meanings bound up with the Lord's Supper transcend that social reality, they are nonetheless functionally embedded in such reality. Thus the sacrament appears in a different light from that appropriate to a theological self-understanding. But of course that is just the goal of a sociological viewpoint. E. Troeltsch wrote with some justification: 'Whoever busies himself with sociological studies and the literature of sociology will doubtless achieve a new attitude to all historical matters and to the objective cultural values which arise in historical life. Everything about causal understanding as well as about the establishment of norms and values is bathed in a new light' (Troeltsch

1925, 705). Of what does this new light consist? There is nothing new in understanding that texts which have been handed down to us deal with social situations, and certainly a sociological point of view helps us better understand these situations. In the final analysis, however, it is not just a matter of the social factors by which people at that time were confronted. It is rather a matter of those factors by which they were shaped while pursuing their goals. The sociology of literature is exegesis *kata sarka*. What Paul finds objectionable, that the Corinthians are humans (1 Cor 3:4), that they are *sarkikoi* (3:3), is the starting point which they take for granted. And indeed it was a very human situation.

There is an obvious contradiction between an early Christian congregation's quarrels and its understanding of itself as an eschato-logical community of love. Playing the reality off against the self-understanding reveals an unrealistic excess. Or one can adopt the radical self-understanding of early Christianity and from that standpoint criticize the realities. We are, however, more likely to be cautious in moving either way once we become aware that the Corinthian conflicts between rich and poor were built into the very structure of things. A community of love would certainly be more easily and consistently achieved within a socially homogeneous group than in groups having internal social stratifications. Anyone wishing to see 'brotherhood'[28] penetrate every social stratum must make allowances for conflicts which arise from the merging of class-specific self-understandings, expectations, norms, and interests. Factions are necessary (*dei haireseis einai*), Paul says, but the sociological *dei* is of a different order from the eschatological *dei* in 1 Cor 11:19, and the factual reality of this statement should be distinguished from its theological intent. Nevertheless, factual reality and theological intent cannot be sundered. They are bound together in the functional context of social action.

---

[28] Cf. Bömer 1963, 178–79: 'Apparently Christianity alone consistently championed in the religious realm the idea of religious brotherhood. The precedents for this were not to be found in the spiritual possession of antiquity but were brought along from Judaism. In the New Testament this idea is already the common possession of the new world religion, and there was no other ancient community of belief in which the equality and brotherhood of all people was set forth so early and consistently as here.'

FURTHER READING

This essay has various points of contact with Theissen's other studies of the social aspects of the church at Corinth (see Theissen 1982) and of early Christianity as a whole (see Theissen 1979; 1993). On the specific issues of social diversity in the congregation and of 'love-patriarchalism', see ch. 7 above and ch. 10 below respectively.

To explore further a social-scientific perspective on the Lord's supper as a 'ritual', see ch. 8 above, and the reading listed there.

On the Lord's supper in the New Testament, well-known works by New Testament scholars include Bornkamm 1969; Schweitzer 1967; Marshall 1980.

The issues and questions opened up here by Theissen are taken up, often with disagreements, in Engberg-Pedersen 1993; Lampe 1991; Horrell 1996a, 86–88, 102–105, 150–55; Meggitt 1998b, 118–22.

10

'Not Many Powerful':
Approaches to a Sociology of Early Christianity

LUISE SCHOTTROFF

INTRODUCTION

In this essay, Luise Schottroff, well-known for her feminist writings on the social history of early Christianity, takes issue with a dominant current consensus in New Testament scholarship. This consensus, founded on the work of Ernst Troeltsch and represented most prominently in the work of Gerd Theissen, maintains that the few socially prominent members of the early Christian communities occupied leading positions within their congregations (cf. ch. 7 above; Maier 1991, 35–39; Clarke 1993) and that the social ethos of these communities may be described with the term 'love-patriarchalism'. In other words, the early Christian communities did not transform established patterns of social relationships nor challenge the hierarchical structure of their society, but accepted and affirmed that those 'above' remained above and those 'below' below. Drawing on Troeltsch's discussion of the Pauline ethic, Theissen summarises love patriarchalism, the ethos which he suggests developed in the Pauline communities, in the following way:

> This love-patriarchalism takes social differences for granted but ameliorates them through an obligation of respect and love, an obligation imposed upon those who are socially stronger. From the weaker are required subordination, fidelity, and esteem. (Theissen 1982, 107)

Focusing particularly upon 1 Cor 1:26–31, Schottroff argues that this Troeltschian consensus gives a distorted and historically inaccurate impression of the character of the early Christian communities. What

First published in German as '"Nicht viele Mächtige": Annäherungen an eine Soziologie des Urchristentums', in *Bibel und Kirche* 1985 (1) 2–8, reprinted in Luise Schottroff, *Befreiungserfahrungen: Studien zur Sozialgeschichte des Neuen Testaments*, Chr. Kaiser/ Gütersloher Verlagshaus: Gütersloh, 1990, pp. 247–53, printed here with permission of the publishers. The English translation was produced by Stuart Dewar in collaboration with me – Ed.

we actually find, she suggests, here in 1 Corinthians and elsewhere in the New Testament, is evidence that in the communities the anticipated eschatological reversal of above and below was brought about: 'The Christian community is the place where this reversal is already being lived out' (p. 285). The rich and powerful gave up their power, prosperity and status (p. 281), and the poor and socially weak, chosen and favoured by God, 'were able . . . to obtain justice, self-worth and education' (p. 283).

Turning explicitly to the concerns of contemporary liberation theology, Schottroff argues that the picture of a community of the poor (which the rich may join insofar as they show solidarity with the poor) which liberation theologians see in the Bible is indeed justified not only theologically but also historically. While some criticise liberation theology for what is perceived to be an over-dependence on Marxist theory, Schottroff maintains that what the liberation theologians have discovered lies firmly rooted in the biblical tradition, and is not an inappropriate imposition. This, she suggests, raises uncomfortable questions both for 'the church of the rich' and New Testament scholarship (p. 286).

Like other feminist and radical scholars, notably Elisabeth Schüssler Fiorenza (1983), Schottroff believes that careful historical-critical study, but without conventional bourgeois and androcentric presuppositions, can challenge the portrait of the early Christian communities which has come to predominate in New Testament scholarship. Some may feel that Schottroff's portrayal of the 'church of the poor', or Fiorenza's view of the early followers of Jesus as a 'discipleship of equals' (Fiorenza 1983, 97ff, esp. 140–54), are somewhat idealised, or that socio-political commitments have led such scholars to see what they want to see. But that raises the question: To what extent have other scholars too – those in what Schottroff calls the bourgeois traditions of scholarship – seen the early Christian communities through the lens of their own social, political, and economic assumptions and commitments? Feminist scholars have certainly powerfully drawn attention to the ways in which androcentric assumptions have often led to translations and interpretations which distort the evidence of the texts (see e.g. Fiorenza 1983, 41–67). Essays like those of Schottroff challenge interpreters to consider the evidence afresh, and to consider carefully the possibility that the New Testament witnesses to the lives of communities which, no doubt partially and failingly, experienced and practised the transformation of their social relationships according to the pattern of the gospel's reversal of above and below.

❧

Ernst Troeltsch and the current consensus in New Testament study

In 1912, E. Troeltsch sketched a picture of the social composition of the early Christian communities, which was directed against a Marxist view of the origins of Christianity. He wished to show that social causes played only an indirect part in the emergence of Christianity (Troeltsch 1912, 31). The 'emergence of Christianity is to be understood not from social history, but rather from the religious history of antiquity' (p. 25). The first Christians at all stages of the development of Christianity in New Testament times belong to the lowest strata. Jesus is a man of the people (p. 27), yet Christianity is *not the creation of a social movement* (p. 15). Christianity is a new *religious* construction. Here, as always, the 'inherently creative, community-forming, religious foundations' are 'the work of the lowest strata' – but not for economic reasons, rather on account of the 'continuity of imagination' (*Ungebrochenheit der Phantasie*), the 'simplicity of the emotional life (*Gemütslebens*)' (p. 27; cf. pp. 29, 78). Troeltsch reckoned that already in Jesus' time isolated 'members of the upper stratum' joined the movement, for he stressed that they were present 'from the beginning' (pp. 25, 33). Jesus' world is one of rural/small-trader relationships (p. 27). The Pauline communities, however, exist in the 'urban world of slaves and the lower middle classes' (p. 70). In these communities, too, there are a few members of the upper classes (pp. 25, 33, 68). Of decisive importance for Troeltsch is the organisation of the unconditional 'community of love' (p. 66), of 'Christian patriarchy' (p. 67), which arose in the Pauline communities. This patriarchy requires 'submission and subordination' from those who are socially inferior, and offers them the 'care of the strong for the weak' (pp. 66, 68). The dominance of the male is 'accepted as the natural order' (p. 71). This Christian patriarchy first made Christianity an organisation suited to a world mission, for the missionary band of disciples, the disorganised believers of Jesus' day, and the religious cooperative 'love-communism' (*Liebeskommunismus*) in the earliest community did not constitute a viable organisation. Despite the 'bourgeois usefulness' (pp. 23–24) of the communities after Paul, 'despite every subjection' (p. 72), the Christians then later destroyed the Roman state, because they had no regard for its institutions. Because of its individualism and universalism, Christianity thus became revolutionary – despite its conservative character. It destroyed pure nationalism, as 'indeed every other purely earthly authority' (p. 72; cf. pp. 73, 80).

Despite many variations, Troeltsch's basic premises remain those of the currently dominant school in this matter. There is a consensus in New Testament scholarship that the members from the upper stratum, even if few in number, occupied leading roles in the communities. Gerd Theissen's characterisation of the structure of the Pauline and post-Pauline communities with the key term 'love-patriarchalism' (*Liebespatriar-chalismus*) has been widely accepted – above all in the relevant discussion in the U.S.A., which pays more attention to these questions than does German New Testament study. The idea that this patriarchal organisation established the success of Christianity, and not the 'itinerant radicalism' of Jesus and his travelling wandering-prophets, also remains within the parameters set out by Troeltsch.[1] The detailed research of Theissen and in the American discussion then also provides the basis for the elaboration of social-historical material relating to individuals considered to be members of the upper stratum, such as Paul himself, or Erastus, the city treasurer of Corinth.[2]

The Marxist historian Heinz Kreissig also stresses above all the role of members of the upper stratum in the communities – as does bourgeois-theological New Testament scholarship in Western Europe and the U.S.A. He even believes that the majority in the communities is made up of 'well-placed craftspeople, traders, members of independent professions'. Paul's information that 'not many' wise, influential, noble people are to be found in the communities (1 Cor 1:26), Kreissig finds 'one-sided' (Kreissig 1967, 91–100, esp. 99). It is interesting to note that the comments of New Testament scholarship stress almost without exception that a Marxist understanding of early Christianity as a revolutionary social movement of the lower classes is to be refuted, although one seeks in vain for such an assessment of early Christianity from Marxist historians – including Friedrich Engels (1882; 1883; 1884)

---

[1] Theissen's relevant articles since 1973 have now been collected in Theissen 1979. On 'love-patriarchalism' see 210, 296, 271. For the debate in the U.S.A., see Meeks 1983, which sums up and develops this discussion.

[2] With reference to Paul, see for instance, Hock 1978; 1979; 1980. For detailed work on Erastus, see esp. Theissen 1979, 238–45.

and Karl Kautsky (1908). Engels considers Christianity to be a religion primarily of members of the lower strata, who are fleeing into an inner realm, who seek a 'religious way out' into 'another world' (1882, 304; 1884, 464). Kautsky believes early Christianity to be a movement of the lumpenproletariat, which subsists through the labour of other people and must be clearly distinguished from 'the modern proletariat' (1908, 364, 500).

The spectre of a Marxist interpretation of early Christianity as a social-revolutionary movement is a product of Christian-bourgeois polemic. For example:

> Given a belief in the class struggle, it is easy to take a group of Galilean peasants, add the community of goods, Paul 'working with his hands', and the 'not many wise . . . not many mighty, not many noble' at Corinth, and thus discover a movement of protest among the working classes. (Judge 1964, 50 [=1960a, 51])

Paul's statements in 1 Cor 1:26–31 and their significance for Christianity in New Testament times

In 1 Cor 1:26–31, Paul reaches back above all to two traditions, which are therefore important for the understanding of the text:

1. He uses classical categories for describing the vertical division of society. 'Above' is to be found education, power, noble ancestry, and scorn for those who are below. Those 'below' are uneducated, powerless, of non-noble origin, despised, and 'nobodies'.

2. Paul refers back to the biblical and Jesus-based concept of the gospel of the poor, in accordance with which, through God's merciful work, those who are 'below' are chosen by God, and the powerful are destroyed by God.

With reference to (1): In his Oration to Rome (*Or.* 26), Aelius Aristides (117–*c.*189 CE), seeks to extol the merits of the Roman Empire, in which the legal opportunity of an appeal to the Emperor establishes an equality for all. 'Here there is a comprehensive and notable equality of the weak with the mighty, the unknown with the famous, the needy with the rich, the simple with the noble.' (*Or.* 26.39)[3] He presupposes

---

[3] Translation [in German] from Klein 1983, 27 [for ET see Behr 1981]. That the equality asserted by Aelius Aristides is a fiction hardly needs to be proven; on this point see Klein 1983, 82 n. 47.

this same division of society in his description of the benefits of Roman civil law. The distinction between Greek and barbarian is said to be no longer relevant, but rather the difference between Romans and non-Romans (*Or.* 26.63). 'You have actually divided all the subjects of your empire . . . into two groups, and everywhere made the educated, the noble, and the powerful into citizens . . . the remaining inhabitants of the empire you consider as subjects and governed.' (*Or.* 26.59) 'On the basis of such a classification of people there are in every city many citizens of yours . . . there is no need of garrisons to hold fortresses; for the most respected and powerful men everywhere protect their own home town in your interests.' (*Or.* 26.64) The rulers in Rome form an alliance with the upper stratum in the cities of subject peoples, and are able therefore to maintain a relatively small and invisible military presence (*Or.* 26.67: 'so that many of the provinces do not even know where their garrison is'). Aelius Aristides may be considered an example of the method of describing the vertical ordering of society, often found in literary documents of antiquity. Paul uses these same categories. Only a few members of the urban upper stratum in Corinth can be found in the Christian communities. They consist overwhelmingly of the town's lower stratum, of male and female slaves, and of independent labourers and tradespeople of both sexes. There is no middle stratum,[4] although in representations of the social history of early Christianity the presupposition is found over and over again that the lowly people in the Corinthian community, like the fishermen of Galilee and the tradespeople Paul, Prisca and Aquila, belong to a middle stratum.[5]

With reference to (2): Paul refers back to the biblical and Jesus-based picture of God. God takes the side of the insignificant, the weak and the powerless. His involvement to their good effects the (eschatological) reversal of above and below. Hannah's song (1 Sam 2:1–10), the Magnificat (Luke 1:46–55), the Beatitudes (Matt 5:3–12 par.), many parables from the Jesus-tradition, the Book of Judith, and Jewish-apocalyptic books express this idea of God. The Jewish people, small in number, oppressed by major powers, experienced over centuries this God on its side. It is no coincidence that women too become representatives of the lifting up of the lowly by God: Hannah, Judith,

---

[4] See esp. MacMullen 1974, 89–90; Alföldy 1975, 83–138; Klein 1983, 83 n. 49.
[5] E.g. Theissen 1979, 28; tradespeople are regarded as members of the middle stratum, for example, by Ollrog 1979, 26.

Mary.[6] In comparing the different expressions of this tradition, one should not proceed by separating them from one another or judging them; nor indeed by assessing a text such as the parable of the rich man and poor Lazarus (Luke 16:19–31) as 'sub-moral' and 'primitive' (on this, see Schottroff and Stegemann 1978, 46–48). A much more helpful comparison is in recognising what is characteristic in each individual version of this tradition. In the Magnificat, hunger plays a striking role; in 1 Cor 1:26–31 it is noteworthy that a small group of people – the Corinthian Christians – are seen as the chosen ones of this God. With their calling (*klēsis*), with God's election of the slaves and workers in Corinth, the eschatological inversion of above and below has begun. That Paul sees this reversal as something eschatological is shown by the verbs with which he depicts the overthrow of the mighty: they are shamed and brought to nothing in the face of God's judgment.

God's revolutionary action, which takes power from the great and raises the lowly, is an eschatological event – for Paul as for the Jesus-tradition – that has now already begun. Paul says that there are also a few members of the upper stratum in the community; certainly one must take this into account based on his formulation in 1 Cor 1:26. The decisive question now for the sociology of early Christianity is what role the members of the upper stratum have in the communities. From the reversal brought about by God's action, it can only be concluded that in the community (and in society), they gave up and lost power, prosperity and status – all their privileges. That this is in fact to be assumed is shown by Paul himself. Paul describes himself admittedly not as a member of the upper stratum, but rather as a free-born person, who in comparison to slaves has an important social privilege. Along with the sharp division of society into above and below, there are still important horizontal boundaries: between free-persons and slaves, men and women, different nationalities. Besides, they do not relativise the vertical division of society. Paul maintains that these boundaries are abolished in the community (Gal 3:28). He even stresses the reversal in the opposition of slaves and free-persons. He, Paul, who understands himself to be free, has become the slave of Christ (see esp. 1 Cor 9:19) and believes that through God's action of election in the community, the roles of slave and free are exchanged (1 Cor 7:22). One should not

---

[6] On the idea of God who reverses social destiny, see Schottroff 1978; see also in Schottroff and Stegemann 1978, 43–45; on the role of Judith, see Fiorenza 1983, 115–18.

underestimate this reversal, as if it were no real change in the enslavement of people; a point which has not been adequately considered in relation to the need to demand the abolition of slavery in the name of Christ. The Christian communities, with their attempt to live the reversal of society, were themselves a social reality, which from the very beginning was perceived as a disturbance of Roman social order. Paul understands himself to be a slave of Christ, and therefore requires no 'reward' or 'pay' from the communities, which were actually obliged to meet his living costs. He works manually in order to demonstrate the fact that he is a slave of Christ (1 Cor 9:17–19). He requires that the escaped slave Onesimus be treated by his Christian owner, Philemon, as a brother in the flesh and in the Lord (Phlm 16). These highly radical steps of transformation for the communities in their life together were in my opinion more effective than a simple proclamation of the equality of all people, or suchlike. The reversal of above and below as the work of the merciful God is the structural principle of Christian life in the communities (cf. also Mark 10:42–45 par.). If, then, members of the upper stratum lived in the communities, they were certainly no longer those who demanded subordination or who brought about in the community only a softened repetition of the pattern of injustice found in society. A patriarchal organisation of the communities as envisaged by Troeltsch and Theissen, moreover, would have been exactly the organisation which, in the opinion of the masters in Rome, comprised the ideal society. Above remains above, below remains below, and the rule from above to below is exercised with 'clementia' [forbearance] (see Seneca's tract with this title). The conflicts between Roman adminis- tration and the Christian communities would be inexplicable if this patriarchy had been a Christian organisational principle from the beginning. E. Schüssler Fiorenza's feminist critique of the idea of (love-) patriarchalism as an organisational principle of early Christian communities goes to the heart of the problem: here patriarchy is legitimised under the banner of historical 'success'. Other forms of organisation which offer more justice are marginalised as 'impractical' (*lebensunfähig*) (Fiorenza 1983, 79–83). Yet the impressive list of women who fulfil leading responsibilities in early Christian communities speaks eloquently: in the communities, the living of God's revolution has been attempted. Patriarchy, which predominated later in Christianity, was incompatible with the God of Israel and of Jesus, who casts down the mighty from their thrones, as Paul clearly insists (1 Cor 1:26–31). The result of God's call was a church of the poor in an unjust society. The manual labourers, the dockworkers and the slaves of Corinth were able here to obtain justice, self-worth and education (*Bildung*).

1 Cor 1:26–31 has representative significance for Christianity in New Testament times, both with regard to socio-historical information, and as the theological basis of life together in the communities. The eschatological reversal of poor and rich is at the centre of Jesus' message according to the synoptic evangelists. Where rich people enter the communities, they give up their wealth and their power, as may be seen in Luke's gospel. Rich people who cannot bear this consequence are taken leave of with sadness and sympathy (Mark 10:17–22 par.). Even at the end of the second century this picture has not fundamentally changed.[7] Chrysostom correctly summarises Paul's position in 1 Cor 1:26–31: most of the disciples had been poor (*penētes*), coarse, uneducated, plagued by hunger, of no importance in the social order, of humble origin. Paul did not hesitate to speak of their poverty, nor to beg for money for the poor.[8]

The approach of liberation theology and its historical and theological justification

In the reading of the Bible in base communities of the poor in Latin America, the concept of the church of the poor in early Christianity is a component of theological reflection. Theological and sociological questions here coincide. The book best known to us that documents this reading of the Bible is the collection by E. Cardenal, *Das Evangelium der Bauern von Solentiname* [ET: *The Gospel in Solentiname*]. For them, Mary who sings the Magnificat, like Jesus and his followers, was poor. The Magnificat and the Beatitudes of Jesus sing of 'the Revolution' (Cardenal 1967, 32–33). The woes against the rich (Luke 6:26ff) show 'that for Christ, humanity is divided into two clearly distinguishable classes. He is for one, and against the other' (Alejandro). 'That is truly revolutionary. Christ says: All who do well today will do badly tomorrow.

---

[7] On the thinking of the synoptic evangelists, see Schottroff and Stegemann 1978. On development in post New Testament times, see the material in Friedländer 1923, 236–40; Harnack 1924, 559–68.

[8] John Chrysostom, *Panégyriques de S.Paul* 4.11 [trans. A. Piédagnel, *Sources Chrétiennes* no. 300, pp. 206–207].

The pancake will be turned over.' (Laureano).[9] The new people of Christ, who are to be free, 'cannot be freed by others; they must free themselves'. The rich should depart (Cardenal 1967, 33) or live in equality with all other people. 'The gospel can also be the liberation of the rich.' Like Christ, the poor must preach the gospel to the rich (Cardenal 1967, 128).

The church of the poor, which Julia Esquivel describes, is the community of the poor, who know God is on their side, and of the rich who show solidarity with the poor. 'The poor who follow Jesus . . . and those who show solidarity with them, *they* comprise the church of the poor' (Esquivel 1983, 26). The situation of the poor of Latin America is recognised in the Bible: they are exploited, despised, marginalised, without rights, ill, homeless. 'The concepts used in the Bible to describe the poor are concrete; the Bible does not spiritualise poverty. The terminology and its application correspond to the list which we have drawn up with reference to this concept in Latin America.' (Esquivel 1983, 6; cf. p. 4). Here it becomes clear why the biblical reading of the poor does not distinguish between the 'theology' and the 'sociology' of early Christianity. 'The Bible, then, is the story of how the poor are lifted up by God, and how they receive hope and faith in the midst of their sorrow, their struggles, and their escape from a situation of oppression and slavery to the fulness of life' (Esquivel 1983, 10). The Bible itself here supplies the explanation of the particular situation (which in other branches of liberation theology is reached through scholarship steeped in Marx):[10] 'For four and a half centuries the majority on the continent had no effective and comprehensible explanation of the causes of injustice and domination. They had believed it was their fate to suffer, and to eat their meagre bread mixed with pain and tears. In the Bible, they discovered a people who suffered just as they did, and were able to liberate themselves, and who were in a position to become a true, worthy and respected people.' 'Thousands of communities of the poor have had this experience throughout the Latin-American continent' (Esquivel 1983, 10).

In conclusion, one can say that the role of the poor in the church of the poor, viewed from the perspective of liberation theology, is that of the self-liberating people. Rich people belong to this church insofar as they show solidarity with the poor; but this solidarity is not to be confused

---

[9] Both citations from Cardenal 1967, 127.
[10] Gutiérrez 1976, 95, etc.

with financial support in the sense of charity, which alters nothing in the situation of the poor or of the rich.

The sociology of early Christianity, which is studied within New Testament scholarship above all in Western Europe and the U.S.A., is bound up with the claim to use historical method. The views of liberation theology about the church of the poor in early Christianity do not make this claim. Nevertheless, I believe I can show, with the methods of bourgeois historical study that I use, that the picture of liberation theology is historically (not just theologically) justified. In view of the findings I have outlined above (the consensus in New Testament scholarship on the one hand, the alternative picture of liberation theology on the other), an over-hasty reaction could be one of historical scepticism: in both positions, the social presuppositions and goals of their representatives are reflected, except that perhaps in New Testament scholarship the requirement of objectivity conceals the interests bound up with that particular standpoint. Such scepticism, however, is in my view unfounded, as New Testament scholarship on this question turns out to be in contradiction to the wording of the texts. This contradiction is sufficient to show that the picture of the church of the poor, at least for the evangelists and for Paul, is more correct than that of patriarchy. In 1 Cor 1:26–31, God's election of the poor and the eschatological destruction of members of the upper stratum is described. The Christian community is the place where this reversal is already being lived out. In it, the poor are God's chosen ones, and not the objects of the welfare, care and concern of the rich. Neither care from above to below nor a leading role of the rich is compatible with the text, nor in my opinion, with other Pauline texts, although this cannot be further discussed here.

Liberation theology has been accused of taking its precepts not from the Bible, but from Marx and other Marxist authors. In the case of Jesus' gospel for the poor, 'every rigid ideological understanding must of course be set aside, like the notion that the poor could be seen as leading the way to a better, classless, society, in which there will be no more injustice. The gospel for the poor . . . is not concerned with showing the poor the role of the proletariat, which comes to them via the classic Marxist doctrine of history.'[11] From a historical point of view, these

---

[11] Lohse 1981, 54. This polemic is directed on the one hand against the ecumenical document 'Für eine mit den Armen solidarische Kirche' ['For a church in solidarity with the poor'] (epd-Dokumentation Nr. 25a, 1980) and on the other against Schottroff and Stegemann 1978.

SOCIAL-SCIENTIFIC APPROACHES TO NEW TESTAMENT INTERPRETATION

sentences are recognisably polemic, as they are written in a context in which the Marxist accusation functions as a disqualifier. Without wishing now to react apologetically to that, one must insist that the concept of God's revolution, which raises the poor and puts down the mighty from their throne, is certainly just a little older than the concept of the leading role of the working class in Marxist revolution. The two concepts cannot be defended in the same way. The roots of the church of the poor actually lie simply in the biblical tradition, even if Christians and Marxists join forces with one another in the struggles of the poor. In my opinion, the sociology of early Christianity cannot concern itself with promoting or defending the claims of Marxism, but with grasping the basic structure of the early church, which the gospel of the poor called into being. The church of the rich and New Testament scholarship have here to face a question which the biblical tradition poses and which cannot actually be ignored.

FURTHER READING

Troeltsch's classic work on *The Social Teaching of the Christian Churches* is available in English as Troeltsch 1931. Theissen's thesis about the ethical radicalism of the synoptic tradition being replaced by an ethos of love-patriarchalism which developed in the Pauline churches is outlined in the closing pages of the essay printed in ch. 3 above. See further Theissen 1982, esp. 107–10, 138–40, 163–64.

Examples of scholars of early Christianity who have accepted Theissen's characterisation of the Pauline ethic include MacDonald 1988, 43–44, 102–22, 202; Kidd 1990, 177–79 (citing both Troeltsch and Theissen with approval); Maier 1991, 35–39. On the social level of the early Christians, see ch. 7 above, and esp. Clarke 1993, who regards the socially prominent as the leaders of the congregations [see further ch. 12 below].

Critics of the love-patriarchalism thesis besides Schottroff include Fiorenza 1983, 79–80; Engberg-Pedersen 1987; Martin 1990, 126–29; Horrell 1996a. One of the main arguments of my recent book is that love-patriarchalism is not an appropriate label for the 'social ethos' of 1 Corinthians, though it does aptly describe later documents such as 1 Clement (see Horrell 1996a, esp. 126–98, 258–72, with further detail and bibliography there. Cf. also Fiorenza's discussion of 'patriarchalisation' in the early church: 1983, 251–342).

For feminist perspectives on the history of early Christianity see Schottroff 1993; 1995; Richter Reimer 1995; Fiorenza 1983/1995a; 1992; 1994/1995b. Feminist writers like Schottroff share the concern for liberation from oppression which is central to liberation theology and liberationist readings of the Bible. For a collection of essays representing a variety of liberationist readings of biblical texts, see Gottwald and Horsley 1993; Sugirtharajah 1991; on Paul, see Elliott 1994. On the challenge of liberation theology to biblical studies see Rowland and Corner 1990 (see also *Introduction* §5; §6.3). For brief introductions to liberation theology, see Boff and Boff 1987; Gibellini 1987.

11

Deviance and Apostasy:
Some Applications of Deviance Theory to
First-Century Judaism and Christianity

JOHN M. G. BARCLAY

INTRODUCTION

In this essay John Barclay makes it clear that he sees himself
essentially as a historian of early Christianity and Judaism in the
Roman period, but one who gladly makes use of the new questions
and insights that social-scientific perspectives can offer (see
Introduction §4). All too often, he points out, 'apostasy' is treated as
though it were 'an objectively definable entity . . . an inherent quality
in certain kinds of behaviour' (p. 297). Drawing cautiously and not
uncritically on the interactionist perspectives on deviance developed
by sociologists in the 1960s and since, Barclay suggests instead that
'deviance', or apostasy, is socially-defined; that is, a certain act or
person is *labelled* deviant by a social group or their leaders, who
thereby 'create' deviance, in some sense, through that process of
labelling. This raises a number of interesting questions: To what extent
are 'norms' applied differently, according to who is doing the labelling
and who is being labelled? Who defines what is deviant, and whose
interests are served by these definitions? Why is there greater pressure
or perceived 'need' to label deviants at some times, or some places,
than at others? To what extent is the creation of 'deviants' a reflection
of power struggles between different groups or individuals, in which
one seeks to exclude or marginalise another by labelling them as
'deviant'?

These questions are particularly relevant to the study of Judaism
and early Christianity, for issues of group-definition and boundaries
are central both to the process whereby 'deviant' Christianity is
eventually deemed to be distinct from its parent Judaism, and to the

definition of boundaries around the developing Christian movement. Previous studies using deviance theory have focused primarily on the question of Jewish–Christian relations. Malina and Neyrey (1988; see ch. 1 above) have examined the 'labelling' of Jesus – both negative and positive – in Matthew's gospel. Anthony Saldarini (1991; further 1994) suggests that the Matthean community, while still essentially Jewish, is labelled 'deviant' by the Jewish authorities and by many members of the Jewish community in the same area. Jack Sanders (1993, esp. 129–51) explains the Jewish punishment of Christian 'deviants' with reference to the identity-crises suffered by Judaism in the first century and especially post-70 CE. One of Barclay's particular emphases is on the diversity and variety within Judaism and Christianity of the first century; hence he explores the ways in which deviance and apostasy may have been defined differently, and the label 'apostate' applied variably, depending on who was doing the labelling and who was being labelled, and what their relative positions of social power or prominence were.

Paul and the Corinthian church provide Barclay with an example of the struggle over the definition of boundaries within early Christianity itself, an issue perhaps less adequately explored to date and where deviance theory offers fruitful insights. Paul is engaged, in 1 Corinthians, in establishing community boundaries; and his differences with the Corinthians over where these boundaries should lie – what counts as deviant? – is one cause of conflict and dispute.

Taken in isolation from other methods and perspectives, this approach to deviance and apostasy could perhaps lead to a neglect concerning the *substance* of differences between and among Jews and Christians in the first century, whether they concerned rules about food, patterns of social interaction, or 'weightier' theological matters such as the Torah, Christology, and so on. But taken in conjunction with a range of other approaches the sociology of deviance raises vital questions and indeed offers a vital corrective to an over-emphasis on questions of 'content' concerning belief and practice. It forces us to raise what the sociologist Peter Berger describes as the sociologist's persistent question: '*Says who?*' (Berger 1963, 80). We must ask who is labelling whom, and how this connects with the power and interests of different social groups. As Barclay suggests, these questions are particularly relevant in connection not only with the conflicts between Jews and Christians, but also with New

Testament documents which expend considerable energy in labelling and 'deviantising' their 'Christian' opponents (esp. the Pastoral Epistles, 2 Peter, Jude; see suggestions for further reading below). We should, at least if we wish to be historians sympathetic to the silent losers whose voices were not recorded, be wary of any assumption of 'rightness' on the part of the canonical author. From a sociological perspective, the polemic is one instrument in the power struggles within the early Christian movement, reflecting the interests of certain groups and marginalising others.

Introduction

Historians of early Christianity are concerned with the phenomenon of deviance in at least two respects. In the first place, we wish to understand the process by which, over a period of three or four generations, this originally Jewish movement was deemed to have deviated sufficiently from Jewish norms to be regarded by its parent community as a distinct social and religious entity. Secondly, we are intrigued by the ways in which the early Christian communities defined their own boundaries, a process which involved excluding those they considered to have deviated from the norms of Christian practice or belief. This double process of definition is central to the phenomenon of early Christianity: its definition as distinct from Judaism and its internal definition of its own identity. The sort of questions which intrigue us are well illustrated by the case of Paul, who was indeed a pivotal figure in the whole process: we want to know how Paul came to be regarded as an apostate by his Jewish contemporaries and how he, in turn, came to reject some adherents of his churches as 'false brothers'.

Sociologists have long been concerned with the processes by which societies define and maintain their boundaries, and special attention has also been accorded to those individuals or groups which deviate from social norms. The 'sociology of deviance' which has flourished under that name since the 1950s (and under other names before that date) might well hold some promise for research focused on the Christian movement as a deviant form of Judaism and on the definition and exclusion of deviants from the early Christian communities. It will not, of course, provide a magic wand with which to solve the many intricate problems of our subject, but we can at least inquire what light, if any, it could shed on the historical processes we struggle to understand. In recent years some attempts have indeed been made to apply deviance theory to the topic of 'the parting of the ways' between Judaism and early Christianity, notably by Anthony Saldarini (1991) and Jack Sanders (1993). My efforts in this direction will be somewhat more modest than theirs in scope and claim but I hope still fruitful in suggesting avenues for further research.[1]

The sociology of deviance: the interactionist perspective

Many kinds of sociological theory have been employed in the analysis of deviant behaviour, as theoretical approaches go in and out of fashion and as different features of the phenomenon are illuminated.[2] Without making monopolistic claims for its value, I wish here to explore the potential of what has been termed the 'interactionist' or 'societal reaction' perspective (sometimes also, rather loosely, 'labelling theory'). This perspective on deviance suddenly rose to prominence in the early 1960s and became the focus of intense interest (and controversy) through the 1960s and 1970s; the value of its contribution is now widely recognized, though (as we shall see) its limitations are also obvious. Drawing on a theoretical framework known as 'symbolic interactionism' (developed by Mead and Blumer), the interactionist perspective received its programmatic expression in Howard Becker's book *Outsiders* (1963) and fitted the mood of the 1960s so perfectly as to become the new orthodoxy in an amazingly short time.[3] The basic features of the interactionist perspective can be summarized under two headings: deviance as a social product and the consequences of labelling.

---

[1] Saldarini combines deviance theory and sect typology in his analysis of the Matthean community, but at a very high level of generality. His conclusions also seem inconsistent: if societies label 'deviants' in defining their boundaries, it makes little sense to insist that 'deviant groups remain part of the whole' (1991, 47). Despite frequent appeals to Erikson (1966, cited as 'Ericson'), Saldarini's thesis runs quite contrary to Erikson's conclusions. Sanders 1993, 129–51, more accurately reflects the sociological discussion but is inclined to rather sweeping generalizations; see further below (Judaism and apostasy). Malina and Neyrey have applied deviance theory to the narrative of Matthew (Malina and Neyrey 1988) and Luke (Malina 1991). But it remains unclear whether their analysis relates to the history of Jesus or to the Gospel narratives; if the latter, it is hard to see what can be achieved beyond renaming the actors and processes in the story.

[2] There are valuable surveys by Pfohl 1985 and Downes and Rock 1988; Davis's survey (1980) is somewhat dense and ideologically biased.

[3] Some of the essential elements of the perspective had been outlined by Lemert 1951; but he was somewhat critical of its later expression in the 1960s (Lemert 1972, 14–25).

Deviance as a social product

The interactionist perspective is essentially a reaction against theories which take deviance to be a particular quality inherent in certain acts or persons; it questions whether deviance is an objectively definable entity at all. If we think we know who or what is deviant and muster quantitative statistics, interactionists insist that the definition of deviance is radically dependent on the societal reaction which behaviour evokes. To quote the now famous words of Becker:

> Social groups create deviance by making the rules whose infraction constitutes deviance, and by applying those rules to particular people and labeling them as outsiders. From this point of view, deviance is not a quality of the act the person commits, but rather a consequence of the application by others of rules and sanctions to an 'offender'. The deviant is one to whom that label has been successfully applied; deviant behaviour is behaviour that people so label. (Becker 1963, 9)[4]

The cutting edge of this definition is that deviance cannot be predicated of acts as such, only of acts as they receive a negative social response or reaction. The point here is not simply that in any given society norms and laws define what is or is not deviant (that is true but also trite). The point is that in actual fact societies apply their own norms differentially, selecting and stereotyping those they choose to mark as deviant, so that only some norm-breakers are actually treated as deviant. Moreover, what makes an act socially significant as deviant is not so much that it is *performed*, as that it is *reacted* to as deviant and the actor accordingly labelled. Lots of people drink heavily, but only some are labelled 'alcoholic' and what would make any individual's drinking significant as deviant in the eyes of others is as and when this reaction (and this label) is elicited. In other words, the interactionist perspective focuses not just on the act itself, but on what is made of the act socially, insisting that this social reaction radically affects the nature, social meaning and implications of the act (Schur 1971, 16). Deviance is, in this sense, the product of social interaction.

The consequences of labelling

If the deviant act becomes socially significant when it receives a social reaction, interactionists are also interested in the further consequences for the actor when he/she receives such a reaction. Of course, negative

[4] Near contemporaneous definitions of this feature of the interactionist perspective can be found in Kitsuse 1962 and Erikson 1962, both reprinted in Becker 1964.

reactions can vary in degree of seriousness and not all labels are equally damaging, but interactionists note the ways in which labels generally affect the identity of those who receive them, how, for instance, one considered an 'alcoholic' often adopts a new role in society. Tracing what they have called 'deviant careers' and the grouping of those labelled into 'deviant associations', researchers following the interactionist perspective have often exposed the detrimental effects of labelling and the confirmation of deviant identity leading to what has been called 'secondary deviance'. They therefore insist that, far from being a static phenomenon, deviance is actually a complex process, in which the on-going relationship between the actor and the reacting society defines what counts as deviant.

In the limited space of this essay, I can only explore some features of this perspective and will focus solely on the first and foundational notion of deviance as a social product. It is clear, I hope, that this perspective contains a strong strand of relativism. Its interest is as much in the labellers ('Who is judging this activity to be deviant?') as in the activity so labelled. Since those who create and apply the rules vary in their judgments from one society to another, and differ within the same society at different times and in differing circumstances, 'deviance' appears to be, in an important respect, 'in the eye of the beholder'. In social-scientific parlance, it is an ascribed as much as it is an achieved status. When it analyses cases of deviance, delinquency, criminality, apostasy or the like, the interactionist perspective is always asking 'Whose definitions of deviance are operative here?' and (as a supplementary question) 'Whose interests do these definitions serve?' I am convinced that sensitivity to these questions could clarify some of the historical matters which interest us. However, first I should note some of the limitations of this approach and the criticisms which have been levelled against it. These will help us to see more precisely what we can and cannot do in utilizing this perspective in our research.[5]

Limitations of the interactionist perspective

Concerning the limitations of this approach, it is important to say at the outset that it is not intended to explain the origins or the motivations

---

[5] Among the most searching critics of this perspective are Gibbs 1966 and Knutsson 1977; a vulgarized version is sharply rejected by the essayists in Gove 1975, where, however, Kitsuse and Schur defend its central notions as properly understood. There are also critical discussions in Rock 1973, 19–26 and Davis 1980, 197–234.

of the deviant act as such. Its focus is, as we have seen, on the reaction
to the act (and the effects of that reaction), not on the originating causes
of the deviation. This peculiar focus has given the impression that the
interactionist perspective views the 'deviant' as merely passive, as one
whose actions are simply pounced upon by arbitrary labelling authorities,
as indeed 'more sinned against than sinning'. When Becker and others
paraded their empathy with the 'deviants' they studied (e.g. Becker 1964,
1–6) in the radical mood of the 1960s, critics suspected them of an
anti-establishment bias which sought to blame deviance on the authorities
for labelling people and so driving them into crime. In fact, political
bias is by no means a necessary consequence of this perspective which
properly is concerned neither to excuse nor to blame: it is simply
interested in how a society (or an interest group within society) selectively
creates its definitions of deviance and how the social significance of an
act that deviates from the norms is radically dependent on the sort of
reaction which it elicits.[6]

If it does not provide an 'aetiology' of deviant acts, neither does the
interactionist perspective in itself explain why societies react as they do
to acts they consider 'deviant'. However, it has been allied to various
forms of explanation which could shed light on this matter. Becker
himself pointed to factors of political and economic power which enable
certain individuals or groups to enforce their definitions of deviancy
(1963, 17–18). Other sociologists have gone further in exploring the
power struggles in which a threatened element in society seeks to identify
and label deviants in accordance with its own interests (Lofland 1969,
13–19; Schur 1980).[7] Such analyses tie deviance theory closely to theories
of social control, and even if the complexities of modern society make it

[6] A careful reading of Becker 1963 shows that he is not guilty of suggesting that the
deviant act itself is irrelevant to the labelling process, as some have charged: he
writes, 'whether a given act is deviant or not depends *in part* on the nature of the
act (that is, whether or not it violates some rule) and *in part* on what other people do
about it' (1963, 9, my emphasis). This led him to some terminological confusion over
the use of the word 'deviant' (e.g. he posits a category of 'secret deviant' which critics
observe is logically problematic for an interactionist perspective). But so long as one
recognizes the distinction between 'deviant' in the weak sense of 'what deviates from
social norms' and 'deviant' in the strong sense of 'what elicits the social reaction that
"something should be done about it"' (see Schur 1971, 24–25), this difficulty is not
insuperable.
[7] Lofland (1969, 14) writes: 'Deviance is the name of the conflict game in which individuals
or loosely organized small groups with little power are strongly feared by a well-organized,
sizeable minority or majority who have a large amount of power.'

exceptionally difficult to trace the influence of competing interest groups, the interactionist perspective certainly invites such an investigation of interests and power where it can be pursued.

On a parallel track, Erikson (1966) combined the interactionist perspective with elements of Durkheimian functionalism, in enquiring what functions reactions to deviance serve for society as a whole. He suggested, and sought to illustrate through a study of seventeenth-century New England, that the labelling of deviants can perform an important function in the boundary maintenance of an insecure community.[8] While his thesis (and its functionalist basis) are now considered too simplistic to be applied to modern industrialized societies, Erikson's work may be of value in suggesting avenues of enquiry concerning the simpler forms of community which we can study in early Judaism and early Christianity. In particular, his study could shed light on the situation of a simply structured community encountering serious ambiguities in its definition of norms; such ambiguities could arise in situations of novelty or transition, where norms are inconsistently applied or have become controversial, or where activities appear borderline in relation to previous precedents.[9] Here there is a good case to be made that the identification of 'deviants' can serve to give an insecure community clarity and security in its social identity. As we shall see, this has particular relevance to the social situation of early Christianity, but it may also be applicable to certain aspects of first-century Judaism.

It would be a mistake to regard the interactionist perspective as a theory operating with clear-cut definitions and testable hypotheses. It is better regarded as a 'sensitizing concept' (Schur 1971, 26, 31) which suggests an angle of enquiry, rather than a 'theory' or 'model' generating predictive hypotheses. Some of its notions can only be loosely defined (since negative social reactions can take many different forms) and it is misunderstood if it is taken to predict that labelling deviants always and

---

[8] 'The deviant is a person whose activities have moved outside the margins of the group and when the community calls him to account for that vagrancy it is making a statement about the nature and placement of its boundaries' (Erikson 1966, 11). Erikson's thesis has been supported and refined by Ben-Yehuda 1985, 23–73.

[9] See Schur 1971, 21 and Lemert 1972, 21–22; the latter insists in this connection that 'no one theory or model will suffice to study the societal reaction; models must be appropriate to the area under study, to the values, norms, and structures identifiable in the area, as well as the special qualities of the persons and their acts subject to definition as deviant' (p. 21).

inevitably sets off a 'deviant career'.[10] In certain respects, therefore, the interactionist perspective can never be established by empirical proof, and its resistance to statistical analysis has caused some frustration among sociologists who regard their subject as a natural science. However, rightly employed this perspective can enable us to ask new questions of the historical material we study: it can suggest some interesting directions in which to look, though not, of course, what we will find when we look there.

Judaism and apostasy

It is remarkable how frequently scholars of Judaism appear to regard 'apostasy' as an objectively definable entity, as an inherent quality in certain kinds of behaviour. Discussions of our topic often work on the assumption that we all know what constitutes apostasy: it is only a matter of detecting the cases which crop up here and there in our sources. Yet 'apostasy', like other deviant labels, is essentially a matter of perspective. One may list activities in which Jews were socially assimilated to their gentile environment and thereby abandoned some aspects of their national traditions, but where such assimilation was regarded as 'apostasy' was a matter which different Jews in different locations and times could define in very different ways.[11] A Jew who was assimilated to the extent of attending a Greek school and visiting the Greek theatre might be considered by some Jews as 'apostate' but fully accepted as an observant Jew by others. Given what we know of the diversity of Jewish practice and belief, it is odd how scholars continue to regard the perspective of the Maccabean literature (for instance) as definitive for Judaism as a whole, as if all Jews contrasted 'Judaism' and 'Hellenism' along the lines of 1 and 2 Maccabees, or all regarded the acquisition of Greek citizenship as tantamount to apostasy (as does 3 Maccabees).[12] Where the author of *The Letter of Aristeas* celebrates the social integration of Hellenized Jews in the Ptolemaic court, 3 Maccabees sees only compromise, inevitably entailing idolatry. Given the divergent expressions of Judaism within

---

[10] Downes and Rock (1988, 183) properly insist that 'interactionism casts deviance as a process which may continue over a lifetime, which has no necessary end, which is anything but inexorable, and which may be built around false starts, diversions and returns.'

[11] I have explored this matter in more detail in relation to the Diaspora in Barclay (1994).

[12] Kasher 1985 is a particularly clear example of this, but by one means the only one; for an earlier essay based on the spurious notion of 'orthodoxy' in Judaism see Feldman 1960.

Palestine before 70 CE and the varieties of Judaism in the Diaspora, we should not be surprised if we find varying definitions of 'deviants' (i.e. 'sinners', 'apostates', etc.) in our Jewish sources.[13] The interactionist perspective suggests that we should regard 'apostate' as a term defined only in relation to the party issuing the label, and what evidence we have from first-century Judaism bears out the truth of this relativistic observation.

I do not mean to suggest that Jewish communities were invariably disunited in their definition of their boundaries or that the definition of 'apostate' was always negotiated anew in each instance. During periods of stability individual Jewish communities could clearly take some definitions for granted and a certain unity of mind is sometimes perceptible both within individual communities and across geographical and temporal bounds. Philo tells us his own opinion on who has 'deserted the ancestral customs', but also indicates the viewpoint of 'the masses' in the Jewish community in Alexandria with which he is largely in accord.[14] We can also discern certain topics (e.g. engagement in 'idolatrous' worship and eating unclean food) on which there appears to have been a fair degree of unanimity across different Jewish communities in our period. Thus we need not suppose that every case of 'deviating' behaviour had to be negotiated from scratch in the community as to its 'deviant' or 'nondeviant' status. Nonetheless, norms do change over time and even where they are generally upheld and applied, exceptions can be allowed in particular circumstances. A homosexual was a 'pervert' only a generation ago, but is less frequently so labelled today, and although most Americans strongly disapprove of adultery, they are prepared to turn a blind eye in certain notable cases. Thus, as the interactionist perspective suggests, when we find a Jew labelled an 'apostate', it is always worth enquiring who is doing the defining and whose interests are involved in this definition.

The case of Tiberius Julius Alexander

Let me take one famous example of an 'apostate' and see what might be suggested by this interactionist perspective. My example is Tiberius Julius Alexander, Philo's nephew, who was born into an exceptionally wealthy

---

[13] On the varying definitions of 'sinner' in Palestinian Judaism see Dunn 1990, 71–77; on diversity in the Diaspora see Barclay 1996.

[14] For his own opinion see, e.g., *Jos.* 254; *Virt.* 182; *Mos.* 1.31; *Spec. Leg.* 1.54–58; 3.29. For the opinion of the masses, *Migr. Abr.* 89–93.

Jewish family in Alexandria in *c*.15 CE.[15] Alexander features as a sceptic in three philosophical treatises written by Philo, but these do not suggest that he was dissociated from the Jewish community or regarded by Philo as an apostate.[16] In his subsequent career we find Alexander prominent in Roman administration, first as *epistrategos* of the Thebaid (42 CE), then as procurator of Judaea (46–48 CE), as a high-ranking officer in the eastern army (63 CE) and then at the very top of the equestrian ladder as Roman governor of Egypt (66–69 CE). It was during this latter period that he had to suppress a Jewish uprising in Alexandria (Josephus, *War* 2.487–498) and in 70 CE, he acted as Titus' advisor and second-in-command at the siege of Jerusalem (*War* 5.45–46; 6.237–242). Thereafter he may have become prefect of the praetorian guard in Rome.

It is striking that when recording these aspects of Alexander's life in his *Jewish War* (late 70s CE) Josephus makes no comment on Alexander's Jewish standing. One can imagine what the members of the Jewish community in Alexandria thought of him when he ordered the Roman troops into their quarter, and from the perspective of the Jewish defenders of Jerusalem he was presumably a traitor and renegade, like Josephus himself (*War* 3.438–442; 5.375). In fact the common fate of Alexander and Josephus as advisors of Titus in the Roman camp and their subsequent honours at Rome may have induced Josephus to omit criticism of Alexander's behaviour, though he presumably knew that his duties involved him in officiating at the worship of Egyptian and Roman deities.[17] If we had only Josephus' *War* we would have no explicit evidence that Alexander was ever regarded as an apostate. It is only in his later work, the *Jewish Antiquities*, that Josephus records that Alexander 'did not remain faithful to his ancestral customs' (*Ant.* 20.100). That was published at a date (93 CE) when Alexander was almost certainly dead. The facts of this case prompt two observations.

First, Alexander's prominent position in Roman government brought no advantage to the Jews either in Alexandria or in Judaea. But if events had turned out differently, if (for instance) he had succeeded in averting

---

[15] His biography has been fully detailed by Turner 1954 and Burr 1955.

[16] *Prov.* 1 and 2 and in *Anim.* Alexander argues against divine providence, but Philo treats him with warmth and respect and has him retract his doubts at the end of *Prov.* 2. As a caution, note the hesitancy of Hadas-Lebel (1973, 23–46) on the authorship of these treatises and the identity of the Alexander featured in them.

[17] We find Alexander in inscriptions honouring Egyptian deities (and their providence!) in *Orientis Graeci Inscriptiones Selectae* 663 and 669; cf. comparable papyri in *Corpus Papyrorum Judaicorum* 418.

violence in Alexandria or had saved Jerusalem, would he still have been castigated as an apostate? To what extent were Jewish communities willing to tolerate compromise among their well-placed members so long as their activities worked to the benefit of Jews? One thinks of the tumultuous welcome accorded to Agrippa I in Alexandria after his enthronement as king by Gaius (38 CE), even though he was well known to be a dishonest bankrupt whose close friendship with Gaius must have involved extensive assimilation (Philo, *Flacc.* 25–30; Josephus, *Ant.* 18.143–239). Agrippa could play an important role on behalf of the Jews; Alexander, as it turned out, could not.

Secondly, Josephus may have regarded Alexander as an apostate at the time he wrote the *War*, but refrained from saying so either because it would have reflected badly on himself (he was also somewhat compromised in his role during the war) or because he could not afford to alienate a man of such influence in Rome. Perhaps he named Alexander an apostate in the *Antiquities* because it was safe to do so only when Alexander was dead (Turner 1954, 63). This might suggest that charges of apostasy, which could cause offence, were made only when those who levelled them could afford to do so.

These observations on the case of Tiberius Julius Alexander are merely illustrative of the sort of questions which arise when we employ the interactionist perspective on deviance to the phenomenon of apostasy. They suggest that we have to rid ourselves of the notion that everyone knows (and everyone then knew) who was an apostate; we need to watch very carefully who was (or was not) defining and applying the label 'apostate', in what circumstances, from what perspective and in whose interests. Our observations on this particular case also suggest the power factors which could be involved in this process, in which it was easier to label the socially weak than the socially strong.

The case of Christians in the first century

Such considerations could be of benefit in investigating the processes by which Christians were edged out of Jewish communities in the course of the first century CE. As I mentioned at the beginning, Jack Sanders has made interesting use of deviance theory in this connection (1993, 129–51). Sanders' question is: 'Why did the leadership of Roman-period Judaism, normally tolerant of diversity, reject and even persecute the various manifestations of Christianity that it encountered?' (p. 129). He considers that cultural (i.e. theological) factors are insufficient to answer this question (pp. 99, 139) and looks for help from deviance theory, especially that functionalist application developed by Erikson which suggested that the identification of deviants helps to clarify and enforce the boundaries of an insecure community. Taking the early Christians to be a new outcrop of deviants whose status raised difficult questions, Sanders points to the tension-laden years in Judaea both before and after the revolt as the crucial factor in driving the threatened Jewish leadership towards identifying and punishing the Christians as deviants (pp. 136–37).

Several features of this analysis are suggestive, but it requires, I suggest, much closer definition. In the first place, it is not clear whether the 'social identity crisis' which Sanders discovers in Judaea (p. 135) was as severe in the pre-70 period as he suggests, or prevalent to any degree in those parts of the Diaspora where we can trace the growth of the Christian movement.[18] Second, it is extremely hard to discern, and impossible to generalize about, what were the issues on which Christians were considered 'deviant'. It is even difficult to see to what degree such issues were novel or ambiguous; perhaps some Christians were dismissed without much ado as 'apostates' since they had clearly flouted laws long regarded as tests of loyalty to Judaism.[19] Third, if its social identity crisis even before 70 CE caused mainstream Judaism to reject Christianity 'when it had normally accepted similar deviance' (p. 136), why did it not also reject those other 'deviant' forms of Judaism in this period? Sanders cites comparable examples of deviance as including Philo, the

[18] The external threats to Palestinian Jews in the pre-70 period which Sanders lists (p. 137) are not quite equivalent to the identity-threatening features of Puritan New England which he takes from Erikson as his model. Arguably, the threat of the statue of Gaius (39–41 CE) made Palestinian Jews not less but more certain of their unity and the limits of their tolerance. In the Diaspora, the Jewish communities in Egypt and Cyrene were certainly troubled during this century, but we cannot trace the rise of Christianity there; and in the places where our record for Christianity is strong (Rome, Greece, Asia Minor) there is little evidence of 'crisis' in the synagogue communities (except perhaps in Rome in the 40s CE).

[19] Sanders (1993, 136) is aware that old and traditional 'crimes' hardly need a social identity crisis to be identified and punished, and thus has to assert that the Christians ('of course') constituted an ambiguous group, a case of 'soft deviance' which either was not or might not have been punished at other times. But this clearly needs to be established in the first place and the situation may have differed greatly between different expressions of Christianity. Sanders is naturally aware of the diversity in early Christianity on such matters as the admission of gentiles, but seems to assume that any welcome of gentiles, even as proper proselytes, was liable to interpretation as deviance (p. 138); that seems to run against the evidence (e.g. Josephus, War 2.454).

Essenes, John the Baptist and the Pharisaic party (pp. 86, 133), none of which was ostracized in the pre-70 era. In fact, if all of these can be regarded as 'similar' in deviance to each other and to Christianity, it appears that the notion of 'deviance' has become far too large a hammer with which to crack this rather delicate nut.

Rather than adopting any such global hypothesis, we should observe that the interactionist perspective suggests that definitions of 'deviance' could vary somewhat between different parties and interest groups in Judaism, and this could help to explain why Christians were in fact so *variously* assessed during the first century. An activity, we recall, is deviant only to the degree to which others react negatively towards it. To some Jews 'Matthean Christians' may have seemed peculiar but not apostate, while other Jews may have considered them to have crossed a crucial boundary out of Judaism. Other Jewish Christians could have evoked different reactions and their gentile Christian adherents may have been variously judged as valuable sympathizers or dangerous diluters of the faith. In fact, given the relativity which is integral to the subject of deviance and the evidence for varying Jewish definitions of sinners and apostates, it may be unhelpful to look for any single issue on which the early Christians made themselves clearly suspect to contemporary Jews. Rather, since deviance is a matter of definition and since the Christians were deviant only as and when they were reacted to as such, we should imagine there to have been a host of variations in local circumstances and a range of reactions to various kinds of Christianity. As we have seen, some of these variations were probably related to power struggles: where the Christians were politically and socially weak it was far easier to 'deviantize' them than where they had a significant power base in numerical or economic terms. Thus, while general social trends in cultural insecurity probably had some part to play in the whole process, we must be ever alert to the innumerable variables of circumstance and personnel through which the earliest Christians sometimes were and sometimes were not rejected by first-century Jews as deviant. It is unfortunate that we can trace very few actual examples of this deviantizing process. Paul is perhaps the best documented and worth considering in some detail.

The case of Paul

From the evidence of his letters it appears that Paul was continually 'endangered' by Jews (2 Cor 11:26) and felt himself 'persecuted' because of his stance on circumcision (Gal 5:11). In one passage he mentions being 'banished' and 'prevented from speaking to Gentiles' (1 Thess 2:15 – its authenticity is questioned by some) and in another revealing comment says he has received the synagogue punishment of the thirty-nine lashes on five occasions (2 Cor 11:24). It appears that even many Christian Jews strongly opposed him; they considered his eating with gentiles sinful (Gal 2:11–17) and his teaching an invitation to libertinism (Rom 3:8). In Acts also the theme of Jewish opposition to Paul is prominent, though perhaps somewhat stereotyped. In that narrative Paul is frequently denounced and expelled from synagogues, and sometimes charged with serious offences. When he arrives in Jerusalem he is met by anxious Jewish Christians who have been told that he teaches 'apostasy' from Moses to the Jews who live among the gentiles, telling them not to circumcise their children or to live in accordance with the Jewish customs (Acts 21:21). Paul's previous fears concerning his reception in Jerusalem (Rom 15:31) are amply fulfilled in his arrest and subsequent trials.

Such evidence suggests that Paul was frequently denounced as an apostate Jew. Such a reaction was not, however, either automatic or immediate. Some Jewish Christians at least some of the time accepted Paul's stance as compatible with their understanding of Judaism (Peter, Barnabas, Prisca and Aquila, for instance) and there is good reason to believe that Paul was initially accepted as a synagogue member in most locations. The thirty-nine lashes were discipline for a synagogue member, not quite the expulsion and ostracism which an officially designated apostate might receive.[20] There were clearly some ambiguities about Paul which elicited varying reactions, and that is not surprising in relation to a man who said he lived as a Jew among Jews, but without reference to the law among gentiles (1 Cor 9:20–21), and whom we find in his letters sometimes celebrating and sometimes denigrating his Jewish credentials (2 Cor 11:22; Rom 11:1; Gal 1:13–14; Phil 3:2–11).

Scholars have recently debated whether Paul was or was not an apostate, but usually without reference to how he was actually perceived in his own day.[21] It should be clear by now that the question requires us to be sensitive to the opinions and judgments of Paul's contemporaries; his deviance, like any other, was in the eye of the beholders. The evidence we have briefly surveyed suggests that many variables could affect their vision of Paul: Jews of different persuasions and in different places reacted

---

[20] See Harvey 1985; Gallas 1990; Horbury 1985.
[21] See e.g. Dunn 1990, 183–214; Räisänen 1985, 543–53; Segal 1990.

differently to this enigmatic figure in their midst. How Paul fared in the Diaspora synagogues perhaps depended on how long he stayed there, what personal animosities he engendered, how his judges at his synagogue trials viewed his defence and what reports (either true or false) they had heard of his behaviour. It is not insignificant that Paul's social position in the Diaspora communities was generally weak: he was a newcomer, of low social status, with no economic or political power base on which to build his defence, and power struggles in the synagogue almost inevitably turned to his disadvantage. Inasmuch as he *was viewed* by his contemporary Jews as an apostate, he *was* (historically speaking) an apostate, and no amount of pleading about the Jewish elements in his theology or the diversity within first-century Judaism can mask or alter that reality.

Early Christianity and the creation of deviants

I have left myself little space to address that other crucial process of definition which characterizes early Christianity, its internal definition of its own boundaries. We may simply observe here, by way of illustration, a particularly intriguing example of the struggle for the definition of Christian identity in the correspondence of Paul with the church in Corinth. One may read the whole of 1 Corinthians as an attempt by Paul to define the boundaries of the Christian community in Corinth, and an integral part of that effort involves Paul labelling as deviant those he considers should be excluded from the church. Indeed this letter contains a statement which almost precisely summarizes Erikson's thesis on the function of deviance in boundary definition. In 1 Cor 11:19 Paul introduces his discussion of the Lord's Supper with the stunning comment that 'there must be divisions (*haireseis*) among you in order that those who are genuine (*dokimoi*) among you may be recognized'. That is a proto-sociological statement if ever there was one! Paul recognizes that the creation of distinctions between the 'genuine' (*dokimoi*) and the 'spurious' (*adokimoi*, cf. 1 Cor 9:27) serves to give the Christian community definition and identity; he even uses a 'functionalist' purpose clause!

Commentators are surprised at this statement, since earlier in the letter Paul deplores party divisions (1 Cor 1:10–12).[22] But in fact Paul

---

[22] Fee (1987, 538) considers the sentence 'one of the true puzzles in the letter'. Barrett (1971a, 262) significantly tones down its meaning and Munck (1959, 136–37) implausibly relegates its reference to the eschatological future.

spends a considerable proportion of this letter indicating where he thinks the proper boundaries of Christian practice lie. Though he does not think the Apollos or Cephas party has deviated significantly from Christian norms, he certainly wants the Corinthians to recognize that the man reported to have had sex with his father's wife (1 Cor 5:1–13) and those who participate in 'idolatry' (1 Cor 10:1–22) and those who mishandle the Lord's Supper (1 Cor 11:17–34) are all to be regarded as 'deviants' who have strayed over the boundary out of the community.[23] Here in this clash between Paul and the Corinthians we see very clearly how 'deviance' is defined by social reaction. The Corinthian Christians do not apparently regard the man mentioned in 1 Corinthians 5 as other than a sexually active brother; Paul insists that he is, and must be publicly labelled as, a *pornos* who is only a 'so-called' brother (5:11). It is fascinating to see here how, in a typical deviance process, Paul selects from this individual's many activities the one feature of which he disapproves and makes that the defining character of his identity: this man does not just *indulge* in some *porneia*, he *is* a *pornos* and must be treated as that, whatever else he might also be in character or behaviour.

In fact a fundamental point of dispute between Paul and the Corinthians is the location of their community boundaries. As I have argued elsewhere (Barclay 1992), Paul thinks the Corinthians are far too comfortable in their social integration, and he spends much of the letter erecting barriers where the Corinthians presently see none. Conversely, he does not treat as deviant some whom other Christians might well have considered such: he does not want to see excommunicated those who are married to non-Christians, or those who are uncircumcised or those who cannot speak in tongues. Throughout 1 Corinthians Paul is creating insiders and outsiders on his own terms and he does so with regard to so many different issues that it was almost inevitable that some Corinthians would take exception to his rulings. He identifies deviants in order to establish boundaries and solidify the identity of the Corinthian community, precisely as Erikson suggests. Unfortunately, in this case it was a policy which backfired disastrously, for he lacked the authority to get his understanding of deviance accepted. Turning to 2 Corinthians we find that resistance to Paul takes the form

---

[23] On 1 Corinthians 5 see Forkman 1972, 139–51; on 1 Cor 11:17–34 see most recently Engberg-Pedersen 1993.

of questioning whether *he* is *dokimos* ('genuine') as a Christian (2 Cor 13:1–7) and Paul has to respond by questioning the Christian status of this whole congregation and by furious invective against opponents whom he castigates as 'false apostles' (2 Cor 11:13). It is easy to recognize here what we have seen throughout this discussion, that 'deviant' labels are being applied as part of a power struggle, here a fundamental battle for control of the Christian tradition.

We could of course trace this same process in other early Christian conflicts, where we are nowadays conscious of how perspectival terms like 'heretic' and 'apostate' are. Even so, I suspect there is still a tendency to take the views of the New Testament authors as somehow containing an inevitable and objective 'rightness' in their definition of deviance. The advantage of the interactionist perspective in this regard is that it continually reminds us to ask whose definitions we are hearing and whose interests they serve. It certainly suggests, for instance, a thoroughly suspicious reading of the Pastorals, 2 Peter, Jude and other polemical documents from the late first century which react against (and perhaps even invent) those 'deviants' who threaten the social structures which the authors represent. In the Pastorals we can see how practices recognized and tolerated by Paul (e.g. celibacy) have become 'deviantized' in the interests of a particular construction of church policy. In the highly fluid conditions of early Christianity, there were almost no 'taken-for-granted' norms which commanded universal assent, and it was open to each group and party to designate deviance in its own way. That the future of Christianity was determined by power contests between different groups is something no historian can deny, at least none with any sociological awareness: such is the way with all human society.

As I said at the outset, deviance theory is no magic wand with which to solve the many intricate problems which confront the historian of early Christianity. It can only be used in conjunction with minute historical analysis of the sources and cannot fill in the gaps which they leave. Its chief benefit, however, is to call into question our assumptions concerning the objective status of phenomena like apostasy and to invite us to pay close attention to the individuals or groups responsible for the application of deviant labels. If it helps to highlight a degree of relativism in the Judaism of this period, it also suggests that the process of 'the parting of the ways' cannot simply be traced in relation to certain absolute boundary marks, but was radically dependent on the particularities of location, personnel and social context in which early Christianity took root.[24]

FURTHER READING

Ample guidance to the relevant literature on this subject may be found in the footnotes to the article. For the classic texts from the sociology of the 1960s see esp. Becker 1963; 1964 and Erikson 1962; 1966. Surveys of the approach are provided by Pfohl 1985 and Downes and Rock 1988. Important recent studies include those of Ben-Yehuda 1985 and Theo 1995. For criticisms of the approach see literature listed above in n. 5.

Other New Testament scholars who have used deviance theory include Malina and Neyrey 1988 (see ch. 1 above); Malina 1991; Saldarini 1991; 1994; Sanders 1993; Pietersen 1997; Still 1999 (esp. ch. 4).

Some of the ideas Barclay sketches here are developed in more detail elsewhere: on the Corinthian church, and Paul's sense that they are rather too integrated into their surrounding culture with too weak a set of boundaries, see Barclay 1992; on the question of Paul's apostasy, Barclay 1995; and on diaspora Jews in the period (including a section on Paul) see Barclay 1996.

Those who wish to consider the polemic in other New Testament epistles in the light of the questions raised by the sociology of deviance and in this essay will find relevant material on the Pastoral Epistles in Horrell 1993 and Pietersen 1997; on 2 Peter and Jude in Horrell 1998 and (on Jude alone) Wisse 1972; Thurén 1997.

Of wider relevance to the whole question of heresy and diversity in early Christianity are Bauer 1972; Dunn 1977; Lüdemann 1996.

[24] I would like to thank my research student Todd Still for his bibliographic assistance and stimulating work on this topic, and the members of the 'Context and Kerygma' conference held in St Andrews in June/July 1994 for their questions and encouragement.

12

Leadership Patterns and the
Development of Ideology in Early Christianity

DAVID G. HORRELL

INTRODUCTION

In the study of early Christianity, as of any other social movement, one obvious area of interest for a social-scientific investigation is that of leadership. How are power and authority exercised and (sometimes, perhaps) concealed? What patterns of leadership exist and how do they develop over time? How are positions and patterns of leadership legitimated and to what extent are they contested?

Whether from a theological, historical or sociological perspective, many studies have recognised and investigated the development of increasingly structured patterns of leadership in Christianity of the first century CE and beyond (for a concise overview, see Maier 1991, 1–5). In the essay below I attempt to focus particularly upon the significance of a shift in the main locus of power and authority from itinerant to resident leaders, a shift connected in part with the deaths of the most prominent itinerant apostles, though contested for some time after that. There is evidence of some conflict over the patterns of leadership and of the various ways in which resident leadership was legitimated in the face of conflict and opposition. The shift of power to resident leaders and the need for legitimation of their position are also connected, I suggest, with the so-called 'household codes', or *Haustafeln*, which serve to focus power increasingly in the male heads of household who are the primary resident leaders of the congregations. The household codes play a part in the process whereby

A revised version of a paper first published in *Sociology of Religion* 58.4 (1997) 323–41, reproduced here by kind permission of the editor. The paper was first presented to the Sociology of Early Christianity Workshop which met in conjunction with the British Sociological Association Study of Religion Group in Twickenham, U.K., in April 1996. I am grateful to the participants for their comments and questions, and especially to the workshop's convenor, Professor Anthony Blasi. I would also like to thank Alastair Logan for his comments on the paper.

this pattern of leadership is given ideological legitimation and in the ideological battle to exclude others – including women and slaves – from power and influence in the community. The diachronic perspective adopted here has been inspired in part by Anthony Giddens' 'structuration theory', which focuses upon the ways in which social life is structured in an ongoing process of reproduction and transformation. Also inspired by Giddens and others is the critical focus on ideology – understood here as the ways in which symbolic and linguistic resources are used to legitimate a particular pattern of domination (see Horrell 1995; 1996a, 45–59).

This study builds upon, yet sometimes disagrees with, earlier work by Gerd Theissen, Bengt Holmberg, Margaret MacDonald, Harry Maier and Alastair Campbell (see suggestions for further reading below). All may agree that there is some degree of development, or 'institutionalisation', evident over time through the first century and beyond, but I suggest that Maier and Campbell have played down the extent of transformation. Am I right, or have I exaggerated the differences between the earlier and later periods? And am I right to suggest that a shift of power from itinerant to resident leadership is a crucial aspect of change, and to connect this with the emergence of the household-code instruction? This study may also raise a wider set of questions: What are the implications of adopting a critical social-scientific perspective on the struggles over leadership in early Christianity? If the household codes are viewed as a form of ideology which legitimates the power and position of the male heads of households and serves their interests as leaders of the community, while at the same time marginalising others, does that imply a hostile critique of such biblical teaching, and of the pattern of leadership it supports? Or can a social-scientific perspective involve an 'unmasking' of the structures whereby power and domination operate, without necessarily judging whether or not that domination is legitimate? Similar questions arise in connection with the applications of deviance theory (see ch. 11 above), while Schottroff's essay (ch. 10 above) shows at least one way in which such critical social analysis might connect with a particular contemporary theological agenda.

1. Introduction

On the subject of leadership patterns, as in so many areas of New Testament sociology, Gerd Theissen has drawn our attention to issues of considerable significance. In his article entitled 'Legitimation and Subsistence: An Essay on the Sociology of Early Christian Missionaries', first published in 1975, Theissen proposed the following thesis:

> there were two types of primitive Christian itinerant preachers, to be distinguished as itinerant charismatics on the one hand and community organizers on the other. The most important difference between them is that each adopts a distinctive attitude to the question of subsistence. The first type arose in the social circumstances of the Palestinian region. The second, represented by Paul and Barnabas, arose in the movement of the mission into Hellenistic territory. Both types work side by side but come into conflict in Corinth. (Theissen 1982, 28)

The itinerant charismatics, Theissen argued, followed the synoptic mission instructions requiring missionaries to depend entirely upon the generosity of others for their material support (Mark 6:7–13; Matt 10:5–15; Luke 9:1–6; 10:1–12). Paul and his co-workers, on the other hand, insisted on working at their own trade to support themselves. While Theissen's sociological reconstructions of the Jesus movement in Palestine and specifically of the role of the wandering charismatics have not gone uncriticised,[1] the essential points of this thesis stand. It is clear from the synoptic mission instructions that Jesus is recorded as commanding his apostles not to take even the minimum of possessions on their travels, not even the bag, staff and mantle characteristic of the Cynic preacher,[2] and to depend on the support and hospitality offered to them (cf. Matt 10:40–42; Mark 9:38–41). It is clear too that Paul knows this instruction of the Lord, even though he himself sets it aside and thereby behaves differently from other itinerant missionaries, Peter and others connected with the Jerusalem church, who were known to the Corinthian congregation (1 Cor 9:1–23; cf. also 1 Cor 4:11–13;

---

[1] See esp. Horsley 1989, 43–50; also Stegemann 1984. Horsley's criticisms, while often valuable, focus primarily upon Theissen's popular book (Theissen 1978) and hardly deal adequately with the detailed essays Theissen published on the subject (see now Theissen 1979; 1993); nor do his criticisms of the wandering charismatics thesis seem to me convincing. [See further ch. 3 above.]

[2] See Crossan 1993, 117–19; Harvey 1982, 218; Theissen 1978, 14–15; Lucian, *Peregrinus* 24.

1 Thess 2:9; 2 Thess 3:6–13). Moreover, the synoptic evangelists, especially Luke, reveal a tendency to downplay the Lord's command to charismatic poverty and to legitimate the Pauline practice of self-support through manual labour (see Matt 10:8; Luke 22:35–36; esp. Acts 20:33–35). Conflict over the issue of material support for itinerant missionaries was evident especially at Corinth, but more widely too.[3]

However, while Theissen has drawn our attention to a sociologically significant conflict between patterns of leadership activity, the two types of missionary leader to which he draws attention share one fundamental characteristic in common. They are both, as Theissen recognises, itinerant forms of leadership. The focus of this essay is the distinction between two forms of leadership which also contrast and conflict in important ways in early Christianity, namely itinerant leadership and resident leadership (that is, leadership from those who are located in a particular community, over which they exercise leadership). I will argue that there are important distinctions to be drawn between these two patterns of leadership, that in general it is legitimate to speak of a development from itinerant to resident leadership in early Christianity, that there is evidence which reflects the tensions and difficulties which the diverse patterns of leadership caused, and that the transference of power from itinerant to resident leadership is a sociologically significant transformation which may be connected with the development of more socially conservative patterns of ethical instruction (especially the 'household codes').[4]

2. Sociological perspectives on authority and leadership

Any sociological discussion of authority and leadership must begin with Max Weber's classic description of the three ideal 'types of legitimate domination': rational-legal, traditional, and charismatic (see Weber

[3] On these various points see further Horrell 1997a; 1996a, 199–237.
[4] Although von Harnack's argument that an early Christian leadership pattern of itinerant apostles, prophets and teachers was replaced by episcopal leadership in local communities has been influential (Harnack 1904, 398–461; 1905, 46–114; see Draper 1995, 298–99), I suggest that insufficient attention has been given to the specific pattern of change from itinerant to resident leadership. Previous studies have tended to focus either (from a theological or historical perspective) upon the development from charismatic freedom to ecclesiastical structure (e.g. von Campenhausen 1969) or (from a sociological perspective) upon the processes of the 'routinization of charisma' and of 'institutionalisation' (e.g. Holmberg 1978; MacDonald 1988).

1968a, 212–301; Eisenstadt 1968, 46–47).[5] In the first type of authority, 'obedience is owed to the legally established impersonal order' and to persons only insofar as it falls within the scope of the authority of their office (1968a, 215–16). In the second type, 'obedience is owed to the *person* . . . who occupies the traditionally sanctioned position of authority' (Weber 1968a, 216): leaders have a 'traditional status' (1968a, 226). Charismatic authority, on the other hand, resides not in a person's occupation of a particular role, office, or social position, but in his or her individual qualities, 'by virtue of which he [*sic*] is considered extraordinary and treated as endowed with . . . exceptional powers or qualities. These are such as are not accessible to the ordinary person, but are regarded as of divine origin . . .' (1968a, 241). Charismatic authority is, for Weber, a 'revolutionary force' (1968a, 244). However, it cannot remain stable, but becomes 'routinised': 'traditionalised or rationalised' (1968a, 246ff; further Eisenstadt 1968).

This Weberian typology has been carefully and critically applied to the structure of authority in the primitive churches by Bengt Holmberg (1978; cf. also Gager 1975, 67–76; Schütz 1975, and on Jesus, Ebertz 1987; Hengel 1981). Clearly, from a Weberian perspective, Jesus is *the* charismatic leader of the Christian movement (though note the critique of Malina 1996a, 123–42). Paul, among others, may be regarded as a 'minor founder' (Holmberg 1978, 155) whose authority is secondary, but nonetheless charismatic. Holmberg also explores the ways in which, from the very earliest times, charismatic authority is routinised in an ongoing process of institutionalisation (see Holmberg 1978, 162–95; MacDonald 1988, 10–18). Over time, according to Holmberg, institutionalisation becomes less 'open', less free in terms of the various directions it may take (1978, 200–202; MacDonald 1988, 12–13). Margaret MacDonald has analysed this process of institutionalisation in relation, *inter alia*, to the development of structures of ministry, employing also the sociological model of a sect developing towards a more 'church'-type institution.

These sociological perspectives offer some valuable tools for describing and understanding the developing patterns of leadership and authority in the earliest churches, and the changes which took place in the

---

[5] They are 'ideal' in that they are not expected to occur historically in their 'pure' form. The types provide a conceptual framework with which the always more complex historical realities can be analysed. See Weber 1968a, 216; cf. also Holmberg 1978, 136–37.

institution over time. However, by describing what is typical, almost inevitable, as institutions develop, they may perhaps lead to a neglect to explore the specific factors which can help to explain change in a particular historical context,[6] and a failure to uncover the power struggles which took place in a *contested* process of development (see Horrell 1993). 'The danger is that the change [may] be "explained" as a typical process of sociological necessity – thereby legitimating and at the same time obscuring what is in fact a process of conflict in which the groups with most power ultimately come to dominate' (Horrell 1996a, 289; see 287–89).

In what follows I shall accept that the pattern of change in leadership structures may broadly be seen as a process in which charismatic authority becomes routinised and moves towards a more 'traditional' type. It also seems evident that the pattern of change in the institution may be characterised, in a generalised way, as the beginnings of a movement from 'sect to church' (MacDonald 1988, 163–66, 200–201). However, I will pay most attention to exploring a specific historical and contextual aspect of the change in leadership patterns – namely the change from itinerant to resident leadership – and will seek to relate this to power struggles in the early church. Holmberg is surely right that institutionalisation might in theory proceed in a number of different directions; that it proceeded in the particular direction it did should be the subject of critical social analysis.

One aspect of Weber's treatment of domination remains particularly relevant in what follows, namely that of legitimation. The types of domination Weber outlined were all forms of *legitimate* domination. In other words, as distinct from authority which is simply imposed by brute force,[7] each of Weber's types of domination depends on an

---

[6] It is often stated that social science is concerned with what is typical whereas history attends to the unique and particular. However, I do not accept that this is a legitimate intellectual 'division of labour'. Some social theorists argue that explanation is essentially contextual – 'most "why?" questions do not need a generalisation to answer them' (Giddens 1984, xix) – and a number of writers have argued for an amalgamation of historical and sociological approaches into social history, or historical sociology (e.g. Burke 1980; Abrams 1982). Moreover, comparative work, often undertaken in the social sciences, need not only imply the search for what is typical; illuminating what is distinctive may equally be a concern. In my view, both wide-ranging theoretical perspectives and specific historical and contextual focus belong together in a socio-historical method. On this whole question see further Horrell 1996a, 22–31.

[7] Though even authority imposed by physical coercion usually attempts also to legitimate ideologically its domination, as was clearly the case in the Roman empire; see Horrell 1996a, 69–73.

acceptance that the domination exercised is legitimate: authority must be granted and acknowledged by the subordinates, as well as claimed by the leader(s). This raises the question, to which we shall give some attention, as to the ways in which particular patterns of leadership were legitimated in the early church.

3. Patterns of leadership in earliest Christianity

In his analysis of the distribution of power in the primitive church, Holmberg outlines a structure in which Jerusalem has a particular status as a centre of authority (Holmberg 1978, 14–57). Paul, while sometimes stressing his independence and vehemently arguing his case, nevertheless acknowledges the importance of the Jerusalem leaders' accepting the legitimacy of his apostleship and gospel (Gal 2:1–10). Next Holmberg explores the structures of authority encompassing Paul and his circle of co-workers, and finally local leadership in the congregations (1978, 58–123).

Although our evidence is scarce, and much of it relates to the Pauline churches, it is clear that the major locus of leadership power and authority in the earliest churches was in the circle of apostolic missionaries such as Peter, James and Paul, even if Paul sometimes had to argue hard to maintain his position as a true apostle. At least in relation to the Pauline congregations, and indeed to churches other than in Jerusalem, these leaders are itinerants. Although Peter, James and John, for example, were based in the Jerusalem community – they were, Paul says, its 'pillars' (Gal 2:9) – they, and others connected with them or with the Jerusalem community, engaged in missionary activity over a wide area. 'Certain people from James' arrived in Antioch, at a time when Peter (Cephas), Paul and Barnabas were there already (Gal 2:11–13). 1 Cor 9:5 refers to the itinerant missionary activity (note *periagein*) of 'the other apostles and the brothers of the Lord, and Cephas'.[8] Jerusalem connections are also evident in the case of those who have come to Corinth and whom Paul denounces as 'false apostles' in 2 Cor 11:12–23. In the early days of their missionary activity, according to Acts, Paul and Barnabas had a specific link with the Antioch community (Acts 11:25–30; 13:1–15:35), although this came to an end, possibly due to the success in Antioch of

---

[8] Note also the evidence mentioned by Eusebius (*EH* 1.7.14) about relatives of Jesus engaged in itinerant missionary activity in Palestine; see further Bauckham 1990, 57–70.

the Judaising faction represented by the 'people from James'.[9] But in Antioch, as in Corinth, it is clear that the major locus of authority was with those who were itinerant missionaries, or at least, with the leading circle in Jerusalem or in local missionaries (Paul and Barnabas) who travelled over a wide area. At Corinth Apollos, also itinerant, at least in relation to Corinth, was also influential, such that different people in the congregation claimed allegiance to Paul, to Peter, or to Apollos (1 Cor 1:10–12).[10]

A considerable number of itinerant missionaries exercised some form of authority and leadership in earliest Christianity. As well as the prominent leading figures, and the nameless others connected with James and the Jerusalem community, we hear also of other co-workers of Paul besides Barnabas. Some of Paul's prominent co-workers – Silvanus, Timothy and Titus – are named as partners in initial missionary activity (2 Cor 1:19), as co-authors of epistles (1 Thess 1:1), or are sent as Paul's authorised representatives (1 Cor 4:17; 16:10–11; 2 Cor 7:5–8:24; see further Holmberg 1978, 58–69; Ollrog 1979). Paul also refers generally to co-workers and labourers (e.g. 1 Cor 16:16), though these were not necessarily itinerant (cf. Phlm 1).[11] Indeed, we should be careful not to draw too sharp a distinction between itinerant and resident leadership. At least some of the leaders of the Jerusalem church are clearly itinerant as well as community-based. There are also examples in the Pauline circle. Prisca and Aquila, for example, are co-workers who have spent time and hosted house-churches in a number of different cities (Rome [Rom 16:3–5], Corinth [Acts 18:2–3] and Ephesus [1 Cor 16:19]). Phoebe is a *diakonos* of the church at Cenchreae, but is travelling to Rome (Rom 16:1–2), and there are many other examples of people who are based in one Christian community travelling with messages or material support for Paul (e.g. Phil 2:25; 1 Cor 16:17).

It is also clear that certain forms of resident leadership did exist within the various Christian communities, although here again evidence is scarce (Holmberg 1978, 96–123). The earliest New Testament letter, 1 Thessalonians, urges the *adelphoi* in Thessalonica 'to respect those

---

[9] See further Taylor 1992, 87–144; Holmberg 1978, 15–34.

[10] Whether there was a 'Christ party', and, if there was, what the declaration of allegiance to Christ meant in contrast to the other slogans of allegiance, remains unclear and much disputed.

[11] On the role of the *ergatēs*, 'ein Terminus technicus für den urchristlichen Missionar', see Haraguchi 1993.

who labour among you, and have charge of you in the Lord and admonish you' (1 Thess 5:12; cf. also Gal 6:6). A number of the gifts listed in 1 Cor 12:4–11 and Rom 12:6–8 and presumably exercised in the communities imply a certain degree of authority or leadership – prophecy, teaching, leading,[12] and so on. Indeed, prophets and teachers are listed second and third in the hierarchy of leading functions Paul outlines in 1 Cor 12:28. Whatever is the precise role or office of the *episkopoi* and *diakonoi* Paul addresses in Phil 1:1, these are clearly people in the congregation with some authority of oversight and ministry.

However, these various references give us few clues as to the precise patterns of leadership or the social position of the leaders. A few references do indicate that people of some social standing at least sometimes acquired roles of leadership and influence. Phoebe, for example, a *diakonos* of the church at Cenchreae, is described as a patron of many (*prostatis pollōn* – Rom 16:1–2). Gaius acts as host not only to Paul, but to the whole of the Corinthian church (Rom 16:23).[13] An important piece of evidence is found in 1 Cor 16:15–18. Here Paul instructs the Corinthians to recognise and submit to the household of Stephanas, since they were the first converts in Achaia and have given themselves to the service of the saints. Paul here accepts to a degree the structure of the household; Stephanas is a leading figure and head of a household (see also 1 Cor 1:16). However, we must be careful to take all the evidence into account here. It will not do to refer only to Stephanas as a leading figure and thus to use this evidence to support the view that 'the household provided the leadership of the church', as Alastair Campbell does (Campbell 1994, 126).[14] Campbell argues that leadership in the earliest churches was provided by the householders in whose houses the congregation met. These leaders were in fact 'the equivalent of elders in all but name' (ibid.). (Campbell argues that the term 'elder', *presbuteros*, was essentially 'a title of honour, not of office, a title that is imprecise, collective and representative, and rooted in the ancient family or household' (1994, 246).) In the first generation, he suggests, when the local church comprised separate groups focused on single households,

---

[12] Rom 12:8 uses the same verb, *proïstēmi*, found in 1 Thess 5:12 to describe leadership.

[13] On these people and their social standing, and more generally on the social level of the Corinthian Christians, see Theissen 1982, 69–119; Horrell 1996a, 91–101. [Also ch. 7 above.]

[14] Andrew Clarke also focuses upon the influential well-to-do members of the Corinthian congregation, and assumes without argument that they may be referred to as the 'leaders' in the church (Clarke 1993).

the actual name 'elders' was inappropriate, but it became inevitable in the second generation, with the expansion of the churches and the linking together of various house-congregations. Concerning the earliest churches he writes:

> The church that met in someone's house met under that person's presidency. The householder was *ex hypothesi* a person of standing, a patron of others, and the space where the church met was his space, in which he was accustomed to the obedience of slaves and the deference of his wife and children. (Campbell 1994, 126)[15]

Harry Maier (1991) similarly emphasises the centrality of the household to understanding the development of ministry structures in the early churches, and maintains that there is in this regard an essential continuity between the situation at the time of Paul and that represented around the turn of the century in the writings of Hermas, Clement and Ignatius. Relatively wealthy householders, Maier suggests, were resident local leaders from the start.

It is certainly clear, both from the Pauline epistles and from Acts, that the earliest Christian communities met in houses, and that in each city 'the church' therefore comprised a number of house-churches (Klauck 1981; Campbell 1994; on Acts, see 152–59). However, while the influence of householders within the earliest congregations should not be denied, neither should their exclusive leadership be assumed. When discussing 1 Cor 16:15–18 Campbell mentions only Stephanas, the head of the household, as a leading figure (1994, 122–23). However, Paul, referring to 'the *household* of Stephanas', urges submission 'to such people (*tois toioutois* – plural!) and to every co-worker and labourer' (16:16). In fact in the following verse he names not only Stephanas, but also Fortunatus and Achaicus (16:17). These last two were most likely members of Stephanas' household, possibly slaves or freedmen (see Fee 1987, 3, 829, 831–32). In the absence of substantive evidence it should not be assumed that all leading roles – co-workers, prophets, teachers, etc. – were filled only or even primarily by heads of household, although such persons were clearly sometimes in dominant positions. Similar comments might be made concerning Philemon, a householder who owns slaves (or at least owns Onesimos) and hosts a church. Yet the

---

[15] Despite the male language (and male heads of households were certainly the norm) Campbell points out that 'the householder could also be a woman, of course' (p. 126). Cf. Col 4:15.

letter Paul writes is addressed also to Apphia and Archippus and indeed to the whole congregation (Phlm 1–2).

In relation to Acts too Campbell 'deduces' that since the early Christians met in homes, then the household structure provided the leaders both in Jerusalem and elsewhere, whom Luke not inaccurately labels 'elders' (Acts 11:30; 14:23; 15:2, 4, etc.; 16:4; 20:17; 21:18; Campbell 1994, 141–75). Prophets and teachers, such as are mentioned at the church in Antioch (Acts 13:1) may be 'supposed' also to be such leading figures within the household hierarchy (Campbell 1994, 164). Yet that presumption seems risky, and without denying Campbell's important focus on the household basis of the early Christian congregations, one may suggest that he has too fully equated household hierarchy and the exercise of leadership. This is especially so in view of the evidence which suggests (*a*) a much wider opportunity to exercise leadership and influence, e.g. through prophecy (1 Cor 14:31), (*b*) a wide and varied circle of co-workers, etc., who should not, *pace* Campbell, be assumed to be drawn only from the circle of heads of household, and (*c*), especially relevant here, the focus of power and authority in the circle of itinerant apostles. Many scholars believe that Luke, writing perhaps in the 80s CE, has read back onto earlier times the leadership terminology of his own day.[16] Certainly due weight should be given to the complete absence of the term *presbuteros* from the genuine Pauline epistles.

Holmberg presents a somewhat more balanced picture, pointing to the existence of *both* 'gifted' persons who fulfil various leadership roles (prophecy, etc.; and no indications are given that they came from only a certain social group), *and* the group of persons whose social and economic position renders them able to provide some forms of leadership (1978, 118); though he too tends to 'presume' that Paul deliberately sought out persons of relative wealth and position as leading figures for the congregation (1978, 107; see 104–107).[17]

But whatever the precise structures of local resident leadership – and there clearly was such leadership in existence – the primary locus of power and authority in the early church was evidently with the itinerant

[16] E.g. Lüdemann 1989, 163: 'Luke imagines that the Church constitution of his time already existed in the time of Paul.' Campbell (1994, 167–69) points out the striking similarities of language regarding church leadership between Acts and the Pastoral Epistles, but does not believe that the emergence of the explicit label 'elders' marks a development in leadership patterns as such from the earlier period; rather that the *term* was not applied in earlier times (see above).

[17] For a contrasting perspective, see Schottroff's essay, ch. 10 above.

missionaries who travelled between the churches, and this is the important point in the context of the present argument. These included the most prominent apostles such as Peter, James and Paul, but many others too – other 'apostles' from the Jerusalem community and other 'co-workers' of Paul's. Certainly in the case of the Pauline churches (for which we have the most direct evidence) the reason for the relatively undeveloped resident local leadership is, as Holmberg states 'the personage of Paul himself. The founder has not left the scene, but is fully and energetically active in his churches' (1978, 117; cf. 158–59).

4. Patterns of conflict and change

As we have already seen, Theissen drew attention to an early and significant conflict over models of itinerant leadership: should the itinerants support themselves, at least in part, through their own labour, or should they entrust themselves entirely to the generosity of supporters in the communities they visit? One danger of the latter model is that itinerant leaders may abuse and take advantage of those who provide support (note Paul's accusation in 2 Cor 11:20, and his self-defence in 12:14–18). This danger is clearly a concern in the *Didache*, or at least in the second half of this probably composite document. In the context represented by the *Didache* (Antioch? late first century?) wandering prophets and teachers are still important and influential figures[18] yet careful instruction is given to congregations to guard against their being taken advantage of by those regarded as less than genuine. Although 'the prophets' seem to be allowed some special freedom in their celebration of the Eucharist (*Did* 10.7) they are to be judged according to the soundness of their teaching (11.1–2, 10; cf. 2 John 10). However the main thrust of the instruction to the congregation concerns limitations on the provision of material support. The congregation has a basic duty to receive and support 'the apostles and prophets', 'according to the ordinance of the Gospel'.[19] But those who come must only stay for one day, or two at most; if they remain three days they are false prophets (11.5). Moreover, they must accept only bread for their journey;

---

[18] See Theissen 1978, 9, but note Patterson 1995, 324.

[19] Lake 1912, 327 n. 1 states that: 'It is unknown to what ordinance the writer refers.' It is surely likely that the reference is to the command of the Lord to the apostles to 'live from the gospel', i.e. to depend upon the communities for support (1 Cor 9:14; and the synoptic mission instructions). Thus the congregation has a responsibility.

if they ask for money, they are false prophets (11.6). There is clearly a danger that prophets will demand precisely these kinds of things: extended board and lodging, and money. The writer of the *Didache* is not one to be taken in by spiritual or charismatic legitimation: 'no prophet who orders a meal in the spirit (*en pneumati*) shall eat of it' (11.9) and 'whosoever shall say in the spirit (*en pneumati*), "Give me money, or something else", you shall not listen to them' (11.12). The possibility of itinerants settling with the community is also recognised and regulated. A 'traveller' who settles must work for their own food (12.3; cf. 2 Thess 3:10). But a true prophet or teacher who settles in the community is 'worthy of their food' (13.1–2; see Matt 10:10; Luke 10:7; 1 Tim 5:17).

Whatever the date of this material in the *Didache*, other evidence confirms that in at least some contexts or some strands of early Christianity, itinerant preachers remained influential at least into the second century. Lucian's account of the life of Peregrinus, a travelling Cynic who for a time became a Christian preacher and who died around 165 CE, satirises not only what Lucian regards as Peregrinus' desire for fame and glory, but also the gullibility (again in Lucian's view) of the Christians who supplied his needs over-generously. Peregrinus was supplied with goods or money (*polla chrēmata*) by the Christians while in prison (*Peregrinus* 13). Later Lucian writes: 'He left home, then, for the second time, to roam about, possessing an ample source of funds in the Christians, through whose ministrations he lived in unalloyed prosperity' (*Peregrinus* 16). Lucian regards wandering Cynic philosophers with the same suspicion, believing their motives to be self-enrichment at the expense of others (*Runaways* 17, 26).

While itinerant apostles, prophets and teachers seem for the *Didache* to represent still an important locus of leadership and authority, the community is given a vital role in discriminating the true from the false. Moreover, significantly, the *Didache* takes some steps to encourage and promote resident leadership.[20] The congregations are urged to 'appoint for themselves' worthy men (*andras*) as *episkopous kai diakonous* (15.1). These people, the writer insists, perform the same service (*tēn leitourgian*) as the prophets and teachers, and should therefore be honoured (15.2).

---

[20] Draper 1995 argues that local resident leadership is being threatened by an increase in the influence of itinerant missionaries. However, the trajectory of change is generally (and in my view more convincingly) argued to be in the opposite direction; see Patterson 1995.

Conflict over the treatment of travelling Christian preachers is also evident in 3 John. Here the writer, describing himself simply as *ho presbuteros* (v. 1),[21] urges the recipient of the letter, Gaius, faithfully to support the *adelphoi* 'even though they are strangers to you'; 'to send them on their way in a manner worthy of God, for they began their journey for the name [of Christ], accepting no support from non-believers' (vv. 5–8). The verb used in verse 6, *propempō*, as Holmberg points out, often conveyed the meaning 'to equip someone with provisions for their journey' (Holmberg 1978, 89). Diotrephes is criticised precisely because he refuses to welcome the itinerant *adelphoi* and prevents others from doing so too, expelling them from the church (vv. 9–10; cf. Gager 1975, 73).

In other New Testament letters, primarily in the Pauline corpus, there is considerable evidence which reveals the increasing prominence and power of resident leadership; a pattern of leadership which, as we have seen, the *Didache* seeks to promote. However, our assessment of this evidence and our understanding of the process and pace of change are obviously dependent upon hypotheses concerning the date and authorship of these letters. The following analysis is based on the view that Colossians and Ephesians are pseudonymous letters which claim Paul's authority in order to present teaching to churches now living in Paul's permanent absence (see Wedderburn and Lincoln 1993). The Pastoral Epistles are also pseudonymous, but are to be dated somewhat later than Colossians and Ephesians, towards the end of the first century. Thus a process of development spanning some decades may be traced through these epistles (see MacDonald 1988). The view that these later Pauline letters are pseudonymous will also affect our interpretation of the purpose of their ascribed authorship and implied recipients.

Colossians and Ephesians reveal little directly about structures of leadership in the churches of their time.[22] In Colossians a number of Pauline co-workers are mentioned, most of whom are mentioned in Paul's short letter to Philemon. These leading figures are described using typically Pauline appellations – *diakonos, doulos Christou, sunergos*, etc. (see Col 1:7; 4:7–17)[23] – though without much being revealed about

---

[21] On the puzzle of this attribution, see Campbell 1994, 207–208.

[22] See MacDonald 1988, 123–38, with particular attention to the implications of the apostle Paul's absence and of the household codes in these letters, on which more below.

[23] The term *sundoulos* (1:7; 4:7) is not found in other Pauline letters, though it occurs in Matthew and Revelation.

their precise roles and functions. If their mention in the letter is a pseudonymous device, adding a sense of authenticity by mentioning Pauline companions known from the letter to Philemon, then we can attach even less significance to any evidence we might glean from these references. Some evidence of the household basis of the congregations is glimpsed in the reference to Nympha, a woman in whose home a congregation meets (Col 4:15).

Personal references to leaders are almost entirely absent from Ephesians, the exception being the mention of Tychicus in 6:21–22, though this reference is lifted verbatim from Colossians 4:7–8 (a sign of the pseudonymity of Ephesians, if not of Colossians, assuming the priority of the latter).[24] The writer of Ephesians clearly regards the 'apostles and prophets' as the foundational leaders of the church, along with 'evangelists, pastors and teachers' (3:5; 4:11–12) though we learn nothing from the letter about who is regarded as legitimately fulfilling such ministries.

In the Pastoral Epistles, however, we find considerable attention given to appropriate structures of leadership and to the qualities and behaviour required from leaders. Here it is clear that the leaders of the churches are resident members of the communities, specifically male heads of households. The leaders are referred to as *episkopoi, diakonoi* and *presbuteroi,* although little is said about their roles and responsibilities which would enable any clear distinctions to be drawn between the functions of the different 'offices'. More attention is given to describing the qualities which must characterise such leaders. As has often been pointed out, these are essentially the stock characteristics of decent and respectable well-to-do persons in Greco-Roman society.[25] The *episkopos,* among other things, 'must manage his own household well, keeping his children submissive and respectful in every way – for if someone does not know how to manage his own household, how can he take care of God's church?' (1 Tim 3:4–5). Deacons likewise must 'manage their children and their households well' (1 Tim 3:12); this wording is surely an indication also that such households often included slaves as well as wife and children.

---

[24] In all 32 words from Col 4:7–8 are repeated in the same order in Eph 6:21–22, though with one addition and one omission in the Ephesians text compared with Colossians.
[25] See Verner 1983, 147–60; Towner 1989, 241; Hanson 1982, 35; Onosander *De imperatoris officio* 1.1.

1 Tim 5:17–18 is an important and revealing reference. The elders who rule well (the verb *proïstēmi* is used as in Rom 12:8 and 1 Thess 5:12), especially those who labour in word and teaching, are to be considered worthy of *diplēs timēs*, 'double honour', which should most probably be taken as a reference to a level of financial support.[26] The legitimation then given in v. 18 for the support of elders – *resident* leaders in the community – is particularly noteworthy, for it uses two citations, both of which had been used in earlier times to legitimate the material support of *itinerant* leaders. The citation from Deut 25:4, 'you shall not muzzle an ox while it is treading out the grain', was used by Paul in 1 Cor 9:9 to underscore the right of the travelling apostles to support. The second citation, apparently referred to by the author of 1 Timothy as 'Scripture' (*hē graphē*) along with Deut 25:4, is the proverb of Jesus from the synoptic mission discourse which explains why the itinerant apostles can expect their support from others: 'the worker is worthy of his wage' (Luke 10:7; cf. Matt 10:10). These scriptural and dominical legitimations for the material support of itinerant missionaries have here become legitimations for the support of *resident* elders.

Assuming that the Pastoral Epistles are pseudonymous, it is most likely that their implied recipients, Timothy and Titus, are indeed implied, fictional, rather than real. The entire literary framework is a pseudonymous device to convey a sense of authenticity and apostolic authority. The letters present themselves as the instruction of Paul to two of his trusted and prominent co-workers. This adds a further kind of legitimation to the appointment and position of the resident leaders. The whole literary context of 1 Timothy, for example, is one in which Paul urges Timothy to remain in Ephesus (1 Tim 1:3) so that he can ensure that sound teaching is followed, so that he can 'teach and urge the duties' which the letter details (6:2b) faithfully guarding what has been entrusted to him (6:20). If the reference to 'laying on of hands' in 5:22 is to a form of 'ordination' – designating certain people as those in a position of leadership – as many commentators think,[27] then Timothy has a special charge to appoint leaders carefully. This responsibility is clearer still in the letter formally addressed to Titus, who, according to the letter, has been left in Crete in order to 'appoint elders in every town' (Titus 1:5). This appointment of leaders is presented as Paul's

---

[26] See Hanson 1982, 101; Campbell 1994, 200–204.
[27] See Hanson 1982, 103; Knight 1992, 239; NRSV: 'Do not ordain anyone hastily . . .'.

explicit instruction – 'as I commanded you'. There follows a list of the qualities required of elders and of the *episkopos* (Titus 1:5–9). Thus the appointment and authority of resident leaders is legitimated as something commanded by Paul and enacted through his most prominent delegates.

In these ways the author of the Pastoral Epistles supports and strengthens the position of the resident leaders in the churches of his time, and he seeks to ensure that positions of leadership are filled by those of an appropriate social standing – male heads of households. The Pastoral Epistles are also fiercely polemical letters which expend considerable energy in labelling the opponents as 'despicable deviants' (e.g. 1 Tim 1:4–7; 4:1–3; 6:3–10; 2 Tim 2:14–26; 3:1–9; Titus 1:10–14).[28] The conventional nature of the polemic (see Karris 1973) means that it is hard to 'mirror read' from the Pastorals much reliable information concerning the beliefs, ethos and practices of the opponents.[29] On the specific subject of leadership among the so-called false teachers, little is revealed. However, it seems clear that the 'false' forms of the faith allow women to take leading roles, or, at least, that women regard themselves as legitimate teachers and propagators of this faith. Why else would the author of 1 Timothy need to make the stern declaration: 'I permit no woman to teach or to have authority over a man; she is to keep silent' (1 Tim 2:12), a declaration which is then undergirded with a legitimation drawn from the Genesis creation narratives (2:13–14)? The young widows are apparently a particular threat; 'some have already turned away to follow Satan' (1 Tim 5:15). The author fears that, outside the structure of the household (5:14), they will roam from house to house, 'saying what they should not say' (5:13). This can hardly with confidence be described as an itinerant form of missionary activity (though it might be that), but at the very least what we seem to encounter is a form of the faith, branded by the author of the Pastorals as false and Satanic, to which women are attracted and which they spread as they move from house to house (see further MacDonald 1988, 187–89). For the author of the letters, who sees an intimate connection between the structure of the household, leadership in the churches, and socially respectable behaviour, such younger widows should 'marry, bear children, and manage their households' (5:14). Forms

[28] A short phrase from the title of Lloyd Pietersen's paper, presented at the same workshop; see now Pietersen 1997.
[29] There have, of course, been many attempts; see further Roloff 1988, 228–39; Schlarb 1990.

of the faith which operate outside of, or present a challenge to, the structure of the household, are a threat.

Within the canonical Pauline corpus, then, a clear trajectory can be seen in which the locus of power and authority shifts from the itinerant apostles, Paul and his co-workers, to the male heads of households resident in the Christian communities, though this resident leadership is still legitimated in Paul's name and through the implied agency of some of his most prominent co-workers. Certainly it is true that a number of householders had significant power and influence in the Pauline communities during Paul's own lifetime. It is also true that the pattern of community life and structure which the author of the Pastoral Epistles urges is not uncontroversially established; it is presented in the context of harsh and vituperative polemic against those who see things differently. The extent of the transformation should not therefore be exaggerated, but neither should it be downplayed.

Evidence from other early Christian epistles from the late first and early second century may also be drawn into this picture. 1 Peter, written from Rome sometime between 75 and 90 CE, though it deals little with structures of leadership in the communities, addresses the elders of the communities to which the letter is sent (1 Pet 5:1–4). These figures, who as Campbell (1994, 206–207 and *passim*) suggests are probably resident leaders of seniority in both faith, age and social position, are urged to exercise their pastoral role and 'oversight' (*episkopountes*)[30] willingly. And those who are younger are instructed to accept the authority of the elders (5:5).

Resident leadership is also the pattern revealed and extolled in *1 Clement*, also written from Rome, and sent to Corinth around the end of the first century (perhaps 95–96 CE; see Horrell 1996a, 238–44). The occasion for the whole letter is the removal of the established presbyters due to a certain rebellion in the Corinthian congregation. The writer of *1 Clement* regards this as an unholy sedition, urges the community to reinstate its rightful leaders and exhorts the troublemakers to depart.[31] His aim is that the 'flock of Christ' should 'be at peace with the appointed presbyters' (*tōn kathestamenōn presbuterōn* – *1 Clem* 54.2). There has been considerable discussion of the forms of ecclesiastical office in *1 Clement*, much of it conducted in terms of the later Protestant–

---

[30] This participle is absent from some texts, though the evidence for its originality is strong; see Michaels 1988, 276.

[31] See *1 Clem* 44.3ff; 47—57; further Horrell 1996a, 244–50.

Catholic agenda (see esp. Fuellenbach 1980). *1 Clement* does not seem to draw a distinction between the role of *presbuteros* and the responsibility for *episkopē* (see 44.4–5) and therefore, despite his mention of the 'strife for the title of *episkopē*' (44.1), a monepiscopal structure does not yet seem to be in view.[32] The author uses various terms for the leadership of the congregation, though *presbuteroi* is the most common (see 1.3; 21.6; 44.5; 47.6; 54.2, etc.). It is interesting that *1 Clement* legitimates the ecclesiastical structures of leadership by claiming for them an apostolic basis (cf. comments on 1 Timothy and Titus above): 'They [sc. the apostles] preached from district to district, and from city to city, and they appointed their first converts, testing them by the Spirit, to be bishops and deacons (*episkopous kai diakonous*) of the future believers' (42.4). Even this, the author asserts, was 'no new method', for scripture itself had written of the appointment of bishops and deacons (42.5); an assertion for which Isaiah 60:17 (paraphrased) serves as a 'proof-text'.[33] Scriptural and apostolic resources are thus used here to legitimate the position and office of resident leaders in the community.

Somewhat later than *1 Clement*, the structure of monepiscopacy does develop and is evidenced most clearly in the writings of Ignatius, bishop of Antioch in the late first and early second century (see Eusebius *EH* 3.22; 3.36). Also at around this time, and also from Asia Minor, we have an epistle of Polycarp, who was bishop of Smyrna. Ignatius' epistles are particularly interesting in the extent to which they reveal a clear concern to strengthen the position of the established leadership: bishop, presbyters and deacons.[34] For example, in his letter to the Philadelphians, Ignatius restates his teaching, which he uttered 'in a great voice, with the voice of God, "Give heed to the bishop, and to the presbytery and deacons"' (*Philad* 7.1).[35] *Ephesians* 6.1 states: 'Therefore it is clear that we must regard the bishop as the Lord himself.' The theological legitimation of the position of the established leaders is more fully set

---

[32] *Contra* Campbell 1994, 211–16, 245; see argument in Horrell 1996a, 247–48. Note that the noun used in 44:1 is not *episkopos* but *episkopē: hoti eris estai epi tou onomatos tēs episkopēs.*

[33] The LXX (the form generally quoted by 1 Clement) reads: *dōsō tous archontas sou en eirēnēi kai tous episkopous sou en dikaiosunēi* ('I will appoint your rulers in peace and your overseers in righteousness').

[34] Lake 1912, 167 summarises thus: 'Ignatius is exceedingly anxious in each community to strengthen respect for the bishop and presbyters. He ascribes the fullest kind of divine authority to their organisation, and recognises as valid no church, institution, or worship without their sanction.' See further Maier 1991, 147–97.

[35] See also *Ephes* 2.2; 4.1; *Magn* 2.1—4.1; 7.1; 13; *Trall* 2.1—3.1, etc.

out in *Trallians* 3.1: 'Likewise let all respect the deacons as Jesus Christ, even as the bishop is also a type of the Father, and the presbyters as the council of God and the college of Apostles'.

The pattern seen most clearly in the Pauline epistles, then, in which a resident structure of leadership develops, based upon the structure of the household and with prominent men as the overseers at the top of the ecclesiastical as well as domestic hierarchy, becomes established broadly as the dominant pattern of leadership in what later emerges as 'orthodox' Christianity. Just as the polemic in the Pastoral Epistles reveals that the 'canonical' pattern of teaching was hardly uncontroversial, so also Ignatius' strenuous appeals to strengthen the authority of the established leadership surely suggest that such leadership was not at the time unquestioned. The establishment of this particular pattern of leadership clearly involved power struggles, in which this 'orthodox' pattern had to be legitimated.[36] Such legitimation, I suggest, is also found in the so-called 'household codes', or *Haustafeln*, though in these codes the focus is not upon the forms of leadership as such, but is often upon the appropriate submission expected of subordinate social groups. The following section therefore seeks to explore the possible links between the emergence of resident leadership and the socially conservative forms of ethical teaching found in these household codes.

5. Household codes and resident leadership

The form, function and origin of the various *Haustafeln* in the New Testament epistles have been much discussed.[37] Though there are both Greco-Roman and Jewish parallels to this pattern of instruction which may be traced back to Plato and Aristotle,[38] the earliest written form of Christian *Haustafel* is found in Colossians, closely paralleled in Ephesians (assuming the priority of Colossians). The Colossian *Haustafel* is compact and formalised, which has suggested to many that it represents a traditional form of Christian instruction significantly earlier than the epistle itself.[39] This may or may not be the case, but we must insist that we have no evidence for an earlier Christian form of the code. 1 Corinthians 7 and 11 cannot be said to reflect elements of a household

---

[36] Cf. the central thesis in the classic work of Bauer 1972.

[37] See esp. Verner 1983; Balch 1981; Yoder 1972, 163–92; Crouch 1973.

[38] See esp. Balch 1981, 23–62; 1986, 81; Aristotle *Politics* 1.2.1–2 (1253b. 1–14).

[39] See e.g. Carrington 1940; Ellis 1986, 484–85, 492.

code, nor do we find such elements elsewhere in the undisputed Paulines (*contra* Ellis 1986, 492). Indeed, as Peter O'Brien rightly points out, if Paul had known of or approved a form of household code it is most surprising that he did not use it in 1 Corinthians (or 1 Thessalonians) where it might have been expected (O'Brien 1982, 218).

The Colossian and Ephesian *Haustafeln* address the same social groups in the same order: wives, husbands, children, fathers, slaves, masters (Col 3:18–4:1; Eph 5:22–6:9). Women, children and slaves are instructed to be submissive; the husbands, fathers and masters are urged to be loving and just in their actions towards those under their care. While these codes do indeed add theological legitimation to the established patterns of domestic domination, providing an ideology for the household, the demand for subordination on the part of the socially inferior is balanced by the demand for justice and consideration on the part of the powerful (see further Horrell 1995, 230–33). The ethos of the instruction is appropriately labelled 'love-patriarchalism', not merely patriarchalism (Theissen 1982, 107; MacDonald 1988, 102–22).

These *Haustafeln* relate to the domestic structure of the Greco-Roman household and display no explicit connection with church leadership or structure. Nevertheless, as MacDonald points out: 'The Colossian and Ephesian Haustafeln represent a placing of power more firmly in the hands of the rulers of the households (husbands, fathers, masters), ensuring that leadership positions fall to members of this group' (1988, 121–22). The significance of this is something to which we shall return.

In view of the evidence for the emergence of resident leadership surveyed briefly above, it is significant that forms of household code instruction appear in the Pastoral Epistles (1 Tim 2:8–6:2; Titus 2:2–10), 1 Peter (2:18–3:7), *1 Clement* (1.3; 21.6–8), Polycarp (*Phil* 4.1–6.3), Ignatius (*Pol* 4–6), *Didache* 4.9–11 and *Barnabas* 19.7. All but the last two – *Didache and Barnabas* – stand to some degree in a Pauline tradition[40] and in this 'trajectory' there are a number of features which

---

[40] The similarities between the epistle of Polycarp and the Pastoral Epistles led to von Campenhausen's theory that Polycarp wrote the Pastoral Epistles; see Lüdemann 1996, 140–41. While there is debate about the extent of Pauline influence on, e.g., 1 Peter and *1 Clement*, some shared knowledge of Pauline traditions seems clear. The same goes for Ignatius (see Bultmann 1953; 1955, 191–99). The *Didache* and *Barnabas*, on the other hand, derive their ethical teaching from a Jewish 'two ways' tradition, in which household-code type material also appears, independently of the Pauline trajectory (see further Carleton Paget 1994, 80–82; Kloppenborg 1995). I am grateful to Alastair Logan for making this point.

are notable in the ways in which this material is used and developed. First, the reciprocity evident in Colossians and Ephesians all but disappears. In 1 Peter, for example, there is an extended admonition to slaves (2:18–25) but no instruction to masters, an extended address to wives (3:1–6) but only a short instruction to husbands (3:7). In *1 Clement* the focus is upon the honour and respect to be paid to those who are leaders, instruction of the young in the fear of God, and the quiet submission expected from women. In 1 Tim 6:1–2 and Titus 2:9–10 slaves are instructed to be submissive and to please their masters, especially Christian masters, with no reciprocal instruction addressed to these Christian masters. A second observation may help to explain this first one. In these later letters it becomes clear that the 'household' pattern of instruction becomes the pattern for the whole church and for the behaviour of its subordinate members in relation to the church's leadership. In *1 Clement* it is the men of the community who are addressed and given the responsibility for ensuring that the others, women and children, behave appropriately.[41] As Campbell has argued, here (and in 1 Peter) the 'elders' seem to comprise a group of men who are senior in faith and prominent in social position (1 Peter 5:5; Campbell 1994, 210–16; cf. Maier 1991, 93, 100). The prominent (male) heads of households have their responsibility *qua* leaders of the community. This is most clear in the Pastoral Epistles, especially 1 Timothy, where the main duties mentioned for the *episkopos* and the *diakonos* are their responsibilities for respectable citizenship and good household management (1 Tim 3:1–13; Titus 1:5–9).[42] This is where the instruction to the socially prominent men of the community is found. The corollary of these requirements is the instructions in the Pastorals that women and slaves must be submissive and appropriately obedient. Women are forbidden to teach or be in authority over men; they must learn in silent submission (1 Tim 2:11–15). The church community is shaped according to the household model; indeed, it is described as the *oikos theou* (1 Tim 3:15), and so the ecclesiastical hierarchy mirrors the domestic and social hierarchy. 'The role of leaders as relatively well-to-do householders who act as masters of their wives, children, and slaves is inseparably linked with their authority in the church' (MacDonald 1988, 214).

[41] See Jeffers 1991, 123; Bowe 1988, 102; Lindemann 1992, 29; Horrell 1996a, 263–72.
[42] See note 25 above.

It is not hard to see that there may be some connection between the development of resident leadership and the use of household code instruction. As the dominant pattern of leadership (at least in the Pauline churches) shifts from itinerant to resident, due particularly to the death of Paul (see further below), so forms of household code instruction become prominent. As the resources of scriptural, dominical and apostolic tradition are used to legitimate the pattern of resident leadership (as we have seen in 1 Timothy, *1 Clement* and Ignatius) so at the same time the resources of the household code are used to insist that the subordinate members of the household, women and slaves, must for the Lord's sake be obedient and submissive. The power struggle to establish such a pattern of leadership is one in which the *Haustafeln* play a part, conferring power upon the male heads of household and providing theological legitimation for the subordination of those who are to be excluded from positions of power and leadership.

6. *Ideological development and leadership patterns – possible connections*

Can more be said about the nature of the connection between the development of resident leadership and the introduction and use of the household codes in early Christianity? This essay has devoted most attention to tracing a trajectory of developing leadership patterns, a trajectory in which an important shift takes place after the death of Paul, when power and authority are increasingly transferred to the resident leaders in each community. I have elsewhere outlined briefly a trajectory of 'ideological development' in Pauline Christianity (Horrell 1995; also 1996a), using 'ideology' in a critical sense to refer to the ways in which language and symbols are used to sustain or legitimate social relations of domination,[43] and focusing therefore upon the ways in which the symbolic resources of Pauline Christianity are increasingly used, especially in the household code material, to add theological legitimation to the established social and domestic hierarchy. These diachronic perspectives have been inspired by a theoretical framework drawn from Anthony Giddens' 'structuration theory', a theory at the

---

[43] This notion of ideology is outlined more fully in Horrell 1996a, 50–53; 1993, 87, drawing on the work of Anthony Giddens, John Thompson, and Terry Eagleton.

heart of which lies a concern to grasp the ways in which social life is structured through an essentially ongoing process of reproduction and transformation.[44]

In earliest Christianity, as far as we can tell, power and authority were exercised primarily by itinerant leaders, especially the apostolic figures Peter, James, Paul, etc., though resident leaders and prominent householders also enjoyed a level of power and influence. As much of the evidence for subsequent development is found in the Pauline and post-Pauline letters, it is difficult to ascertain the extent to which the pattern of change is essentially one which characterises the Pauline churches, though if this is the case then certainly the pattern of resident leadership becomes more widespread towards the end of the first century and beyond.

One obvious catalyst for the transition was the death of the primary charismatic itinerant apostles. Since the deaths (or rather, executions) of James, Peter and Paul all most likely happened within a few years of one another in the 60s CE[45] then a number of the most prominent apostolic leaders were removed from the scene at a similar point in time.[46] This may therefore have had a cumulative and significant impact at a particular period. It is interesting, for example, that both Pauline and Petrine traditions, often in conflict in an earlier period (e.g. Gal 2:11–16), after the deaths of the great apostles, are drawn together in an increasingly powerful Roman Christianity (cf. 1 Peter; 2 Pet 3:15–16; *1 Clem* 5.1–7).[47]

After Paul's removal from the scene, something effected perhaps initially and partially by periods of imprisonment but then completely by his death, the power and influence of resident leaders in the Pauline churches increased. It is still in Paul's name, however, and with Paul's 'authority' therefore, that the position of these leaders is legitimated. Colossians and Ephesians are written in Paul's name, and crucially they contain the first written formulations of the Christian household codes which focus power in the male heads of households. The increasing

---

[44] See Horrell 1995, 224–27; 1996a, esp. 45–59.
[45] For the death of James, brother of Jesus, in 62 CE see Josephus *Ant.* 20.200. The executions of Peter and Paul are generally reckoned to have taken place when Nero made Christians scapegoats for the fire of Rome in 64 CE (see Tacitus *Annals* 15.44; *1 Clem* 5.4–7; discussion in Michaels 1988, lvii–lxi, though Michaels disputes the evidence for Peter's martyrdom).
[46] On the impact of the death of Paul, see MacDonald 1988, 86–158; Maier 1991, 112–13.
[47] See further Bauer 1972, 95–129, 229–40.

power and prominence of these well-to-do male leaders may be inextricably linked with the formulation of teaching which reinforces their position, regulates their 'office' (elucidating their responsibilities and the necessary qualifications of respectability and social position), makes the household model increasingly dominant,[48] and marginalises and deviantises those who have a different view of the faith and its consequent social embodiment. These 'deviants', whose perspectives and interpretations we can but glimpse and guess at, include women, whom the author of the Pastoral Epistles is at pains to exclude from positions of authority and leadership (1 Tim 2:11–15). Younger widows are clearly regarded as an especially dangerous group; they are particularly prone to be attracted to what the author regards as false teaching – perhaps a form of teaching which encouraged them to remain unmarried and to engage in teaching or missionary activity free from the structure of subservience into which marriage and the household placed them (1 Tim 5:11–16). The author advises incorporation into a household structure (5:14). Hence the epistle to Titus urges an important teaching responsibility upon older women: they are to instruct and encourage the younger women to love their children and their husbands, to work well in the home (*oikourgos*) and to be submissive to their husbands (Titus 2:3–5). *1 Clement* similarly places the responsibility for leadership upon the men of the community and requires from women the virtue of quietness (*1 Clem* 1.3; 21.6–8). 1 Timothy 6:1–2 also hints that some slaves expected the fact that they and their Christian masters were now *adelphoi* to make a difference to the character of their relationship (cf. Phlm 16). In view of this, the author urges slaves with Christian owners not to use the fact that they are all *adelphoi* as a reason to serve their owners less; on the contrary, they should serve a Christian master 'all the more'. Ignatius is clearly aware of slaves who think that the church should use its money to purchase their freedom. He insists that

---

[48] Balch (1986, 98–100) points out that the household context – and therefore the household codes also – becomes less prominent and less relevant as the church develops and grows as an institution. This may be right, up to a point, but the household code does not perhaps become as irrelevant to the church of the second century and beyond as Balch suggests, especially if recent arguments about the persistence of house-churches (meeting in private dwellings in rooms *not* set aside exclusively for church use) into the late second or early third century are correct (see e.g. Lampe 1987, 307–20; Brent 1995, 398–412). Such forms of instruction are still found in the Apostolic Fathers; moreover as the Pauline corpus becomes 'recognised', 'authorised', accepted as orthodox and eventually canonical, so the household code and its social ethos are there encapsulated and preserved as a basis for Christian social relations. (See also Campbell 1994, 228–35.)

they should 'endure slavery to the glory of God'; their desire to be set free at the church's expense shows that they are in danger of becoming 'slaves to desire' (*douloi epithumias* – *Pol* 4.3).

The emergence of patterns of resident leadership, the marginalising of opposing viewpoints, and the development of theological ideology, especially in the household code material, therefore, are all apparently connected. They are tied together as part of an ongoing process in which certain people use their position of power to formulate teaching which, at the same time, reinforces and sustains that power. The polemical arguments, and the force with which certain things 'need' to be said, permit glimpses of alternative viewpoints which remind us that power and position were not attained or sustained without a struggle – an ideological battle. Resident leaders needed legitimation to sustain their position, and various forms are used in the early Christian epistles we have surveyed: scriptural (1 Tim 5:18; *1 Clem* 42.5); dominical (1 Tim 5:18); apostolic (*1 Clem* 42.2–4; Ign *Trall* 2.2; pseudonymity of the post-Paulines) and theological (Ign *Trall* 3.1, etc.).[49] Similar forms of legitimation are used ideologically to undergird the subordination of others (1 Tim 2:11–15, etc.) and here the theological ideology of the household codes plays a major part: it is the Christian duty of wives, children and slaves to submit in fear to their male superiors, who are to be served and revered 'as the Lord' (see Col 3:23–24; Eph 5:22–24; 6:5–8; further Horrell 1995, 231–32).

7. Conclusion

As I reiterate the thesis of this essay and draw together the threads of its argument, I begin with some qualifications. Although I have sought to illuminate a pattern of change and transformation, it cannot be suggested that what we discover in this process is a sharp disjunction or a complete change. Householders and resident leaders were present and influential within the very earliest Christian (at least in the Pauline) communities. Moreover, a sharp and clear distinction between itinerant and resident leadership cannot be sustained. Some itinerant apostles were also connected with a particular community (especially Jerusalem; also Paul's

---

[49] Other viewpoints also, of course, required and attempted their own legitimations, as, for example, the legacy and memory of Paul is presented in the Acts of Paul and Thecla, used (probably) in turn as a legitimation for women's leadership for some time after it was written (see Tertullian *De baptismo* 17).

early connection with Antioch, etc.); some resident leaders travelled between various Christian communities (e.g. Prisca and Aquila). From the beginning the leaders of the church at Jerusalem were of major importance; the 'pillars' of the community there were also itinerant apostles with influence over a wide area. There are clear similarities here with the pattern of later years, when power and influence became concentrated in certain geographical centres, Antioch and especially Rome (see Brown and Maier 1983), with leading figures who came to be known as bishops having an influence over a wide area. Travelling between churches and areas also of course remained an essential feature of life in early Christianity. A further qualification is that, while I have tried to cast the net of the investigation somewhat more widely, much of the evidence for the pattern of change and for the emergence of resident leadership has been drawn from the Pauline epistles. One may of course question how unique and specific this evidence is to the Pauline churches, though in the absence of much other early evidence the Pauline material has to have a central place in any such investigation. It may be, nevertheless, that the contrast between Paul himself and the later pattern of resident leadership is most strong – stronger, perhaps, than that between the other apostles and later resident leaders. Paul, after the link with the Antioch community ended, had no particular community as his base (unlike Peter and James, etc.); he remained unmarried (contrast the practice of the other apostles noted in 1 Cor 9:5); he encouraged others, notably widows, not to (re)marry (1 Cor 7:7–8, 26–40); he insisted upon self-support through his own manual labour (again in contrast to Peter and 'the other apostles'; 1 Cor 4:12; 9:4–18; 1 Thess 2:9); and he embodied and taught a radical social ethos which was often opposed to the position and interests of the socially strong (see Horrell 1996a).

However, while it would be inappropriate therefore to mount a thesis arguing for a radical or disjunctional change at a point in the development of early Christianity, it is vitally important for historians of early Christianity to attend to and seek to explain the patterns of trans-formation which are revealed even in our limited sources. Those who wish to root later developments strongly in earliest tradition (thus conferring upon them the legitimation of primitive authenticity) are often unwilling to do this.[50] A similar criticism applies, I suggest, to the

---

[50] See e.g. Ellis 1986; also Hauke 1988, 389, on 1 Cor 14:34–35, who argues that this command to women to be silent stems from a word of Jesus on this subject (the ultimate Christian legitimation?!).

theses of Campbell (1994) and Maier (1991). While they have valuably drawn attention to the influence of relatively well-to-do householders as leading figures within the Christian communities from the earliest times, they have given too little attention to the significant changes which took place over time, especially following the death of Paul and other first generation itinerant leaders. Giddens' structuration theory, by contrast, is built on the following premise: '*Unser Leben geht hin mit Verwandlung,* Rilke says: Our life passes in transformation. This is what I seek to grasp in the theory of structuration' (Giddens 1979, 3).

My thesis may therefore be restated. I have attempted to draw attention to the important but neglected distinction between itinerant and resident leadership in earliest Christianity, though with the qualifications noted above. It is hardly new to study the emerging pattern of what may be termed ecclesiastical offices, the development of the threefold structure of bishops, presbyters and deacons. Yet due attention has perhaps not been given to the importance of the shift from itinerant to resident leadership, nor to the relationship between the latter and the emergent forms of ethical instruction which support the household structures upon which the resident pattern of leadership is based. As a broad trajectory it would seem to be legitimate to speak of a development or transformation from itinerant to resident leadership in earliest Christianity – though hardly, of course, an even or consistent trajectory – and there is evidence which reveals the tensions and difficulties which the diverse and changing patterns of leadership caused. Moreover, the transference of power from itinerant to resident leadership is a sociologically significant transformation which is inextricably connected with the development of more socially conservative patterns of ethical instruction (especially the 'household codes'). The emergence of patterns of resident leadership, the marginalising of opposing viewpoints, and the development of theological ideology, especially in the household code material, therefore, are all apparently connected – connected in the ideological battle to sustain and legitimate the power and position of the resident male leaders and the household structure upon which their leadership was based.

FURTHER READING

The classic sociological discussion of 'types of legitimate domination' is Weber 1968a, 212–301; see also Eisenstadt 1968. A detailed and critical application of Weberian perspectives to leadership and authority as reflected in the Pauline epistles is found in Holmberg 1978, whose work is in turn influential on MacDonald's (1988) broader study of institutionalisation (see ch. 8 above; both authors also make use of Berger and Luckmann 1967; see ch. 4 above). Note however Malina's (1996a, 123–42) critique of the use of such Weberian perspectives in New Testament study.

A concise summary of Giddens' 'structuration theory' may be found in Giddens 1982, 28–39; see further Giddens 1984 and the bibliographical appendix in Horrell 1996a, 313. On ideology see Giddens 1979, 165–97; Thompson 1984; Eagleton 1991. My own more detailed use of these theoretical perspectives can be found in Horrell 1995; 1996a.

For an influential study of authority and the development of leadership structures from a more traditional historical perspective, see von Campenhausen 1969 (for further examples, and an argument for a social-scientific perspective see MacDonald 1988, 4–9). Recent studies have shown much greater interest in social context and in using tools from the social sciences: see Theissen 1975a; Gager 1975, 67–76; Schütz 1975; Holmberg 1978; MacDonald 1988; Maier 1991; Taylor 1992; Campbell 1994.

13

Social-Scientific Criticism of a Biblical Text:
1 Peter as an Example

JOHN H. ELLIOTT

INTRODUCTION

In 1981 John Elliott published *A Home for the Homeless*, a ground-breaking contribution to the study of 1 Peter which applied insights from the social sciences to the study of this epistle using a method which Elliott termed 'sociological exegesis' (1981, 7–13; 1986a, 1). In the intervening years Elliott's terminology and method have developed and evolved, while continuing to build on that foundational study. The extract reproduced here is taken from a recent book in which Elliott introduces the methods of social-scientific criticism (Elliott 1993). What follows below is a concise attempt to sketch the contours of a wide-ranging social-scientific approach using 1 Peter as an example. After setting out the range of questions which comprise such an approach, Elliott considers the 'situation' of the Petrine text: its authors and audience, and their geographical and social location. He then moves to consider the 'strategy' of the letter: its aims and purpose as a vehicle of persuasion intended to have an impact upon the communities to which it is sent. For Elliott, 'the form of Christianity depicted in 1 Peter is that of a messianic *sect*' (p. 351), and the letter seeks to promote the solidarity and cohesion of the sect as a community experiencing hostility and social estrangement in the world, whose members live as 'holy nonconformists' (p. 349), members of the 'household of God'.

One aspect of this perspective on 1 Peter is Elliott's argument that the terms 'strangers and resident aliens' (1 Pet 1:1, 17; 2:11) should be taken not as metaphorical, 'theological' descriptions of the Christian believers, but as an indication of their actual social and political status (below p. 347; see Elliott 1981, 21–58). Most scholars, however, have not found this suggestion convincing (see Best 1983a; Feldmeier 1992; Achtemeier 1996, 82, 174–75).

Another major point of debate concerns Elliott's view that 1 Peter intends 'to promote both the internal solidarity of the sectarian movement, and its external distinction from Gentile motives and manners' (1981, 231). An alternative point of view has been proposed by David Balch (Balch 1981), and maintained in debate with Elliott (see Balch 1986; Elliott 1986b; also Wire 1984). According to Balch, 1 Peter represents a move towards greater accommodation or assimilation to the dominant Greco-Roman culture. In order to lessen the hostility they experience, the Christians are urged to conform to the social norms of the day, as far as is possible without compromising their commitment to Christ. Such assimilation is evident especially, Balch suggests, in the 'household code' (1 Pet 2:11–3:12). Personally I find this latter perspective, on the whole, more convincing (see Horrell 1998, 45–47).

Whatever the disagreements, this approach to 1 Peter sets out a range of questions which together form a model of how social-scientific criticism may be practised. It is important to note that Elliott does not deny the importance of the traditional methods of biblical criticism; on the contrary, he assumes their necessity (p. 341). But building upon the insights those methods provide, social-scientific methods enable the interpreter to build up a picture of the community situation which the text addresses (and of that from where it is written) and of its strategy for shaping and affecting that situation.

The specific aim of social-scientific criticism, as a dimension of the exegetical enterprise, is to expose, examine and explain the specifically social features and dimensions of the text, its author(s), recipients, and their relations, its social context, and its intended impact. Its general objective is the analysis, synthesis, and interpretation of the social as well as literary and ideological (theological) dimensions of a text, the correlation of these textual features, and the manner in which it was designed as a persuasive vehicle of communication and social interaction, and thus an instrument of social as well as literary and theological consequence (Elliott 1981/ 1990a, 8–9; see also Gottwald 1985 in regard to Old Testament texts).

To illustrate the process of such a textual investigation it will be useful
to focus on one particular text, which we can then discuss in greater
detail. Inasmuch as New Testament texts vary in the amount of explicit
social information they contain regarding authors and audiences and
their social situations, it is advisable to begin with a document that
contains a maximum, or at least sufficient, amount of relevant data.
Examination of such a text can then serve as a methodological model
for interrogating other texts where such detail is more implicit than
explicit. For our purposes, then, let us examine the letter of 1 Peter.

At least three reasons prompt this choice. First, as a letter, 1 Peter
contains more explicit information about its situation than do, say, the
Gospels or other writings where information must be inferred from
implicit details. Second, 1 Peter offers one of the most sustained
statements of the New Testament on the relation of the community of
believers to their social environment. Thus this text provides not
only a ready amount of explicit data but also a systematic statement that
allows us to study in detail its correlation of situation and strategy. A
final motive for this choice is to acquaint readers with the resources that
this document offers to those interested in the social-scientific criticism
while simultaneously introducing readers to one of the more neglected
but fascinating 'stepchildren' of the New Testament canon.

In the outline of method that follows I shall presume that the
conventional exegetical operations have already taken place, namely,
text criticism, literary criticism, historical criticism, source/form/
tradition criticism, and redaction criticism. On the basis of these analyses
it is clear that 1 Peter is a genuine letter sent in the name of the apostle
Peter by a circle of Petrine associates in Rome to fellow Christians of
Asia Minor in order to console and exhort the brotherhood there to
remain steadfast in loyalty and hope despite their suffering at the hands
of hostile neighbors.[1]

With regard to 1 Peter, as with all biblical writings, two sequential
fields or arenas of social interaction might be analyzed: (*a*) an original
and narrower field of interaction and (*b*) a subsequent and wider field
of interaction. The immediate field of social interaction in which a text
serves as a vehicle of social exchange concerns the original historical and

[1] For my more extensive discussions of these details see e.g. Elliott 1979, 1981, 1982,
1986b, and 1992b. Conclusions drawn from these analyses will also be used in the
discussion that follows.

social setting of the communication: its author(s) and addressees (actual and implied), and their respective geographical and social locations, the nature of their relationship, the circumstances that precipitated the writing, and the manner in which the text is designed to serve as a vehicle of their interaction.

A wider field of interaction that could be investigated subsequent to the text's composition, delivery, and reading/hearing would involve the circumstances of its actual reception and effect upon, first, its targeted audience and then upon subsequent audiences in varying times and places. This would involve a tracing and examination of the text's so-called history of reception and impact (*Wirkungsgeschichte*), its canonical history, and its role in later theological, liturgical, and spiritual tradition. Such an extended investigation is of crucial importance for ascertaining the knowledge and attitudes that inform current readers of a text such as 1 Peter and their theological as well as social perceptions. We are all shaped in our reading and understanding of biblical texts by the history that precedes us. An excellent example of the contribution such an investigation can make to the study of a New Testament writing is the multivolume commentary of Ulrich Luz on the Gospel of Matthew (1990, etc.). For the limited purposes of this present study, however, we shall restrict our attention to a treatment of only the immediate field of interaction, that of the original author(s) of 1 Peter and its original addressees.

In regard to this immediate field of interaction, our aim is to determine the text's situation and strategy and their correlation, that is, the social situation as perceived and portrayed by its author, the author's strategy in portraying and speaking to this situation, and the nature of the relationship of situation and strategy.

To explore these issues, we pursue a series of questions that might be addressed to any biblical document (see Elliott 1990a, xxv-xxvi).

1. Who are the explicitly mentioned (or implied) *readers-hearers* of this document? What is their geographical location? What is their social composition? What is their relationship to the author(s)? To what social networks might they belong, and what is their social location in general? What are the social and cultural scripts, plausibility structures, and particular traditions and beliefs that readers are presumed to share with the author(s)? Can this information be supplemented by further historical and social data external to the writing and organized by social-scientific

and cross-cultural models appropriate to the data at hand? Can a social profile of the audience be constructed?

2. Who is the explicitly mentioned or implied *author-sender* of the text? If the document is anonymous, what can be inferred about the author's identity and on what basis? If the document is ascribed to one or more authors or senders (as, for example, 1–2 Thessalonians), what information on these persons is available outside the text? If the text is pseudonymous (ascribed to someone other than its actual author), how is this determined and what was the motive? What is the relationship of intended audience and author-sender(s)?

3. How is the *social situation* described in the text? What information is explicitly provided or implied? What information is stressed through repetition, reformulation, or emphatic placement? Can further information on the situation be supplied from external sources? Does external information confirm or contradict internal information?

4. How does the author(s) *diagnose and evaluate* the situation? What phenomena are singled out for approval, commendation, disapproval, condemnation, or necessary change? What ideas, beliefs, values, norms, and sanctions are invoked or involved in this evaluation?

5. How is the *strategy* of the text evident in its genre, content (stressed ideas, dominant terms and semantic fields, comparison and contrasts, traditions employed and modified, semantic relations), and organization (syntax and arrangement, line of thought and argumentation, integrating themes, root metaphors, ideological point of view, and in narrative, the mode of emplotment of the story [romance, satire, comedy, tragedy])?

6. What *response* does the author(s) seek from the targeted audience (as perhaps indicated in explicit statements of reasons and goals for writing and response expected)? What part does this play in the author's overall strategy?

7. How does the author attempt to *motivate and persuade* the audience? To what shared goals, values, norms, sanctions, and traditions is appeal made? What are the modes and means of rhetorical argument employed? Are any dominant symbols or 'root metaphors' used to characterize and express the collective identity and action of the audience and the author(s)? How do these features figure in the author's overall strategy?

8. What is the nature of the situation and strategy of this text as seen from a social-scientific *etic perspective* [see below n. 3 – Ed.] with the aid of historical and comparative social-scientific research? What social system

constitutes the larger context of this writing? What are its dominant institutions and the Christian group's relations to these institutions? Are there comparable groups in comparable situations (Qumran, apocalyptic groups, coalitions and factions; cross-culturally comparable groups and movements [sectarian, millenarian, or brotherhoods and fictive kin groups]; and such)? What are the prevailing social and cultural scripts? What social issues and problems are at stake – Conflicting groups with competing interests and ideologies? Problems concerning group identity, organization, order, and cohesion? Issues regarding roles and statuses, internal and external social interaction? Tensions regarding norms, values, goals, world-views, and plausibility structures? How does the document conceptualize, symbolize, and articulate the relation of patterns of belief and patterns of behavior? How does the text explain, justify, and legitimate emphasized social relations and behavior, thereby providing a plausible and persuasive rationale for the integration of experience and aspiration, hope, and lived reality? How is the document constituted to be an effective instrument of rhetorical persuasion and social interaction? To what social model(s) does the strategy of the text conform (for example, strategies of coalitions, factions, sects, reform movements)?

9. What are the *self-interests and/or group interests* that motivated the author(s) in the production and publication of this document? How are they expressed or able to be inferred? What *ideology* is discernible in this document, and how is it related to the interests of the author and the group the author represents? How does this ideology compare and contrast with ideologies of other contemporary groups or social entities, and what are its distinguishing characteristics? How do interests and ideology reckon in the writing's overall strategy?

Such questions guided the investigation of 1 Peter in *A Home for the Homeless*; they might profitably inform a social-scientific exegetical analysis of any biblical document.[2]

Let us turn now to 1 Peter in particular, its immediate field of inter-action, and its situation and strategy.

The *strategy* of this text, we recall, concerns its pragmatic dimension. How did its author or authors design this communication as a specific response to a specific situation? How was it constructed to have a specific

---

[2] For further types of guiding questions, see Berger 1977, 234–39 and Kee 1989, 65–69.

and persuasive effect upon its intended recipients? Because it is the situation as known or presupposed by an author which determines the strategy of his or her response, our first phase of inquiry involves a determination of the situation presupposed by 1 Peter.

Here we might consider what Lloyd Bitzer (1968) has stated regarding the situational nature of all rhetoric (efforts at persuasion), since it applies to the biblical texts as well. Rhetorical discourse comes into existence, he notes (1968, 5–6), as a response to a situation in the same sense that an answer comes into existence as a response to questions or as solutions to problems. Second, a text (oral or written) is given rhetorical significance by the situation in the same manner as are answers to questions or solutions to problems. Third, a rhetorical situation must exist as a necessary condition of rhetorical discourse. Fourth, a situation is rhetorical insofar as it needs and invites discourse capable of participating in a situation and altering its reality. Fifth, discourse is rhetorical insofar as it functions (or seeks to function) as a fitting response to a situation that invites it. Sixth, the situation controls the rhetorical response in the same sense that questions control answers and problems control solutions.

A 'rhetorical situation,' Bitzer thus summarizes, involves three constituents: '[1] a complex of persons, events, objects and relations presenting [2] an actual or potential exigency which can be completely or partially removed [or altered] if [under prevailing social and natural constraints] [3] discourse, introduced into the situation, can constrain human decision or action so as to bring about the significant modification of the exigency' (Bitzer 1968, 6).

This concept of rhetorical situation provides a useful model for examining New Testament writings such as 1 Peter as instances of rhetorical discourse. It suggests as determinative features of a text's situation not only a specific 'exigency' or 'occasion' but also the social relation of author(s) and audience, and the constellation of factors not only constraining an author's response (author's capabilities, creativity, and communicational conventions) but also conditioning the circumstances of author and audience on the whole (general geographical, economic, social, cultural setting). Furthermore, Bitzer's stress on the fitness of the response (1968, 10–11) suggests attention to what we refer to as the correlation of situation and strategy. In examining these features of a text, social-scientific criticism complements rhetorical criticism in its capacity to clarify the social dimensions of these features and their correlation.

To analyze the *situation* of the Petrine text, then, its intended audience and their geographical and social location, the circumstances of the audience, and the authors-senders of the document, we examine the following:

1. The audience addressed

a. Geographical location of addressees: Pontus, Galatia, Cappadocia, Asia, and Bithynia (1 Pet 1:1). These are Roman provinces of Asia Minor comprising about 129,000 square miles of territory. Much of the rural interior of this area was sparsely populated and only lightly urbanized. This address presupposes the wide spread of Christianity throughout Asia Minor and beyond the mission activity of Paul (none in Pontus, Cappadocia, and Bithynia), a rural setting (in contrast to Paul's urban communities), and a date of composition allowing for such expansion.

b. Identity and social location of addressees

- members of a worldwide suffering Christian 'brotherhood' (2:17; 5:9).

- a mix of free persons (2:16) and slaves (2:18–20), with status and roles established by conventional civic (2:13–17) and domestic (2:18–20) norms, but behavior motivated by appeal to the 'Lord' (2:13), God's will (2:15) and the Lord's example (2:21–25).

- a mix of males and females (wives directly addressed in 3:1–6; husbands in 3:7), with status and roles established by conventional social norms but behavior motivated by appeal to the example of the holy matriarchs of Israel (3:5–6), the hope of recruitment (3:1), and the notion of husbands and wives as 'coheirs of the grace of life' (3:7).

- a mix of older and younger persons (in perhaps both biological age and years as Christians, 5:1–5a), with status and roles established by conventional social norms but behavior motivated by appeal to fidelity to the will of God (5:2–3), hope of divine reward (5:4), and mutual humility (5:5b–6; cf. 3:8).

- a mix of converts of both gentile (1:14, 17; 4:1–4) and Jewish origin, the latter indicated by the frequent appeal to Scripture (1:16, 24; 2:4–10; 3:10–12; etc.), biblical persons as models (matriarchs, Sarah, 3:5–6; Noah and family, 3:20), and abundant Jewish tradition that would have had its greatest effect upon those directly familiar with this tradition (see 1:1, 13, 14–16, 17–19, 23–25; 2:2–3, 4–10, 22–25; 3:5–6, 10–12, 14–15; 4:14, 17–18; 5:5, 8–9, 13).

- economic and social status: 'strangers and resident aliens' (1:1, 17; 2:11) whose social and legal rights were curtailed and who were frequently the object of suspicion, slander, and abuse from the natives, who were endemically hostile to strangers and suspicious of their commitments to local standards of obligation and morality. (On the conditions and status of resident aliens in Asia Minor; expropriation of land and reduction of agrarian natives to 'resident aliens'; Christian mobility as traders and missionaries; prevailing suspicion toward strangers, and so on, see Elliott 1981/1990a, 21–58.)

2. The author-senders

'Peter, apostle of Jesus Christ' (1:1) is cited as the chief person in whose name and under whose authority this letter was written. In 5:1 he is portrayed as a 'fellow-elder, witness of the sufferings of the Christ, also sharer in the glory about to be revealed.' Simon Peter was a leading figure of the early church who, according to tradition, died in Rome (c.65–67 CE) after a substantive ministry there. Because the circumstances of the letter presume a date after the apostle's death (wide dissemination of Christianity in Asia Minor; 'Babylon' as surrogate for Rome only after 70 CE; sectarian disengagement of 'Christians' [4:16] from Judaism), with high probability 'Peter' represents the authoritative figure in whose name and authority the letter was written.

The conclusion of the letter, however, also indicates other persons and factors associated with the composition and dispatch of the letter:

- Silvanus, 'a faithful brother' (5:12), is identified and endorsed as the person 'through' whom the letter was delivered. He is probably identical with the Silas mentioned in Acts 15, who was a colleague of Peter in the Jerusalem church and co-deliverer of the letter from Jerusalem to Antioch.

- Personal greetings are sent from 'Mark, my son' (5:13), a further colleague and possibly protégé of Peter earlier on in Jerusalem (Acts 12:1–17; cf. 15:37–39) and later, according to tradition (Papias), also in Rome, and from

- 'the co-elect' [brotherhood]. ('Church' or 'wife' [of Peter] has been suggested as implied here, but 'brotherhood,' which is used in 2:17 and 5:9, is the more likely implied term.)

- 'Babylon' (5:13), used as a biblically flavored term for the capital of world empire, and after 70 CE as a designation for Rome as the destroyer of Jerusalem, implies Rome as the location of the senders of the letter and its place of composition. The terms 'diaspora' (1:1) and 'Babylon' (5:13) signal the similar vulnerable social situation of both addressees and senders living as strangers and aliens in foreign and hostile regions.

Thus, 1 Peter is a letter composed by a circle of Christians in Rome associated with the apostle Peter (core in-group). This letter was sent in his name (and under his legitimating authority) to members of the Christian brotherhood living as strangers and resident aliens in the provinces of Asia Minor.

3. The social situation as described and diagnosed in 1 Peter

The problem most explicit in 1 Peter and most directly addressed is that of adverse social relations between the Christians of Asia Minor and their neighbors. Hostility on the part of the latter had led to the innocent suffering of the former. Ignorance on the part of the natives concerning the addressees (2:16; 3:15) prompted slander, reviling, reproach, and abuse of the Christians as 'evildoers' and social deviants (2:12, 16; 3:9, 13, 15, 16; 4:14, 16; cf. 5:9). Such abuse, in turn, led to fear (3:6, 14) and unjust suffering (1:6; 2:19, 20; 3:14, 17; 4:15, 19; 5:10) on the part of the believers. This picture of strained social relations between the Christian movement throughout the Mediterranean basin and its neighbors can be corroborated and supplemented by evidence from other contemporary Christian writings (Mark 13 and par.; Acts; letters of Paul; Hebrews; James; 1–2 John; and Revelation). Greco-Roman sources on this period are far fewer and are restricted to events at Rome under Nero (c.64–65 CE) (Tacitus, Annals 15.44; Suetonius, Life of Nero 16) and Bithynia-Pontus under Trajan (c.111–112 CE) (Pliny, Epistles 10.96–97). These external sources, however, do corroborate in general the unorganized sporadic outbreak of local hostility against Christians, as the Christian writings illustrate the debilitating effects of such opposition on internal Christian cohesion and commitment.

In response to this situation, the letter declares that the addressees through faith in Jesus Christ, the elect and holy one of God (2:4; 1:19), have become the elect and holy people of God (2:4–10). The rejection and suffering they experience unite them with their rejected and suffering Lord (2:18–25; 3:13—4:6; 4:12–16). Nevertheless, they can live with hope, for as Christ was raised from death and exalted by God, so they too can anticipate a certain salvation. They are God's reborn children, his household and family (1:3—2:10; 4:17), and form a distinctive brotherhood in the world (2:17; 5:9). Their divine calling requires a separation from a formerly ignorant way of life and the responsibility of living as holy nonconformists (1:14–16) who renounce all Gentile vices (2:1, 11; 4:2–4). Such resistance to evil, endurance in doing good, and fidelity to Christ will, with God's help, enable them to 'stand firm in the grace of God' (5:12) and even lead their detractors to 'glorify God on the day of visitation' (2:12, RSV).

4. The situation (and strategy) of 1 Peter from an etic perspective

The response offered in 1 Peter is theologically eloquent and moving. But what of its power to persuade and move to social action? What are the social dynamics that are presupposed in this overtly religious communication? Why might the recipients find this a persuasive piece of communication? If they act in accord with what the letter says and urges, what will be the social consequences? With these questions we shift consideration of so-called *emic* data and begin to look at the bigger social picture from an *etic* perspective.[3]

What social aim lies behind the heavy stress on the collective identity of the addressees, their depiction as an 'elect race,' 'royal residence,' 'priestly community,' God's special people (2:9), gathered flock (2:25, 5:2), and a 'brotherhood' of the reborn (2:17; 5:9)? What does the application of these traditional epithets for Israel to the messianic community imply about its social relation to Judaism? What does their distinctive label as 'Christians' (4:16) and the stress on their superiority over Judaism (1:4, 10–12) also imply about this relationship? What social circumstances are reflected in the lumping together of all nonbelievers as 'Gentiles' (2:12; 4:3), including even Jews? For what social reasons is such emphasis laid on the distinction of believers versus nonbelievers (1:14–16; 2:7–10; 3:1–6, 13–17; 4:1–6, 12–19), union with God and Jesus Christ (1:3–5, 10–12; 2:4–10, 18–25; 3:13–4:6; 4:12–19; 5:1–5, 6–11) versus resistance to the Gentiles (1:14–17; 2:11; 4:2–4) and the devil (5:9)? What social reasons may have prompted the exhortation to 'brotherly love,' mutual service, respect, and material

---

[3] [*Emic* terminology is that which is 'native', or internal, to the culture, community, or document under investigation – i.e. the terminology which the insiders themselves use; *etic* analysis, on the other hand, uses terminology which is external, or foreign, to that context, drawn from another discourse, i.e. often, the analytical and critical concepts of social-science – Ed.]

support (1:22; 3:9; 4:7–10; 5:1–5)? What sense is there to urging distinctiveness and resistance, on the one hand, while, on the other, hoping for a conversion of unbelievers (2:12; 3:2)? What might be the social implications of their paradoxical identification as both 'strangers and resident aliens' (*paroikoi*) (2:11; cf. 1:1, 17) and yet 'household of God' (*oikos tou theou*) (2:5; 4:17)? What might happen to the social integration and emotional commitment of the community if faith and hope, in the face of suffering, give way to disillusionment and despair? In sum, what are the social circumstances presupposed in this writing, and how might the letter's strategy be understood as outlining an effective response to this situation?

A more complete analysis than can be demonstrated here would also examine further social and cultural features of the environment that are encoded in the text. This would include the general inimical relations of strangers and natives; the institution of kinship and household and its significance in the ancient world; the use of familial and household metaphors in imperial programs and propaganda and the political ramifications of its contrary use in 1 Peter (see Elliott 1981/1990a, 174–80); the social conditions of Jews and Christians in the diaspora and in Asia Minor in particular; conventional concerns regarding social order, status and roles; the social scripts regulating relations in the civic, public sphere (strangers vs. natives; in-groups and out-groups) and in the private, domestic sphere (kinship systems; owners–slaves; husbands– wives; elders–younger persons); modes of social interaction (ranging from assimilation to conflict); processes of status degradation and status elevation; modes of internal group governance; the institutions of slavery, hospitality; and encoded aspects of the culture, including the values and scripts concerning honor and shame, male–female relations, prayer and patronage; personality structures (group-oriented rather than individualistic); and attitudes toward suffering and physical discipline as occasions for demonstrating courage and fortitude.

The specific social situation and strategy of 1 Peter can be more fully construed with the aid of an etic model. The picture of the Christian movement presented in the letter is that of an in-group of believers loyal to Jesus as the Messiah who are living as strangers and aliens among the provincials of Asia Minor. While originally a faction within Judaism, this messianic movement to which these believers belong is now at a stage of social and ideological dissociation from mainstream Judaism. The community is distinguished from Jews of the region in terms of its faith in Jesus as Messiah (1:2, 3–12, 18–21; 2:4–10, 21–25; 3:15; 3:18–4:6; 4:12–16; 5:4), its inclusion of non-Jews (1:14–17; 4:2–4), its heavenly rather than territorial inheritance (1:4), and its superiority to Israelite prophets because of its reception of the word of the good news (1:10–12, 22–25). Nonbelieving Jews are associated with nonbelieving pagans as 'Gentiles' (2:12; 4:3), an out-group hostile to the brotherhood and responsible for Jesus' death.

Thus the form of Christianity depicted in 1 Peter is that of a messianic *sect*. Once a faction within Judaism, it is now dissociated from its parent body socially and ideologically and is known by the distinctive label 'Christian' (4:16). The honors, divine favor, and tradition once associated exclusively with Israel are now appropriated by the followers of Jesus Christ and are applied exclusively to the Christian believers as God's fictive kin group (children of God, household of God, brotherhood).

Features typical of sectarian communities, as indicated by social-science research, include their emergence under conditions of social tension and conflict; their initial stage as a protest group within a larger corporate entity; their gradual marginalization and then dissociation from their original parent body because of 'deviant' stances taken toward central issues of corporate identity, exercise of power, and moral behavior; their experience of social disapproval, harassment, and pressures urging conformity; their conception of themselves as an elect and elite community favored with special grace and revelation; a rigorous moral code and demand for exclusive allegiance; a separatist response toward all 'outsiders'; and further related strategies for asserting their collective identity, assuring internal social cohesion, and maintaining ideological commitment.

Virtually all of these characteristics of sectarian groups are evident in the portrait painted of the Christian movement in 1 Peter. In fact, this holds true for many of the New Testament writings and thus suggests that the model of the sect provides a useful heuristic concept for analyzing early Christianity as a social movement. For 1 Peter in particular, this model offers a conceptual framework for envisioning the dilemma facing the Christians and the strategy shaping the address of this situation.[4]

---

[4] For the relevant sociological literature on the typical conditions and features of sectarian formation, examinations of early Christianity as a Jewish sect, and the application of this model to 1 Peter, see Scroggs 1975 [ch. 2 above]; Wilde 1978; Elliott 1981/1990a (using the work of Bryan Wilson on sects).

In regard to the dilemma described in 1 Peter, the Christians were, in the minds of their neighbors, no longer mainstream Jews but 'messianists,' 'Christ-lackeys' (*Christianoi*, 4:16). Therefore they no longer enjoyed the political and legal privileges of ethnic Jews. Ignorance and suspicion of the new movement led to slander of 'evildoing' and the pressure to conform to pagan standards of morality. Increased hostility resulted in innocent suffering. Continued unjust suffering could lead to despair, loss of hope, uncertainty over the surety of salvation and divine protection, and eventually defection. Pressures from outside the group could also lead to internal disorder, the breakdown of roles and properly ordered relations, and conflict over differing ways to remedy the situation. Wholesale defection from the community, in turn, would diminish its already small numbers and seriously endanger the very viability of the movement, let alone its missionary success. The situation, in other words, had serious implications for the continued survival of Christianity in Asia Minor as a missionary movement.

The Petrine author seems to have viewed the predicament as severe, for this communication tackles these problems head on. This brings us to a consideration of the letter's strategy as viewed in the light of sectarian strategies in general.

5. The sectarian strategy of 1 Peter

The strategy of 1 Peter is to empower and motivate its addressees to meet the challenge posed by their abuse in society and their unjust suffering. In more comprehensive (etic) terms, its strategy is three-fold.

First, it affirms the *distinctive collective identity* of the believers, their union with God, Jesus Christ, and one another as the reborn children of God, the elect and holy people of God, the family of the faithful (1:2; 1:3—2:10), and asserts their holy distinction from and moral superiority over the outsider Gentiles (2:11—4:19). The Christian community, it is asserted, constitutes a privileged in-group favored by God and distinct from and superior to all out-groups.

Second, it encourages *internal solidarity and cohesion* through a binding obedience of, and subordination to, the divine Father's will (1:14, 17, 21; 2:13, 15, 18–20, 21; 3:17; 4:19; 5:6), loyalty to Jesus Christ (1:8; 2:7, 13; 3:15; 4:14, 16), and the constant love (emotional attachment), mutual respect, humility (status acceptance), hospitality (generosity), and service toward one another (1:22; 3:8; 4:8–11; 5:1–5).

Third, it promotes a *steadfast commitment* to God, Jesus Christ and community (1) by providing a plausible rationale for innocent suffering (solidarity with the sufferings of Jesus Christ [2:21–25; 3:13—4:6; 4:12–16], suffering as a 'test' of loyalty [1:6, 4:12] and as a sign of the Spirit's presence [4:14]); (2) by stressing the hope of vindication and salvation through union with the vindicated and exalted Christ (1:3–12, 18–21; 2:2–10, 24–25; 3:18—4:6, 12–19; 5:10–11); and (3) by depicting the Christian community as a 'brotherhood' (2:17; 5:9) a 'household of the Spirit/of God' (2:5; 4:17), a family of God in which 'reborn' converts (1:3, 23; 2:2) are 'obedient children' (1:14) of a heavenly 'Father' (1:2, 3, 17) bound with God the Father in holiness (1:14–16; 2:5, 9) and with each other in 'brotherly and sisterly love' (1:22–23; 3:8; 4:8; cf. 5:12–13). Christians, in other words, form a fictive kin group, a community bound by the loyalties and reciprocal roles of the natural family – a potent notion of community in a culture where religion is embedded in kinship!

Acting in this fashion, the addressees will be able to resist (2:11) the pressures of a 'devilish' society (5:8–9) urging conformity to out-group modes of conduct once renounced (1:14–16; 4:1–4), to stand firm in the grace of God (5:12), and even to win erstwhile detractors to the faith (2:12; 3:2). Subordination to civic and domestic authority for the sake of good order and the 'doing of good' may allay opponents' suspicions. But such submission and conduct are ultimately not a sign of compromise but a testimony to the believers' fidelity to the will of God and solidarity with Jesus Christ (2:11—5:11).

The letter does not ignore or downplay the precarious predicament of the believers as objects of abuse and reproach in society. Rather, it acknowledges the reality of this situation but balances it with the assurance that believers who are strangers and aliens in society (*paroikoi*) have a secure home and place of identity and belonging in the household of God (*oikos tou theou*). Thus the terms *paroikoi* and *oikos tou theou* function as social as well as theological correlates to describe the paradoxical condition of the addressees as identical to that of their crucified and exalted Lord – rejected by humans but elevated by God as the elect and holy family of God.

In this communication of consolation and exhortation, the reality of fictive kinship serves as a powerful means for affirming and promoting the distinctive communal identity, social cohesion, and moral responsibilities of the believers in the civic and domestic realms. The process of salvation and conversion is pictured as a 'rebirth' (1:3, 23; cf. 2:2) initiated by God the 'Father' (1:2, 3, 17). Those who have been reborn have become God's 'children' (1:14) and heirs (1:4; 3:7, 9), sharing in his holiness and subject to his will (1:14–16; 2:13–3:9; 5:1– 5) and protected by his power and care (1:5; 4:19; 5:6–7, 10). As 'brothers and sisters' through faith, they are bound to one another by familial loyalty and love (1:22–23; 3:8; 4:8). As 'household stewards' of God's grace (4:10), they emulate household servants (2:18–20) and Jesus the servant of God (2:21–25) in their subordination to the will of God. As 'elders' and 'youth' of the family, they owe one another mutual respect (5:1–5). As a community, the reborn believers constitute a family on the way from rebirth to growth to consolidation (1:3–2:10), a 'household' of God (2:5; 4:17), a 'brotherhood' of faith in a hostile environment (2:17; 5:9).

This declaration of the Christian community as the household of God builds on the traditional conception of household and family as the fundamental unit of society and on house and home as that chief place of identity, security, acceptance, and belonging. This is, moreover, an appropriate symbol for the early Christian movement in which Christian households formed the basis, focus, and locus of Christian mission. Finally, in 1 Peter it serves not only as a comprehensive symbol for integrating various metaphors for salvation, God, believers, and community but also for addressing the specific situation of its intended recipients.

Their situation is one of social estrangement and alienation as *paroikoi* in society. But this condition, 1 Peter asserts, need not be deplored as a bane; to the contrary, it can be embraced as a blessing in disguise. Strangers they are and holy, set apart strangers they are to remain. Their vocation is to resist the pressures and encroachments of a hostile society (2:11–12; 5:8–9) and to stand firm in the grace of God (5:12). Such a life of holy nonconformity is possible because in the community of the faithful the strangers in society (*paroikoi*) have found a home (*oikos*) with God.[5]

Thus the factors of alienation in society versus 'at-homeness' with God play a central and decisive role in the correlation of the situation and strategy of 1 Peter. The letter represents a typically sectarian 'response to the world' (B. Wilson) and more specifically that of a 'conversionist

---

[5] On a similar depiction of the Christian community as the 'household of God' in the Pastorals, see Verner 1983; on familial symbolism in Paul, see von Allmen 1981; and on the Christian household churches, see Klauck 1981.

sect' which urges conversion as a realignment of loyalties, ethical transformation, and involvement in a community of the 'reborn' as the most effective means for personal and social survival and access to salvation. In such a response to the world, an ethic of resistance and nonconformity based on a claim of special divine favor and moral superiority is combined with an insistence upon group solidarity, ideological commitment, and attractive conduct which can win others to the cause.

6. *Interests and Ideology*

The self-interests or group interests that motivate the composition and dispatch of this letter are, as typical of all biblical writings, difficult to ascertain. Self-interests, in contrast to altruistic interests, are generally concealed from view and thus from critique. In many cases they can only be inferred from the content and strategy of a text and from what is known about its producers. In the case of 1 Peter, we are dealing with a communication between a Petrine group in Rome and a segment of the Christian brotherhood in Asia Minor. The sole overt expression of purpose occurs at the conclusion of the letter: 'I have written briefly to you, exhorting and witnessing fully that this is the grace of God; stand fast in it!' (5:12). It is clear, however, from the very genre of the communication – a personal letter from a group of Petrine colleagues at Rome (including Silvanus, Mark, and the co-elect brotherhood there) to a segment of the brotherhood in Asia Minor – that the senders are interested in affirming and maintaining personal ties with their fellow believers in Asia Minor. They are likewise interested in assuring their cohorts in the faith that they share not only the same traditions but also the same experience of alienation and suffering (5:1) that is common to all believers (4:12–13; 5:9). Such commonalities of belief and experience strengthen the 'ties that bind' and build bridges that can be traveled in both directions. The letter and the personal presence of their representative, Silvanus, would forge a bond upon which the Roman Christians could count if and when it was required in the future. This letter, moreover, extended the sphere of influence of the Roman group abroad in a manner similar to that of *1 Clement* addressing the Christians of Corinth. Such influence abroad, in turn, would enhance the prominence and stability of the Christians at Rome. The advantageous position of the Roman Christians, located as they were at the hub of political and cultural power, would make this community an ideal center for the congregation of the 'faithful everywhere' (Irenaeus, *Adv. Haer.* 3.3.2), the coalescence of traditions, the convergence and distribution of information, and eventually the exercise of powerful influence throughout the Mediterranean region.

In terms of ideology, it is clear that the senders of the letter are concerned with strengthening their suffering fellow believers in Asia Minor through a theological conception of the privileged status and distinctive communal identity and responsibility which is theirs as God's favored people, the elect and holy family of God. This ideology of the Christian community as the household of God served as a means for promoting internal sectarian cohesion and commitment while at the same time distinguishing and insulating the Christian in-group from other social groups, including Jews, other cults, and voluntary associations, as well as from the pretensions of imperial propaganda celebrating the emperor as 'father of the fatherland' (*pater patriae*) (see Elliott 1981/ 1990a, 174–80). It offers a powerful contrast to the imperial ideology of the Roman emperor whose goal was to legitimate himself as 'caring father' over a worldwide region of vanquished peoples now proclaimed to be his *patria.* By contrast, the authors of 1 Peter assert that God alone is the father of the Christian household and that, while the emperor deserves respect, as do all persons, God alone is the object of their awe and reverence (2:17). It is God's will that is the ultimate criterion of good conduct and it is Jesus Christ alone who serves as the enabler and example of obedience. Thus the household ideology serves as a plausible social as well as religious rationale for the encouragement of Christian resistance to alien pressures urging conformity and as a veiled critique of imperial paternalistic pretensions.

First Peter, we can thus conclude, was composed and dispatched by a Petrine group in Rome writing in the name and after the death of its leading figure, the apostle Peter. Reflecting in its content the confluence of diverse Christian traditions typical of the communities at Rome, this letter bearing the authority of the apostle Peter stresses the solidarity of believers at Rome with suffering co-believers in Asia Minor and throughout the world. Within the worldwide Christian movement this demonstration of solidarity and support would soon result, as undoubtedly hoped, in the prestige and renown of the church at Rome. Over against the ideologies of other contemporary groups competing for membership and allegiance, the household ideology of 1 Peter, with its roots in the family structures of the region as well as in the history of ancient Israel, and its concretization in fraternal support and solidarity, provided Christians with a powerful means for gaining new members and maintaining commitment. Over against an imperial ideology proclaiming the emperor as 'father of the fatherland' (with the rights and powers of a *paterfamilias*), 1 Peter and its household ideology assured Christians in Asia Minor that God alone is father and judge and that it is this God alone to whom God's family owes fear and reverence (1 Pet 2:17). Finally, the ideology of the Christian community as the household of God provides a persuasive rationale for suffering Christians to 'stand firm' (5:12) and 'resist' (5:8), for while in society they were strangers and aliens (*paroikoi*), in union with God and the Christ they constituted the reborn household (*oikos*) of God.

On the whole, analyzing 1 Peter in terms of a sectarian model has provided a heuristic means for surfacing the underlying social dynamics explicit in this writing and clarifying the manner in which the various content, themes, and organizing metaphors have been integrated to form a coherent and persuasive communication able to motivate its audience to an effective form of social action.

Examination of other New Testament writings as expressions of sectarian consciousness is a promising endeavor that has already yielded some fruitful results.[6] The success of such study will be measured by the degree to which the sectarian model, like all models, provides a means for surfacing latent social dynamics hitherto unconsidered and for clarifying the social as well as theological correlation of a document's situation and strategy.

FURTHER READING

For a wide-ranging introduction to social-scientific criticism, further information on the approach outlined here, and extensive bibliography, see Elliott 1993. On the use of sect models in New Testament studies see ch. 2 above, and Elliott 1995a, which examines the transition in early Christianity – originally a Jewish messianic movement – from 'faction' to 'sect'.

[6] See e.g. Meeks 1972, 1985, 1986; Scroggs 1975 [ch. 2 above]; Wilde 1978; Stanley 1986; Rensberger 1988; White 1988.

Elliott's approach to 1 Peter is first set out, in detail, in Elliott 1981, and defended in Elliott 1986b. Elliott 1995b analyses the ways in which 1 Peter's presentation of the gospel reflects the pivotal honour/shame values of its ancient Mediterranean context (see further ch. 5 above).

Critical discussions of Elliott's work on 1 Peter may be found in Best 1983a; Hemer 1985; Balch 1986; Holmberg 1990, 92–95; Feldmeier 1992. A particularly valuable review of both Elliott (1981) and Balch (1981) is Wire 1984.

Abbreviations

Most abbreviations used in this book follow standard or easily recognisable forms (see e.g. the list in the *Journal of Biblical Literature* 107 (1988) 579–96). Abbreviations used in the Bibliography for Commentary or Monograph series, etc., follow the *JBL* conventions. Listed below are only the abbreviations of journals used in the Bibliography, to enable students and others unfamiliar with the abbreviations to locate articles without difficulty. ET stands for English Translation.

Bib	*Biblica*
BTB	*Biblical Theology Bulletin*
CBQ	*Catholic Biblical Quarterly*
ExpT	*Expository Times*
Int	*Interpretation*
JAAR	*Journal of the American Academy of Religion*
JBL	*Journal of Biblical Literature*
JSNT	*Journal for the Study of the New Testament*
JTS	*Journal of Theological Studies*
NovT	*Novum Testamentum*
NTS	*New Testament Studies*
SJT	*Scottish Journal of Theology*
ZNW	*Zeitschrift für die neutestamentliche Wissenschaft*
ZTK	*Zeitschrift für Theologie und Kirche*

Bibliography

ABRAMS, P. 1982 *Historical Sociology*, Shepton Mallet: Open Books.

ACHTEMEIER, P. J. 1996 *1 Peter*, Hermeneia; Minneapolis: Fortress Press.

ADAM, A. K. M. 1995 *What is Postmodern Biblical Criticism?* Minneapolis: Fortress Press.

ADKINS, A. W. H. 1960 *Merit and Responsibility: A Study in Greek Values*, Oxford: Oxford University Press.

ALFÖLDI, A. 1970 *Die monarchische Repräsentation im römischen Kaiserreiche*, Darmstadt: Wissenschaftliche Buchgesellschaft.

ALFÖLDY, G. 1975 *Römische Sozialgeschichte*, Wiesbaden: Franz Steiner Verlag. ET 1985.

—— 1985 *The Social History of Rome*, trans. D. Braund and F. Pollock, London and Sydney: Croomhelm.

—— 1986 *Die römische Gesellschaft: Ausgewählte Beiträge*, Wiesbaden: Franz Steiner Verlag.

ALLMEN, D. VON 1981 *La famille de Dieu: La symbolique familiale dans le paulinisme*, Orbis Biblicus et Orientalis 41; Göttingen: Vandenhoeck & Ruprecht.

ANDERSON, B. and ZELDITCH, M. JR. 1964 'Rank Equilibration and Political Behaviour', *Archives européenes de sociologie* 5, 112–25.

ANDERSON, J. C. and MOORE, S. D. 1992 *Mark and Method: New Approaches in Biblical Studies*, Minneapolis: Fortress Press.

ANDRESEN, C. 1971 *Die Kirchen der alten Christenheit*, Die Religionen der Menschheit 29, 1/2; Stuttgart.

ATKINS, R. A. JR. 1991 *Egalitarian Community: Ethnography and Exegesis*, Tuscaloosa and London: University of Alabama Press.

AUDET, J. P. 1958 *La Didachè: Instructions des apôtres*, Paris.

BAECHLER, J. 1975 *Revolution*, Oxford: Basil Blackwell.

BALCH, D. L. 1981 *Let Wives Be Submissive: The Domestic Code in 1 Peter*, SBL Monograph Series 26, Chico, CA: Scholars Press.

—— 1986 'Hellenization/Acculturation in 1 Peter', in C. H. Talbert (ed.), *Perspectives on First Peter*, Macon, GA: Mercer University Press, 79–101.

BAMMEL, E. 1952 'Philos tou Kaisaros', *Theologische Zeitschrift* 77, 5–10.

—— 1961 'Matthäus 10, 23', *Studia Theologica* 15, 79–92.

BARBER, B. 1968 Introduction to 'Social Stratification', *International Encyclopedia of the Social Sciences*, vol. 15, 288–96.

BARCLAY, J. M. G. 1992 'Thessalonica and Corinth: Social Contrasts in Pauline Christianity', *JSNT* 47, 49–74.

—— 1994 'Who was considered an Apostate in the Diaspora?', paper presented to the Conference on Tolerance and its Limits in Early Judaism and Christianity, Jerusalem. Now in G. N. Stanton and G. G. Stroumsa (eds), *Tolerance and Intolerance in early Judaism and Christianity*, Cambridge: Cambridge University Press, 1998, 80–98.

—— 1995 'Paul among Diaspora Jews: Anomaly or Apostate?', *JSNT* 60, 89–120.

—— 1996 *Jews in the Mediterranean Diaspora from Alexander to Trajan*, Edinburgh: T&T Clark.

BARRETT, C. K. 1961 *Luke the Historian in Recent Study*, London: Epworth Press.

—— 1971a *A Commentary on the First Epistle to the Corinthians*, 2nd edn; BNTC, London: A&C Black.

—— 1971b 'Paul's Opponents in II Corinthians', *NTS* 17, 233–54.

BARRETT, D. B. 1968 *Schism and Renewal in Africa: An Analysis of Six Thousand Contemporary Religious Movements*, Nairobi: Oxford University Press.

BARTCHY, S. S., 1973 *Mallon Chrêsai: First-Century Slavery and the Interpretation of 1 Corinthians 7:21*, SBLDS, 11. Missoula, MN: Scholars Press.

BARTELS, K. and HUBER, L. (eds) 1965 *Lexicon der alten Welt*, Zurich and Stuttgart.

BARTH, K. 1918 *Der Römerbrief*, ET (of the 6th edn) *The Epistle to the Romans*, London: Oxford University Press, 1933.

BARTLETT, D. L. 1978 'John Gager's *Kingdom and Community*: A Summary and Response', *Zygon* 13, 109–22.

BARTON, S. C. 1986 'Paul's Sense of Place: An Anthropological Approach to Community Formation in Corinth', *NTS* 32, 225–46.

—— 1992 'The Communal Dimension of Earliest Christianity: A Critical Survey of the Field', *JTS* 43, 399–427.

—— 1993 'Early Christianity and the Sociology of the Sect', in F. Watson (ed.), *The Open Text: New Directions for Biblical Studies?*, London: SCM Press, 140–62.

—— 1995 'Historical Criticism and Social-Scientific Perspectives in New Testament Study', in Green (ed.) 1995, 61–89.

—— 1997 'Social-Scientific Criticism', in Porter (ed.) 1997, 277–89.

BARTSCH, H. W. 1962 'Der korinthische Missbrauch des Abendmahls: Zur Situation und Struktur von I Korinther 8–11', *Entmythologisierende Auslegung: Aufsätze aus den Jahren 1940–1960*, Hamburg, 169–83.

BASSLER, J. M. 1979 'The Impartiality of God: Paul's Use of a Theological Axiom', PhD dissertation, Yale University.

BAUCKHAM, R. J. 1990 *Jude and the Relatives of Jesus*, Edinburgh: T&T Clark.

BAUER, W. 1972 *Orthodoxy and Heresy in Earliest Christianity*, London: SCM Press (ET of 2nd German edn, 1964).

BEARE, F. W. 1960 'The Sabbath was Made for Man?', *JBL* 79, 130–36.

BECKER, H. S. 1963 *Outsiders: Studies in the Sociology of Deviance*, New York: Free Press.

—— (ed.) 1964 *The Other Side: Perspectives on Deviance*, New York: Free Press.

BEHR, C. A. 1981 *P. Aelius Aristides, The Complete Works, vol. 2*, Leiden: E. J. Brill.

BELO, F. 1974 *Lecture Matérialiste de l'Évangile de Marc*, Paris: Éditions du Cerf. ET 1981.

—— 1981 *A Materialist Reading of the Gospel of Mark*, trans. M. O'Connell, Maryknoll, NY: Orbis Books.

BEN-YEHUDA, N. 1985 *Deviance and Moral Boundaries*, Chicago: University of Chicago Press.

BENOIT, P. 1952 'Prétoire, Lithostroton et Gabbatha', *Revue Biblique* 59/5, 13–50.

BERGER, K. 1970 *Die Amen-Worte Jesu*, BZNW 29, Berlin.

—— 1977 'Soziologische Fragen', in *Exegese des Neuen Testaments: Neue Wege vom Text zur Auslegung*, Heidelberg: Quelle & Meyer, 218–41.

BERGER, P. L. 1954 'The Sociological Study of Sectarianism', *Social Research* 21, 467–85.

—— 1958–59 'Sectarianism and Religious Sociation', *The American Journal of Sociology* 64, 41–44.

—— 1963 *Invitation to Sociology: A Humanistic Perspective*, Harmondsworth: Penguin.

—— 1969 *The Sacred Canopy*, Garden City, New York: Doubleday. UK title: *The Social Reality of Religion*, London: Faber & Faber.

—— and LUCKMANN, T. 1967 *The Social Construction of Reality: A Treatise in the Sociology of Knowledge*, Garden City, NY: Doubleday; Harmondsworth: Penguin.

BERNAYS, J. 1879 *Lucian und die Kyniker*, Berlin.

BEST, E. 1972 *A Commentary on the First and Second Epistles to the Thessalonians*, BNTC, London: A&C Black; New York: Harper & Row.

—— 1983a 'Review of J. H. Elliott, *A Home for the Homeless*', *SJT* 36, 554–55.

BEST, T. F. 1983b 'The Sociological Study of the New Testament: Promise and Peril of a New Discipline', *SJT* 36, 181–94.

BETZ, H. D. 1972 *Der Apostel Paulus und die sokratische Tradition*, BHTh 45, Tübingen: Mohr.

BIBLE AND CULTURE COLLECTIVE 1995 *The Postmodern Bible*, London and New Haven: Yale University Press.

BIENERT, W. 1954 *Die Arbeit nach der Lehre der Bibel: Eine Grundlegung evangelischer Sozialethik*, Stuttgart.

BITZER, L. F. 1968 'The Rhetorical Situation', *Philosophy and Rhetoric* 1, 1–14.

BLALOCK, H. M. JR. 1967 'Status Inconsistency, Social Mobility, Status Integration, and Structural Effects', *American Sociological Review* 32, 790–801.

BLANK, J. 1959 'Die Verhandlung vor Pilatus: Jo 18:28—19:16 im Lichte johanneischer Theologie', *Biblische Zeitschrift* 3, 60–81.

BLASI, A. J. 1988 *Early Christianity as a Social Movement*, New York: Peter Lang.

BLINZLER, J. 1957 '*Eisin eunouchoi*: Zur Auslegung von Mt 19,12', *ZNW* 48, 254–70.

BOFF, L. and BOFF, C. 1987 *Introducing Liberation Theology*, Tunbridge Wells: Burns & Oates.

BOGATYREV, P. G. and JAKOBSON, R. 1929 'Die Folklore als eine besondere Form des Schaffens', in *Donum Natalicium Schrijnen*, Nijmegen and Utrecht, 900–13.

BÖMER, F. 1963 *Untersuchungen über die Religion der Sklaven in Griechenland und Rom IV*, AAWLM.G, 10, Mainz.

BORNKAMM, G. 1969 'Lord's Supper and Church in Paul', in *Early Christian Experience*, London: SCM Press, 123–60.

BOUWMAN, G. 1969 'La pécheresse hospitalière (Lc VII, 36–50)', *Ephemerides theologicae Lovanienses* 45, 172–79.

BOWE, B. E. 1988 *A Church in Crisis: Ecclesiology and Paraenesis in Clement of Rome*, HDR 23, Minneapolis: Fortress Press.

BOWERSOCK, G. W. 1965 *Augustus and the Greek World*, Oxford: Clarendon Press.

BOWKER, J. 1973 *Jesus and the Pharisees*, Cambridge: Cambridge University Press.

BREHM, J. W. and COHEN, A. R. 1962 *Explorations in Cognitive Dissonance*, New York: Wiley.

BRENT, A. 1995 *Hippolytus and the Roman Church in the Third Century: Communities in Tension before the Emergence of a Monarch-Bishop*, VCSup 31; Leiden: E. J. Brill.

BRONEER, O. 1951 'Corinth: Center of St. Paul's Missionary Work in Greece', *Biblical Archaeologist* 14, 78–96.

BROOTEN, B. 1977 '"Junia . . . outstanding among the Apostles" (Rom 16:7)', in L. Swidler and A. Swidler (eds), *Women Priests: A Catholic Commentary on the Vatican Declaration*, New York: Paulist Press, 141–44.

BROWN, P. 1972 *Religion and Society in the Age of Saint Augustine*, London: Faber & Faber.

BROWN, R. 1965 *Social Psychology*, New York: Free Press.

BROWN, R. E. 1970 *The Gospel According to John, XIII-XXI*, New York: Doubleday.

—— and MAIER, J. P. 1983 *Antioch and Rome: New Testament Cradles of Catholic Christianity*, London: Geoffrey Chapman.

365

BRUNT, P. A. 1965 '"Amicitia" in the Late Roman Republic', *Proceedings of the Cambridge Philological Society* 191, 1–20.

BUCHANAN, G. 1964–65 'Jesus and the Upper Class', *NovT* 7, 195–209.

BULTMANN, R. 1953 'Ignatius and Paul', in *Existence and Faith: Shorter Writings of Rudolf Bultmann*, London: Fontana Books, 1964, 316–29.

—— 1955 *Theology of the New Testament, vol. II*, London: SCM Press.

—— 1957/1961 *Die Geschichte der synoptischen Tradition*, 5th edn 1961, Göttingen. ET 1963/1972.

—— 1960 *Jesus Christ and Mythology*, London: SCM Press.

—— 1965 *Theology of the New Testament*, 2 vols, London: SCM Press.

—— 1972 *The History of the Synoptic Tradition*, trans. J. Marsh, Oxford: Blackwell.

—— 1985 *New Testament and Mythology and Other Basic Writings*, trans. and ed. S. M. Ogden, London: SCM Press.

BURKE, P. 1980 *Sociology and History*, London: George Allen & Unwin.

BURR, V. 1955 *Tiberius Julius Alexander*, Antiquitas 1, Bonn: Rudolf Habelt.

CADOUX, C. J. 1925 *The Early Church and the World*, Edinburgh: T&T Clark.

CAMPBELL, R. A. 1994 *The Elders: Seniority within Earliest Christianity*, Edinburgh: T&T Clark.

CAMPENHAUSEN, H. VON 1969 *Ecclesiastical Authority and Spiritual Power in the Church of the First Three Centuries*, London: A&C Black.

CARCOPINO, J. 1940 *Daily Life in Ancient Rome*, New Haven.

CARDENAL, E. 1967 *Das Evangelium der Bauern von Solentiname*, vol. 1, Wuppertal. ET: *The Gospel in Solentiname*, Maryknoll, NY: Orbis.

CARLETON PAGET, J. 1994 *The Epistle of Barnabas: Outlook and Background*, WUNT 2nd series 64; Tübingen: Mohr.

CARNEY, T. F. 1975 *The Shape of the Past: Models and Antiquity*, Lawrence, KS: Coronado Press.

CARRINGTON, P. 1940 *The Primitive Christian Catechism*, Cambridge: Cambridge University Press.

CARROLL, R. P. 1979 *When Prophecy Failed: Cognitive Dissonance in the Prophetic Traditions of the Old Testament*, New York: Seabury.

CARTER, T. L. 1997 '"Big Men" in Corinth', *JSNT* 66, 45–71.

CARTLEDGE, P. 1994 'The Greeks and Anthropology', *Anthropology Today* 10/3, 3–6.

CASE, S. J. 1923 *The Social Origins of Christianity*, Chicago.

—— 1933 *The Social Triumph of the Ancient Church*, New York.

CATCHPOLE, D. R. 1993 *The Quest for Q*, Edinburgh: T&T Clark.

CHADWICK, H. 1965 *Origen, Contra Celsum*, Cambridge: Cambridge University Press.

CHALCRAFT, D. J. (ed.) 1997 *Social-Scientific Old Testament Criticism: A Sheffield Reader*, Sheffield: Sheffield Academic Press.

CHANCE, J. K. 1994 'The Anthropology of Honor and Shame: Culture, Values and Practice', *Semeia* 68, 139–51.

CLARK, E. A. 1979 *Jerome, Chrysostom, and Friends: Essays and Translations*, Studies in Women and Religion, New York and Toronto: Mellen.

CLARK, E. T. 1937 *The Small Sects in America*, New York.

CLARKE, A. D. 1993 *Secular and Christian Leadership in Corinth: A Socio-historical and Exegetical Study of 1 Corinthians 1–6*, Leiden: E. J. Brill.

COHEN, B. 1975 'La Notion d' "ordo" dans la Rome antique', *Bullétin de l'Association G. Budé*, 259–82.

COHN, N. 1970 *The Pursuit of the Millennium: Revolutionary Millenarians and Mystical Anarchists of the Middle Ages*, London: Temple Smith.

COLLART, P. 1937 *Phillipes: Ville de Macédoine depuis ses origines jusqu' à la fin de l'époque romaine*, École française d'Athènes travaux et mèmoires 5, Paris: Boccard.

CONZELMANN, H. 1954 *Die Mitte der Zeit. Studien zur Theologie des Lukas*, Tübingen: Mohr.

—— 1960 *The Theology of St. Luke*, trans. G. Buswell, New York: Harper & Row; London: Faber & Faber.

—— 1969a *An Outline of the Theology of the New Testament*, New York: Harper & Row.

—— 1969b *Der erste Brief an die Korinther*, 11th edn; Göttingen: Vandenhoeck & Ruprecht. ET 1975.

—— 1975 *1 Corinthians*, Philadelphia: Fortress Press.

COPE, L. 1969 'Matthew XXV, 31–46: "The Sheep and the Goats" Reinterpreted', *NovT* 11, 32–44.

COUNTRYMAN, L. W. 1989 *Dirt, Greed and Sex: Sexual Ethics in the New Testment and Their Implications for Today*, London: SCM Press.

CROSSAN, J. D. 1993 *Jesus: A Revolutionary Biography*, Harper: San Francisco.

CROUCH, J. E. 1973 *The Origin and Intention of the Colossian Haustafel*, FRLANT 109, Göttingen: Vandenhock & Ruprecht.

CULLMANN, O. 1925 'Les récentes études sur la formation de la tradition évangélique', *Revue d'Histoire et de Philosophie religieuses* 5, 564–79.

—— 1956 'Eschatology and Missions in the New Testament', in W. D. Davies and D. Daube (eds), *The Background of the New Testament and Its Eschatology*, Cambridge: Cambridge University Press, 409–21.

—— 1959 *The Christology of the New Testament*, Philadelphia: Westminster Press.

DAHL, N. A. 1951 'Adresse und Proömium des Epheserbriefs', *Theologische Zeitschrift* 7, 241–64.

—— 1967 'Paul and the Church at Corinth according to I Corinthians 1:10–4:21', in W. Farmer *et al.* (eds), *Christian History and Interpretation: Studies presented to J. Knox*, Cambridge: Cambridge University Press, 313–35. Reprinted in *Studies in Paul*, Minneapolis: Fortress Press, 1977.

DALY, M. 1986 *Beyond God the Father: Towards a Philosophy of Women's Liberation*, London: Women's Press.

DAUBE, D. 1956 *The New Testament and Rabbinic Judaism*, London: Athlone Press.

DAUTZENBERG, G. 1969 'Der Verzicht auf das apostolische Unterhaltsrecht: Eine exegetische Untersuchung zu 1 Kor 9', *Bib* 50, 212–32.

DAVIS, N. J. 1980 *Sociological Constructions of Deviance: Perspectives and Issues in the Field*, 2nd edn, Dubuque: W. C. Brown.

DEGENHARDT, H. J. 1963 *Besitz und Besitzverzicht in den Lukanischen Schriften*, diss.: Wurzburg.

DEISSMANN, G. A. 1911 *Paulus: Eine kultur- und religions- geschichtliche Skizze*, Tübingen: Mohr; ET 1957: *Paul: A Study in Social and Religious History*, 2nd edn, New York: Harper & Row.

—— 1923 *Licht vom Osten*, 4th edn; Tübingen: Mohr; ET 1927.

—— 1927 *Light from the Ancient East: The New Testament Illustrated by Recently Discovered Texts of the Graeco-Roman World*, London: Hodder & Stoughton.

DERRETT, J. D. M. 1965 'Law in the New Testament: The Parable of the Talents and Two Logia', *ZNW* 56, 184–95.

—— 1979 '"Where two or three are convened in my name . . .": A Sad Misunderstanding', *ExpT* 91, 83–86.

—— 1995 'The Evil Eye in the New Testament', in Esler (ed.) 1995b, 65–72.

DIBELIUS, M. 1934 *From Tradition to Gospel*, trans. B. L. Woolf, London: Ivor Nicholson & Watson.

—— 1937 *An die Thessalonicher I, II; An die Phillipper*, HNT 11, Tübingen: Mohr.

DOBSCHUTZ, E. VON. 1904 *Christian Life in the Primitive Church*, New York.

DODD, C. H. 1963 *Historical Tradition in the Fourth Gospel*, Cambridge: Cambridge University Press.

DODDS, E. R. 1965 *Pagan and Christian in an Age of Anxiety*, Cambridge: Cambridge University Press.

DONAHUE, J. 1971 'Tax Collectors and Sinners', *CBQ* 33, 39–61.

—— 1973 *Are You the Christ? The Trial Narrative in the Gospel of Mark*, SBLDS 10; Missoula: Scholars Press.

DOUGLAS, M. T. 1963 'Techniques of Sorcery Control in Central Africa', in J. Middleton and E. Winter (eds), *Witchcraft and Sorcery in East Africa*, London: Routledge & Kegan Paul, 123–41.

—— 1966 *Purity and Danger: An Analysis of the Concepts of Pollution and Taboo*, London: Routledge & Kegan Paul.

—— 1967 'Witch Beliefs in Central Africa', *Africa* 37, 72–80.

—— (ed.) 1970 *Witchcraft Confessions and Accusations*, London: Tavistock Publications.

—— 1982 *Natural Symbols: Explorations in Cosmology*, London: Barry & Rockcliff (1970 edn); London: Routledge & Kegan Paul.

DOWNES, D. and ROCK, P. 1988 *Understanding Deviance: A Guide to the Sociology of Crime and Rule Breaking*, 2nd edn, Oxford: Clarendon Press.

DRAPER, J. 1995 'Social Ambiguity and the Production of Text: Prophets, Teachers, Bishops, and Deacons and the Development of the Jesus Tradition in the Community of the *Didache*', in Jefford (ed.) 1995, 284–311.

DUDLEY, D. R. 1937 *A History of Cynicism*, London: Methuen.

DUKE, P. D. 1985 *Irony in the Fourth Gospel*, Atlanta: John Knox

DUNGAN, D. 1971 *The Sayings of Jesus in the Churches of Paul*, Philadelphia: Fortress Press.

DUNN, J. D. G. 1977 *Unity and Diversity in the New Testament: An Inquiry into the Character of Earliest Christianity*, 2nd edn, 1990; London: SCM Press.

—— 1990 *Jesus, Paul and the Law*, London: SPCK.

DURKHEIM, É. 1964 *The Elementary Forms of Religious Life*, trans. J. W. Swain, London: George Allen & Unwin.

DUVERGER, M. 1964 *Introduction to the Social Sciences*, London: George Allen & Unwin.

EAGLETON, T. 1991 *Ideology: An Introduction*, London and New York: Verso.

EBERTZ, M. N. 1987 *Das Charisma des Gekreuzigten: Zur Soziologie der Jesusbewegung*, WUNT 45; Tübingen: Mohr.

ECK, W. 1971 'Das Eindringen des Christentums in den Senatorenstand bis zu Konstantin d. Gr', *Chiron* 1, 381–406.

EDWARDS, O. C. JR. 1983 'Sociology as a Tool for Interpreting the New Testament', *Anglican Theological Review* 65, 431–48.

EHRHARDT, A. 1947/48 'Sakrament und Leiden', *Evangelische Theologie* 7, 99–115.

EISENSTADT, S. N. (ed.) 1968 *Max Weber on Charisma and Institution Building*, Chicago and London: University of Chicago Press.

ELLIOTT, J. H. 1979 *1 Peter: Estrangement and Community*, Chicago: Franciscan Herald Press.

—— 1981 *A Home for the Homeless: A Sociological Exegesis of 1 Peter, Its Situation and Strategy*, Philadelphia: Fortress Press.

—— 1982 *James, I-II Peter/Jude*, J. H. Elliott and R. P Martin, Minneapolis: Augsburg Publishing House.

—— 1985 'Review of W. A. Meeks, *The First Urban Christians*', *Religious Studies Review* 11, 329–35.

—— 1986a 'Social-Scientific Criticism of the New Testament: More on Methods and Models', in J. H. Elliott (ed.), 'Social Scientific Criticism of the New Testament and Its Social World', *Semeia* 35, 1–33.

ELLIOTT, J. H. 1986b '1 Peter, its Situation and Strategy: A Discussion with David Balch', in C. H. Talbert (ed.), *Perspectives on First Peter*, Macon, GA: Mercer University Press, 61–78.

—— 1990a *A Home for the Homeless: A Social-Scientific Criticism of 1 Peter, Its Situation and Strategy, with a New Introduction*. Minneapolis: Fortress Press.

—— 1990b 'Paul, Galatians and the Evil Eye', *Currents in Theology and Mission* 17, 262–73.

—— 1992a 'Matthew 20:1–15: A Parable of Invidious Comparison and Evil Eye Accusation', *BTB* 22, 52–65.

—— 1992b 'Peter, First Epistle of', *Anchor Bible Dictionary* 6, 89–99.

—— 1993 *What is Social-Scientific Criticism?*, Minneapolis: Fortress Press. UK title: *Social-Scientific Criticism of the New Testament*, London: SPCK, 1995.

—— 1995a 'The Jewish Messianic Movement: From Faction to Sect', in Esler (ed.) 1995b, 75–95.

—— 1995b 'Disgraced Yet Graced: The Gospel according to 1 Peter in the Key of Honor and Shame', *BTB* 25, 166–78.

ELLIOTT, N. 1994 *Liberating Paul: The Justice of God and the Politics of the Apostle*, New York: Orbis; Sheffield: Sheffield Academic Press.

ELLIS, E. E. 1986 'Traditions in 1 Corinthians', *NTS* 32, 481–502.

ENGBERG-PEDERSEN, T. 1987 'The Gospel and Social Practice According to 1 Corinthians', *NTS* 33, 557–84.

—— 1993 'Proclaiming the Lord's Death: 1 Corinthians 11:17–34 and the Forms of Paul's Theological Argument', in D. M. Hay (ed.), *Pauline Theology, II: 1 and 2 Corinthians*, Minneapolis: Fortress Press, 103–32.

ENGELS, F. 1882 'Bruno Bauer und das Urchristentum', in *Marx-Engels Werke*, vol. 19, 297–314. ET in Marx and Engels 1957.

—— 1883 'Das Buch der Offenbarung', in *Marx-Engels Werke*, vol. 21, 9–15. ET in Marx and Engels 1957.

—— 1884 'Zur Geschichte des Urchristentums', in *Marx-Engels Werke*, vol. 22, 449–73. ET in Marx and Engels 1957.

ERIKSON, K. T. 1962 'Notes on the Sociology of Deviance', *Social Problems* 9, 307–14.

—— 1966 *Wayward Puritans: A Study in the Sociology of Deviance*, New York: John Wiley & Sons.

ESLER, P. F. 1987 *Community and Gospel in Luke–Acts: The Social and Political Motivations of Lucan Theology*, SNTSMS 57, Cambridge: Cambridge University Press.

—— 1992 'Glossolalia and the Admission of Gentiles into the Early Christian Community', *BTB* 22, 136–42.

—— 1994 *The First Christians in their Social Worlds: Social-Scientific Approaches to New Testament Interpretation*, London: Routledge.

—— 1995a 'Introduction: Models, Context and Kerygma in New Testament Interpretation', in Esler (ed.) 1995b, 1–20.

—— (ed.) 1995b *Modelling Early Christianity*, London and New York: Routledge.

—— 1998a 'Review of D. G. Horrell *The Social Ethos of the Corinthian Correspondence*', *JTS* 49, 253–60.

—— 1998b *Galatians*, London and New York: Routledge.

ESQUIVEL, J. 1983 *Die Kirche des Armen, ihr Glaube und ihre Kämpfe*, ESG Essen.

EVANS-PRITCHARD, E. E. 1937/1976 *Witchcraft, Oracles and Magic Among the Azande*, Oxford: Clarendon Press.

FEE, G. D. 1987 *The First Epistle to the Corinthians*, NICNT, Grand Rapids, MI: Eerdmans.

FELDMAN, L. H. 1960 'The Orthodoxy of the Jews in Hellenistic Egypt', *Jewish Social Studies* 22, 215–37.

FELDMEIER, R. 1992 *Die Christen als Fremde*, Tübingen: Mohr.

FESTINGER, L. 1957 *A Theory of Cognitive Dissonance*, Stanford, CA: Stanford University Press.

——, RIECHEN, H. W. and SCHACHTER, S. 1956 *When Prophecy Fails: A Social and Psychological Study of a Modern Group That Predicted the Destruction of the World*, New York: Harper & Row.

—— *et al.* 1964 *Conflict, Decision and Dissonance*, London: Tavistock.

FILSON, F. V. 1939 'The Significance of the Early House Churches', *JBL* 58, 109–12.

FINLEY, M. I. 1973 *The Ancient Economy*, Sather Classical Lectures 43, Berkeley: University of California Press.

FIORENZA, E. S. 1983/1995a *In Memory of Her: A Feminist Theological Reconstruction of Christian Origins*, 2nd edn 1995; London: SCM Press.

FIORENZA, E. S. 1992 *But She Said: Feminist Practices of Biblical Interpretation*, Boston, MA: Beacon Press.

—— (ed.) 1994/1995b *Searching the Scriptures*, 2 vols, London: SCM Press.

FLORY, M. B. 1975 'Family and "Familia": A Study of Social Relations in Slavery', PhD dissertation, Yale University.

FORD, J. M. 1969 '"Mingled Blood" from the Side of Christ (John xix.34)', *NTS* 15, 337–38.

FORKMAN, G. 1972 *The Limits of the Religious Community*, ConBNT 5, Lund: C. W. K. Gleerup.

FOSTER, G. 1967 'The Image of Limited Good', in J. Potter, M. Diaz, and G. Foster (eds), *Peasant Society: A Reader*, Boston: Little, Brown & Co., 300–23.

FRIEDRICH P. 1977 'Sanity and the Myth of Honor: The Problem of Achilles', *Journal of Psychological Anthropology* 5, 281–305.

FRIEDLÄNDER, L. 1910 *Darstellungen aus der Sittengeschichte Roms in der Zeit von August bis zum Ausgang der Antonine*, 8th edn, Leipzig.

—— 1923 *Darstellung aus der Sittengeschichte Roms, vol. III*, Leipzig 1923 (reprint Aalen 1964).

FUCHS, E. 1971 *Jesus, Wort und Tat*, Tübingen: Mohr.

FUELLENBACH, J. 1980 *Ecclesiastical Office and the Primacy of Rome: An Evaluation of Recent Theological Discussion of First Clement*, Washington, DC: Catholic University of America Press.

FÜGEN, H. N. 1970 *Die Hauptrichtungen der Literatursoziologie*, 4th edn, Bonn.

FUNK, R. W. 1976 'The Watershed of the American Biblical Tradition: The Chicago School, First Phase, 1892–1920', *JBL* 95, 4–22.

GAGER, J. G. 1975 *Kingdom and Community: The Social World of Early Christianity*, Englewood Cliffs, NJ: Prentice-Hall.

—— 1979 'Review of Grant, Malherbe and Theissen', *Religious Studies Review* 5, 174–80.

—— 1981 'Some notes on Paul's Conversion', *NTS* 27, 697–704.

—— 1983 'Review of B. J. Malina, *The New Testament World*', *Int* 37, 194–97.

GALLAS, S. 1990 '"Funfmal vierzig weiger einen . . ." Die an Paulus vollzogenen Synagogalstrafen nach 2 Kor 11, 24', *ZNW* 81, 178–91.

GAMBLE, H. A. JR. 1977 *The Textual History of the Letter to the Romans: A Study in Textual and Literary Criticism*, Grand Rapids, MI: Eerdmans.

GARNSEY, P. 1970 *Social Status and Legal Privilege in the Roman Empire*, Oxford: Clarendon Press.

—— and SALLER, R. 1987 *The Roman Empire: Economy, Society and Culture*, London: Duckworth.

GARRETT, S. 1988 'Review of B. J. Malina, *Christian Origins and Cultural Anthropology*', *JBL* 107, 532–34.

—— 1990 'Review of M. Y. MacDonald, *The Pauline Churches*', *JBL* 109, 151–54.

—— 1992 'Sociology of Early Christianity', in D. N. Freedman (ed.), *Anchor Bible Dictionary*, vol. 6, New York: Doubleday, 89–99.

GÄRTNER, B. 1965 *The Temple and the Community in Qumran and the New Testament*, Cambridge: Cambridge University Press.

GAYER, R. 1976 *Die Stellung des Sklaven in den paulinischen Gemeinden und bei Paulus: Zugleich ein sozialgeschichtlich vergleichender Beitrag zur Wertung des Sklaven in der Antike*, Europäische Hochschulschriften series 23, Theologie 78, Bern: Peter Lang.

GEALY, F. D. 1962 'Asiarch', in *The Interpreter's Dictionary of the Bible*, vol. 1, 259.

GEERTZ, C. 1966 'Religion as a Cultural System', in M. Banton (ed.), *Anthropological Approaches to the Study of Religion*, London: Tavistock Publications, 1–46.

GEORGI, D. 1964 *Die Gegner des Paulus im 2. Korintherbrief: Studien zur religiösen Propaganda in der Spätantike*, Neukirchen-Vluyn; Neukirchener Verlag. ET: *The Opponents of Paul in Second Corinthians*, Edinburgh: T&T Clark, 1987.

—— 1965 *Die Geschichte der Kollekte des Paulus für Jerusalem*. Theologische Forschung, 38, Hamburg-Bergstedt: Evangelischer Verlag. ET: *Remembering the Poor*, Nashville, TN: Abingdon Press, 1992.

GERHARDSSON, B. 1964 *Memory and Manuscript*, ASNU 22, Uppsala.

GIBBS, J. P. 1966 'Conceptions of Deviant Behaviour: The Old and the New', *Pacific Sociological Review* 9, 9–14.

GIBELLINI, R. 1987 *The Liberation Theology Debate*, London: SCM Press.

GIBLIN, C. H. 1984 'Confrontations in John 18,1–27', *Bib* 65, 219–32.

GIBLIN, C. H. 1986 'John's Narration of the Hearing before Pilate (John 18, 28–19,16a', *Bib* 67, 221–39.

GIDDENS, A. 1979 *Central Problems in Social Theory*, London and Basingstoke: Macmillan.

——— 1982 *Profiles and Critiques in Social Theory*, London and Basingstoke: Macmillan.

——— 1984 *The Constitution of Society: Outline of the Theory of Structuration*, Cambridge: Polity Press.

——— 1993 *Sociology*, 2nd edn, Cambridge: Polity Press.

GILL, R. 1977 *Theology and Social Structure*, London and Oxford: Mowbray.

——— (ed.) 1996 *Theology and Sociology: A Reader*, new and enlarged edn, London: Cassell.

GILMORE, D. (ed.) 1987 *Honor and Shame and the Unity of the Mediterranean*, Special Publication of the American Anthropological Association, no. 22; Washington, DC: American Anthropological Association.

GOFFMAN, I. 1957 'Status Consistency and Preference for Change in Power Distribution', *American Sociological Review* 22, 275–81.

GOOCH, P. D. 1993 *Dangerous Food: 1 Corinthians 8–10 in Its Context*, Waterloo, Ontario: Wilfred Laurier University Press.

GOODY, E. 1970 'Legitimate and Illegitimate Aggression in a West African State', in M. Douglas (ed.), *Witchcraft Confessions and Accusations*, New York: Tavistock Publications, 207–44.

GORDON, J. D. 1997 *Sister or Wife? 1 Corinthians 7 and Cultural Anthropology*, JSNTSup 149, Sheffield: Sheffield Academic Press.

GOTTWALD N. K. 1985 'The Interplay of Text, Concept, and Setting in the Hebrew Bible', in *The Hebrew Bible – A Socio-Literary Introduction*, Philadelphia: Fortress Press, 595–609.

——— and HORSLEY, R. (eds) 1993 *The Bible and Liberation: Political and Social Hermeneutics*, London: SPCK.

GOVE, W. R. (ed.) 1975 *The Labelling of Deviance: Evaluating a Perspective*, New York: John Wiley & Sons.

GRANT, F. C. 1926 *The Economic Background of the Gospels*, London.

——— 1950, *An Introduction to New Testament Thought*, New York.

GRANT, R. M. 1977 *Early Christianity and Society: Seven Studies*, New York: Harper & Row.

GRÄSSER, E. 1960 *Das Problem der Parusieverzögerung in den synoptischen Evangelien und in der Apostelgeschichte*, Berlin: Alfred Toppelmann.

—— 1969–70 'Jesus in Nazareth', *NTS* 16, 1–23.

GRASSI, A. J. 1964–65 'The Five Loaves of the High Priest', *NovT* 7, 119–22.

GREEN, J. B. (ed.) 1995 *Hearing the New Testament: Strategies for Interpretation*, Grand Rapids, MI: Eerdmans.

GREEN, M. 1970 *Evangelism in the Early Church*, London: Hodder & Stoughton.

GREEVEN, H. 1968–69 'Ehe nach dem Neuen Testament', *NTS* 15, 365–68.

GROSS, L. (ed.) 1959 *Symposium on Sociological Theory*, New York: Row Peterson & Company.

GRUNDMANN, W. 1969 *Das Evangelium nach Lukas*, ThHNT 3, Berlin.

GÜLZOW, H. 1969 *Christentum und Sklaverei in den ersten drei Jahrhunderten*, Bonn.

GUTIÉRREZ, G. 1976 *Theologie der Befreiung*, 2nd edn, Munich. ET: *A Theology of Liberation*, London: SCM Press, 1988.

GÜTTEMANNS, E. 1979 *Candid Questions concerning Gospel Form Criticism: A Methodological Sketch of the Fundamental Problems of Form and Redaction Criticism*, trans. W. G. Doty, Pittsburgh: Pickwick Press.

HADAS-LEBEL, M. 1973 *De Providentia I et II: Les oeuvres de Philon d'Alexandrie*, Paris: Cerf.

HAENCHEN, E. 1959/1961 *Die Apostelgeschichte*, 12th edn, Göttingen: Vandenhoeck & Ruprecht. ET: *The Acts of the Apostles: A Commentary*, Philadelphia: Westminster; Oxford: Blackwell, 1971.

—— 1966 *Der Weg Jesu*, Berlin.

HAHN, F. 1965 *Das Verständnis der Mission im Neuen Testament*, WMANT 13. 2nd edn, Neukirchen-Vluyn, ET: *Mission in the New Testament*, trans. F. Clarke, SBT 47, London: SCM Press.

HAMPSON, D. 1996 *After Christianity*, London: SCM Press.

HANSON, A. T. 1982 *The Pastoral Epistles*, NCBC, London: Marshall, Morgan & Scott.

HARAGUCHI, T. 1993 'Das Unterhaltsrecht des frühchristlichen Verkündigers. Eine Untersuchung zur Bezeichnung *ergatēs* im Neuen Testament', *ZNW* 84, 178–95.

HARDYCK, J. A. and BRADEN, M. 1962 'Prophecy Fails Again: A Report of a Failure to Replicate', *Journal of Abnormal and Social Psychology* 65, 136–41.

HARNACK, A. VON 1884 *Lehre der Zwölf Apostel nebst Untersuchungen zur ältesten Geschichte der Kirchenverfassung und des Kirchenrechts*, TU 2, 1–2, Leipzig.

—— 1904/1908 *The Mission and Expansion of Christianity in the First Three Centuries*, vol. 1, London: Williams & Norgate; New York: Putnam.

—— 1905/1908 *The Mission and Expansion of Christianity in the First Three Centuries*, vol. 2, London: Williams & Norgate; New York: Putnam.

—— 1924 *Die Mission und Ausbreitung des Christentums*, vol. 2, 4th edn, Leipzig.

HARRINGTON, D. J. 1980 'Sociological Concepts and the Early Church: A Decade of Research', *Theological Studies* 41, 181–90.

—— 1988 'Second Testament Exegesis and the Social Sciences: A Bibliography', *BTB* 18, 77–85.

HARTMAN, L. 1997 *'Into the Name of the Lord Jesus': Baptism in the Early Church*, Edinburgh: T&T Clark.

HARVEY, A. E. 1982 '"The Workman is Worthy of His Hire": Fortunes of a Proverb in the Early Church', *NovT* 24, 209–21.

—— 1985 'Forty Strokes Save One: Social Aspects of Judaizing and Apostasy', in *Alternative Approaches to New Testament Study*, London: SPCK, 79–96.

HASLER, V. 1969 *Amen*, Zurich and Stuttgart.

HAUKE, M. 1988 *Women in the Priesthood? A Systematic Analysis in the Light of the Order of Creation and Redemption*, San Francisco: Ignatius Press.

HEMER, C. J. 1985 'Review of J. H. Elliott *A Home for the Homeless*', *JSNT* 24, 120–23.

HENGEL, M. 1968 *Nachfolge und Charisma: eine exegetisch-religionsgeschichtliche Studie zu Mt 8 21f. und Jesu Ruf in die Nachfolge*, BZNW 34, Berlin: Alfred Töpelmann. ET Hengel 1981.

—— 1969 *Judentum und Hellenismus*, 2 vols, Tübingen: Mohr; ET: *Judaism and Hellenism*, London: SCM Press, 1974.

HENGEL, M. 1973 *Eigentum und Reichtum in der frühen Kirche*, Stuttgart: Calwer Verlag; ET: *Property and Riches in the Early Church*, London: SCM Press, 1974.

—— 1977 *Crucifixion*, London: SCM Press.

—— 1981 *The Charismatic Leader and His Followers*, Edinburgh: T&T Clark.

HENNECKE, E. (ed.) 1959–64 *Neutestamentliche Apokryphen*, 3rd edn, revised by W. Schneemelcher, 2 vols, Tübingen: Mohr. ET: *New Testament Apocrypha*, R. McL. Wilson (ed.) 2 vols 1963–65, Philadelphia: Westminster; London: Lutterworth.

HERZFELD, M. 1980 'Honour and Shame: Problems in the Comparative Analysis of Moral Systems', *Man* 15, 339–51.

HICKLING, C. J. A. 1975 'Is the Second Epistle to the Corinthians a Source for Early Church History?', *ZNW* 66, 284–87.

HIGGINS, A. J. B. 1952 *The Lord's Supper in the New Testament*, London: SCM Press.

HOCK, R. F. 1978 'Paul's Tentmaking and the Problem of His Social Class', *JBL* 97, 555–64.

—— 1979 'The Workshop as a Social Setting for Paul's Missionary Preaching', *CBQ* 41, 438–51.

—— 1980 *The Social Context of Paul's Ministry: Tentmaking and Apostleship*, Philadelphia: Fortress Press.

HOEHNER, H. 1972 *Herod Antipas*, Cambridge: Cambridge University Press.

HOFFMANN, P. 1972 *Studien zur Theologie der Logienquelle*, NTA NF 8, Münster.

HOFFMANN-AXTHELM, D. 1968 'Loisys l'Évangile et l'Église: Besichtigung eines zeitgenössischen Schlachtfeldes', *ZTK* 65, 291–328.

HÖFLER, A. 1935 *Der Sarapishymnus des Aelios Aristeides*, Tübinger Beitrage zur Altertumswissenschaft 27, Stuttgart/Berlin.

HOLL, K. 1908 'Das Fortleben der Volkssprachen in Kleinasien in nachchristlicher Zeit', *Hermes* 43, 240–54.

HOLLADAY, C. H. 1977 *Theios Aner in Hellenistic Judaism*, SBLDS 40, Missoula, MT: Scholars Press.

HOLMBERG, B. 1978 *Paul and Power: The Structure of Authority in the Primitive Church as Reflected in the Pauline Epistles*, Lund: C. W. K. Gleerup.

HOLMBERG, B. 1990 *Sociology and the New Testament: An Appraisal*, Minneapolis: Fortress Press.

HOMMEL, H. 1966 'Herrenworte im Lichte sokratischer Überlieferung', *ZNW* 57, 1–23.

HORBURY, W. 1985 'Extirpation and Excommunication', *Vetus Testamentum* 35, 13–38.

HORNUNG, C. A. 1977 'Social Status, Status Inconsistency, and Psychological Stress', *American Sociological Review* 42, 623–38.

HORRELL, D. G. 1993 'Converging Ideologies: Berger and Luckmann and the Pastoral Epistles', *JSNT* 50, 85–103.

—— 1995 'The Development of Theological Ideology in Pauline Christianity: A Structuration Theory Perspective', in Esler (ed.) 1995b, 224–36.

—— 1996a *The Social Ethos of the Corinthian Correspondence: Interests and Ideology from 1 Corinthians to 1 Clement*, Edinburgh: T&T Clark.

—— 1996b, 'Review of Dale B. Martin, *The Corinthian Body*', *JTS* 47, 624–29.

—— 1997a '"The Lord commanded . . . But I have not used . . ." Exegetical and Hermeneutical Reflections on 1 Cor 9.14–15', *NTS* 43, 587–603.

—— 1997b 'Review of N. Elliott, *Liberating Paul*', *Biblical Interpretation* 5, 285–87.

—— 1998 *The Epistles of Peter and Jude*, Epworth Commentary; London: Epworth Press.

HORSLEY, R. A. 1989 *Sociology and the Jesus Movement*, New York: Crossroad.

—— 1993 *Jesus and the Spiral of Violence: Popular Jewish Resistance in Roman Palestine*, Minneapolis: Fortress Press.

HURD, J. C. 1965 *The Origin of 1 Corinthians*, London: SPCK.

JACKSON, E. F. 1962 'Status Consistency and Symptoms of Stress', *American Sociological Review* 27, 469–80.

—— and BURKE, P. J. 1965 'Status and Symptoms of Stress: Additive and Interaction Effects', *American Sociological Review* 30, 556–64.

JEFFERS, J. S. 1991 *Conflict at Rome: Social Order and Hierarchy in Early Christianity*, Minneapolis: Fortress Press.

JEFFORD, C. N. (ed.) 1995 *The* Didache *in Context: Essays on Its Text, History and Transmission,* NovTSup 77; Leiden: E. J. Brill.

JEREMIAS, J. 1955 *The Parables of Jesus,* New York.

—— 1958 *Jesus' Promise to the Nations,* London: SCM Press.

—— 1969 *Jerusalem in the Time of Jesus,* Philadelphia: Fortress Press.

JEWETT, R. 1986 *The Thessalonian Correspondence: Pauline Rhetoric and Millenarian Piety,* Philadelphia: Fortress Press.

JOHNSON, C. 1968 *Revolutionary Change,* London: University of London Press.

JUDGE, E. A. 1960a *The Social Pattern of the Christian Groups in the First Century: Some Prolegomena to the Study of New Testament Ideas of Social Obligation,* London: Tyndale Press.

—— 1960b 'The Early Christians as a Scholastic Community', *Journal of Religious History* 1, 4–15, 125–37.

—— 1964 *Christliche Gruppen in nichtchristlicher Gesellschaft,* Wuppertal. German trans. of Judge 1960a.

—— 1968 'Paul's Boasting in Relation to Contemporary Professional Practice', *Australian Biblical Review* 16, 37–50.

—— 1980 'The Social Identity of the First Christians: A Question of Method in Religious History', *Journal of Religious History* 11, 201–17.

—— and THOMAS, G. S. R. 1966 'The Origin of the Church at Rome: A New Solution?', *Reformed Theological Review* 25, 81–94.

KANTER, R. 1972 *Commitment and Community,* Cambridge.

—— 1973 'Family Organization and Sex Roles in American Communes', in *Communes: Creating and Managing the Collective Life,* New York, 287–307.

KARRIS, R. J. 1973 'The Background and Significance of the Polemic of the Pastoral Epistles', *JBL* 92, 549–64.

KÄSEMANN, E. 1954–55 'Sätze heiligen Rechtes im Neuen Testament', *NTS* 1, 248–60. ET in *New Testament Questions of Today,* London: SCM Press, 1969.

—— 1959 'Eine paulinische Variation des Amor Fati', *ZTK* 56, 138–54. ET in *New Testament Questions of Today,* London: SCM Press, 1969.

—— 1960 'Die Anfänge christlicher Theologie', *ZTK* 57, 162–85. ET in *New Testament Questions of Today,* London: SCM Press, 1969.

KÄSEMANN, E. 1964 'The Pauline Doctrine of the Lord's Supper', in *Essays on New Testament Themes*, SBT 41, London: SCM Press, 108–35.

—— 1968 'The Beginnings of Christian Theology,' in *New Testament Questions of Today*, London: SCM Press, 1969, 82–107.

—— 1969 'Paul and Early Catholicism', in *New Testament Questions of Today*, London: SCM Press, 236–51.

—— 1971 *Perspectives on Paul*, Philadelphia: Fortress Press.

KASHER, A. 1985 *The Jews in Hellenistic and Roman Egypt: The Struggle for Equal Rights*, Tübingen: Mohr.

KASTING, H. 1969 *Die Anfänge urchristlicher Mission*, Munich.

KAUFFMANN, F. 1958 *Methodology in the Social Sciences*, New York: The Humanities Press.

KAUTSKY, K. 1908/1921 *Der Ursprung des Christentums. Eine historische Untersuchung*, Stuttgart; 11th edn 1921; ET 1925.

—— 1925 *Foundations of Christianity: A Study in Christian Origins*, London: Orbach & Chambers.

KECK, L. E. 1974 'On the Ethos of Early Christians', *JAAR* 42, 435–52.

KEE, H. C. 1985 'Sociology of the New Testament' in P. Achtemeier (ed.), *Harper's Bible Dictionary*, San Francisco: Harper & Row, 961–68.

—— 1989 *Knowing the Truth: A Sociological Approach to New Testament Interpretation*, Minneapolis: Fortress Press.

KELBER, W. H. 1983 *The Oral and Written Gospel: The Hermeneutics of Speaking and Writing in the Synoptic Tradition, Mark, Paul and Q*, Philadelphia: Fortress Press.

——, KOLENKOW, A., SCROGGS, R. 1971 'Reflections on the Question: Was there a Pre-Markan Passion Narrative?', *SBL 107th Annual Meeting: Seminar Papers*.

KENT, J. H. 1966 *Corinth: Results of Excavations conducted by the American School of Classical Studies at Athens, vol. 8, part 3; The Inscriptions 1926–1950*, Princeton: Princeton University Press.

KIDD, R. M. 1990 *Wealth and Beneficence in the Pastoral Epistles. A 'Bourgeois' Form of Early Christianity?* SBLDS 122, Atlanta, CA: Scholars Press.

KIPPENBERG, H. G. 1970 'Versuch einer soziologischen Verortung des antiken Gnostizismus', *Numen* 17, 211–31.

KITSUSE, J. I. 1962 'Societal Reaction to Deviant Behaviour: Problems of Theory and Method', *Social Problems* 9, 247–56.

KLAUCK, H.-J. 1981 *Hausgemeinde und Hauskirche im frühen Christentum*, Stuttgarter Bibelstudien 103, Stuttgart: Katholisches Bibelwerk.

KLEIN, R. 1983 *Die Romrede des Aelius Aristedes*, Darmstadt: Wissenschaftliche Buchgesellschaft.

KLEMM, H. G. 1969–70 'Das Wort von der Selbstbestattung der Toten', *NTS* 16, 60–75.

KLOPPENBORG, J. S. 1995 'The Transformation of Moral Exhortation in *Didache* 1–5', in Jefford (ed.) 1995, 88–109.

KNIGHT, G. W. III 1992 *The Pastoral Epistles: A Commentary on the Greek Text*, NICNT; Grand Rapids, MI: Eerdmans.

KNOPF, R. 1900 'Über die soziale Zusammensetzung der ältesten heidenchristlichen Gemeinden', *ZTK* 10, 325–47.

—— 1920 *Die Lehre der zwölf Apostel*, HNT suppl. vol. 1, Tübingen.

KNUTSSON, J. 1977 *Labelling Theory: A Critical Examination*, Stockholm: Scientific Research Group.

KORNEMANN, E. 1900 'Collegium', in A. Pauly, G. Wissowa and W. Kroll (eds), *Real-Encyclopädie der klassischen Altertumswissenschaft*, vol. 4.1, cols. 380–480.

KRAUSS, S. 1925 'Die Instruktion Jesu an die Apostle', *Angelos* 1, 96–102.

KREISSIG, H. 1967 'Zur sozialen Zusammensetzung der frühchristlichen Gemeinden im ersten Jahrhundert u.Z', *Eirene* 6, 91–100.

—— 1969 'Die Landwirtschaftliche Situation in Palästina vor dem Judäischen Krieg', *Acta Antiqua* 17, 223–54.

KRESSEL, G. M. 1994 'An Anthropologist's Response to the Use of Social Science Models in Biblical Studies', *Semeia* 68, 153–60.

KRETSCHMAR, G. 1964 'Ein Beitrag zur Frage nach dem Ursprung frühchristlicher Askese', *ZTK* 61, 27–67.

KUHN, H. W. 1971 *Ältere Sammlungen im Markusevangelium*, StUNT 8; Göttingen.

KUHN, K. G. and STEGEMANN, H. 1962 'Proselyten', Pauly-Wissowa, *Realencyclopädie der classische Altertumswissenschaft*, supp. vol. 9: cols 1248–83.

KÜMMEL, W. G. 1973 *Einleitung in das Neue Testament*, 17th edn, Heidelberg: Quelle & Meyer. ET 1975.

—— 1975 *Introduction to the New Testament*, Nashville and New York: Abingdon Press.

KÜNZI, M. 1970 *Das Naherwartungs-Logion Mt 10,23*, Tübingen.

KUSS, O. 1971 *Paulus: Die Rolle des Apostels in der theologischen Entwicklung der Urkirche, Auslegung und Verkundigung*, III, Regensburg.

KYRTATAS, D. J. 1987 *The Social Structure of the Early Christian Communities*, London and New York: Verso.

LAKE, K. 1912 *The Apostolic Fathers*, vol. 1, Loeb Classical Library, Cambridge, MA: Harvard University Press.

—— and CADBURY, H. J. (eds) 1933 *The Acts of the Apostles*, edited by F. J. Foakes Jackson and Kirsopp Lake: Vol. 4. *English Translation and Commentary*; Vol. 5: *Additional Notes*; reprint. Grand Rapids, MI: Baker, 1979.

LALAND, E. 1959 'Die Martha-Maria-Perikope Lukas 10, 38–42: Ihre kerygmatische Aktualität für das Leben der Urgemeinde', *Studia Theologica* 13, 70–85.

LAMPE, P. 1987 *Die stadtrömischen Christen in den ersten beiden Jahrhunderten: Untersuchungen zur Sozialgeschichte*, WUNT 2nd series 18; Tübingen: Mohr (2nd edn 1989).

—— 1991 'Das Korinthische Herrenmahl im Schnittpunkt hellenistisch-römischer Mahlpraxis und paulinischer Theologia Crucis (1 Kor 11, 17–34)', *ZNW* 82, 183–213.

LANDVOGT, P. 1908 *Epigraphische Untersuchungen über den oikonomos: Ein Beitrag zum hellenistischen Beamtenwesen*, Strasbourg: Schauberg.

LEE, C. 1971 'Social Unrest and Primitive Christianity', in S. Benko and J. O'Rourke (eds), *The Catacombs and the Colosseum: The Roman Empire as the Setting of Primitive Christianity*, Valley Forge: Judson, 121–38.

LEE, T. 1986 *Studies in the Form of Sirach 44–50*, SBLDS 75; Atlanta, CA: Scholars Press.

LEENHARDT, F. J. 1948 'La Place de la femme dans l'Église d'après le Nouveau Testament', *Études théologiques et religieuses* 23, 3–50.

LEEUW F. VAN DER 1938 *Religion in Essence and Manifestation*, London.

LEGASSE, S. 1963–64 'Jesus a-t-il annoncé la Conversion Finale d'Israel (A propos de Marc X, 23–27)?', *NTS* 10, 480–87.

LEMERT, E. M. 1951 *Social Pathology*, New York: McGraw-Hill.

—— 1972 *Human Deviance, Social Problems, and Social Control*, 2nd edn, Englewood Cliffs, NJ: Prentice Hall.

LENSKI, G. E. 1954 'Status Crystallization: A Non-vertical Dimension of Social Status', *American Sociological Review* 19, 405–13, reprinted in Seymour Martin Lipset and Neil J. Smelser (eds), *Sociology: The Progress of a Decade*, Englewood Cliffs, NJ: Prentice Hall 1961, 485–94.

—— 1956 'Social Participation and Status Crystallization', *American Sociological Review* 21, 458–64.

LEON, H. J. 1960 *The Jews of Ancient Rome*, Philadelphia: Jewish Publication Society.

LIETZMANN, H. 1927 *Petrus und Paulus in Rom*, Berlin/Leipzig.

—— 1933 *An die Römer*, 4th edn, HNT 8, Tübingen: Mohr.

—— 1949 *An die Korinther* I/II, HNT 9, Tübingen: Mohr.

—— 1979 *Mass and the Lord's Supper: A Study in the History of Liturgy*, Leiden: E. J. Brill.

LIGHTFOOT, J. B. 1880 *The Epistle of St. Paul to the Galatians*, 6th edn; reprinted Grand Rapids, MI: Zondervan, 1978.

—— 1913 *Saint Paul's Epistle to the Philippians*, reprinted Grand Rapids, MI: Zondervan, 1953.

LINDARS, B. 1961 *New Testament Apologetic*, Philadelphia: Westminster Press.

LINDEMANN, A. 1992 *Die Clemensbriefe*, HNT 17, Tübingen: Mohr.

LIPSET, S. M. 1968 'Social Class', *International Encyclopedia of the Social Sciences*, vol. 15, 296–316.

LIPSIUS, R. A. and BONNETT, M. (eds), 1891 *Acta Apostolorum Apocrypha*, 3 vols., reprinted Darmstadt: Wissenschaftliche Buchgesellschaft, 1959.

LOFLAND, J. 1969 *Deviance and Identity*, Englewood Cliffs, NJ: Prentice Hall.

LOHSE, E. 1981 'Das Evangelium für die Armen', *ZNW* 72, 51–64.

LOISY, A. 1904 *L'Évangile et l'Église*, 3rd edn, Bellevue.

LÜDEMANN, G. 1989 *Early Christianity According to the Traditions in Acts: A Commentary*, London: SCM Press.

—— 1996 *Heretics: The Other Side of Early Christianity*, London: SCM Press.

LÜHRMANN, D. 1980 'Neutestamentliche Haustafeln und antike Ökonomie', *NTS* 27, 83–97.

LUZ, U. 1990 *Matthew 1–7*, Edinburgh: T&T Clark.

MacDONALD, D. 1979 'Virgins, Widows, and Paul in Second-Century Asia Minor', in P. J. Achtemeier (ed.), *Society of Biblical Literature 1979 Seminar Papers*, Missoula, MT: Scholars Press, 169–84.

MacDONALD, M. Y. 1988 *The Pauline Churches: A Socio-historical Study of Institutionalization in the Pauline and deutero-Pauline Writings*, SNTSMS 60, Cambridge: Cambridge University Press.

MacINTYRE, A. 1981 *After Virtue: A Study in Moral Theory*, London: Duckworth.

MacMULLEN, R. 1974 *Roman Social Relations 50 BC to AD 284*, New Haven and London: Yale University Press.

MAGIE, D. 1950 *Roman Rule in Asia Minor to the End of the Third Century after Christ*, 2 vols. reprinted New York: Arnop, 1975.

MAIER, H. O. 1991 *The Social Setting of the Ministry as Reflected in the Writings of Hermas, Clement and Ignatius*, Dissertations SR Vol 1. Canadian Corporation for Studies in Religion; Ontario: Wilfred Laurier University Press.

MAIR, L. 1969 *Witchcraft*, New York: World University Library.

MALEWSKI, A. 1966 'The Degree of Status Incongruence and Its Effects', in Reinhard Bendix and Seymour M. Lipset (eds), *Class, Status and Power: Social Stratification in Comparative Perspective*, New York: Free Press; London: Macmillan, 303–308.

MALHERBE, A. J. 1977a *Social Aspects of Early Christianity*, Baton Rouge and London: Louisiana State University Press.

—— 1977b 'The Inhospitability of Diotrephes', in J. Jervell and W. A. Meeks (eds), *God's Christ and His People: Studies in Honour of Nils Alstrup Dahl*, Oslo, Bergen and Tromso: Universitetsforlaget, 222–32.

—— 1983 *Social Aspects of Early Christianity*, 2nd edn, Philadelphia: Fortress Press.

MALINA, B. J. 1981 *The New Testament World: Insights from Cultural Anthropology*, Atlanta, CA: John Knox; London: SCM Press 1983.

—— 1982 'The Social Sciences and Biblical Interpretation', *Int* 37, 229–42.

—— 1985a *The Gospel of John in Sociolinguistic Perspective*, 48th Colloquy of the Center of Hermeneutical Studies, Herman Waetjen (ed.); Berkeley: Center for Hermeneutical Studies.

—— 1985b 'Review of W. Meeks, *The First Urban Christians*', *JBL* 104, 346–49.

MALINA, B. J. 1986a *Christian Origins and Cultural Anthropology: Practical Models for Interpretation*, Atlanta: John Knox Press.

—— 1986b 'Normative Dissonance and Christian Origins', *Semeia* 35, 35–59.

—— 1987 'Wealth and Poverty in the New Testament and its World', *Int* 41, 354–67.

—— 1991 'Conflict in Luke–Acts: Labelling and Deviance Theory', in Neyrey (ed.) 1991a, 97–122.

—— 1993 *The New Testament World: Insights from Cultural Anthro-pology*, rev. edn, Louisville, KY: Westminster/John Knox Press.

—— 1996a *The Social World of Jesus and the Gospels*, London: Routledge.

—— 1996b 'Understanding New Testament Persons', in Rohrbaugh (ed.) 1996, 41–61.

—— 1997 'Review of R. Stark, *The Rise of Christianity*', *CBQ* 59, 593–95.

—— and NEYREY, J. H. 1988 *Calling Jesus Names: The Social Value of Labels in Matthew*, Sonoma, CA: Polebridge.

—— and NEYREY, J. H. 1991a 'Honor and Shame in Luke–Acts: Pivotal Values of the Mediterranean World', in Neyrey (ed.) 1991a, 25–66.

—— and NEYREY, J. H. 1991b 'First-Century Personality: Dyadic, Not Individualistic', in Neyrey (ed.) 1991a, 67–96.

—— and NEYREY, J. H. 1996 *Portraits of Paul: An Archaeology of Ancient Personality*, Louisville, KY: Westminster/John Knox Press.

—— and ROHRBAUGH, R. L. 1992 *Social-Science Commentary on the Synoptic Gospels*, Minneapolis: Fortress Press.

MARQUARDT, J. 1884 *Römische Staatsverwaltung II*, Leipzig.

MARSHALL, I. H. 1980 *Last Supper and Lord's Supper*, Exeter: Paternoster Press.

MARTIN, D. B. 1990 *Slavery as Salvation: The Metaphor of Slavery in Pauline Christianity*, New Haven and London: Yale University Press.

—— 1991 'Ancient Slavery, Class and Early Christianity', *Fides et Historia* 23, 105–13.

—— 1993 'Social-Scientific Criticism', in McKenzie and Haynes (eds) 1993, 103–19.

—— 1995 *The Corinthian Body*, London and New Haven: Yale University Press.

MARTINDALE, D. 1959 'Sociological Theory and the Ideal Type', in L. Gross (ed.), *Symposium on Sociological Theory*, New York: Row Peterson & Company, 57–91.

MARX, K. and ENGELS, F. 1957 *On Religion*, Moscow: Foreign Languages Publishing House.

MARXSEN, W. 1969 *Mark the Evangelist: Studies on the Redaction History of the Gospel*, New York: Abingdon Press.

MAY, D. M. 1991 *Social-Scientific Criticism of the New Testament: A Bibliography*, Macon, GA: Mercer University Press.

MAYER, A. 1983 *Der zensierte Jesus: Soziologie des Neuen Testaments*, Olten: Walter Verlag.

MAYES, A. D. H. 1989 *The Old Testament in Sociological Perspective*, London: Marshall Pickering.

MCKENZIE, S. L. and HAYNES, S. R. 1993 *To Each Its Own Meaning: An Introduction to Biblical Criticisms and Their Application*, Louisville, KY: Westminster/John Knox Press.

MCKINNEY, J. C. 1966 *Constructive Typology and Social Theory*, New York: Meredith Publishing Company.

MCVANN, M. 1991 'Rituals of Status Transformation in Luke-Acts: The Case of Jesus the Prophet', in Neyrey (ed.) 1991a, 333–60.

MEEKS, W. A. 1967 *The Prophet-King: Moses Traditions and the Johannine Christology*, NovTSup 14; Leiden: E. J. Brill.

—— 1972 'The Man from Heaven in Johannine Sectarianism', *JBL* 91, 44–72.

—— 1974 'The Image of the Androgyne: Some Uses of a Symbol in Earliest Christianity', *History of Religions* 13, 165–208.

—— 1975 'The Social World of Early Christianity', *Bulletin of the Council on the Study of Religion* 6/1, 1, 4–5.

—— 1982 'The Social Context of Pauline Theology', *Int* 36, 266–77.

—— 1983 *The First Urban Christians: The Social World of the Apostle Paul*, New Haven and London: Yale University Press.

—— 1985 'Breaking Away: Three New Testament Pictures of Christianity's Separation from Jewish Communities', in J. Neusner, E. S. Friechs (eds), *To See Ourselves as Others See Us: Christians, Jews, Others in Late Antiquity*, California: Scholars Press, 93–115.

—— 1986 *The Moral World of the First Christians*, Philadelphia: Westminster Press.

MEEKS, W. A. 1993 *The Origins of Christian Morality: The First Two Centuries*, London and New Haven: Yale University Press.

—— 1996 'The Ethics of the Fourth Evangelist', in R. A. Culpepper and C. C. Black (eds), *Exploring the Gospel of John*, Louisville, KY: Westminster/John Knox Press, 317–26.

—— and WILKEN, R. L. 1978 *Jews and Christians in Antioch in the First Four Centuries of the Common Era*, SBL Sources for Biblical Study, 13; Missoula, MT: Scholars Press.

MEGGITT, J. J. 1994 'Meat Consumption and Social Conflict in Corinth', *JTS* 45, 137–41.

—— 1996 'The Social Status of Erastus (Rom 16:23)', *NovT* 38, 218–23.

—— 1998a 'Review of B. J. Malina, *The Social World of Jesus and the Gospels*', *JTS* 49, 215–19.

—— 1998b *Paul, Poverty and Survival*, Edinburgh: T&T Clark.

MERTON, R. K. and ROSSI, A. K. 1950 'Reference Group Theory and Social Mobility' in Robert K. Merton and P. Lazarsfeld (eds), *Continuities in Social Research*, Glencoe, IL: Free Press, 40–105.

MICHAELIS, J. R. 1965 'Apostolic Hardships and Righteous Gentiles', *JBL* 84, 27–37.

MICHAELS, J. R. 1988 *1 Peter*, WBC 49, Waco, TX: Word Books.

MILBANK, J. 1990 *Theology and Social Theory: Beyond Secular Reason*, Oxford: Blackwell.

MILLER, D. E. 1979 'Sectarianism and Secularisation: The Work of Bryan Wilson', *Religious Studies Review* 5, 161–74.

MILLS, C. WRIGHT 1978 *The Sociological Imagination*, Harmondsworth: Pelican.

MILLS, E. W. 1983 'Sociological Ambivalence and Social Order: The Constructive Use of Normative Dissonance', *Sociology and Social Research* 67, 279–87.

MOFFATT, J. 1918–19 'Discerning the Body', *ExpT* 30, 19–23.

MORITZ, K. P. 1785–90 *Anton Reiser*, trans. P. E. Matheson; London and New York: Humphrey Milford, 1926.

MOULTON, J. H. and MILLIGAN, G. 1963 *The Vocabulary of the Greek New Testament*, London.

MOXNES, H. 1988a 'Honor and Righteousness in Romans', *JSNT* 32, 61–77.

MOXNES, H. 1988b 'Honor, Shame and the Outside World in Paul's Letter to the Romans', in J. Neusner (ed.), *The Social World of Formative Christianity and Judaism*, Philadelphia: Fortress Press, 207–18.

—— 1996 'Honor and Shame', in Rohrbaugh (ed.) 1996, 19–40.

MÜHLMANN, W. E. 1962 *Homo Creator*, Wiesbaden.

—— and MÜLLER E. W. 1966 *Kulturanthropologie*, Köln / Berlin.

MUNCK, J. 1959 *Paul and the Salvation of Mankind*, London: SCM Press.

MUNZ, P. 1972 'Die soziologische Verortung des antiken Gnostizismus', *Numen* 19, 41–51.

MURDOCK, G. P. 1980 *Theories of Illness: A World Survey*, Pittsburgh: University of Pittsburgh Press.

MURPHY-O'CONNOR, J. 1976 'The Non-Pauline Character of 1 Corinthians 11:2–16?', *JBL* 95, 615–21.

MYERS, C. 1988 *Binding the Strong Man: A Political Reading of Mark's Story of Jesus*, Maryknoll, NY: Orbis Books.

NAGY, G. 1979 *The Best of the Achaeans*, Baltimore: The John Hopkins University Press.

NEUENZEIT, P. 1960 *Das Herrenmahl. Studien zur Paulinischen Eucharistieauffassung*, StANT 1; München.

NEUSNER, J. 1963 *Fellowship in Judaism*, London.

—— 1971 *The Rabbinic Traditions About the Pharisees Before 70* (3 Vols), Leiden: E. J. Brill.

—— 1973 *From Politics to Piety*, Englewood Cliffs, NJ: Prentice Hall.

NEWTON, M. 1985 *The Concept of Purity at Qumran and in the Letters of Paul*, SNTSMS 53, Cambridge: Cambridge University Press.

NEYREY, J. H. 1985 *Christ is Community*, Wilmington, DE: Michael Glazier, Inc.

—— 1986a 'Body Language in 1 Corinthians: The Use of Anthro-pological Models for Understanding Paul and his Opponents', *Semeia* 35, 129–70.

—— 1986b 'The Idea of Purity in Mark's Gospel', *Semeia* 35, 91–128.

—— 1986c 'Witchcraft Accusations in 2 Cor 10–13: Paul in Social-Science Perspective', *Listening* 21, 160–70.

—— 1987 'Jesus the Judge: Forensic Process in John 8:21–59', *Bib* 68, 509–42.

NEYREY, J. H. 1988a *An Ideology of Revolt: John's Christology in Social-Science Perspective*, Philadelphia: Fortress Press.

—— 1988b 'Bewitched in Galatia: Paul and Cultural Anthropology', *CBQ* 50, 72–100.

—— 1990 *Paul in Other Words: A Cultural Reading of his Letters*, Louisville: Westminster / John Knox Press.

—— (ed.) 1991a *The Social World of Luke–Acts: Models for Interpretation*, Peabody: Hendrickson.

—— 1991b 'Ceremonies in Luke–Acts: The Case of Meals and Table Fellowship', in Neyrey (ed.) 1991a, 361–87.

—— 1995 'The Footwashing in John 13:6–11: Transformation Ritual or Ceremony?', in L. M. White and O. L. Yarbrough (eds), *The Social World of the First Christians*, Minneapolis: Fortress Press, 198–213.

NIEBUHR, H. R. 1929 *The Social Sources of Denominationalism*, New York.

NINEHAM, D. 1976 *The Use and Abuse of the Bible: A Study of the Bible in an Age of Rapid Cultural Change*, London: SPCK.

—— 1982 'The Strangeness of the New Testament World', Part I *Theology* 85, 171–77, Part II, *Theology* 85, 247–55.

NISBET, R. A. 1953 *The Quest for Community*, New York.

NOCK, A. D. 1961 'Review of H. J. Schoeps, *Paul: The Theology of the Apostle in Light of Jewish Religious History*', *Gnomon* 33, 582.

O'BRIEN, P. T. 1982 *Colossians, Philemon*, WBC 44, Waco, TX: Word Books.

OGLETREE, T. W. 1983 *The Use of the Bible in Christian Ethics*, Philadelphia: Fortress Press.

OLLROG, W.-H. 1979 *Paulus und seine Mitarbeiter: Untersuchungen zu Theorie und Praxis der paulinischen Mission*, WMANT 50; Neukirchen-Vluyn: Neukirchener.

ORR, W. F. and WALTHER, J. A. 1976 *I Corinthians: A New Translation*, Anchor Bible, 32; Garden City, NY: Doubleday.

OSIEK, C. 1984 *What Are They Saying About the Social Setting of the New Testament?*, revised and expanded edn 1992; New York: Paulist Press.

—— 1989 'The New Handmaid: The Bible and the Social Sciences', *Theological Studies* 50, 260–78.

PAGELS, E. H. 1979 *The Gnostic Gospels*, New York: Random House.

PAMMENT, M. 1981 'Witch-hunt', *Theology* 84, 98–106.

PATTERSON, S. 1995 '*Didache* 11–13: The Legacy of Radical Itinerancy in Early Christianity', in Jefford (ed.) 1995, 313–29.

PERISTIANY, J. D. (ed.) 1965 *Honor and Shame: The Values of Mediterranean Society*, London: Weidenfeld & Nicolson.

—— and PITT-RIVERS, J. (eds) 1992 *Honor and Grace in Anthropology*, Cambridge: Cambridge University Press.

PERRIN, N. 1967 *Rediscovering the Teaching of Jesus*, New York: Harper & Row.

PESCH, W. 1960 'Zur Exegese von Mt 6, 19–21 und Lk 12, 33–34', *Bib* 41, 356–78.

PETERSEN, N. 1985 *Rediscovering Paul: Philemon and the Sociology of Paul's Narrative World*, Philadelphia: Fortress Press.

PETTIGREW, T. F. 1967 'Social Evaluation Theory: Convergences and Applications' in David Levine (ed.), *Nebraska Symposium on Motivation 1967*, Lincoln: University of Nebraska Press, 241–311.

PFOHL, S. J. 1985 *Images of Deviance and Social Control: A Sociological History*, New York: McGraw-Hill.

PIETERSEN, L. 1997 'Despicable Deviants: Labelling Theory and the Polemic of the Pastorals', *Sociology of Religion* 58/4, 343–52.

PIPPIN, T. 1997 'Ideological Criticisms, Liberation Criticisms, and Womanist and Feminist Criticisms', in Porter (ed.) 1997, 267–75.

PITT-RIVERS, J. 1977 *The Fate of Shechem or the Politics of Sex: Essays in the Anthropology of the Mediterranean*, Cambridge: Cambridge University Press.

PLEKET, H. W. 1985 'Review of W. Meeks, *The First Urban Christians*', *Vigiliae Christianae* 39, 192–96.

POLAND, F. 1909 *Geschichte des griechischen Vereinswesens*, Preisschriften der fürstlich Jablonowskischen Gesellschaft, 38; Leipzig: Teubner.

PORTER, S. E. (ed.) 1997 *Handbook to Exegesis of the New Testament*, Leiden: E. J. Brill.

POTTERIE, I. DE LA 1989 *The Hour of Jesus. The Passion and Resurrection of Jesus According to John*, New York: Alba House.

QUESNELL, Q. 1968 'Made Themselves Eunuchs for the Kingdom of Heaven', *CBQ* 30, 335–58.

RADICE, B. (trans.) 1969 *The Letters of the Younger Pliny*, Harmondsworth: Penguin.

RÄISÄNEN, H. 1985 'Galatians 2:16 and Paul's break with Judaism', *NTS* 31, 543–53.

REDEKOP, C. 1962 'The Sect Cycle in Perspective', *Mennonite Quarterly Review* 36, 155–61.

REEKMANS, T. 1971 'Juvenal's Views on Social Change', *Ancient Society* 2, 117–61.

REINHOLD, M. 1970 *History of Purple as a Status Symbol in Antiquity*, Bruxelles: Latomus.

RENSBERGER, D. 1988 *Johannine Faith and Liberating Community*, Philadelphia: Westminster Press.

REX, J. 1969 *Key Problems of Sociological Theory*, London: Routledge & Kegan Paul.

RICHARDSON, C. C. (ed.) 1953 *The Library of Christian Classics*, vol. 1: *Early Christian Fathers*, Philadelphia: Westminster Press.

RICHARDSON, H. N. 1962 *Interpreter's Dictionary of the Bible*, New York.

RICHARDSON, P. 1969 *Israel in the Apostolic Church*, Cambridge: Cambridge University Press.

RICHTER, P. J. 1984 'Recent Sociological Approaches to the Study of the New Testament', *Religion* 14, 77–90.

RICHTER REIMER, I. 1995 *Women in the Acts of the Apostles: A Feminist Liberation Perspective*, Minneapolis: Fortress Press.

RICOEUR, P. 1970 *Freud and Philosophy: An Essay on Interpretation*, New Haven.

RIESENFELD, H. 1957 *The Gospel Tradition and Its Beginnings*, London: Mowbray.

—— 1962 'Vom Schätzesammeln und Sorgen – ein Thema urchristlicher Paränese' in *Neotestamentica et Patristica: Festschrift für O. Cullmann*, NovTSup 6, Leiden: E. J. Brill, 47–58.

ROBBINS, V. K. 1996a *The Tapestry of Early Christian Discourse: Rhetoric, Society and Ideology*, London and New York: Routledge.

—— 1996b *Exploring the Texture of Texts: A Guide to Socio-Rhetorical Interpretations*, Valley Forge, PA: Trinity Press International.

ROBINSON, J. M. 1964 'LOGOI SOPHŌN: Zur Gattung der Spruchquelle Q', in *Zeit und Geschichte: Festgabe für R. Bultmann*, Tübingen, 77–96.

ROCK, P. 1973 *Deviant Behaviour*, London: Hutchinson & Co.

RODD, C. S. 1981 'On Applying a Sociological Theory to Biblical Studies', *Journal for the Study of the Old Testament* 19, 95–106.

—— 1988 'Review of P. F. Esler, *Community and Gospel*', *ExpT* 99, 129–30.

ROHDE, J. 1968 *Rediscovering the Teaching of the Evangelists*, London: SCM Press.

ROHRBAUGH, R. L. 1984 'Methodological Considerations in the Debate over the Social Class Status of Early Christians', *JAAR* 52, 519–46.

—— 1995 'Legitimating Sonship – A Test of Honour: A Social-Scientific Study of Luke 4:1–30', in Esler (ed.) 1995b, 183–97.

—— (ed.) 1996 *The Social Sciences and New Testament Interpretation*, Peabody, MA: Hendrickson.

ROLOFF, J. 1970 *Das Kerygma und der irdische Jesus*, Göttingen.

—— 1988 *Der erste Brief an Timotheus*, EKKNT 15; Zürich: Benziger; Neukirchen-Vluyn: Neukirchener.

ROSTOVTZEFF, M. 1929 *Gesellschaft und Wirtschaft im Römischen Kaiserreich* 2, Leipzig. ET: *The Social and Economic History of the Roman Empire*, vol. 2, 1926; rev edn. 1957; Oxford: Clarendon Press.

ROWLAND, C. C. 1985 *Christian Origins: An Account of the Setting and Character of the most Important Messianic Sect of Judaism*, London: SPCK.

—— and CORNER, M. 1990 *Liberating Exegesis: The Challenge of Liberation Theology to Biblical Studies*, London: SPCK.

SALDARINI, A. J. 1991 'The Gospel of Matthew and Jewish-Christian Conflict', in D. L. Balch (ed.), *Social History of the Matthean Community*, Minneapolis: Fortress Press, 38–61.

—— 1994 *Matthew's Christian-Jewish Community*, Chicago and London: University of Chicago Press.

SAMPLEY, J. P. 1977 '*Societas Christi*: Roman Law and Paul's Conception of the Christian Community', in J. Jervell and W. Meeks (eds), *God's Christ and His People: Studies in Honour of Nils Alstrup Dahl*, Oslo, Bergen and Tromsö: Universitetsforlaget, 58–74.

—— 1980 *Pauline Partnership in Christ: Christian Community and Commitment in Light of Roman Law*, Philadelphia: Fortress Press.

SANDERS, E. P. 1990 'Jewish Association with Gentiles and Galatians 2:11–14', in R. T. Fortna and B. R. Gaventa (eds), *The Conversation Continues: Studies in Paul and John in Honour of J. Louis Martyn*, Nashville, TN: Abingdon Press, 170–88.

SANDERS, J. T. 1993 *Schismatics, Sectarians, Dissidents, Deviants: The First One Hundred Years of Jewish-Christian Relations*, London: SCM Press.

SASAKI, M. S. 1979 'Status Inconsistency and Religious Commitment', in Robert Wuthnow (ed.), *The Religious Dimension: New Directions in Quantitative Research*, New York, San Franciso, and London: Academic Press, 135–56.

SCHAEFER, H. 1962 'Prostatēs', Pauly-Wissowa, *Realencyclopädie der classische Altertumswissenschaft*, supp. vol. 9; cols 1288–304.

SCHELER, M. 1960 *Die Wissensformen und die Gesellschaft*, 2nd edn, Leipzig.

SCHLARB, E. 1990 *Die gesunde Lehre. Häresie und Wahrheit im Speigel der Pastoralbriefe*, Marburg: N. G. Elwert.

SCHMITHALS, W. 1971 *Gnosticism in Corinth*, Nashville, TN: Abingdon Press.

SCHNACKENBURG, R. 1982 *The Gospel According to St. John*, New York: Crossroad.

SCHNEEMELCHER, W. 1959 'Das Problem der Sprache in der Alten Kirche', in *Das problem der Sprache in Theologie und Kirche: Referate vom Deutschen Ev. Theologentag 27–31. Mai in Berlin*, 55–67.

SCHNEIDER, J. 1968 'Timē', in G. Kittel and G. Friedrich (eds), trans. G. Bromiley; *Theological Dictonary of the New Testament*, Grand Rapids, MI: Eerdmans, vol. 8, 169–80.

SCHOEPS, H. J. 1961 *Paul: The Theology of the Apostle in the Light of Jewish Religious History*, Philadelphia: Westminster Press.

SCHOLDER, K. 1987 *The Churches and the Third Reich. Vol.1: Preliminary History and the Time of Illusions 1918–1934*, London: SCM Press.

SCHÖLLGEN, G. 1988 'Was wissen wir über die Sozialstruktur der Paulinischen Gemeinden?', *NTS* 34, 71–82.

SCHOTTROFF, L. 1978 'Das Magnificat und die älteste Tradition über Jesus von Nazareth', *Evangelische Theologie* 38, 293–313.

—— 1985 '"Nicht viele Mächtige", Annäherungen an eine Soziologie des Urchristentums', in *Befreiungserfahrungen: Studien zur Sozialgeschichte des Neuen Testaments*, Theologische Bücherei Band 82; München: Chr. Kaiser Verlag, 247–56.

—— 1993 *Let the Oppressed Go Free: Feminist Perspectives on the New Testament*, Louisville, KY: Westminster/John Knox Press.

—— 1995 *Lydia's Impatient Sisters: A Feminist Social History of Early Christianity*, London: SCM Press.

—— and STEGEMANN, W. 1978 *Jesus von Nazareth, Hoffnung der Armen*, Stuttgart. ET 1986.

SCHOTTROFF, L. and STEGEMANN, W. 1986 *Jesus and the Hope of the Poor*, Maryknoll, NY: Orbis.

SCHOTTROFF, W. and STEGEMANN, W. (eds) 1984 *God of the Lowly: Socio-historical Interpretation of the Bible*, Maryknoll, NY: Orbis.

SCHRAGE, W. 1964 *Das Verhältnis des Thomasevangeliums zur synoptischen Tradition und zu den koptischen Evangelienübersetzungen*, BZNW 29; Berlin.

SCHREIBER, J. 1967 *Theologie des Vertrauens*, Hamburg.

SCHROEDER, D. 1959 'Die Haustafeln des Neuen Testaments: Ihre Herkunft und ihr theologischer Sinn', D. Theol dissertation, Hamburg.

SCHULZ, S. 1972 *Q: Die Spruchquelle der Evangelisten*, Zurich.

SCHUR, E. M. 1971 *Labelling Deviant Behaviour: Its Sociological Implications*, New York: Harper & Row.

—— 1980 *The Politics of Deviance: Stigma Contests and the Uses of Power*, Englewood Cliffs, NJ: Prentice-Hall.

SCHÜRMANN, H. 1959 'Zur Traditions und Redaktionsgeschichte von Mt 10, 23', *Biblische Zeitschrift* 3, 82–88.

—— 1969 *Das Lukasevangelium*, HThK 3/1, Freiburg.

SCHÜTZ, J. H. 1975 *Paul and the Anatomy of Apostolic Authority*, SNTSMS 26, Cambridge: Cambridge University Press.

—— 1977 'Steps toward a Sociology of Primitive Christainty: A Critique of the Work of Gerd Theissen', Paper presented to the Social World of Early Christianity Group of the American Academy of Religion / Society of Biblical Literature, 27–31 December 1977.

—— 1982, 'Introduction' in Theissen 1982, 1–23.

SCHWEITZER, A. 1959 *The Quest of the Historical Jesus*, New York: Macmillan.

SCHWEIZER, E. 1967 *The Lord's Supper According to the New Testament*, Facet Books Biblical Series 18, Philadelphia: Fortress Press.

SCROGGS, R. 1965 'The Exaltation of the Spirit by Some Early Christians', *JBL* 84, 359–73.

—— 1972 'Paul and the Eschatological Woman', *JAAR* 40, 283–303.

—— 1975 'The Earliest Christian Communities as Sectarian Movement', in J. Neusner (ed.), *Christianity, Judaism and Other Greco-Roman Cults, Studies for Morton Smith at Sixty*, Leiden: E. J. Brill, 1–23.

—— 1980 'The Sociological Interpretation of the New Testament: The Present State of Research', *NTS* 26, 164–79.

SEBESTA, J. L. 1976 'Dine with Us as an Equal', *Classical Bulletin* 53, 23–26.

SEELEY, D. 1990 *The Noble Death: Graeco-Roman Martyrology and Paul's Concept of Salvation*, JSNTSup 28, Sheffield: JSOT Press.

SEGAL, A. F. 1990 *Paul the Convert: The Apostolate and Apostasy of Saul the Pharisee*, New Haven: Yale University Press.

SELBY, H. A. 1974 *Zapotec Deviance: Stigma Contests and the Uses of Power*, Englewood Cliffs, NJ: Prentice Hall.

SHERWIN-WHITE, A. N. 1963 *Roman Society and Roman Law in the New Testament*, Oxford: Clarendon Press.

—— 1965 'The Trial of Christ', in *Historicity and Chronology in the New Testament*, Theological Collections 6; London: SPCK, 97–116.

SMALLWOOD, E. M. 1976 *The Jews Under Roman Rule*, Leiden: E. J. Brill.

SMELSER, N. J. 1971 'Alexis de Tocqueville as Comparative Analyst', in I. Vallier (ed.), *Comparative Methods in Sociology: Essays on Trends and Applications*, Berkeley, Los Angeles and London: University of California Press, 19–47.

SMITH, J. Z. 1975 'The Social Description of Early Christianity', *Religious Studies Review* 1, 19–25.

—— 1978 'Too Much Kingdom, Too Little Community', *Zygon* 13, 123–30.

SMITH, M. 1956 'Palestinian Judaism in the First Century', in M. Davis (ed.), *Israel: Its Role and Civilisation*, New York.

—— 1980 'Pauline Worship as Seen by Pagans', *Harvard Theological Review* 73, 241–49.

SNOW, D. A. and MACHALEK, R. 1983 'The Convert as a Social Type', in R. Collins (ed.), *Sociological Theory*, San Francisco: Josey Bass, 259–89.

SODEN, H. VON 1951 'Sakrament und Ethik bei Paulus', in *Urchristentum und Geschichte*, Tübingen, 239–75. Abridged ET in W. Meeks (ed.), *The Writings of St. Paul*, New York, 1972, 257–68.

SPINOZA, B. DE 1670 *Tractatus Theologico Politicus*, ET R. Willis, 1862, London.

STÄHLIN, G. 1938 '*isos ktl.*' in G. Kittel and G. Friedrich (eds), *Theologisches Wörterbuch zum Neuen Testament*, vol.3, 343–56.

STANLEY, J. E. 1986 'The Apocalypse and Contemporary Sect Analysis', in K. H. Richards (ed.), *SBL Seminar Papers 1986*, Atlanta, GA: Scholars Press, 412–21.

STARK, R. 1986 'The Class Basis of Early Christianity: Inferences from a Sociological Model', *Sociological Analysis* 47, 216–25.

—— 1996 *The Rise of Christianity: A Sociologist Reconsiders History*, Princeton: Princeton University Press.

STARK, W. 1967 *The Sociology of Religion Vol. 2: Sectarian Religion*, London.

STAUFFER, E. 1956 'Agnostos Christos. Joh.ii.24 und die Eschatologie des vierten Evangeliums', in W. D. Davies and D. Daube (eds), *The Background of the New Testament and Its Eschatology*, Cambridge: Cambridge University Press, 281–99.

STE CROIX, G. E. M. DE 1975 'Early Christian Attitudes to Property and Slavery', in D. Baker (ed.), *Church, Society and Politics; Studies in Church History* 12; Oxford: Blackwell.

—— 1981 *The Class Struggle in the Ancient Greek World from the Archaic Age to the Arab Conquests*, Ithaca, NY: Cornell University Press; London: Duckworth.

STEGEMANN, W. 1984 'Vagabond Radicalism in Early Christianity? A Historical and Theological Discussion of a Thesis Proposed by Gerd Theissen', in W. Schottroff and W. Stegemann (eds) 1984, 148–68.

STEINBERG, L. 1983 *The Sexuality of Jesus in Renaissance Art and in Modern Oblivion*, New York: Pantheon/October.

STILL, T. 1999 *Thlipsis in Thessalonica: Paul and the Thessalonian Christians in Conflict with Outsiders*, JSNTSup; Sheffield: Sheffield Academic Press, forthcoming.

STOWERS, S. K. 1985 'The Social Sciences and the Study of Early Christianity', in W. S. Green (ed.), *Approaches to Ancient Judaism Vol. 5, Studies in Judaism and its Greco-Roman Context*, Atlanta, GA: Scholars Press, 149–81.

STUHLMACHER, P. 1975 *Der Brief an Philemon*, EKKNT; Zurich: Einsiedeln; Cologne: Benziger; Neukirchen: Erziehungsverein.

SUGIRTHARAJAH, R. S. (ed.) 1991 *Voices from the Margin: Interpreting the Bible in the Third World*, London: SPCK.

SWIDLER, L. 1979, *Biblical Affirmations of Women*, Philadelphia: Westminster.

SYDOW, C. W. VON 1948 'On the Spread of Tradition', in *Selected Papers on Folklore*, Copenhagen, 11–43.

TANNEHILL, R. C. 1967 *Dying and Rising With Christ: A Study in Pauline Theology*, BZNW 32, Berlin: Alfred Töpelmann.

TAYLOR, H. F. 1973 'Linear Models of Consistency: Some Extensions of Blalock's Strategy', *American Journal of Sociology* 78, 1192–215.

TAYLOR, N. H. 1992 *Paul, Antioch and Jerusalem: A Study in Relationships and Authority in Earliest Christianity*, JSNTSup 66; Sheffield: Sheffield Academic Press.

—— 1997a 'Paul, Pharisee and Christian: The Gentiles, the Law, and the Salvation of Israel in Light of Cognitive Dissonance Theory' *Theologia Viatorum* 24, 45–65. First published in Italian in *Religioni e Societa* 24 (1996) 22–39.

—— 1997b 'Paul for Today: Race, Class, and Gender in the Light of Cognitive Dissonance Theory', *Listening* 32, 22–38.

—— 1998 'Cognitive Dissonance and Early Christianity: A Theory and its Application Reconsidered' *Religion and Theology* 5, 138–53.

THEISSEN, G. 1973 'Wanderradikalismus. Literatursoziologische Aspekte der Überlieferung von Worten Jesu im Urchristentum', *ZTK* 70, 245–71. ET in Theissen 1993, 33–59.

—— 1974a 'Soziale Integration und sakramentales Handeln: Eine Analyse von 1 Cor. XI 17–34', *NovT* 24, 179–205. Cited by Meeks from Theissen 1979. ET in Theissen 1982, 145–74.

—— 1974b 'Soziale Schichtung in der korinthischen Gemeinde', *ZNW* 65, 232–72. Cited by Meeks from Theissen 1979. ET in Theissen 1982, 69–119.

—— 1974c 'Theoretische Probleme religions-soziologischer Forschung und die Analyse des Urchristentums', *Neue Zeitschrift für systematische Theologie* 16, 35–56. ET in Theissen 1993, 231–54.

—— 1975a 'Legitimation und Lebensunterhalt. Ein Beitrag zur Soziologie urchristlicher Missionare', *NTS* 21, 192–221. Cited by Meeks from Theissen 1979. ET in Theissen 1982, 27–67.

—— 1975b 'Die soziologische Auswertung religiöser Überlieferungen', *Kairos* 17, 284–99. Cited by Meeks from Theissen 1979. ET in Theissen 1982, 175–200.

—— 1975c 'Die Starken und Schwachen in Korinth: Soziologische Analyse eines theologischen Streites', *Evangelische Theologie* 35, 155–72. Cited by Meeks from Theissen 1979. ET in Theissen 1982, 121–43.

—— 1978 *The First Followers of Jesus*, London: SCM Press; US title: *Sociology of Early Palestinian Christianity*, Philadelphia: Fortress Press.

—— 1979 *Studien zur Soziologie des Urchristentums*, WUNT 19, Tübingen: Mohr.

THEISSEN, G. 1982 *The Social Setting of Pauline Christianity*, ed. and trans. J. H. Schütz, Edinburgh: T&T Clark.

—— 1985 'Review of W. Meeks, *The First Urban Christians*', *Journal of Religion* 65, 111–13.

—— 1987 *Psychological Aspects of Pauline Theology*, trans. J. Galvin, Edinburgh: T&T Clark.

—— 1988 *Studien zur Soziologie des Urchristentums*, 3rd edn; WUNT 19, Tübingen: Mohr.

—— 1993 *Social Reality and the Early Christians: Theology, Ethics and the World of the New Testament*, trans. M. Kohl, Edinburgh: T&T Clark.

—— and MERZ, A. 1998 *The Historical Jesus: A Textbook*, London: SCM Press.

THEO, A. 1995 *Deviant Behavior*, 4th edn; New York: HarperCollins.

THOMASON, B. C. 1982 *Making Sense of Reification: Alfred Schutz and Constructionist Theory*, London: Macmillan.

THOMPSON, J. B. 1984 *Studies in the Theory of Ideology*, Cambridge: Polity Press.

THURÉN, L. 1997 'Hey Jude! Asking for the Original Situation and Message of a Catholic Epistle', *NTS* 43, 451–65.

TIDBALL, D. J. 1983 *An Introduction to the Sociology of the New Testament*, Exeter: Paternoster; reissued under the title *The Social Context of the New Testament*, Carlisle: Paternoster, 1997.

TOWNER, P. H. 1989 *The Goal of Our Instruction: The Structure of Theology and Ethics in the Pastoral Epistles*, JSNTSup 34, Sheffield: JSOT Press.

TRACY, D. 1978 'A Theological Response to *Kingdom and Community*', *Zygon* 13, 131–35.

TROELTSCH, E. 1912 *Die Soziallehren der christlichen Kirchen und Gruppen, Gesammelte Schriften I* (reprinted 1919); Tübingen. ET 1931.

—— 1925 *Gesammelte Schriften IV*, H. Baron (ed.), *Aufsätze zur Geistesgeschichte und Religionssoziologie*, Tübingen.

—— 1931 *The Social Teaching of the Christian Churches, vol. 1*; London: George Allen & Unwin; New York: Macmillan.

TUCKETT, C. M. 1996 *Q and the History of Early Christianity*, Edinburgh: T&T Clark.

TURNER, E. G. 1954 'Tiberius Julius Alexander', *Journal of Roman Studies* 44, 54–64.

TURNER, J. H. 1987 'Analytical Theorizing', in A. Giddens and J. H. Turner (eds), *Social Theory Today*, Cambridge: Polity Press, 156–94.

TURNER, V. W. 1969 *The Ritual Process: Structure and Anti-Structure*, Chicago: Aldine Publishing Co.

—— 1974 *Dramas, Fields and Metaphors*, Ithaca, NY: Cornell University Press.

UNNIK, W. D. VAN 1964 'Die Rucksicht auf die Reaktion der Nicht-Christen als Motiv in der altchristlichen Paränese', in W. Eltester (ed.), *Judentum, Urchristentum, Kirche: Festchrift für Joachim Jeremias*, BZNW 26, Berlin: Akademie, 221–33.

URBACH, E. E. 1964 'The Laws Regarding Slavery as a Source for Social History of the Period of the Second Temple. The Mishnah and Talmud', *Papers of the Institute of Jewish Studies Vol. 1*, 1–50.

VALLIER, I. (ed.) 1971 *Comparative Methods in Sociology: Essays in Trends and Applications*, Berkeley, Los Angeles and London: University of California Press.

VERNER, D. C. 1983 *The Household of God: The Social World of the Pastoral Epistles*, SBLDS 71, Chico, CA: Scholars Press.

VIELHAUER, P. 1965 'Gottesreich und Menschensohn in der Verkündigung Jesu', in *Aufsätze zum Neuen Testament*, Munich, 55–91.

VOGT, J. 1939 *Kaiser Julian und das Judentum: Studien zum Weltanschauungskampf der Spätantike*, Morgenland 30; Leipzig: Morgenland.

—— 1975 'Der Vorwurf der sozialen Niedrikeit des frühen Christentums', *Gymnasium* 82, 401–11.

WAELE, F. J. DE 1961 *Corinthe et Saint Paul*, Paris.

WAINWRIGHT, G. 1971 *Eucharist and Eschatology*, London: Epworth Press.

WALKER, W. O. JR. 1975 '1 Corinthians and Paul's Views Regarding Women', *JBL* 94, 94–110.

WALLACE, A. F. C. 1956 'Revitalization Movements', *American Anthropologist* 58, 264–81.

WALTER, N. 1962 'Zur Analyse von Mc 10, 17–31', *ZNW* 53, 206–18.

WATSON, F. 1986 *Paul, Judaism and the Gentiles: A Sociological Approach*, SNTSMS 56, Cambridge: Cambridge University Press.

WATSON, F. 1990 'Review of M. Y. MacDonald *The Pauline Churches*', *JTS* 41, 191–94.

WEAVER, P. R. C. 1967 'Social Mobility in the Early Roman Empire: The Evidence of the Imperial Freedmen and Slaves', *Past and Present* 37, 3–20. Reprinted in M. I. Finley (ed.), *Studies in Ancient Society*, London: Routledge & Kegan Paul, 1974, 121–41.

WEBER, M. 1949 *The Methodology of the Social Sciences*, Glencoe.

—— 1963 *The Sociology of Religion*, Boston.

—— 1968a *Economy and Society: An Outline of Interpretive Sociology, vol. 1*, G. Roth and C. Wittich (eds); Berkeley and Los Angeles, CA: University of California Press.

—— 1968b *The Methodology of the Social Sciences*, New York: The Free Press.

WEDDERBURN, A. J. M. and LINCOLN, A. T. 1993 *The Theology of the Later Pauline Epistles*, Cambridge: Cambridge University Press.

WEIDINGER, K. 1928 *Die Haustafeln: Ein Stück urchristlicher Paränese*. UNT 14, Leipzig: Hinrichs.

WEISS, J. 1910 *Der erste Korintherbrief*, Göttingen: Vandenhoeck & Ruprecht.

—— 1937 *The History of Primitive Christianity vol. 2*, New York.

WERNER, M. 1957 *The Formation of Christian Dogma*, New York: Harper & Bros.

WHITE, L. J. 1986 'Grid and Group in Matthew's Community: The Righteousness/Honor Code in the Sermon on the Mount', *Semeia* 35, 61–90.

WHITE, L. M. 1988 'Shifting Sectarian Boundaries in Early Christianity', *Bulletin of the John Rylands Library* 70, 7–24.

WILDE, J. A. 1978 'The Social World of Mark's Gospel: A Word About Method', in P. Achtemeier (ed.), *SBL Seminar Papers 1978*, vol. 2; Missoula, MT: Scholars Press, 47–40.

WILLER, D. 1967 *Scientific Sociology: Theory and Method*, Englewood Cliffs, NJ: Prentice-Hall.

WILSON, B. R. 1961 *Sects and Society: A Sociological Study of Three Religious Groups in Britain*, London: Heinemann.

—— 1963 'A Typology of Sects', in R. Robertson (ed.), *Sociology of Religion*, Harmondsworth: Penguin, 1969, 361–83.

WILSON, B. R. 1967 *Patterns of Sectarianism: Organisation and Ideology in Social and Religious Movements*, London: Heinemann.

—— 1973 *Magic and the Millennium: A Sociological Study of Religious Movements of Protest Among Tribal and Third-World Peoples*, London: Heinemann.

WIRE, A. 1984 'Review of J. H. Elliott, *A Home for the Homeless* and D. L. Balch, *Let Wives be Submissive*', *Religious Studies Review* 10, 209–16.

WISSE, F. 1972 'The Epistle of Jude in the History of Heresiology', in M. Krause (ed.), *Essays in the Nag Hammadi Texts in Honour of A. Böhlig*, Leiden: E. J. Brill, 133–43.

WITHERINGTON, B. III. 1995 *Conflict and Community in Corinth: A Socio-Rhetorical Commentary on 1 and 2 Corinthians*, Grand Rapids, MI: Eerdmans.

—— 1998 *The Acts of the Apostles: A Socio-Rhetorical Commentary*, Grand Rapids, MI: Eerdmans.

WORSLEY, P. 1970 *Introducing Sociology*, Harmondsworth: Penguin.

YINGER, J. M. 1946 *Religion in the Struggle for Power*, Durham.

YODER, J.H. 1972 *The Politics of Jesus*, Grand Rapids, MI: Eerdmans.

ZETTERBERG, H. L. 1954 *On Theory and Verification in Sociology*, New York: The Tressler Press.

Index of Biblical References

(including Apocryphal/Deuterocanonical Books)

24:25	185	9:30	169
24:26	159, 171	9:34	64
		10	174
John		10:3–4	165
1:9–10	165	10:17	174
1:34	164, 168	10:17–18	170, 172
1:41	164, 168	10:18	160, 174
1:46	169	10:19	32
1:49	164, 168	10:24	168
3:2	164	10:26–27	165
3:8	169	10:29	170
3:13	169	10:33	168
3:14	167	11:47–48	158
3:16	165	11:50–53	172
4:19	168	11:51	173
4:42	42, 165, 168	12:1–8	163
5:18	168, 172	12:13	168
5:19–29	165, 168	12:13–15	164
5:20	168	12:16	162
5:22	168, 171	12:23	167
5:23	160	12:27	170
5:26	168	12:27–28	165
5:27	168, 171	12:28	159, 165
5:36–38	165	12:31	165, 171
6:14	164, 168	12:32	167
6:15	164, 168	12:32–33	172
6:38	169	12:42	64, 161
6:41–42	169	12:47	165
6:52	258	13:1–2	169
6:62	169	13:1–3	165
7:26	156, 164	13:3–5	163
7:27–28	169	13:6–11	246
7:39	159	13:31	168
8:14	169	13:31–32	167
8:23	164, 167, 169	14:30	165
8:44	32	16:2	64
8:48	32	16:11	165
8:52	32	16:30	165
8:53	168	17:1	165, 167
9:17	156, 164	17:1–5	165
9:22	64	17:5	159, 165, 167–68
9:22–23	161	17:24	165, 168
9:24	61	18:1–11	159, 163
9:29	169	18:3	163

Index of Modern Authors